DEBATING TRANSCENDENCE

Comparative Theology / Thinking Across Traditions

SERIES EDITORS
Loye Ashton and John Thatamanil

This series invites books that engage in constructive comparative theological reflection that draws from the resources of more than one religious tradition. It offers a venue for constructive thinkers, from a variety of religious traditions (or thinkers belonging to more than one), who seek to advance theology understood as "deep learning" across religious traditions.

DEBATING TRANSCENDENCE

Creatio ex Nihilo and *Sheng Sheng*

BIN SONG

Fordham University Press NEW YORK 2026

Copyright © 2026 Fordham University Press

All rights reserved. No part of this publication may be reproduced, stored in a retrieval system, or transmitted in any form or by any means—electronic, mechanical, photocopy, recording, or any other—except for brief quotations in printed reviews, without the prior permission of the publisher.

Fordham University Press has no responsibility for the persistence or accuracy of URLs for external or third-party Internet websites referred to in this publication and does not guarantee that any content on such websites is, or will remain, accurate or appropriate.

Fordham University Press also publishes its books in a variety of electronic formats. Some content that appears in print may not be available in electronic books.

Visit us online at www.fordhampress.com.

For EU safety/GPSR concerns: Mare Nostrum Group B.V., Mauritskade 21D, 1091 GC Amsterdam, The Netherlands, gpsr@mare-nostrum.co.uk

Library of Congress Cataloging-in-Publication
Data available online at https://catalog.loc.gov.

Printed in the United States of America
28 27 26   5 4 3 2 1

First edition

*This book is dedicated to
Master Jue Zhen (覺真長老, 1933–2015),
who extended his hand to me
when it was needed most during the formation of this book.*

CONTENTS

Introduction 1

1 Comparative Theology as a Liberal Art 14

2 Comparative Theology as a Science 39

3 The Transcendence Debate in the History of Christian-Ru Interaction 53

4 Methodologies of Comparative Theology, Religion, and Philosophy for the Progress of the Transcendence Debate 75

5 *Creatio ex Nihilo* from Plato to Augustine 86

6 *Creatio ex Nihilo* in Continuum: Aquinas, Descartes, Schleiermacher, and Tillich 121

7 *Sheng Sheng* as *Generatio ex Nihilo* from Confucius to Wang Bi 145

8 *Generatio ex Nihilo* in Continuum: Zhou Dunyi, Zhu Xi, Cao Duan, and Luo Qinshun 199

Conclusion: Comparative Reflections on the Transcendence Debate 237

Acknowledgments 271

Glossary 275

Notes 277

Index 313

DEBATING TRANSCENDENCE

Introduction

Background and Emergence

Let's begin this book by sharing some personal stories. After all, regardless of the type of intellectual narrative one may aspire to construct, we remain humans living in specific contexts.

I was born as a precursor of millennials and grew up in the final two decades of the twentieth century in mainland China. My hometown was situated in a suburban environment, nestled within the inner mountainous region of the Shandong Peninsula in East China. Within a dozen miles to the east, I could return to the rural village where my parents and grandparents were born and grew up. According to the inscription on a stone in the village gate, this village was established in the late Ming dynasty (1368–1644 CE) as ancestors fled from end-of-dynasty wars and famine. Within seventy-seven miles to the west, I could visit the city of Qufu, where Confucius (551–479 BCE, also known as Kongzi) was born.

For those well-versed in the intellectual history of mainland China during the final two decades of the twentieth century, this era eludes simple categorization. It teemed with uncertainty, excitement, and a yearning for prosperity amid a tumultuous interplay of despair and hope that felt almost predestined. The scars of the Cultural Revolution (1966–76) lingered in the collective consciousness, yet staunch supporters of the ruling government periodically evoked nostalgia for Maoist China's revolutionary fervor. The influx of Western ideas reintroduced more than two thousand years of intellectual heritage to Chinese scholars, amid a whirlwind of premodern, modern, and postmodern influences that they endeavored to navigate. Religious practices resurged, encompassing Western faiths like Christianity and indigenous ones like Buddhism and

Daoism. However, despite this resurgence, the prevailing atheistic education imposed by the ruling party left much of the populace wary of religion, particularly Western religions. Traditional Chinese culture, deeply influenced by Ruism,[1] experienced a revival both intellectually and socially. However, vestiges of the anti-Ruist sentiment prevalent in the early twentieth century, which attributed China's perceived backwardness during the era of Western colonialism to Ruism, endured in the cultural fabric. At the close of the twentieth century, a shared aspiration for economic prosperity unified the Chinese population. Intellectually, no single trend dominated, as diverse ideologies vied for prominence in their pursuit of survival and advancement.

Given the location where I was born, it is no wonder that my upbringing was influenced most by the Ru tradition. As a child, I regularly participated in family and communal rituals in the village, such as sweeping ancestral tombs on specific dates each month; visiting and kowtowing in the family shrine, where a long and elaborate diagram of our family tree hung behind an offering table; and joining other important festival rituals such as parades and feasts. However, when I asked for the reasons behind the details of these practices, the answers I received from the elders in my family were always very vague. The best explanation they could offer was that these were prescribed by Confucius. I now understand that the relative ignorance among my extended family members about the philosophy behind these rituals is due to the huge educational gap created by the ten-year absence of formal education during the Cultural Revolution. However, as a young child, I was simply confused by the seemingly empty rituals I was forced to perform regularly.

One of the most annoying aspects of these ritual performances was the divination practice based on the *Classic of Change*, an important Ruist classic that also happens to be a central focus of this book. I was often driven for hours to a remote village where a famous diviner lived. The diviner would have me throw coins on the ground and then deliver his predictive verdict on various issues, mostly in response to questions posed by my parents: What university I could attend, what spouse and how many children I might have, what city I would live in, and so on. Since the process was completely out of my control, and my family indeed set their expectations for my life based on these divinations, I felt powerless in the face of these powerful questions and answers.

These experiences deeply motivated me to study Confucius's thought and the Ru tradition he helped to transmit and nurture. I felt the need to quench my curiosity about the reasons behind the rituals and to regain autonomy over my future planning. All of this drove me to embark on a journey of reading Ruist classics when I entered university.

Shutting myself up in the university library day after day and relying on the simple expedient of reading while simultaneously transcribing ancient Chinese philosophical texts on paper, I had a few very blissful and transient religious experiences. Although there is no space here to describe these experiences,[2] this whole book can be seen as a long-overdue result of such experiences. In order to understand what ontological references these experiences might hold, and how to maintain and integrate them into daily life amid the rapidly changing intellectual and societal milieu in mainland China and elsewhere, I could not avoid learning and pondering the concept of "transcendence."

Given that I devote a full chapter to exploring all possible meanings of "transcendence" that comparative scholars in the Christian-Ruist context have addressed, suffice it to say at this point that the transcendent dimension of one's worldview functions like the ridge beam in architecture. It is the highest organizing principle, implicating itself broadly across all dimensions of one's way of life, thereby making one's lifestance appear as a whole. This overarching effect of the discourse on transcendence is particularly prominent in cross-cultural studies of worldviews and lifestances.

For instance, during my immersive study of ancient Ruist classics, the viewpoint I encountered most frequently among Christian believers and liberal-minded Chinese intellectuals aiming to reform Chinese politics was that there is no transcendent element in traditional Ruist culture. They argued that for Ruism, all ethics are consumed in human relationships, individual autonomy succumbs to various forms of authority, and, hence, there is no way to achieve genuine spiritual liberation and democratic political reforms. This free-floating academic street talk carried some residual influence from the anti-Ruist intellectual trend of the early twentieth century. However, upon deeper analysis, it actually continued a long-enduring intellectual debate, which I term the "transcendence debate," spanning all major periods of historical interaction between the Christian and Ruist traditions ever since the sixteenth century, when Matteo Ricci embarked on his missionary journey to Ming China. In the context of the reform period in mainland China starting in the 1980s, it can also be seen as a potent narrative perpetuated by vying ideologies to advance their causes in public discourse.

But is this viewpoint true? Can a nontranscendent classical discourse, such as Ruism, engender and sustain a way of life with strong moments of religious experience? Absent a transcendent dimension, can Ruism truly adapt to modern life and even make further contributions to human civilization that are irreplaceable by other traditions? All my subsequent years of learning after graduating from university were deeply driven by these questions, which I believe are crucial not only for me but also for a comparative understanding of traditional Chinese culture in general.

I believe that the anecdotes and experiences of my upbringing shared above should leave my readers with no doubt that the profound impact of questions surrounding transcendence on the everyday life of individuals is difficult to overstate. The exact locus of controversy in the ongoing "transcendence debate" between Christianity and Ruism focuses on determining if the Ruist concept of *Tian* (heaven, cosmos, or the universe), or its more precise metaphysical referent, *Taiji* (Ultimate Limit), can be regarded as the origin of the existing world, and consequently, as transcendent in comparison to Christian notions of the Creator-God. As I will elaborate in chapter 3, Christian scholars, Ru scholars, and independent comparativists have all contributed to this debate, each being motivated to engage with it by their unique social and political contexts. Their divergent conclusions often align with and serve these underlying motives. For example, affirming a more transcendent dimension in the Christian worldview would have undoubtedly aided the proselytizing efforts of early Christian missionaries, whereas counterarguments by twentieth-century Ru scholars were largely aimed at affirming the autonomous nature of Ruism in response to the encroachment of Western culture. Moreover, independent comparative philosophers in the twenty-first century may seek to challenge Western cultural dominance and explore genuine alternative philosophical frameworks by denying any transcendent dimension within traditional Ru discourse.

Reflecting on my academic formation since college, I have come to realize that no scholarly group is entirely free from social or political motivations, even when engaging with what may seem like the most abstract metaphysical questions humans can ask: Where does the world come from? Why is there anything at all, rather than nothing? Because of the differing motives of those involved in the transcendence debate, they often selectively cite particular sources and employ varying definitions of transcendence to support conclusions that align with their aims. This has led to an unusually complex and confusing status quo in the debate, with a broad diversity of scholarly views on display.

Is there hope for constructing a more scientific and systematic framework for comparison, one that could answer the central debated question in a way that minimizes biases stemming from individual motives and maximally addresses the concerns raised by participants in the ongoing debate? Evidently, the need for a new comparative methodology must precede any solid answer to the debated question itself. As a scholar who identifies with Ruism, I feel a particular urgency regarding this methodological question. To this day, Ruism has yet to establish a stable vocabulary for engaging with the Western discipline of "theology," where many of the contested issues in the ongoing debate have been posed and discussed primarily by the Christian side. What could "theology" possibly mean for Ruism? Can we find an appropriate definition of "theology," and by extension "comparative theology," that allows Ruism not only to respond to posed questions but to do so using a vocabulary that is authentic to its own historical formation? If so, what is the relationship between this theology and "philosophy," another Western discipline with which contemporary Ru scholarship seems more comfortable engaging?

With these emerging questions simmering and intensifying in my mind, my interest in the transcendence debate grew exponentially during my visiting research on religious experience in classical Chinese thought at the Harvard-Yenching Institute from 2011 to 2013, where I was introduced to the works of Liu Shu-hsien (1934–2016) on the subject. As I delved deeper into this complex and impactful matter, I formed the ambition to pursue a PhD in theological or religious studies in the US, building on the philosophical training I had obtained in China and France, to enhance my academic abilities to address the debate. I was fortunate enough to be admitted to graduate programs in theology and religious studies at Boston University, where I had the opportunity to take courses from prominent scholars in the field of comparative theology, including those affiliated with the Boston Theological Interreligious Consortium. This consortium allowed me to study at both Boston College and Harvard University, where I learned from renowned scholars such as Catherine Cornille, Francis X. Clooney, and Kimberley C. Patton.

Working closely with Robert Neville, John Berthrong, and Stephen Angle, all either founders of or sympathetic with "Boston Confucianism," further enhanced my spiritual identity as a Ru scholar. In 2014, I founded the Boston University Confucian Association, a student organization focused on group readings, community dinners, summer retreats, and scholarly speeches, which became a weekly occurrence until 2018. Since the fall of 2018, I have been teaching philosophy, religion, and theology comparatively in a liberal arts setting at Washington College, one of the oldest institutions of its kind in the US. As I continue to refine the craft of teaching, my passion for contributing to the ongoing discourse on comparative theology remains as strong as ever.

In a nutshell, as a culmination of my decades-long exploration and practice of Ruist spirituality since my late teens, the crux of this book is to offer a resolution to the transcendent versus immanent controversy from the perspective of a Ru scholar and comparative theologian. The following chapters outline my approach to achieving this.

Chapter Outline

Comparison within traditions is not a neutral endeavor. The traditions being compared inevitably shape the process, nature, and comparative method employed. In the following chapters, my approach to comparison is informed by my foundation as a Ru scholar. As I will demonstrate, from a Ru perspective, comparative theology is best understood as both a liberal art and a science. The significance of this concept will be explicated in the first two chapters of the book. Accordingly, these opening chapters will primarily serve as an introduction to thinking from a Ru standpoint, while also offering a secondary introduction to comparative theology as interpreted through a Ru lens.

In chapter 1, "Comparative Theology as a Liberal Art," I survey various definitions of "theology" and conclude that comparative theology, while referencing Aristotelian and Ruist approaches to contemplating ultimate reality, should be pursued in this book as a rooted, nonconfessional liberal art. I argue that Ruism can learn from other traditions in a theology of religions, which I describe as a "seeded, open inclusivism."

Given that the transcendence debate revolves around metaphysics, chapter 2, "Comparative Theology as a Science," confronts modern skepticism about metaphysics and posits that comparative theology related to metaphysics can be approached as a science. By adopting a broader understanding of the process by which feedback from reality can refine metaphysical hypotheses, I contend that Ru metaphysics can be viewed as a science in its own historical context, and thus, Ruism can and should be a valuable participant in global metaphysical conversations.

With this larger framework in place, I proceed to address the transcendence debate from chapter 3 onward. Following Jonathan Smith's insight, which I will delve into more extensively in later chapters, I assert that any comparative study of religions must address three essential questions: Why am I making this comparison? How am I conducting it? And, importantly, so what are the implications?

Chapter 3, "The Transcendence Debate in the History of Christian-Ru Interaction," focuses on the "why" question by clarifying the purpose of this comparative project. I examine three stages of Christian-Ru interaction, from Matteo Ricci in the sixteenth century to the present day. By surveying major scholarly contentions, I show how Christian scholars, Ruist scholars, and independent comparativists have used different definitions of "transcendence," selected varying texts and figures, and utilized disparate methodologies to argue their contentions, leading to a confusing state of the debate. Among all these definitions, the question of whether there is an ontological dimension of transcendence in Ruist thought remains the most controversial, not only among scholars associated with different traditions but even among those who proclaim a shared association. Furthermore, among all ideas of disputants in the debate surveyed in this study, the Christian understanding of divine creation as *creatio ex nihilo* and the Ruist understanding of the cosmic creativity of *Tian* as *sheng sheng* (生生, birth birth) are the most frequently referenced. This analysis of the current state of the transcendence debate provides the rationale for selecting these two ontological ideas as the central foci of this book's comparative study, and it also affords further methodological guidance on how to tackle the debate.

Chapter 4, "Methodologies of Comparative Theology, Religion, and Philosophy for the Progress of the Transcendence Debate" is dedicated to investigating a variety of methodologies for comparative studies of religion, including comparative theology, comparative religion, and comparative philosophy of religion. After careful consideration, I have selected and constructed the most appropriate methodology for my situation. Specifically, I reaffirm my project as a rooted, nonconfessional comparative theology that combines Robert Neville's pragmatist use of "vague category" and Jonathan Smith's hermeneutical "situational thinking."

"Conclusion: Comparative Reflections on the Transcendence Debate," answers the "so what" question, presenting the broader implications of this project. I respond to major viewpoints and arguments presented by comparative scholars involved in the historical transcendence debate, as investigated in chapter 3, and reach conclusions regarding various topics addressed by the debate, such as the relationship between ontology and cosmology, the mystical expression of the ineffability of divine creativity, theodicy, and how to incorporate Platonism into Ruist metaphysical thought. From a comparative perspective, I provide my direct answer to whether the Ruist idea of Ultimate Limit is transcendent when compared with Christian ideas of the Creator God. In the end, I present my own constructive Ru theology in its preliminary form and hint at directions for future comparative studies on related topics.

Chapters 5 through 8 provide the necessary comparative data for the final analysis, and hence, form the backbone of this book. Rather than comparing singular figures or texts, I have chosen to compare traditions because of the complex nature of the transcendence debate. Scholars have used various texts and figures from both traditions to support their views, but these views do not necessarily represent the entire tradition. By focusing on the continuity and renewal of the ideas of *creatio ex nihilo* and *sheng sheng* within each tradition, I hope to shed light on the broader picture of the debate.

However, I am aware of the criticism that the more materials one deals with, the less accurate their descriptions tend to be. To address this, I have carefully chosen the most important moments in each tradition to present the most relevant data for comparison. These moments include the seeds of thought, the first systematic expressions, and significant innovations in early modern times. As the transcendence debate was initially introduced by the Christian perspective, and since I am writing in English, I will first cover the Christian survey, followed by the Ruist survey. Once I conclude my examination of the intellectual history of *creatio ex nihilo*, I will introduce a category called "creation," alongside related concepts such as "ontological dependence" and "transcendence," which will be deliberately vague to allow for an easier comparison of original Ruist materials. The structure of these backbone chapters is outlined as follows.

In the Greek-European Christian tradition of philosophical theology,[3] which has been heavily involved in the transcendence debate, Augustine of Hippo was the first philosophical theologian to construct a systematic theology centered on the concept of *creatio ex nihilo* following the Council of Nicaea. Thus, my exploration of the concept of *creatio ex nihilo* in the Christian tradition will be divided into two parts.

In chapter 5, "*Creatio ex Nihilo* from Plato to Augustine," I will investigate the significant intellectual trends that influenced Augustine's ideas regarding *creatio ex nihilo*. These trends include the exegetical tradition of *Genesis* in early Christianity, Plato's ontological cosmology, Middle Platonism, the first philosophical formulation of *creatio ex nihilo* by Theophilus of Antioch, Plotinus's Neoplatonism, and the Gnosticism represented by early Christian polemicists. The primary concept under investigation will be that of "creation," as well as related ideas such as "matter," "time," and "evil." The goal of this chapter is to address the "why" and "how" questions regarding the emergence of the concept of *creatio ex nihilo* during this period.

In chapter 6, "*Creatio ex Nihilo* in Continuum: Aquinas, Descartes, Schleiermacher, and Tillich," I will examine the further development of the concept of *creatio ex nihilo* following Augustine by exploring the works of four theologians and philosophers: Thomas Aquinas, René Descartes, Friedrich Schleiermacher, and Paul Tillich. I will justify this selection based on the proposed comparative methodology. First, I will exclude the nonmainstream theology of Christian mysticism, as it is not typically discussed in the transcendence debate. Second, less innovative thinkers who repeat the same ideas as pioneering thinkers will also be left out. Third, significant thinkers such as Spinoza and Hegel, who addressed the problem of divine creation but not in the way of *creatio ex nihilo*, will also be omitted. Finally, contemporary theorists later than Paul Tillich will not be included, as their significance is still being debated.

The positive rationale for this selection is as follows: Thomas Aquinas is one of the most analytical thinkers in the tradition of *creatio ex nihilo* in its medieval, Scholastic expression, and he provided a detailed analysis of *creatio ex nihilo* based on its Augustinian interpretation. René Descartes's theory of "created eternal truth" breaks new ground concerning the intelligibility of the created world, making the traditionally theistic logic behind *creatio ex nihilo* more comparable to nontheism. Friedrich Schleiermacher invests the idea of *creatio ex nihilo* with rich existential interpretations, and his metaphysical analysis of the relationship between God and the created world is emblematic and suitable for my comparative purpose. Finally, Paul Tillich is one of the most recent systematic thinkers of *creatio ex nihilo*, whose philosophy not only provides innovative solutions to traditional issues such as theodicy but also significantly influences the thought of contemporary Chinese Ru philosophers like Liu Shu-hsien.

For Ruism, the first appearance of an idea similar to *creatio ex nihilo* is found in the commentaries of Wang Bi (226–249 CE) and Han Kangbo (332–380 CE) on the *Dao De Jing* and the *Classic of Change*. This idea is related to their philosophical interpretation of the *sheng sheng* of Ultimate Limit, and I refer to their concept as "generatio ex nihilo," as the creative power of Ultimate Limit was understood to be constantly active without a creator standing behind the scenes. To comprehend this nontheistic concept of *generatio ex nihilo*, a similar investigation of the intellectual history of ancient Chinese cosmology is needed.

Chapter 7, "*Sheng Sheng* as *Generatio ex Nihilo* from Confucius to Wang Bi," is dedicated to exploring how scholarly debates within the traditions of ancient Chinese cosmology led to the emergence of the concept of *generatio ex nihilo* in Wang Bi and Han Kangbo. This chapter will highlight the consistent controversy between the Daoist understanding of the *Dao*'s creativity as one of "cosmological succession" and the Ruist understanding of *Tian*'s creativity as one of "ontological dependence." Key texts and thinkers include the *Dao De Jing*, the *Xici* of the *Classic of Change*, the *Zhuang Zi*, the *Lü Annals of Spring and Autumn*, the *Huainanzi*, the *Weft Book* of the *Classic of Change*, the commentary of Zheng Xuan (127–200 CE) on the *Classic of Change*, and Wang Bi and Han Kangbo.

Ru metaphysics, centered around the *sheng sheng* of Ultimate Limit, was significantly developed during the Song through Ming periods, pioneered by the ethical metaphysics of Zhou Dunyi (1017–1073 CE) and underpinned by Zhu Xi's interpretation of Zhou's works. Thus, chapter 8, "*Generatio ex Nihilo* in Continuum: Zhou Dunyi, Zhu Xi, Cao Duan, and Luo Qinshun," will focus on Zhou Dunyi and Zhu Xi, followed by two Ruist thinkers, Cao Duan (1376–1434 CE) and Luo Qinshun (1465–1547 CE), to indicate how Zhu Xi's followers challenged his metaphysical system and how we might refine Zhu Xi's thought on *sheng sheng* for our comparative purpose.

After completing these investigations, a detailed and final comparison of *creatio ex nihilo* and *sheng sheng* will be conducted to highlight their similarities and differences. In other words, the book will provide a well-delineated range of comparative data and a rigorously devised methodology, culminating in "Conclusion: Comparative Reflections on the Transcendence Debate." Thus, the three crucial moments for each tradition are Plato's *Timaeus* versus the *Xici*, Augustine of Hippo versus Wang Bi, and Descartes versus Zhu Xi. For the intellectual histories of *creatio ex nihilo* and *sheng sheng* in Christianity and Ruism, all other related ideas can be seen either in the work of seminal predecessors or as responding consequences to these thinkers and texts.

Regarding my comparative studies of the two intellectual histories, three caveats need to be presented. First, although the history of ideas is the primary methodology used in chapters 5 to 8, each philosopher's or theologian's thought will be examined not mainly from the perspective of their intellectual biographies but rather from a relational perspective of their ideas to the development of the concepts of *creatio ex nihilo* or *sheng sheng* within each tradition. Unless a change in a thinker's ideas on creation can significantly influence our understanding of a corresponding stage in one of the compared traditions, their ideas will be presented as a more or less coherent whole in relation to other thinkers within each tradition.

Moreover, since continuity of ideas and their significance to the transcendence debate is the central concern, I will include selected secondary literature reviews on each thinker and text mainly in endnotes, rather than in the main text, to keep the reader's focus on the systematic nature of the core argument that this book will make. This approach to systematically treating historical materials is dictated by the comparative nature of this project. As entailed by the fallibilist methodology of comparison I present in chapters 2 and 4, theses presented via this approach are intrinsically vulnerable to rational criticism if any expert on any individual philosopher or text can provide corrections for the presentation of each thinker or text concerned. For those specialists who deem such a systematic, tradition-based approach to comparison to be too ambitious to be achieved by a single comparativist, despite my firm belief that big and significant questions raised in the transcendent debate warrant such ambition, please rest assured that the comparative fallibilism I advocate in this book welcomes these experts' potential criticism of this book's interpretations of individual thinkers or texts. Such criticism will be incorporated, if not by me, then by a larger collective effort that refines the current project in the future.

Second, as someone spiritually rooted in the Ru tradition, I aim to provide an impartial reading of all selected thinkers and texts across the two intellectual histories, especially with regard to Christian theologians in chapters 5 and 6. Here, "impartiality" is understood through the fallibilist methodology of comparison. However, I am mindful that my theological education at Boston University, under the guidance of prominent Protestant theologians, may have influenced my study of Christian sources, with both the advantages and limitations that such a formation entails. Therefore, the fallibilist methodology of comparison invites readers to apply the same level of scrutiny and critique to this implicit influence as to any other.

Third, a number of texts on early Chinese cosmology addressed in chapter 7 are under philological debate regarding authorship and date of composition. However, since the survey of intellectual histories is for the purpose of comparison concerning the transcendence debate, my focus will primarily be on how these texts have been received philosophically in the Ru tradition. Alternative versions of these texts may be discussed to enhance the philosophical argument. However, unless newly developed philology significantly modifies the philosophical understanding of their received versions, I will not invest much time in setting out philological details in later chapters. The philosophical approach to textual analysis equally welcomes philological criticism.

Major Arguments

The major arguments and comparative conclusion of this book are as follows: The emergence of the idea of *creatio ex nihilo* from Plato to Augustine championed the ontological dependence of cosmic realities upon the Creator God. During this epoch of Western history, philosophers and theologians held a view of divine creation as a process in which divine intelligence infused ideas and forms into a primordial state of being, thereby giving rise to diverse realities. However, Descartes's theory of "created eternal truth" conceptualized divine creation as not being constrained by any rule of intelligence. This Cartesian voluntarism pushed the theistic vocabularies of creation to their limit such that it allowed for a de-anthropomorphic subtradition within the main theistic tradition of *creatio ex nihilo*. Schleiermacher and Tillich refined Descartes's thought.

In ancient China, there were two distinctive cosmologies: One is Daoist, pioneered by the *Dao De Jing*; and the other is Ruist, initiated by the *Xici*. When Wang Bi employed the ontology in the *Xici* to interpret the cosmogony of *Dao De Jing*, his understanding of Ultimate Limit influenced the Ru tradition to reach an idea of creation similar to *creatio ex nihilo*. Accordingly, Ultimate Limit's creativity can be characterized as *generatio ex nihilo*, an unconditioned, constantly creative cosmic power without a creator operating behind the scenes. Zhou Dunyi and Zhu Xi refined Wang Bi's thought.

The Ru tradition of *generatio ex nihilo* provides the most apt comparison to the de-anthropomorphic subtradition of *creatio ex nihilo*. If we define transcendence as what is indeterminate and ontologically unconditioned by the existing world, the Ruist idea of *sheng sheng* of Ultimate Limit as *generatio ex nihilo* can be recognized as not only containing a similarly and legitimately transcendent dimension specifying ontological relationships among cosmic realities. It is even more transcendent, namely, more rigorously following the logic of ontological unconditionality, than the mainstream theistic Christian understanding of divine creation.

1 Comparative Theology as a Liberal Art

The fundamental question this book seeks to address is how a Ru scholar can engage in comparative theology (CT) today. Specifically, for scholars who identify with Ruism as a comprehensive way of life, what is the significance of learning from other comprehensive traditions? To answer this, I propose a Ruist project akin to the Christian theology of religions, which provides a general framework for a Ruist CT. In doing so, I clarify what "theology" means in the context of Ruism, how comparative a Ru theology can be, and why theological comparison is vital to Ruism. To establish this framework, I position Ruism within the terms and concepts that scholars currently employ to map the relatively new discipline of CT. Chapter 1 is dedicated to accomplishing this task.

Comparative Theology as Theology

Contemporary discussions among scholars on the nature of comparative theology usually begin with defining the concept of "theology" and then consider why and how a comparative approach is essential to it. Francis X. Clooney's influential works have played a key role in these discussions, as various scholars have responded to, agreed with, disagreed with, or critically engaged with his version of comparative theology. For us, Clooney's approach serves as a useful starting point to envision a possible Ruist comparative theology and to consider whether his methodology aligns with a Ruist perspective.

The CT that Clooney advocates for is predicated on two fundamental assumptions. The first is the existence of a state of consciousness known as "faith" toward a definitive form of divine revelation. As a result, a need to "understand" this faith arises, given that human beings must employ languages, symbols, and concepts characteristic of their respective culture and history to live out their faith. In keeping with the Catholic Scholastic tradition, theology is, therefore, a "faith seeking understanding" that is grounded in a given faith. Clooney argues that the need for CT arises from the fact that contemporary theologians no longer live in cultures and histories that constrain them to a single set of cultural devices.[1] It is important to note that Clooney recognizes the impact of other faiths on the cultural devices of other traditions, and so the way he positions his own faith vis-à-vis other faiths is critical to his "faith seeking understanding." The second operational premise of Clooney's CT is the requirement of a preexisting, clearly defined faith community, which he calls the "home tradition." While studying other traditions is expected to offer fresh theological insights, comparative theologians following Clooney's model must demonstrate "continued loyalty" to their home community during the process of comparison. They must also continually reaffirm the significance of the "fresh theological insights" obtained through comparison for their home tradition.

Clooney's concrete comparative works reveal that the "fresh theological insights" obtained through comparison cannot revise or modify preexisting faith statements in his home tradition. Instead, these insights serve to "intensify" his awareness of how specific his own faith is,[2] based on a deep understanding of other traditions. This result confirms the normativity of the two premises of Clooney's comparative theology. In other words, Clooney's faith is based on a determinate and unalterable form of divine revelation, as articulated by orthodox council creeds, such as Nicaea and Chalcedon, in the Catholic tradition.[3] Thus, cultural devices brought in by the theologian cannot substantially modify that foundational expression of faith in his home tradition. Clooney does not seek to subsume other faiths within his own. The only possible outcome of comparison, in his view, is to highlight the specificity of each faith alongside another. Therefore, the project that Clooney pursues is more about "comparing theologies" than "comparative theology," since external cultural devices cannot substantially modify the established understanding of his faith.[4]

Keith Ward and Robert C. Neville proposed alternative understandings of "theology" and "comparative theology," and both of them are landmark figures in the contemporary study of CT. Because I will have a detailed analysis of Neville's methodology of CT in chapter 4, I will concentrate on Ward's work here.

Ward defines comparative theology "not as a form of apologetics for a particular faith but as an intellectual discipline which enquires into ideas of the ultimate value and goal of human life, as they have been perceived and expressed in a variety of religious traditions."[5] Ward furthermore stresses that "there is nothing to prevent a comparative theologian from being committed to one religious tradition, even a very authoritarian one, unless that authority prohibits such a study [CT]." But the CT of Ward's type does require "being prepared to revise beliefs if and when it comes to seem necessary." Although Ward is writing "from within one (Anglican) strand of the Christian tradition," he intends to "articulate that tradition in a global context" and explore what light other traditions in turn shed on his Christian beliefs.[6]

Obviously, Ward's CT operates on a quite different understanding of "theology" from Clooney's. "Divine revelation" for Ward involves both indeterminate and determinate aspects:[7] an ultimately indeterminate mystery pertaining to the final value of human existence is revealed through a determinate expression of it in a specific linguistic community and history. Since no determinate expression exhausts the mystery, "theology" is summoned to explore all available cultural devices to contemplate the living and developing reality of the once partially revealed mystery in a global context. Theology in this sense is intrinsically comparative since no single determinate expression of the mystery is treated as final and complete. This does not mean that the work of a comparative theologian cannot start from a baseline, because a determinate manifestation of the mystery in a linguistic community needs to be set in an initial position to point the theologian to the mystery. Nevertheless, the ever-expanding and diversifying manifestations of the mystery demand that the theologian be ready to revise their previous specific understanding of it. In my view, the revision in question would not bring too much concern of conversion for Ward since no determinate revelation exhausts the mystery, and all revisions would simply add to his original exposure to divine revelation without completely abandoning it.[8]

To sum up, for Clooney, the task of theology is to hold faith in a specific and predetermined form of divine revelation, and then to seek out cultural devices to understand it. In the study of comparative theology, this established faith will be enhanced in comparison with other expressions of faith from around the world. However, for Ward, faith and understanding occur simultaneously in any instance of divine revelation. In Ward's view, critical theological reflection is a crucial part of any particular expression of faith, and theology is thus inherently comparative because of the interplay between the indeterminate and determinate aspects of divine revelation.

Both Clooney and Ward self-identify as Christian, albeit belonging to different denominations. Their comparative works are supposed to be strongly accepted as types of both "theology" in general and "comparative theology" in particular. However, their works are treated unevenly in the scholarship of CT, and a number of voices have emerged to doubt whether CT of Ward's type can be counted as theology. For instance, in a recent book charting the terrain of CT, Paul Hedges emphasizes that "Clooney grounds his method in the 'faith seeking understanding' principle, which as far as anything is may be said to be the sine qua non of any definition of theology as a first-order discipline," whereas "the paradigms of Neville and Ward are to some degree forms of comparative religion or philosophy and so somewhat distinct."[9] Hedges's characterization of Ward's work is striking because Ward insists that his work is "primarily concerned with the meaning, truth, and rationality of religious beliefs," and thus should be distinguished from "religious studies," which objectively observe religions and do not seek truth central to one's faith.[10] Hedges also accepts a similar standard to distinguish comparative theology from comparative religion in that the former "asks the question of truth and validity," while the latter does not.[11]

So, what exactly precludes Hedges from fully recognizing Ward's work as comparative theology? The answer lies in the principle of "faith seeking understanding," as articulated by Clooney, which Hedges views as the sine qua non of theology. According to Hedges, no matter whether a comparativist seeks religious truth or not, as long as they are not faithfully committed to an unalterable set of expressions of divine revelation, and accordingly, have no clearly bounded community to speak to as an insider, their work is not theology, let alone comparative theology.

It is remarkable that Ward's fine intellectual endeavor to seek all available cultural devices to contemplate truth concerning the ultimate value of human life cannot even be counted as theology. Hedges's reflective work evidently uncovers an assumption prevalent in the English-writing academy about how to define theology. My following argument is that in the West, this assumption of theology—defined as a Scholastic "faith seeking understanding"—exists only after the historical division between philosophy and theology, that is, after Christianity became established in late antiquity and medieval Europe. However, this definition of theology cannot adequately represent how theology was envisioned by ancient Greek philosophers. This misrepresentation leads to two consequences: First, CT theorists, such as Hedges, cannot discern that a project of Ward's type is congenial to "theology" integral to ancient Greek philosophy. Second, this blind spot on the origin of theology hinders reflective CT theorists and first-order CT theologians (who seek religious truth comparatively) from discovering alternative resources to do CT today. The second point is of special significance to my project because to envision a Ruist CT, we need to ensconce the key term "theology" and its related ones such as "revelation" and "home tradition" in a more hospitable resource so that contemporary readers can readily comprehend the nature of a Ruist CT. Emphatically, the expansion of the vista of "theology" to its Greek cognate resonates with the emphasis of contemporary CT to decenter, albeit not to abandon Christianity, and thus to explore historical resources to transform CT into a genuinely global discipline.

Theology from Ancient Greece to Medieval Europe

To my claim that ancient Greek philosophy provides an alternative resource to enrich the contemporary understanding of theology, it is conceivable for CT scholars to have an initial reaction such as: Wasn't "theology" just part of philosophy back then, and thus, a purely argumentative and rational discourse aiming for intellectual truth, pursued in a way that is anything but religiously significant? Didn't it lack the very existential grip by ultimate religious truth and the consequential transformation of people's whole personality, two indispensable implications of "theology" understood today?

Unfortunately, this reaction commits an error of anachronism when assuming the relationship between philosophy, theology, and religion as such. The conception that philosophy is merely an argumentative discourse on intellectual matters deprived of religious significance is possible only after Christian Scholasticism took hold and accordingly treated philosophy as a subservient tool to parse out the Christian theology. And the authority of the theology derives from divine revelation in the biblical scripture as elaborated by the orthodox doctrines of the Church. In other words, this subordinate role of philosophy transpires simultaneously with the conception of theology as "faith seeking understanding" discussed above. To argue for an alternative resource of CT in ancient

Greek philosophy, we need to transcend the concerned period of medieval Christianity, and see into how philosophy, theology and religion were apprehended in the ancient world.

In this regard, Pierre Hadot's meta-philosophical work on ancient philosophy as a way of life,[12] together with Wilfred C. Smith's genealogical study of religion,[13] helps contemporary readers to understand the origin and evolution of each contested term (philosophy, theology, and religion) before established Christianity. I will present my understanding as follows:

Philosophy in the ancient world is primarily a way of life, the nature of which is best manifested by varying spiritual exercises aiming to transform people's vision of the world and metamorphize people's whole personality. These spiritual exercises pertain to the training of attention, ways of dialogue, how to read, how to live in the face of death, and so on. Philosophical discourse is the abstract and conceptual aspect of these exercises; it is inseparable from the latter, but in the final analysis, discourse is not the central focus of philosophy as a way of life. Theology, as indicated by Aristotle's example, which I will analyze later, is integral to philosophy as a way of life. It utilizes rational devices to investigate the cosmic truth that reveals ultimate values of human existence, and the resulting awareness of the truth is incorporated into spiritual exercises practiced by schools of ancient Greek thought.[14]

Religion in the ancient world connotes primarily the innermost feeling of devotion and piety, and the accompanying awareness of what is mightily incumbent upon one to do when one is performing rituals, ceremonies, taking oaths, or other cultic observances designed to bind an individual and community to some transcendent reality. It is more about doing, feeling, and existential states of those ritual performers, rather than concepts, doctrines, or rational persuasions.

Before established Christianity, the comparison between philosophy and religion can be conducted as follows: they aimed at largely the same target, but relied upon different means. Rites played a less prominent role in philosophers' life, and accordingly, philosophers did not consider the assistance of divine grace as the most necessary exercise, and did not make of humility, penitence, and obedience the most important virtues. Accordingly, philosophers after Socrates in ancient Greece rarely formed exclusive membership communities, and schools built by philosophers, such as Plato's Academy, were "a place for free discussion, and ... within it there was neither scholastic orthodoxy nor dogmatism."[15] Despites all these differences, both philosophical and religious practices aim to connect human beings to some cosmic, transcendent reality that reveals ultimate values of human life, and thus, to transform their whole personality.

Because of this shared commitment of philosophy and religion in the ancient world, when Christianity was rising, it was possible for Christian thinkers such as Augustine of Hippo to state that "philosophy, that is, an assiduity for wisdom, is not something different from *religio* (the worship of God)."[16] However, the establishment of Christianity in medieval Europe radically changed the meanings of philosophy, theology, and religion. Per the established view, Christianity is the genuine religion, that is, the right way to the worship of God, and its authority over humans' faithful life is based upon God revealed in the biblical scripture and articulated by orthodox doctrines of the Church. Henceforth, "theology" arises to address a need to understand the specific divine revelation in cultures and histories; for this reason, "philosophy" serves as a necessary analytic tool to help theology seek to understand an established faith. The radical change of meanings of "philosophy" vis-à-vis "theology" is visible: in ancient Greece, theology was part of philosophy as a way of life which had rich spiritual and religious significances. However, per their transformed meanings in the Christian world, philosophy was deprived of these significances, and treated instead as an intellectual enterprise to focus upon concepts, argumentation, and rationalization. In turn, theology was no longer as open to competitive or complementary views from plural resources, as philosophy as a way of life once meant it to be. This innovated form of theology utilized available cultural devices to preach or defend an established set of faith statements enshrined as orthodox within a clearly bounded religious community. Here, how Clooney's understanding of "theology" stands within the evolutionary history of the term should become comprehensible.

Shouldn't contemporary scholars of CT pay attention to the alternative meaning of "theology" in ancient Greek philosophy that has such a rich spiritual and religious implication? In the following sections, I will analyze one concrete example of this type of theology in Aristotle's works, and explain why this theology is more amenable to our understanding of the CT of Ward's type, and more important, why it is more conducive to the Ruist CT.

Comparative Theology as a Liberal Art

In Aristotle's architectonic philosophy, theology is located in metaphysics, and implicates itself extensively in biology, physics, ethics, politics, and education. I will briefly describe the structure of the philosophy before reflecting upon its theological nature.

After using four causes to explain natural phenomena in the celestial and sublunar worlds in *Physics* and *On the Heavens*, Aristotle starts to investigate the first cause, the Unmoved Mover, for the entire chain of explanatory causes in his *Metaphysics*. By the same token, after enumerating five elements in the universe, their respective natural positions and natures, in *Physics* and *On the Heavens*, Aristotle's *Metaphysics* explores what it means to be a substance in general in addition to attributes predicated on a substance, such as qualities, quantities, relatives, and so on. Thus, metaphysics, per Aristotle and its various expressions in later Western philosophy, can be defined as an inquiry into the most generic features of beings so as to define the boundary conditions of a worldview. With the guidance of this inquiry, humans can inquire further into concrete domains of the world.

Metaphysics construed as a rational and open inquiry into generic traits of beings leads to an interesting idea of "theology (*theologike*)."[17] For Aristotle, theology is necessarily part of metaphysics. While metaphysics defines the boundary conditions of a worldview, theology can be seen as lying at the cusp of these boundaries. In other words, taking the Unmoved Mover (which is the first cause of the existing world) as theology's unique object of inquiry, Aristotle's theology transformed the idea of deity prevalent in ancient Greek folklore and mythology into an ultimate Being which attracts the same extent of rational investigation as all other domains of human knowledge. In a further analysis, this first Unmoved Mover is identified as "Nous" (thought or intellect), a pervading energy (*energeia*) of pure activity, which moves the other parts of the world like an object of perception triggering perception while itself remaining unmoved.[18] As the ultimate efficient cause, Nous is involved in a perpetual process of contemplating itself; and all existing beings in the world, while moved by Nous, change, grow, and strive for it as their final cause.

The practical wisdom (*phronesis*) propounded by Aristotle in his ethics also has a final cause. Following his teacher Plato, Aristotle defines the Unmoved Mover of Nous as the ultimate "Good," and thinks the purpose of practical wisdom, which adjudicates good or bad in concrete situations, is to create conditions of a human life that resembles the divine life of Nous as much as possible. Therefore, for Aristotle, the best life of human beings is pure contemplation upon all beings in the world. However, the union between human life and its final cause, Nous, is mysterious and beyond what any philosophical discourse can describe. The unitary experience happens momentarily and instantaneously, and can never achieve the state of divinity unique to the perpetual self-contemplative life of Nous.[19] So, human life on the earth unfolds as a ceaseless process of self-perfection guided by both practical wisdom and its ultimate holy cause.

Politics should be organized according to the same principle prevailing in ethics. For Aristotle, an ideal state creates conditions for its citizens to enjoy leisure so as to practice the best life of contemplation. The education fit for the citizens should be genuine "liberal arts" defined in the sense, first, that nothing useful is downplayed. This is because practical wisdom is required for human beings to live through concrete situations to create conditions for the noblest way of life in contemplation. Second, useful subjects cannot be taught merely because they are useful. Otherwise, they would make humans a machine, and thus, be deprived of full intellectual and personal growth.[20] An education of liberal arts should therefore enlighten citizens in all subjects necessary for humans' full flourishing (*eudaimonia*). Since good human life is envisioned in Aristotle's ethics as a ceaseless process, education is also a lifelong project.

With the Aristotelian theology construed as such, it would be comprehensible why I think the CT of Ward's type is closer to Aristotle than to Aquinas.

Aristotle's theology is intrinsically comparative. This is indicated not only by the facts that, first, Aristotle's investigation of the ultimate cosmic cause starts from discussing previous theologians, natural philosophers, and mythologists in various areas of the world known to him;[21] and second, his theological conclusions are subject to further scrutiny and debate within the schools he created or influenced. Also, all beings in the world are worth knowing as a goal of contemplation because the continually unfolding divine reality of Nous is manifested in every nook and cranny of the existing world. Through contemplating them, human life enjoys its highest good while striving to become the self-contemplative Nous. In other words, Aristotle's theology contains an internal impetus to go outside for comparative and comprehensive studies of all beings in the world.

It is evident that Aristotle's theology is not a purely intellectualist endeavor, but has its rich religious import.[22] The dynamic between the ultimate Nous and humans' endless self-perfecting activities toward it is comparable to varying visions of human life shaped by spiritual exercises in many religious traditions. In particular, although the language of "divine revelation" does not prevail in the Aristotelian philosophy, Aristotle's longing for the mystical union with Nous, and his awareness of the radical limitedness of philosophical discourse in understanding the union, make that language not completely alien to his philosophy. In terms we once utilized to analyze the difference between Clooney and Ward, we can say that the ultimately indeterminate and ineffable Nous is revealed in Aristotle's architectonic philosophical discourse. The discourse is determinate, yet keeps unfolding, revisable and perfectible, as human contemplation of world phenomena deepens and expands.

Nowadays, Aristotle's type of theology is normally characterized as "natural theology" or "philosophical theology," and accordingly is thought of as merely focusing on human reason. Based on the above analysis, I conclude that this is a mischaracterization of Aristotle's work, a mischaracterization made possible only after established Christianity took away the rich spiritual and religious significance of ancient Greek thought, and accordingly displaced philosophy as a subservient analytic tool. In contemporary discussions of CT, we do not need to hold on to this mischaracterization.

Conceivably, the remaining hesitancy among contemporary readers of CT to fully recognize Aristotle's theology as theology seems to be this: Apparently, Aristotle's theology did not have a clearly bounded community to speak to. However, whether a faithful community can only be built upon the theological model of "faith seeking understanding" remains controversial.[23] Aristotle built his school, and included theology as part of liberal arts education. Following this Aristotelian model of liberal arts, faithful, noble-minded, and open-minded learners can nurture simultaneously their spiritual and their intellectual life within a variety of educational communities. These educational communities of liberal arts are indeed not equivalent to any exclusive membership community based on unalterable faith statements; however, seen as a whole, they are an anchored, long-standing, and growing community. In particular, per the Aristotelian model, this community of liberal arts does not exclude overt religious affiliates as long as these affiliates do not absolutize and reify their own determinate understanding of faith, and hence, would like to incorporate the practice of their faith and the learning of the world into an organic way of life. I believe that when Ward states that comparative theology is compatible with one's religious commitment, and he writes comparative theology as an Anglican Christian, the community he envisions is close to the one I just described.

Now, let me summarize my major claims and arguments before we move on to the possibility of Ruist CT.

The CT of Clooney's type follows a definition of theology as "faith seeking understanding" and thus pivots upon faith toward a determinate form of divine revelation pronounced in a clearly bounded home tradition. This is essentially a Scholastic project, which results in the intensification of the specificity of each faith understood similarly in varying traditions.

The CT of Ward's type conceptualizes theology as a continual human endeavor of utilizing available cultural devices to contemplate ultimate reality. It may start from a determinate form of divine revelation in one tradition, but intends to revise, enrich, and advance this form while continually learning other traditions. While sharing a general Protestant mentality, this is also distinctively an Aristotelian project, which enables Ward to embed his overt religious affiliation within a broader consciousness of human community portrayable as one of liberal arts.

Contemporary scholars find it problematic to fully recognize Ward's work as theology because their understanding of "theology" is shaped by how this term is understood after established Christianity in medieval Europe. In tandem with the establishment, philosophy is divested of its rich spiritual and religious imports, and degraded as a purely intellectual endeavor. However, in contemporary discussions of CT, it is important to recover the pre-Christian conception of theology, particularly because, first, this conception enables us to grasp other theologies in non-Christian traditions; and second, it broadens the audience of CT to all people who cherish the value of liberal arts and hence seek the truth of ultimate reality from plural perspectives. An important caveat is that this pre-Christian understanding of theology is not incompatible with Christianity. To the contrary, Aristotle's theological thought has been absorbed into the Christian tradition of philosophical theology; and more important, as indicated by the case of Ward,[24] a Christian can still embed their religious affiliation within this general Aristotelian framework of theology as a liberal art, and thus practice CT as a Christian.

Ruist Theology as a Liberal Art

It remains uncontroversial to characterize Confucius as an educator. It is also an easy argument to make that the Ruist pedagogy which Confucius's thought helped to incubate is similar to the Aristotelian "liberal arts." Just look at how strikingly similar these two statements by Aristotle and Confucius, respectively, on the purpose of education are:

> Any occupation, art, or science, which makes the body or soul or mind of the freeman less fit for the practice or exercise of excellence, is mechanical.[25]

> An exemplary person does not learn to be a utensil-like thing (器).[26]

For Aristotle and Confucius, any aspect of education to preclude the broad and continual intellectual and personal growth of individuals will make them either a "machine" or a "utensil," that is, be illiberal or ignoble, and thus less than a human. However, the question remains whether "theology" registers prominently in Ruist liberal arts. Scholars' occasional mischaracterization of the Ru tradition as solely focusing on ethics and politics, without a substantive metaphysical dimension, is due to their overlooking that the *Classic of Change* (*Yijing*), to which Confucius contributed his own interpretative thought,[27] has an everlasting influence on Ruist metaphysics. Because the classic is essential to my comparative work in the following chapters, I will briefly discuss it here to lay out a basic vocabulary for considering a Ruist theology.

Metaphysics is translated into Chinese as 形而上學, literally "a learning about things beyond shape," and this translation derives from a verse in the *Xici* (*Appended Texts*) of the *Classic of Change*, "What lies beyond shape is called the *Dao*, and what lies within shape is called the utensil-like things (形而上者謂之道, 形而下者謂之器)."[28] The underlying idea of this verse is that concrete things have a shape and can be studied like a utensil since each of them, with its concrete characteristics, serves a specific relationship to the human world. However, if this kind of study is also seen as a kind of art or technology that is limited to a specific domain of worldly phenomena, then there is another sort of learning that delves into how things in general originate, evolve, change, and, thereby, dynamically and harmoniously fit together. In a Ruist term, a learning delving into these more generic features of things in the world takes "Dao," or the Way, as its objective. Its major task is to investigate layers upon layers of "principle (理, *li*)"[29] in order to understand how things in varying worldly domains dynamically and harmoniously interrelate. For instance, from the most to less generic, terms used to characterize these principles are *yin/yang* vital-energies; four seasons; five phases (metal, wood, water, fire, and earth); eight trigrams (each of which represents one pattern of evolving harmonies in the world, such as Qian [creativity], Kun [receptivity], and Kan [risk]); sixty-four hexagrams; and so on. In a word, notwithstanding being embedded in a different linguistic and cultural system, Ruism has a metaphysical system which delves into the most generic features of things in the world, and hence, defines the boundary conditions of a Ruist worldview. In this sense, Ruist metaphysics can be compared to its Western counterparts, which are influenced by Aristotle.

Is there a "theological" dimension of Ruist metaphysics? While investigating the most generic features of things in the world, the aforementioned Ruist metaphysical text is also immensely interested in probing the origin of the world. For instance, one verse tells us that there is a sequence of ontological dependence among the aforementioned principles. "There is Ultimate Limit in the Change. Ultimate Limit creates two modes. Two modes create four images. Four images create eight trigrams."[30] In other words, the change of eight patterns of evolving harmonies in the world (eight trigrams) depends upon one of the four seasons or five phases (four images). The changing of the four seasons or five phases is furthermore conditioned by one of the *yin/yang* vital-energies, and the *yin/yang* vital-energies ultimately derive from an ontological creative origin called Ultimate Limit. In the long-standing commentarial tradition of the *Yijing*, there are two major conceptions of Ultimate Limit. One says it is the all-pervading cosmic field of vital-energy (氣, *qi*), the self-movement and further differentiation of which generate all things in the world. Another says that it is the supreme ontological principle which generates both cosmic vital-energy and all other secondary principles accounting for how vital-energies unfold and change in pattern.

Regardless, both interpretations see Ultimate Limit as the *Dao* of the cosmos, which, per the literal meaning of *Dao* as "the Way," makes the cosmos take place and start to work. Can this Ruist discourse of Ultimate Limit (or the cosmic *Dao*) be counted as theology?[31] As a rational inquiry into the ultimate cause of the cosmos, it surely can. Nevertheless, theism does not register prominently in the Ruist intellectual history of metaphysics initiated by the *Yijing*. *Dao*, albeit a constant signifier of ultimate reality, is not typically conceived of by Ruist thinkers as a creator deity, standing behind the cosmic scene and dictating its unfolding. Because of this, a more appropriate term to describe the mode of theology in Ruism may be "dao-logy," rather than "theo-logy." However, we also need to remember that even for Aristotle, his idea of God is very different from the one prominent in ancient Greek folklore and mythology. In the history of Christian philosophical theology, we also frequently encounter thinkers who modified the theistic idea of God into a de-anthropomorphized abstract force, such as Aquinas's "pure act to be," Tillich's "ground of being," and other mystical conceptions of God. Therefore, if modified to include a non-theistic mode, "theology" is surely suitable to describe that dimension of Ruist metaphysics which investigates the ultimate cause of the world and its intricate relationship to concrete worldly phenomena.

Noticeably, the vigor of broad and continual learning expressed by the Ruist pedagogy of liberal arts represents the spirit of "ceaseless self-strengthening" of an exemplary person,[32] and in the *Yijing*'s metaphysical-ethical system, this spirit furthermore manifests the *sheng sheng* constantly creative power of the cosmic *Dao*. Just as Aristotle's theology presents the first cosmic principle for human ethical deeds, and ultimately grounds his vision of liberal arts education, we find a similar ideological continuum between theology, metaphysics, ethics, and pedagogy in the Ruist case.

My argument so far is summarized as follows: For the clarification of whether Ruism has a theology, we bad better not take the Scholastic project of theology as "faith seeking understanding" as a comparative point. This is because the project requires a loyal allegiance to a determinate form of divine revelation established as "faith" at first, and then, to use human devices to understand it, a language which Ruism does not quite speak. However, Aristotle understands theology as an open and rational inquiry into ultimate reality, and it is integral to philosophy as a way of life with liberal arts as its pedagogical emphasis. I find that this Aristotelian theology is conducive to the characterization of Ruism (as Ruism is represented by the rich interpretative and commentarial tradition of the *Classic of Change*) as being equipped with a rich theological dimension. Because the key component "theo-" in the Aristotelian case does not prioritize any theistic conception, theology as such is particularly fit for us to depict the dimension of Ruist discourse that addresses the ultimate origin of the cosmos and human society. Therefore, in the following chapters, whenever a Ruist theology is mentioned, theology will be meant by the analyzed Aristotelian fashion.

Nevertheless, since Ruism has a theology practiced as a liberal art, the crucial question remains: How comparative is it? Since we interpret it using an Aristotelian term fit for Ward's Christian CT, has Ruist theology indicated features similar to the CT of Ward's type? What attitude did Ruism indicate to other peer comprehensive traditions in the ancient Chinese context? To answer these questions, I will use one very concrete example, Wang Longxi's (1498–1583 CE) understanding of the relationship among three teachings (Ruism, Daoism, and Buddhism), to present a Ruist theology of religions as a "seeded, open inclusivism."

Seeded, Open Inclusivism

Wang Longxi studied with Wang Yangming (1472–1529 CE), a landmark Ruist in the Ming dynasty, and is considered to be the founder of the "Middle Zhe" school of Wang Yangming's followers. Wang Longxi's thought continues his teacher's instruction on the pivotal significance of "conscientious knowing (良知)," an innate moral awareness, in Ruist self-cultivation, and emphasizes the spontaneous and liberating nature of this awareness. I will provide more elaborate analysis of Wang Longxi's thought in connection to the Ruist debate on the nature of knowledge in chapter 2. Here, what is of greatest interest is Wang Longxi's thought on the relationship between Ruism, Daoism, and Buddhism. Wang Longxi's reflection on the relationship took place in a very special time: the late stage of the *Daoxue* movement (道學, the learning of Dao, also termed Neo-Confucianism), when the three mentioned teachings all had established their long lineages. Therefore, envisioning the relationship from a theological perspective became an urgent topic for Ruist thinkers. In my view, Wang Longxi's thought on this topic distinctively represents the spirit of Ruist theology as a liberal art, and thus can be used to instantiate how Ruist theology comparatively looks at other traditions. In the following, I will present my original translations of Wang Longxi's three key writings on this topic before laying out my final analysis.[33] Because Wang Longxi's words in these writings are philosophically dense, I will provide my brief annotation to them whenever needed.

Text 1: A Response to the "Hall of the Three Teachings"

The Three Teachings all arose long ago. Lao spoke of "void," yet the teachings of the sages[34] also speak of "void." The Buddha spoke of "tranquility," yet the teachings of the sages also speak of "tranquility." So what distinguishes them? Today's Ru do not consider the original similarities between these [Three Teachings], treating the other two as heretical, but this is not a sensible view.

At the time of the Spring and Autumn Period, Buddhism had not yet entered China. Lao, however, witnessing the decadence of late Zhou culture and seeking to restore its foundations, regarded the practice of ritual as a sign of inadequate loyalty and trustworthiness.[35] This approach is similar to that of Kongzi, who once said that when it came to adopting rituals, he would rather follow the example of commoners than that of aristocrats.[36] Kongzi, furthermore, went to the Zhou capital and asked questions of Lao, for he later said that he had heard Lao Dan speak about all sorts of things. He therefore did not consider Lao an interloper.

Xiangshan[37] once said: "We Ru have our own heretics, for anyone who does not follow our original lineage [of teaching], but searches beyond it in the company of strange teachers, is a heretic." Yet Kongzi said, "Do I have any knowledge? No, I have no knowledge," meaning that one's conscientious knowing is initially without knowledge; and, "When a commoner asks me a question, I am completely blank" (*Analects* 9:8)— the expression "completely blank" referring to void and tranquility. Yanzi was an excellent student of Kongzi's; he said [of Yanzi]: "He's almost there, isn't he? For he frequently empties himself" (*Analects* 11:19). This was high praise! Ru of the Han dynasty made etiquette, formalities, rules, and procedures the subject of their learning and thus ignored their true goal: "complete emptiness" (as it is called).[38]

When Buddhists started to enter into China, they took charge of instructing the people, seeking to transform the disorder of their Five Aggregates[39] and restore their purity. They cultivated their three virtues[40] completely, they passed through the Six Realms[41] exhaustively, and they concentrated everything into a single thought. They demonstrated the nature of emptiness constantly, and used every difference between the sages and the common people as an occasion to advance their particular instructions. In its lowest form, however, Buddhism withers human initiative and sets out to discard ritual and law, sinking utterly into nihilism and oblivion. This is a gloomy sort of emptiness, accepted only by second-rate disciples, and was not part of Buddhism's original teachings.

From birth, humans are endowed by Heaven and Earth with a certain centeredness, each sharing a common nature. They do not begin life divided into sects, with some born Ruist, some Daoist, and others Buddhist. They are, however, all endowed with conscientious knowing, which is the genius of human nature. It brings together Heaven and Earth and everything in between into one reality, thereby encompassing all the Three Teachings. It does not submit to conventions or standards, nor is it mired in thoughts and deeds. Nothingness and being give rise to one another, and yet, [conscientious knowing] cannot be said not to exist. Stillness and motion follow one another, and yet, [conscientious knowing] cannot be said to be extinct. It likes what the common people like and dislikes what they dislike, nor is it detached from the affections and reciprocities at the heart of human relationships. From it the achievements of the sages are derived. Those who learn from the Buddha or Lao in order to restore their human nature as their foremost aim, and do not fall prey to illusions or fantasy, are simply Daoist or Buddhist Ru (道釋之儒). Among us Ru, any who would use their wisdom selfishly, failing to embrace all things and manifest the aims of our tradition, would be a Ruist heretic (儒之異端). Like the difference between one *hao* and one *li*,[42] the distinctions between these schools are very subtle. If our own Ruist teachings are understood clearly, we can confirm what is true of the other two traditions. We must get to the marrow [of Ruism], which cannot be fathomed by mere words or thought. Yet some of our Ruist confrères cannot get to the foundations of our own teachings or understand them, and so they vainly set out to castigate others with senseless clamor. This will only incur disrespect from the other two traditions and prove that we have no grasp of our own. The gentleman of Lu Yuzhong composed "The Hall of the Three Teachings" and asked for a word of approval from me in support of his teachings. I have therefore written this response and send it to him.

Text 2:

A friend asked: "Even though Buddhism is unavoidably skewed, its theories on the heartmind and human nature are nevertheless quite refined and subtle, for metaphysical realities are their principal concern. We Ru speak of rectifying human relationships, and so we cannot avoid discussing material realities, but because Ruist teachings on the heartmind and human nature have been buried and disregarded for so long, it is currently difficult for us to transcend our materialistic tendencies. If we could borrow from their way in order to galvanize our own understanding, this would not necessarily be unhelpful for our learning."

Master Wang answered: "What you have just said may seem true, but it is not. Reality cannot be separated into either metaphysical or material parts, nor have we Ru ever failed to speak of void, of tranquility, of subtlety, and of mystery, all of which have been passed down by countless sages who guarded these esoteric teachings.[43] If we follow and comprehend these, our ultimate aim shall be that which encompasses all of the Three Teachings. Ever since the learning of the sages was obscured, subsequent Ru have rejected the essentials laid down by their countless sages, believing that such topics belong to the Buddhists. Whenever emptiness and tranquility are mentioned, they consider it heresy and refuse to have any more to do with them. They do not realize that what the Buddhists speak of was originally the great Ruist way, but instead they want to adopt the way of Buddhism to enter into [wisdom]. What a great pity!

"Both the Immortalists and the Buddhists furnish learning for life beyond this human world. Although Buddhism arrived in China much later, during the Tang and Yu dynasties, men like Chao and Xu were already living a similar way of life.[44] But the learning of the sages prevailed during the Tang and Yu dynasties, and so while Chao and Xu dwelt in the mountains like common trees or rocks and were left to live and mature on their own, they were still part of the great unity fostered by Yao and Shun. There is, after all, in every generation that type of person who is simple, quiet, and detached, and cannot bear worldly matters; nor would the likes of Yao and Shun ever force them to. Because the learning of the sages was later obscured, however, the Ru of the Han dynasty insisted on debating abstract theories, miring themselves in models, classifications, formalities, and paradigms, and holding these up as the highest truths. They lost sight of the living substance of human nature, which is ever changing and flowing, and thus they were criticized and mocked by the Daoists and Buddhists who thereby managed to expand their own influence. We Ru are unaware of the great patrimony which was originally ours, and instead we willingly yield it to others. What a terrible tragedy!

"My late teacher (Wang Yangming) used to compare this to a house with three rooms. Originally, during the Tang and Yu dynasties, all three of the rooms were in our possession, and even people like Chao and Xu resided therein. In subsequent generations the learning of the sages was no longer able to maintain its preeminence, and so it was left with only the central room, having willingly yielded the rooms on the left and right to Buddhism and Daoism. As our Ruist teachings declined day by day, while Buddhist and Daoist teachings flourished day by day, we Ru willingly conceded our inferiority and hoped that by borrowing from the others we might still endure. Later, even our one central room was imperiled by our inability to ensure even our own survival, for many left and affiliated themselves with the other [two rooms]. Thus we gradually lost our patrimony without ever having realized it.

"For us Ru today, is the situation really any different? Occasionally there arise bold and exceptional scholars who cannot bear to lose everything so willingly, and so, as a matter of personal duty, they strive to uphold the truth and put the Buddhists and Daoists in their place. Such persons, however, are unable to seek the roots of things or entertain subtleties, nor can they cultivate themselves from within. They merely wish to strike up a reputation for righteousness and to triumph through sheer willfulness. With respect, all this does is to fuel the criticisms of the Daoists and Buddhists.

"My late master's teaching on conscientious knowing is the wondrous crux of all the Three Teachings. If we can start realizing this now and no longer adulterate it with any other bits of knowledge, then the others will obediently return to us, for—as they say—true teaching and heresy cannot coexist. This cannot be achieved through quarrelsome talk."

Text 3:

A gentleman, Lu of Wutai, asked about Buddhism and Daoism, to which Master Wang replied: "The teachings of these two traditions are different from our Ruist ones. However, they can still be taught alongside Ruism and are not being abandoned because they too have the Way within them.

"Everyone has a heartmind. Buddhism maintains that it arises before one is conceived by one's parents, and thus they have sayings such as 'before being born to one's parents,' and, 'free from the slightest entanglement.' They call their approach to self-cultivation, 'illuminating the heartmind and perceiving one's nature.' Daoists maintain that [the heartmind] arises before an infant is delivered from its mother's womb, and thus they have sayings such as 'at the infant's first cry, even Mount Tai lost its footing,' and 'one's heartmind was once formed in liveliness and purity, but now it has forgotten the breath of infancy.' They call their approach to self-cultivation 'mending the heartmind and refining one's nature.' We Ru, however, maintain that [the heartmind] arises during one's childhood, and thus we have sayings such as 'in childhood we come to know love and reverence . . . without studying or thinking about them,' and 'a great man has not lost the heartmind of his ruddy youth.' We call our approach to self-cultivation 'preserving the heartmind and nourishing one's nature.'[45]

"To consider the heartmind before birth is Buddhism, with its teachings of immediate enlightenment and returning to the void. To consider the heartmind after delivery from the womb is Daoism, with its teachings on refining essences, vital-energies, and spirits in order to return to the void. Two words: 'conscientious knowing'—these encompass all the Three Teachings. The embodiment of conscientious knowing is essence, its diffusion is vital-energy, and its wondrous operation is spirit; there are not three positions on this. Conscientious knowing is the void; there is no 'Oneness' to return to. This is the learning of the sages!

"If we fixate on the period before birth, we neglect the infant's delivery from the womb. If we fixate on the moment of the infant's delivery from the womb, we neglect its childhood. Childhood, however, provides a complete picture—of Heaven and Earth, and everything in between whenever we nurture and guide, raise and arrange them—yet without excluding those moments onto which the Daoists and Buddhists have latched. Any other approach cannot help but resort to false assumptions: either striving to conflate the Three Teachings as one and the same, or rejecting them as essentially different, neither of which is our understanding of the relationship between them."

These three included texts aim to illustrate Wang Longxi's understanding on the relationship between the Three Teachings (*sanjiao*): Ruism, Daoism, and Buddhism. Here is my analysis of it concerning the questions asked by this chapter:

The Way generates everything in the universe and it endows a heartmind (心) to each human being with a distinctive human nature. This is a basic fact that Wang Longxi thinks is acknowledged by all traditions. As such, when Wang expresses his view that Daoism and Buddhism also have the Way in their own distinctive modes, he reveals a profoundly pluralistic awareness shared by many other Ru and other spiritual practitioners of his day: Different traditions cultivate human relationships with the Way in different ways.

Nevertheless, Wang believes that Ruism has become the most comprehensive tradition, the insights of which into the Way potentially encompass all valuable insights furnished by the other two traditions. This characterizes Wang's view on the intertraditional relationship as a Ruism-centered inclusivism.

We must note a significant qualifier for this Ruist inclusivism: Wang does not believe that classical Ruism has exhausted all possibilities for further growth. Rather, Ruism continues to change and transform over time. On the one hand, great Ruist philosophers (such as Wang Yangming) furnished new paradigms for the tradition, thereby enriching and developing it. On the other hand, as admitted by Wang Longxi himself, Ruism continues to incorporate elements from the other traditions through a prudent judgment of their efficacy in articulating the universal and ultimately ineffable Way, thereby synthesizing them into a growing, organic body of human wisdom which nevertheless maintains continuity with classical Ruism. In short, the "inclusivism" Wang Longxi envisions is dynamic and open, rather than static and closed.

By way of comparison, this type of inclusivism is different from two of the most studied cases of inclusivism in the Christian tradition. Karl Rahner's (1904–1984 CE) theory of "anonymous Christianity" presumes that any valuable element from other traditions make them anonymously Christian. Jacques Dupuis's (1923–2004 CE) inclusivism, on the contrary, acknowledges the possibility for Christianity to learn new insights from other traditions, although he still maintains a historical "eschaton" toward which all traditions must strive. In other words, in Jacques Dupuis's vision, all traditions are supposed to fit into a ready-made Christian framework of world history so as to achieve ultimate salvation.[46] These two types of inclusivism are essentially "closed" in the sense that both believe that ultimate truth has already been achieved within one tradition, and with respect to this truth, the tradition need not develop.

In Wang Longxi's vision of Ruist inclusivism, however, he neither entertains an idea of an eschaton where human efforts to know and follow the Way can stop, nor does he believe that any valuable insight from other traditions is necessarily already present within the Ruist tradition. In a word, Wang's understanding of the relationship between Ruism and other traditions can be described as a "seeded, open inclusivism," undergirded by a pluralistic consciousness: There are multiple traditions in the world addressing varying aspects of the same cosmic and human Way. Ruism, however, from its earliest origins, has generated seeds of thought which have the great potential to encompass all valuable insights from the plurality of traditions. In time, Ruism continues to change and transform, so as to incorporate more and more elements from other traditions in order to better know the Way and tackle new challenges in human society.

The notion of "open inclusivism" within the theology of religions has piqued the interest of CT theorists. Two notable examples in this context will be examined as follows. Catherine Cornille differentiates between "closed inclusivism" and "open inclusivism" by providing examples primarily from Christian comparative theologies.[47] As defined in this chapter, the "open inclusivism" practiced by confessional Christian comparative theologians discussed by Cornille remains closed, because it assumes an unchangeable standard of truth, albeit minimal, within their home tradition. In contrast, Wang Longxi's inclusivism, conducted within a Ruist framework, is genuinely open because nothing within Ruism has been absolutized. Historically, the Ru tradition has been devoted to a distinct set of lifestyle traits, such as humanism, cosmic harmony, self-cultivation, and social and political activism. However, none of these commitments has been solidified into unalterable doctrine or dogma. Utilizing the biological metaphor of a "seed," I would argue that for a Ruist comparativist, insights from other traditions may alter the genetic code in the "seed," leading to the development of new epigenetic traits within Ruism over time.

Drawing upon Paul J. Griffiths's work on religious diversity, John J. Thatamanil expressed "a genuine sympathy and appreciation for open inclusivism." This is because Griffiths's version of open inclusivism acknowledges that religious traditions are genuinely different but not incommensurable, and that not all truth claims made by other traditions are already found in Christian traditions. Consequently, Griffiths's open inclusivism affirms the possibility of interreligious learning. However, due to Griffiths's adherence to a problematic concept of religion that asserts religions are incompossible with one another and no one can simultaneously inhabit more than one religious life, Thatamanil believes Griffiths's Christian open inclusivism cannot generate intrinsic interest in the aims of other religions. Thus, it falls short of being a robust theology of religions that promotes interreligious learning.[48]

The "seeded, open inclusivism" of Ruism that I advocate, inspired by Wang Longxi's historical writing, aims to fulfill all the criteria of a theology of religions or, in Thatamanil's terms, a "theology of religious diversity" that is suitable for interreligious learning.[49] Notably, this Ruist open inclusivism is based on a proactive reflection on the definitions of religion and theology discussed earlier. As a result, it abandons the mindset of treating religions as hermetically sealed, incompossible wholes, and refrains from claiming the superiority of Ruism as a whole over other religions. I believe that Ruism holds the potential to develop a system that incorporates truth claims from other traditions. However, the focus of this belief lies in the ongoing, ceaseless process of including, rather than in the attainment of inclusion itself. The manner in which this Ruist open inclusivism addresses the truth claims of other traditions will be elaborated on in the following discussion.

A Ruist Comparative Theology as a Liberal Art

Wang Longxi's theology of religions, characterized as a "seeded, open inclusivism," together with our previous discussions on the CT of Ward's type and Aristotle's theology as a liberal art, equips us with concepts and historical instances to elaborate on the nature of Ruist CT.

A Ruist CT conducted in the contemporary context would be a liberal art par excellence. It starts from the study and practice of the rooted tradition of Ruism, including all its historical and geographical expressions, and then continually incorporates wisdom from all over the world as evolving objective situations require and its intrinsic impetus urges. I deliberately use the term "the rooted tradition" rather than Clooney's "home tradition" because a "root" is an anchored living-being, always undergoing adaptation, revision, and growth, which is very different from the image that a bulwarked "home" evokes. In this sense, no determinate manifestation of the cosmic *Dao*, as articulated by varying thinkers and texts in historical Ruism, would be treated by contemporary Ru as final and complete; yet, while intrinsically longing for learning new determinate manifestations, Ru would not completely abandon their previously learned ones either. Neither dogmatism nor conversion. All they try to achieve is to organically inherit, sustain, and grow the tradition through cultivating themselves a creative, meaningful, and fulfilling individual human life within the community of humanity in varying and evolving life situations.

Since no determinate expression of the cosmic *Dao* is treated as an unalterable final disclosure, a Ruist CT is not confessional. This implies that a rooted Ruist way of life does not preclude "impartiality" as an achievable goal in comparative studies. In more concrete terms, a Ruist scholar of CT should and can understand compared theses accurately and evaluate compared points unbiasedly. However, the "impartiality" sought here does not derive from any transcendent bird's-eye view decoupled from concrete perspectives initiated by traditions. Rather, as I will elaborate on in chapters 2 and 4, "impartiality" in the study of CT is achievable through a hypothetical process of cross-traditional reading using the pragmatist method of "vague category." This method does not prohibit scholars from perceiving a certain issue from a traditional perspective, including a Ruist one, but it does lead to the revision of the perception when new perspectives are learned and incorporated.

This rooted, impartial, and nonconfessional nature of Ruist CT also implies that while comparing Ruism with other comprehensive traditions, Ruists, as inspired by Wang Longxi's thought analyzed above, would neither strive to conflate varying traditions as one and the same, nor reject them as incommensurably different. In other words, no judgment about "similarities" or "differences" will be delivered before an actual comparison is rigorously conducted. In certain cases, a Ruist comparativist may encounter views from other traditions that they disapprove of. As long as it is based on an accurate understanding of those views, well-argued and susceptible of scholarly debate, the disapproval is a legitimate result of comparison. In other cases, a Ruist comparativist may encounter the genuine uniqueness of theses or motifs in compared traditions, for which they cannot find any comparable counterpart in the Ru tradition. At this moment, the ineffable, continually unfolding nature of the cosmic *Dao* will prepare the Ruist comparativist well to accept and marvel at the genuine novelty that emerges from the process of comparative studies. However, whether and how to organically incorporate the novelty into the historical body of Ru wisdom will depend upon Ru scholars' continual efforts.

Finally, while doing CT, a Ruist scholar is surely writing for anyone who can comfortably identify themselves as a Ru. However, per the above analysis, since Ruism is not an exclusive membership tradition, the identity of "Ru" is not entailed by the commitment to any unalterable faith declaration or performance. Rather, the identification depends upon whether one would like to study, practice, and wrestle with all historical and contemporary expressions of Ru wisdom as one irrevocable component of one's own way of life. Since I characterize Ruist CT as a liberal art par excellence, the sustainable yet fluid identity of Ru will be immersed in the broader community of all who are intrigued by shared problems and issues in human lives. In more concrete terms, this community will be potentially extended to all of humanity, and will include anyone who cherishes the value of liberal arts education. In chapter 3, I will specify three kinds of audiences that are involved in my Ruist project of comparative theology centered on the issue of transcendence; as shall be indicated, these audiences can all be seen as part of the broader community of liberal arts I envision here.

2 Comparative Theology as a Science

The construal of theology as part of metaphysics integral to philosophy as a way of life, which is replete with religious significances, puts any project of comparative theology (CT) in a prominent spot. This is because the name of "metaphysics" has been tarnished since the time of early modern philosophy, and historical voices reverberate in the contemporary academy, doubting whether metaphysics can afford any legitimate knowledge.

Can theology and metaphysics be pursued as a science? This question is uniquely challenging for the CT project I am pursuing, because, as argued in chapter 1, whenever "metaphysics" and "theology" are mentioned, they now include their Ruist instantiations. Consequently, we can ask related questions as follows: Can theological pursuit in the Ru tradition afford scientific knowledge as well? Will the way in which theology is pursued in the Ru tradition revise our sense of "science," currently implied mainly by Western sources?

This chapter will answer all these leading questions in three steps: First, since the terms used to formulate the central question of this chapter (i.e., how can theology and metaphysics be pursued as a science?) derive from a Western origin, I will analyze those terms and answer the question using Western sources. Second, drawing upon my knowledge of the Ru tradition, I will advocate for enriching our vocabulary to include non-Western traditions, so as to facilitate a global conversation on metaphysics and theology. Last, I will canvass the distinction between the Western and Ru metaphysics in general, and seek valuable insights for the particular comparative project on Christianity and Ruism.

Metaphysics and Its Challenge from Modern Science

As discussed in chapter 1, metaphysics, per Aristotle and its various expressions later in Western philosophies, can be defined as a rational and open inquiry into the most generic features of things so as to define the boundary conditions of a worldview, under the guidance of which humans can inquire further into concrete domains of the world. Theology lies at the cusp of those metaphysical boundaries and takes the ultimate cause of the existing world, that is, ultimate reality, as its unique object of inquiry. Relying upon the all-encompassing nature of metaphysical discourse, theology implicates itself pervasively within varying aspects of daily human life: scientific inquiries, education, ethics, politics, and so on. For Aristotle, metaphysics was surely a science because he believed science implies the application of the universal logic of human reason (that is, the Aristotelian logic of categorization and syllogism) to the investigation of particular objects so as to constitute a method fit for each domain of human knowledge.[1] Therefore, the object of metaphysics and theology as "being qua being," that is, the most generic traits of things insofar as they exist, is certainly a specific domain of human knowledge open to inquiry and rational debate.

From this standpoint, science is essentially a humanistic endeavor. It takes the formal, logical rules of human reason, and the feedback furnished by objective scrutiny, as the sole authority, which is then vulnerable to further critique and refinement. As substantiated by Aristotle, both metaphysics and theology were historically pursued as a science.

Nevertheless, during the time of modern scientific revolution, humanity's understanding of science was renewed. The model of science is now conceived of as a formal system of mathematical symbols, each of which refers to a specific aspect of reality. Through mathematical systems, the consequences of any hypothesis about studied reality can be referred to measurable facts in laboratories, observatories, and social surveys so that the truth of the original hypothesis be temporarily secured. It is the exact mapping between the deductive relationship among mathematical symbols and the causal relationship among natural phenomena that has generated the greatest power for science to transform nature. For the exact knowledge of natural causalities can now be utilized to invent technologies in order to harness part of causal chains in nature for producing desirable effects.

Given this renewed vision of science, it is not surprising that the aforementioned distrust of metaphysics in modern times continues to arise. Metaphysics, for its modern critics, is just too abstract and speculative. There seems to be no way to settle any metaphysical claim because it is hard, if not impossible, to deduce measurable consequences from it, and thus, have its seemingly ethereal claims landed in concrete realities. For instance, Rudolf Carnap views that if a statement, such as metaphysical ones, cannot be verified by observable facts, then it is just meaningless![2]

Nonetheless, despite these critiques, philosophers, theologians, and scientists are continually asking and attempting to resolve great metaphysical questions. In the twentieth century, we witnessed the formation of robust metaphysical systems, such as the development of process thought by Alfred Whitehead, as well as the flourishing of philosophical theology by Christian thinkers, such as Friedrich Schleiermacher, Paul Tillich, and Robert Neville, to name a few this book will focus on later. All these metaphysicians and theologians considered their pursuits to be undoubtedly scientific, because these pursuits all pertain to rational constructions of human intelligence about perceived realities, and the efficacy of these constructions are subject to further critique and reconstruction due to the continuous feedback furnished by the objective traits of evolving realities. In other words, metaphysics and theology are currently pursued as a scientific endeavor.

Addressing the Criticisms

Nonetheless, it would not satisfy those modern critics of metaphysics to merely point out the fact that metaphysics and theology have continued to thrive despite their critiques. After all, it was Kant who averred that although metaphysics cannot be pursued as a science, it is still a tendency intrinsic to human reason, so that people will continue to conjure up metaphysical systems and be accordingly involved in metaphysical controversies, yet with no hope of eventually obtaining any settlement on them.[3] This means that in order to convince modern readers of the scientific nature of metaphysics and theology, we also need to explain how the pursuit of metaphysics and theology as a science is possible while using terms that are accessible to those modern critics and, thus, addressing concerns raised by them. In the following, I will use two steps to propose such an explanation. First, I will refute some of Kant's key arguments against the scientific nature of metaphysics, and utilize some of his reflections on the regulative role of metaphysical ideas to channel a more positive assessment of metaphysics. Second, I will follow the tradition of critical rationalism in the philosophy of science to explain how metaphysics can fit into the scientific method.

Three major points make up my critique of Kant's suspicion of the scientific nature of metaphysics. First, Kant's critique of the ambivalent nature of metaphysical debates failed to take into consideration the full range of metaphysical legacies before him, and hence did not do justice to what is at stake in those metaphysical reasonings. For example, Kant thinks the thesis that "time has a beginning" versus its antithesis "time is infinite" can both be refuted as false. Accordingly, human reason will necessarily be trapped in an antinomy where no criterion helps to decide the truth of competing metaphysical theses.[4] Nevertheless, the metaphysical tradition of *creatio ex nihilo* before Kant clearly differentiates the cosmologically temporal sense of the beginning of time versus the ontologically nontemporal one. In Thomas Aquinas's thought, for instance, the beginning of the temporal sequence of cosmic events can either exist or not. However, whether having a temporal beginning or not, the cosmos still ontologically depends upon an ultimate creative "pure act to be" which initiates all modes of cosmic times in a nontemporal way. Hence, "time has a beginning" and "time is infinite" can indeed both be true, and why this is so depends upon particular metaphysical traits, cosmological or ontological, we are talking of about the phenomenon of time.[5] Evidently, Kant's analysis of the antinomy surrounding the concept of time oversimplified Aquinas's metaphysical argument, which undermines his critique of metaphysics in general.

Second, Kant demands metaphysical knowledge be synthetic a priori and then denies such a status of knowledge to metaphysics based upon the reason that the pure categories of human understanding cannot be applied to the whole of human experience.[6] Nevertheless, a fallibilist epistemology can readily dismiss Kant's approach. Metaphysical knowledge, despite pertaining to the most generic features of things in the world, does not need to be a priori. Often functioning as deeper assumptions about the structural features of an inquisitive worldview, metaphysical knowledge derives from various sources of human experience and guides, implicitly or explicitly, the application of human intelligence to investigating concrete domains of the world. As I'll elaborate later, taking the more concrete knowledge of the objective world as a system of peripheral epistemic statements, metaphysical knowledge at its core is susceptible of being continually tested, adjusted, and readapted in order to guide humans to engage more effectively those evolving realities. In other words, it is the debatable, a posteriori, and correctible nature of metaphysical knowledge that makes it on a par with any other scientific endeavor.

Third, Kant's evaluation of metaphysical knowledge is not entirely negative. He thinks that despite being unable to furnish certain knowledge, metaphysics provides human reason with ideas to regulate the application of pure categories of human understanding so that derived empirical knowledge can progress.[7] For instance, although metaphysics cannot produce certain knowledge about the beginning of time, the idea of "beginning of time" can still regulate human understanding's use of the category of causality so that scientists would try to find the beginning of time or a more original cause of the cosmos in the long run.

In my view, it is the regulative role of metaphysics in scientific inquiries that speaks to its own scientific nature, because whether one specific version of metaphysics can regulate scientific inquiries well is one important criterion to debate the efficacy of such metaphysical knowledge. For instance, in the history of modern science, René Descartes was the first scientist who came up with a comprehensive mechanical cosmology to provide a physical account for the heliocentric Copernican astronomy. However, Descartes's physics was replaced later by Newton's, and one major reason for Descartes's theory to have lost favor among scientists is that compared with Newton's metaphysical assumption of atomism, Descartes's idea of body as "extension" precludes the existence of vacuum.[8] As a result, it is not easy for Descartes to isolate an ideal status of those natural phenomena under investigation in order to build a mathematical model of them for testing hypotheses and predicting future outcomes. In other words, Descartes's metaphysics produced physical reasoning that was too complicated and, in this sense, it did not regulate the concerned scientific enquiries well and was replaced by scientists with a more viable alternative.

In a nutshell, Kant did not do justice to the rich legacy of metaphysics before him; and theses listed in his antinomies for the sake of debunking the scientific nature of metaphysics are actually debatable. A fallibilist epistemology makes Kant's doubts about the a priori status of metaphysical knowledge misplaced; and using Kant's own terms, whether a metaphysical view can well regulate scientific inquiries is one significant criterion to judge its scientific efficacy. Given these reflections on Kant, it would not be difficult for us to explain how metaphysics and theology can be pursued as a scientific endeavor in a more positive way.

A significant improvement of Imre Lakatos's philosophy of science upon Karl Popper's theory on the demarcation of science versus pseudoscience is that Lakatos emphasizes the holistic nature of scientific theories, which he called a "research program" consisting of a core of central theses and more auxiliary hypotheses.[9] Popper's criteria for distinguishing science from pseudo-science (i.e., testability, refutability, and falsifiability) is kept by Lakatos; however, per Lakatos, in order to ensure that the scientific nature of a specific piece of human knowledge is retained, we need to evaluate the falsifiability of an entire research program to which that piece of human knowledge belongs. The process of such an evaluation may be complicated and time-consuming, involving all available criteria of scientific truth, but in theory, the evaluation is still viable, just as the raised case of Descartes versus Newton indicated. Therefore, the right place for metaphysics and theology in a scientific research program lies at the core of its central theses.

How to Incorporate Non-Western Metaphysics and Theologies into a Global Conversation

Under the subheading "Ruist Theology as a Liberal Art" in chapter 1, I provided a basic set of vocabulary drawing on the Ruist commentarial tradition of *Yijing* to discuss Ruist metaphysics and theology in light of Aristotle's comparable ideas. This being the case, can metaphysics and theology, while including the Ruist case as a family member, still be pursued as a scientific endeavor?

Science, per the above analysis, is a symbolic construction by human intelligence about reality, and the construction is vulnerable to further critique and revision within a scientific community owing to the continuous feedback furnished by perceived realities. Particularly according to the work of Joseph Needham on the history of science in ancient China, it is evident that Ruist metaphysics can inspire modern scientists to create more robust conceptual tools to capture the biological, organic, and process aspects of worldly phenomena so as to contribute to the positive sciences. However, for appreciating that Ruist metaphysics and theology were historically pursued as a scientific endeavor in their own right, we need to broaden our understanding regarding both how realities are perceived and what kind of feedback realities can furnish to refine a Ru thinker's symbolic construction.

In the model of modern scientific methodology discussed above, realities to revise scientific hypotheses are perceived mainly with a detached attitude. In other words, realities are perceived as data loaded with metrics, and they are obtained by objective observers through controlled experiments in laboratories, observatories, or social surveys, with a minimal involvement of the subjective traits of those observers themselves, such as emotions, characters, biographies, and so on. Correspondingly, the purpose of scientific construction is to locate the natural causalities linking varying aspects of reality with an expectation that the resultant knowledge can be put to further technological use. In contrast, the primary purpose of Ruist metaphysics and theology is not to represent reality objectively with a strong motive toward controlling it. Instead, the metaphysical and theological contemplation of Ruist thinkers serves a series of ethical, social, and political goals premised upon the self-transformation of those thinkers themselves. This also means that while continually debating each other, Ruist thinkers tend to draw upon a much broader range of human experience to substantiate and critique varying metaphysical and theological stances.[10]

It is of crucial importance to grasp this characteristic of Ruist theological debate because when we compare Christianity and Ruism regarding the theological controversy in question in the following chapters, criteria to adjudicate the truth of each compared metaphysical view will go beyond the usual ones in the discourse of modern sciences such as the logical coherence of ideas, the correspondence of ideas to observed realities, and the predictive power of theories. I will use a concrete example from the intellectual history of Ruism to indicate why this is so.

The Example of Ruist Metaphysical Debate on Self-Cultivation

The Ruist program of self-cultivation is specified by the classical text, the *Great Learning*, as consisting of eight steps: It starts from an investigation of things (格物), followed by attaining the needed knowledge (致知). Individuals can then make their intentions authentic (誠意) and rectify their heartmind (正心) further while cultivating their sense of self (修身). In this way, one can be dedicated to aligning one's family (齊家) and governing one's country (治國); and eventually, one can contribute to bringing harmony and peace to everything under the heavens (平天下). In the commentarial tradition of this text, two lineages of thought furnished widely different interpretations. One is called the learning of principle (理學), which embraces a more extrinsic style of learning and self-cultivation and demands that the entire program should focus on investigating the principles of things so as to understand how realities in the cosmic and human realms fit together. The other lineage is called the learning of heartmind (心學), which interprets the character "knowledge (知)" as "conscientious knowing (良知)" and insists that the fulcrum of the entire program is to rediscover and maintain an ethical mindfulness so that one's innate moral consciousness can be firmly applied to correcting things and affairs in the world. There are two pithy phrases to illustrate the difference between these two interpretations. For the latter, the heartmind is the principle of things (心即理),[11] so that an individual's self-cultivation should focus on preserving humanity's instinctive sense of ethics in any situation. However, the former, although it also acknowledges that the heartmind can comprehend the principles of reality (心具理),[12] denies that the principles of things can be entailed by the immediate interaction between outside things and the human heartmind. In other words, there are objective traits to the principles of things that exceed the direct grasp of the heartmind, so we must continue our learning in order to digest and include more principles in our heartmind.[13]

To make my point in the prior paragraph, we need first to understand that despite proposing divergent views, these two lineages of Ru thought both draw from a wide range of human experience to substantiate their understanding of key terms in the text. For instance, according to Cheng Yi (1033–1107 CE), a pioneering Ru philosopher for the learning of principle, studies about the external world with the help of books, ethical experience through empathizing with and assessing the deeds of human fellows, and firsthand practical dealings with human affairs[14] are all perceived as sources of realities to implement Cheng's investigation of principles of things, which (according to our analysis in chapter 1) is a richly metaphysical and theological pursuit. By the same token, for thinkers in the lineage of the learning of heartmind, such as Wang Longxi (1498–1583 CE), multiple ways are recognized as reaching "conscientious knowing," and thus having individuals become aware of the ontological bond between humans and the cosmic *Dao*. Wang notes, "There are three ways someone might achieve awareness (悟): Some achieve it through words, some achieve it through quiet-sitting, and some achieve it through effort and practice amid the changing circumstances of daily living."[15] Compared to Cheng Yi's statement, Wang impressively emphasizes that Ruist spiritual practices, such as quiet-sitting, are also important sources of reality that contribute to the refinement of one's learning and personhood.

Not only did Ruist thinkers muster all available sources of human experience to substantiate their metaphysical and theological inquiries, they also debated with each other in such a multifaceted way. As mentioned above, the idea that the heartmind is the principle in the learning of heartmind implies that the conscientious knowing of humankind, as an innate sort of moral realization, encompasses all possible principles of things in the world. Thus, self-cultivation should be merely about rediscovering and preserving this intrinsic moral consciousness, rather than studying extensively the outside world. To this idea, thinkers in the lineage of the learning of principle, such as Luo Qinshun (1465–1547 CE), propounded a powerful counterargument. "The heartmind is that by which humans are aware and sensitive [of things in the world]. It is where principles come in and reside. Why did they [i.e., thinkers in the learning of heartmind] think that heartmind is the principle, and thus, investigating the principles of things has just been reduced into investigating the heartmind?"[16] In other words, for Luo, the heartmind is one thing among many things, and each of these myriad things has its own unique principle to be investigated. Therefore, a more plausible approach to self-cultivation is to investigate principles of both the outside world and the heartmind so as to understand how all of them can fit together, rather than focusing predominantly on just one side of the equation.

Throughout Luo's writing, we find that he used at least three methods to exposit his own view of heartmind and debate his fellow Ruists in the learning of heartmind. First, he asserts that the discourse about conscientious knowing should follow a coherent ontological logic:

> If we say humanity's conscientious knowing is equal to the principle of the cosmos, then we would have to think human nature and human awareness are just one thing. However, in my view, we should differentiate these two. The reality of human nature derives from the original state of human life (天性之真乃其本體), while human awareness is just the wondrous function of human nature (明覺自然乃其妙用). Human nature is endowed by the constantly creative power of the cosmos at

the beginning of humanity's birth, but human awareness can only start to function after humans are born. If we have the original state at first, we can expect its function to follow suit. But we cannot take the function as the same as its original state.[17]

Here, Luo utilizes the traditional Ruist metaphysical terms of "original state (體)" and "function (用)" to specify the correct ontological order of metaphysical entities. The principle of the cosmos (天理) is the original state of human life, which endows a specific nature to the human species, and that nature is manifested through the function of human awareness. In this way, human awareness comes at the end, rather than at the beginning, so that the identification of human awareness with the principle of the cosmos made by the learning of heartmind is misplaced.

Second, Luo doubts whether views proposed by the learning of heartmind can benefit people's actual practice of self-cultivation. He says,

> If we think people's conscientious knowing is equal to the principle of the cosmos, then what seems easy and simple will be practiced at first, and what needs labor and effort (工夫) will follow. But what follows shall be normally delayed. . . . If we say the principle of the cosmos is not equal to conscientious knowing, then what seems easy and simple will be arranged afterwards, and what needs labor and effort will be practiced at first. Then, people will rush to do what is the number one priority.[18]

In other words, if we think all we need to do for self-cultivation is to rediscover and maintain our innate moral consciousness, this seemingly easy and simple approach will make the laborious process of learning new principles of things unnecessary. In Luo's view, the practical consequence of this approach will undermine the genuine goal of Ruist self-cultivation; that is, the goal to transform human individuals during the process of learning and tackling things and affairs in the world.

Third, Luo refers to a commonsense observation of facts to refute the metaphysical claim "conscientious knowing is the principle of the cosmos" by the learning of heartmind. He says,

> If we consider conscientious knowing as being the principle of the cosmos, should we think as a result that the myriad things between heaven and earth all have this conscientious knowing? For the sublimity of heaven, it is difficult for us to perceive it; for mountains, rivers, and the broad earth, I did not find they have conscientious knowing, as well. There are really many things in the world, and our knowledge cannot

easily cover them; for grass, wood, metal, and stone, I really did not find they have any conscientious knowing.... We should know that the nature of each of the myriad things is nothing but their principle. Even for those things that have no consciousness whatsoever, they have their own principles. If this is not the case, then we cannot say that they have their own natures and there would then be things that do not have their own natures (which is absurd). From this perspective, we must be clear that conscientious knowing is not what the principle of the cosmos is all about.[19]

In other words, because each and every thing in the universe has a principle to account for how components of the thing can dynamically and harmonious fit together and how the thing can coexist with other things, and because not everything has the same degree of "awareness" or "consciousness," the moral conscientious knowing of humankind cannot be equivalent to what the principle of the cosmos implies.

Among all three arguments, the first and third refer respectively to the philosophical coherence of concepts and the existence of facts to critique metaphysical and theological views, which are comparable to the way similar views would be argued in the framework of a modern scientific methodology. However, the second argument points to the practical dimension of metaphysical and theological discourse, which takes the self-transformation of personhood as its primary goal. I therefore conclude that if we expand our understanding about how human experiences are furnished to refine preestablished symbolic systems, it is clear that Ruist metaphysics and theology were likewise historically pursued as a scientific endeavor.

The Harmonization of Western-Ruist Metaphysics and Theologies

The phenomenon in which metaphysics and theology are deeply involved in the self-transformation of personhood is not uniquely Ruist. As discussed in chapter 1, this idea is central to philosophy as a way of life in ancient Greek thought as well.[20] Readers may already have a sense that the very efforts of my inquiries into issues on comparative metaphysics and theology aim to bring traditions together, while highlighting and focusing on distinctive features of each tradition. But why do we need to do so? Why do we need to broaden our understanding of "science" so as to include non-Western metaphysics and theologies in a global conversation? To put it simply, that is because none of the compared traditions (the Western and Ruist ones) are perfect, even when being assessed according to their own historically envisioned goals.

Regarding the role of metaphysics in the origination and development of modern science, without any exaggeration, I realize that without Platonism, there would have been no modern science. The prioritization of the Ideal over the material world in Platonism allows a mindset to see concepts, mathematical symbols, and their intricate interrelationships as constituting an independent realm of realities that deserves to be studied alone for its own sake. This Platonic interest in the intelligible world was quickly translated into Aristotle's contemplation of pure knowledge, which was seen as the perfect happiness of human beings. In medieval times, it helped systemize the Christian idea of a divine *Logos*, and the world was accordingly seen as obeying basic rules and laws in a divine plan even before the world was created. In modern times, the revival of Platonism was at the very core of the scientific projects pursued by pioneers such as Copernicus, Galileo, Descartes, and others. For Karl Popper, his metaphysics of three worlds, especially the world of objective knowledge, is obviously an offspring of Platonism, and it is the very interaction between the human mental world and the objective physical world as mediated by the world of objective knowledge that powers the development of science.[21]

The reason I highlight the metaphysics of Platonic dualism is that in the Ruist metaphysical and theological tradition, concepts and mathematical ideas have never been studied alone for their own sake. If any deductive relationships among these concepts and ideas are revealed, the resultant knowledge is either used to interpret classics, such as the *Classic of Change*, or quickly related to broader worldly phenomena so as to serve the distinctive Ruist goals of individual self-cultivation, social management, and politics. In other words, for the Ruist thinkers who have come under my purview, the world has not been perceived as susceptible to pure intellectual analysis, and the idea of a Platonic "intelligible world" has usually never come to their mind.[22] Since this idea represents a significant difference between Western and Ruist metaphysical and theological traditions, we can therefore discuss further the pros and cons of each tradition.

The value of Western metaphysics, as it is embodied by Platonic dualism and its accompanying idea of an intelligible world, consists in its contribution to a unique attitude toward objective knowledge, which further promotes the formation of modern science. However, I will point out two of its major negative consequences. One, the pursuit of knowledge for the sake of knowledge itself implies that the ethical evaluation of how pure knowledge is applied to technology in human society at large is severed from the production of that knowledge. The resulting chasm of fact and value in human consciousness has caused major humanitarian crises since the twentieth century, such as environmental disasters and the escalating threat of nuclear war. Two, the narrative of "divine plan" in major Western religions, which was historically fueled by the ontological priority of Platonic Ideas over materials, indicates an uncompromisingly exclusive tendency which has led to major religious conflicts among groups, nations, and civilizations. In modern times, these conflicts were addressed by the institutional arrangement of the separation of church and state in liberal democracies. However, the relentless interruption of religion into public discourse speaks to the difficulty in keeping the two apart, and the increasing diversification of faiths and cultures in major democratic countries also makes classical Western philosophical wisdom untenable for many.

As for Ruist metaphysics and theology, although it has not yet been essential to the formation of modern science, its advantage seems to be exactly what can alleviate those negative impacts generated by Western metaphysics and theology. By "its advantage," I mean Ruism's holistic, unifying, and harmonizing mindset that is essential to the sustainability of any civilization. Apart from the above example of metaphysical argumentation, I would like to use two further ones to illustrate the point. First, in the history of ancient East Asia, Ruism has contributed to a robust set of basic ethical standards oriented toward the harmonization of human relationships so that people in varying levels of civilization (from individuals, families, and communities all the way up to societies and countries) can live together and co-thrive. The program of self-cultivation in the *Great Learning* analyzed above serves as an instance of those Ruist ethical standards leading to civilizational co-thriving. Second, Ruist metaphysics has indicated an incredibly open-minded, accommodating, and inclusive potential throughout the intellectual history of ancient Chinese thought. During the Han dynasty of China (206 BCE–220 CE), Ruism adopted major elements in non-Ruist ancient Chinese philosophies such as Daoism and Legalism, and achieved its first intellectual synthesis around the second century BCE, which became an ideological backbone of Chinese society in later times. In the Song through Ming dynasties of China (960–1644 CE), Ru thinkers adopted major achievements of Buddhist and Daoist philosophies, which marked the second apex of ancient Chinese thought. And its impacts were broadly manifested in East Asian countries and constituted the foundation of their modernization. More important, I believe the third synthesis of Ruism is under way because of its encounter with Western philosophies and religions beginning around the sixteenth century. During this ongoing process, the Ruist theology of religions termed "seeded open inclusivism" in chapter 1 provides a noble ideal for contemporary Ru scholars to pursue.

Given the distinction and imperfections of the compared traditions, I believe what is urgent for the agenda of Western metaphysical and theological study is to regain the unity of human knowledge and human praxis without undermining its scientific sharpness. During the process, non-Western traditions such as Ruism can undoubtedly provide further insights that will be integral to a new era of global wisdom. On the other side, Ruists need to think about how to incorporate the Platonic conception of an intelligible world and its related valuable Western metaphysical and theological ideas into their own lexicon about world principles so that a mandate of harmonization between the West and the East can be carried out more fully in this new era. The comparative project that this book will carry on, despite not directly tackling the inclusion of Platonism into the Ru tradition, will hopefully contribute some insights on it.

Last but not least, the emphasis of the Ruist metaphysical tradition on grounding intellectual ideas upon social realities furnishes a special guidance for the following project of Ruist CT: Since the study of CT is not for the sake of comparison but rather for the purpose of tackling concerned theological problems, I will furthermore submit that a Ruist CT would not tackle theological problems for purely intellectual reasons, although it does not exclude those reasons either. I will argue in the next chapter that these problems are actually implicated by a long-standing historical debate. In other words, the non-dualistic characteristic of Ruist metaphysics guides the implementation of a Ruist CT as a rooted tradition incorporating novel thoughts and responsive to historical situations.

3 The Transcendence Debate in the History of Christian-Ru Interaction

Significant exchanges of religious and philosophical ideas between Christianity and Ruism began with the arrival of Catholic missionaries in China during the sixteenth and seventeenth centuries. Since then, as primarily reflected in international English-language historiography and scholarship, three stages of Christian-Ru interaction can be identified: the first stage being the aforementioned, the second involving Protestant missionaries visiting China in the mid-nineteenth century, and the third commencing around World War II and continuing to evolve. In all three stages, a persistent "transcendence debate" exists, yet remains unresolved.[1] This debate concerns the controversy over whether the Ruist concept of *Tian* (heaven, cosmos, or the universe), or its metaphysically more accurate referent *Taiji* (Ultimate Limit), is transcendent when compared to Christian notions of the Creator God.

This ongoing transcendence debate necessitates an updated response from a Ruist perspective. I must examine the points of contention among scholars and attempt to find ways to resolve the debate. This addresses "why" I am motivated to pursue this comparative project and identifies the social reality upon which my comparison of metaphysical and theological ideas is based.

Chapter 3, therefore, selects representative figures to survey the transcendence debate across its three historical stages, pinpoints the contested issues, and ultimately suggests a comparative methodology to progressively engage in the ongoing debate. Emphatically, the analysis in this chapter does not attempt to provide exhaustive studies of all figures that, associated with different traditions, have been involved in the historical debate. Neither does this chapter aim to isolate each identified stage of Christian-Ru interaction and provide unique scholarship to each of them.

Rather, the focus is to identify patterns, repetitive themes, and concepts across the stages of the debate to orient the further study of the intellectual histories of transcendent creation in compared traditions, and ultimately to locate questions that the final conclusion of this comparative project must address.

The First Stage
MATTEO RICCI (1552–1610 CE) AND HIS FOLLOWERS

As the initiator of the first stage of interaction regarding transcendence, Matteo Ricci's *The True Meaning of the Lord of Heaven* is a magnum opus that exemplifies Ricci's missionary strategy, described by scholars as "accommodation." On one hand, it attempts to find similar theistic terms and ideas, such as *Tian* or *Shangdi* (supreme deity), in pre-Confucian Ruist classics to demonstrate that this form of "original Ruism" contains seeds of truth capable of accommodating the spread of the Christian message. On the other hand, it argues that these original theistic Ruist ideas were later corrupted by the naturalizing and humanizing mainstream Ruist teachings, which were first developed by Confucius and then refined by his followers up until Song and Ming Ruism, the flourishing form of Ruism during Ricci's time. Ricci believed that by accommodating the Christian message within an indigenous Chinese mindset, his mission could fulfill the potential of truth seeded in original Ruism and consequently correct the nontheistic contaminants of later Ruism.[2]

If the first part of Ricci's missiology can be viewed as a creative reinterpretation of pre-Confucian Ruist classics aimed at bridging the hermeneutical gap between the two traditions, its second part implies a significant theological challenge arising from the fact that, by Ricci's time, Ruism had developed a highly sophisticated form of metaphysics based on classical Ruist texts such as the *Xici* (*Appended Texts*) of the *Yijing* (*Classic of Change*), which I analyze initially in chapter 1.

In *Xici*, *Tian* is not conceived as a supreme deity reigning above the heavens and controlling the destinies of human society, as it once was in pre-Confucian Ruist classics. Instead, *Tian* is considered an all-encompassing and perpetually creative cosmic power that brings all things in the universe into existence, without a creator orchestrating from behind the scenes. Within this all-inclusive existential field of *Tian*, *Xici* also explores layers of principles (*li*) that elucidate the origin and order of the ever-changing cosmic entities, among which the *yin* and *yang* vital-energies (*qi*) are particularly prominent. In other words, for explanatory purposes, the alternation and interaction of *yin* and *yang* vital-energies are regarded in *Xici* as the most pervasive principles, as the verse "one *yin* and one *yang* is called the Way" aptly summarizes. However, with another enigmatic verse, "*Taiji* (Ultimate Limit) generates two modes,"[3] *Xici* endeavors to identify a singular principle that can account for the origin of cosmic vital-energies. In short, *Xici* presents a potentially comprehensive cosmology that not only describes the general characteristics of cosmic changes but also indicates the ontological origin of the entire universe. As mentioned earlier, this Ruist cosmology was later developed, during Ricci's time, by Song through Ming Ruist thinkers such as Zhou Dunyi (1017–1073 CE), Zhu Xi (1130–1200 CE), and Luo Qinshun (1465–1547 CE) into a dominant metaphysical worldview among Ru literati.

Challenged by the sophisticated form of Ruist cosmology that his mission sought to fulfill, Ricci needed to prove why his Christian counterpart was superior. He adopted two methods: First, Ricci introduced Ru literati to the most sophisticated Christian doctrine of creation in his time—that of Thomas Aquinas, which centers on *creatio ex nihilo*—using accessible Chinese language and concepts. Second, using Scholastic vocabulary, Ricci differentiated between two kinds of ontological entities that are either "self-sustaining" (substance) or "dependent-upon others" (attributes). Ricci took the literal meaning of *Taiji* as explained in Zhu Xi's metaphysics and argued that *Taiji* was merely a general name for all kinds of principles, such as the musical forms played by instruments or the geometrical figures embodied in furniture. As such, *Taiji* would not be able to sustain itself and, therefore, could not be considered the origin of the cosmos.[4]

Following Ricci, Catholic missionaries developed similar arguments regarding the ontological status of *Taiji*. For instance, while maintaining Aquinas's conception of divine creation as a process in which God formulates ideas and forms in His divine intelligence into His divine plenitude of being, Julius Aleni (艾略儒, 1582–1649) and Alexandre de la Charme (孙璋, 1695–1767) construed *Taiji* as the formless "primary material (元質, *yuanzhi*)," equivalent to the Ruist idea of "primordial vital-energy (元氣, *yuanqi*)."[5] They further interpreted Aquinas's idea of divine "plenitude of being" as *yuanzhi* in Chinese and concluded that *Taiji*, as *yuanzhi*, must have been created by the Christian God.

Clearly, whether interpreting *Taiji* as a general principle or as primordial vital-energy, Ricci and his followers all regarded the ontological status of *Taiji* as inferior to the Christian God. For them, the Christian God was more transcendent since He alone could be the origin of cosmic realities, including the reality of *Taiji*.

COUNTERARGUMENTS FROM RUIST SCHOLARS

Considering the abundant heritage and extensive theoretical possibilities of Ruist metaphysics during Ricci's era, it is not surprising that Ruist scholars would reject Ricci's and his followers' arguments. Following the publication of Ricci's work, a series of counterarguments quickly emerged. Two examples will help illustrate the situation.

Addressing the claim that Ultimate Limit is merely an attribute-like principle and therefore cannot sustain itself, Huang Zhen cited a verse from the Ruist canon, the *Zhong Yong*: "The Way [which, according to Huang Zhen, also signifies Ultimate Limit and the singular supreme principle] cannot be abandoned for even a moment. If it can be abandoned, it is not the Way." He contended that all human and cosmic realities rely on the creativity of Ultimate Limit. As a result, the Ultimate Limit sustains itself, rather than depending on others.[6]

Moreover, whether Ultimate Limit is perceived as an attribute-like principle or as the "primary material"–like vital-energy, neither interpretation aligns with the ultimate ontological status of Ultimate Limit as recognized by the *Xici* and Zhu Xi's interpretation. For this reason, Chen Houguang stated:

> Matteo Ricci knows neither *Tian* nor *Shangdi*. How can he comprehend the Ultimate Limit? Ultimate Limit is the source of principles, so it cannot be regarded merely as one principle. Ultimate Limit is the origin of vital-energy, so it cannot be considered merely as vital-energy. Retracting, it has no beginning, so it can initiate things. Advancing, it has no end, so it can complete things.[7]

These Ruist counterarguments offer a glimpse into the intensity of the transcendence debate during its initial phase. Regrettably, as the debate unfolded alongside the worsening "Rites Controversy," which eventually led to the official ban of Christian missionaries from China in 1721, there were no signs of mutual understanding from either party. In relation to the outcome of the debate's initial stage, Yu Chunxi's words are revealing: "If the teaching of the Lord of Heaven [i.e., Christianity] gains a foothold in China, there will be nothing in Ruism's doctrine of Ultimate Limit . . . that can be committed to."[8] This statement was meant to convey that, as observed by this Ru scholar, Christianity and Ruism were mutually exclusive concerning the contested metaphysical issue.[9]

The Second Stage: James Legge

James Legge (1815–1897), a British Congregationalist missionary, took center stage in the second phase of the transcendence debate. Legge's scholarship on Ruism reiterated essential elements of Ricci's missiology: He maintained that pre-Confucian original Ruism was a monotheism advocating belief in the same Christian God; he believed this pure monotheistic faith became corrupted in later Ruism; and thus, by spreading the Christian message in China, missionaries would provide opportunities for Chinese people to rediscover and come closer to the religious truth ultimately revealed by Christianity.[10] Given Legge's enhanced philological skills and more open Protestant mindset, a struggle between his scholarly commitment to critical analysis and his missionary piety is evident within his numerous translations and studies of Ruist classics.

When annotating the Ruist cosmology in the *Xici*, Legge observed that the alternation and interaction between *yin* and *yang* vital-energies are considered by this Ruist classical text to be the all-pervasive principle, explaining the dynamics and order of cosmic changes. However, regarding the deeper question of whether these cosmic vital-energies are "eternal or created," Legge's interpretation of Ruist thought remained ambiguous.[11] He sometimes denied that the text had contributed anything substantial to this question, stating that "neither creation nor cosmogony was before the mind of the author whose work I am analyzing."[12] Nevertheless, faced with the rich commentarial tradition of later Ruism that had pondered this question extensively, Legge believed that this tradition had been contaminated by Daoist philosophy and was, therefore, "more Taoist than Confucian."[13]

In Legge's view, what is the correct answer furnished by original Ruism regarding the origin of *yin* and *yang* vital-energies? In annotating another verse in the *Xici*, "What is unfathomable through *yin* and *yang* is the numinous and wonderful,"[14] Legge wrote:

> Confucius felt that all which appeared in the *Yi* did not account for all that took place in the world of fact.... Confucius felt, I believe, that in all phenomena there was the presence and doing of God, the potency that "spreads undivided and operates unspent," an immanent spirit, and yet not to be confounded with the matter which He molds and changes.[15]

Clearly, Legge believed that according to Confucius's view in the *Xici*, the creator of *yin* and *yang* vital-energies is the spiritual power of the Christian God, referred to as *Shangdi* in Chinese. This power is immanent through the activities of vital-energies while simultaneously transcending them. This also implies that Legge's conception of *Taiji* refers to the same power.

In other words, if we were to ask Legge whether the Ruist idea of *Tian* or *Taiji* is transcendent in comparison with the Christian God, Legge would answer "yes" because, for him, *Tian* or *Taiji* is the Christian God. Regrettably, there are no words in the *Xici* that can conclusively validate Legge's interpretation. The prevailing nontheistic cosmological tradition in Ruism following the composition of the *Xici* did not support Legge's perspective either. During Legge's era, the arrival of Christian missionaries was perceived by Chinese scholars as a harbinger of Western colonialism. The ensuing suspicion and unease impeded productive engagement between Christianity and the Ru tradition. Consequently, Legge's assertion of *Tian*'s transcendent status as God primarily functioned as a self-affirming monologue, which elicited minimal reaction from his contemporary Ruist audience.

The Third Stage

The third stage of Christian-Ru interaction began around World War II when the unstable geopolitical situation led prominent Chinese intellectuals to relocate to Hong Kong or Taiwan and forced numerous East Asians to emigrate to Western societies. Three major types of scholars are involved in this interaction: Christian scholars who are typically ordained priests or pastors in various Christian orders; contemporary Ru philosophers who grew up in the greater Chinese area, assert a Ru identity in their scholarship, and strive to present Ruism to the Western academy using a comparative approach; and other Western comparativists who either have no obvious religious affiliation or advocate for "multiple religious affiliations," contending that religious affiliates should not introduce undue bias into the comparative study of religions.

CHRISTIAN SCHOLARS

The work of Julia Ching, one of the most influential religious scholars in the Christian-Ru interaction during the late twentieth century, presented complex perspectives on the transcendence debate. Ching says: "Confucianism has not developed any doctrine of creation."[16] And:

> The Confucian tradition has never developed a theory of creation *ex nihilo*. The later substitution of the word Heaven (*Tian*) for that of on-High also strengthened the direction of immanence and the idea of a spontaneous creation. Besides, the word "Heaven" lacks inherently a notion of personality, and its increasing usage has been accompanied by an evolution in the meaning of the world itself—in a mystical, perhaps "pantheistic" direction.[17]

Despite these seemingly contradictory statements, we can attempt to understand Ching's perspective as follows: If, according to Christianity, creation is understood as being brought forth by a supreme deity standing outside the world and creating it from nothing, Ruism has no similar concept. Instead, according to mainstream Ruist teaching, *Tian* overlaps with the world, leading to the world being perceived as a process of spontaneous emergence that sustains and perpetuates itself. In this sense, Ching's understanding of *Tian* is similar to that of early Catholic missionaries who believed that *Tian* refers to the nature of the existing world and thus cannot be seen as a creative origin that transcends the world.

However, the term "transcendent" can be applied to the Ruist discourse if it alternatively signifies "the realm beyond man."[18] In Ching's view, Ruism advocates for an ethical form of transcendence, as it teaches that through self-cultivation, individuals can manifest *Tian*'s cosmic creativity within human society and, in turn, realize humanistic values with implications that extend beyond the human realm.

Another example I will examine regarding contemporary Christian responses to the transcendence debate is Hyo-Dong Lee's pneuma-centric comparative theology. Lee's CT aims to develop an Asian contextual theology that upholds the sovereignty of the Asian embodiment of Christian truth and counteracts traditional Eurocentric Christianity, characterized by the colonialist power of metaphysical "Oneness" and sociopolitical "empire."[19] Lee observes that the prevalence of "psychophysical energy" (*qi*) confirms the interconnectedness of the "many" cosmic events, thus promoting the democratic power of cosmic entities (which Lee refers to as the "multitude") in the overall process of cosmic creation. This Ruist concept aids Christianity in reclaiming the status of "spirit" from its marginalized position in traditional hierarchical Trinitarian theology, allowing for a postmodern innovation of Christian theology attuned to contexts and the multitude.

Lee's approach to CT contributes a fascinating perspective to the transcendence debate. He recognizes that in some aspects of the Ru tradition, psychophysical energy is not considered ultimately real, as beyond this energy, Ru thinkers like Zhu Xi acknowledged a more transcendent creative origin of the cosmos. Consequently, traditional Ruism shares the notion of "ontological hierarchy" among its core metaphysical concepts, which is comparable to the Christian Trinity. However, since this similarity does not support the intent of his CT, Lee encourages revisiting the more *Qi*-centric[20] aspects of Zhu Xi's thought, or exploring other *Qi*-centric thinkers in the Ru tradition, such as Yin-Senzhu or Su-un. In other words, if "transcendence" is understood as "a deeper ontological context unconditioned by that which depends on it,"[21] Lee asserts that Ruism possesses a comparable idea regarding creation, but this aspect of Ruist thought is simply not accessible for Lee's theology.

The final Christian scholar whose perspective on the transcendence debate I will analyze is Paulos Huang. Although he acknowledges the creative agency of *Taiji* advocated by traditional Ru metaphysicians, Huang distinguishes "create" from "produce" with this explanation: "'Producing' implies that the source of the world has no personality, and that the producer and the world are of the same substance. 'Creating' implies that the creator of the world has personality, and that the creator and the world are of different substances."[22] Consequently, Huang argues that *Taiji*'s creativity cannot be considered "creating" in the full Christian sense, since unlike *Shangdi*'s personalistic traits, "when *Taiji* is considered as the source of all things in the world, the producer and the world are of the same substance, bearing no distinction between the world and the producer."[23]

By asserting the ultimate creative power of *Shangdi*, a pre-Confucian theist idea, rather than *Taiji*, a post-Confucian naturalized idea, as being akin to the Christian Creator God, Huang's view aligns with Ricci's and Legge's discourse on original Ruism. However, Huang more subtly differentiates between two conceptions of transcendence: an "objective-lying-beyond-the-limits" versus an "actively-to-go-beyond-some-limit," and he refers to the former as "ontological or external transcendence" and the latter as "internal transcendence." Since *Taiji* is regarded as producing rather than creating, Huang questions "whether in Neo-Confucianism *Taiji* is an objective-lying-beyond-the-limits (of the finite, of knowledge, of the subject, of that which falls within the power of knowledge, and so on)."[24] Nonetheless, since Ruism generally asserts that the cosmos is a process of constant change, and that humans should strive for continuous moral self-cultivation to achieve the ultimate cosmic values of human life, Huang concedes that the second conception of transcendence as "actively-to-go-beyond-some-limit" or "internal transcendence" resonates with Ruism.

In other words, in Huang's view, although *Taiji* is considered as "producing" the world, it remains part of the world. In this sense, *Taiji* does not transcend. However, since Ruist exemplary humans aim to be cosmic and the cosmos is always changing, humans are transcending themselves.[25]

CONTEMPORARY RU PHILOSOPHERS

I will continue my analysis by examining three exemplary contemporary Ru philosophers: Mou Zongsan, Liu Shu-hsien, and Tu Wei-ming.

Beginning in the 1970s, Mou Zongsan (1909–1995) used the phrase "being both transcendent and immanent" in numerous works to characterize the Way of *Tian* and its significance to the ethical-metaphysical worldview of Ruism.[26] When Mou described the Way of *Tian* as transcendent, he meant that as an all-encompassing and continuously creative cosmic power, *Tian* generates everything in the universe, including human existence. *Tian* is both the ontological origin of human existence and the foundation of humanistic values promoted by Ruist ethics. In accordance with how Christian scholars have discussed the term, Mou's thought addresses the conception of *Tian*'s "transcendence" as both a "realm beyond humans" (Julia Ching) and a capacity to "actively go beyond some limit" (Paulos Huang). However, it does not address the "ontological transcendence" that was the focus of Huang, Lee, and possibly other early Christian missionary scholars. In other words, as long as *Tian* can be portrayed as the origin of moral values and a self-generating cosmic power that consistently transcends its current state, Mou would not disagree with his Christian interlocutors on the idea that *Tian* is transcendent. However, Mou remained silent on whether *Tian* can represent an ultimate reality external to the created world and thus be considered an unconditioned ontological entity.

Around the 1970s, Mou Zongsan's student, Liu Shu-hsien (1934–2016), published a series of articles in English on Ru religiosity and the transcendence of *Tian*. Among these articles, the most concise statement is as follows:

> Now the Confucian approach to the problem of transcendence and immanence becomes clear. Heaven is transcendent in the sense that it is an all-encompassing creative power which works incessantly in the universe. It is not a thing, but it is the origin of all things. And it cannot be detected by sense perceptions, because its "operations have neither sound nor smell." But Heaven is also immanent in the sense that it penetrates deep in every detail of the natural order, in general, and of the moral order of man, in particular. But Heaven in no sense should be regarded as something completely beyond nature; on the contrary, it is that which constitutes the warp and woof of nature. As for man, he is beyond any doubt a creature in the world and hence a part of the natural order.[27]

Since "Heaven" (*Tian*) is both transcendent and immanent, Liu characterized its form of transcendence as "immanent transcendence," contrasting it with the "pure transcendence" of the Christian God, "who created, but is not part of, the world."[28]

Liu Shu-hsien clearly provided a reassuring answer to the key question of whether *Tian* could be considered the origin of the world. As for the subtler question of whether *Tian* is identical to the world, Liu's response is more nuanced: He emphasizes that *Tian* is not a thing, and in contrast, the pure transcendence of the Christian God makes God a creator who is not part of the world. Consequently, we can infer that in Liu's mind, if we define the "world" as the sum of all actual things in any conceivable modes of past, current, and future moments of time, Liu would still insist that *Tian* is the origin of the world and therefore cannot be identical to the world. However, if we push Liu one step further and ask him about the "ontological transcendence" specified by Huang and Lee—whether *Tian* ontologically transcends the world in the sense that it can be seen as "a deeper ontological context unconditioned by that which depends on it"—since Liu always emphasizes that the creating *Tian* is immanent in the world, we cannot derive a clear answer from him.

In other words, to understand more precisely the relationship between *Tian* and the world in Ruist metaphysics, we need sharper concepts that allow us to more accurately compare Ruism with its Christian counterpart. These concepts should help answer questions such as: Is it legitimate to describe the ultimate creativity of *Tian* as "being ontologically unconditioned"? Also, if *Tian* is also immanent in the world, does this mean that *Tian*'s creativity depends on things in the world, or does it merely imply that *Tian*'s creativity can be manifested in the changing cosmic realities in their actual ways? Moreover, following Mou's thought that the ultimate reality conceived by Ruism "cannot be grasped by empirical experience,"[29] Liu's thought addresses a related epistemological question of whether the cognitive capacity of human beings can fully comprehend *Tian*'s all-encompassing creativity. In light of these pending questions, I believe participants need to differentiate between ontological and epistemological senses of "priority" before continuing the transcendence debate: *Tian* may be ontologically prior to the world in the sense that it creates the world, while *Tian* may be epistemologically posterior to the world in the sense that only through the world can we know anything about *Tian*.

The last contemporary Ru philosopher I will analyze is Tu Wei-ming (1940–). Tu once eloquently argued that "because of its ceaselessness, it [the creative power of *Tian*] does not create in a single act beyond the spatio-temporal sequence. Rather, it creates a continuous and unending process in time and space. It is therefore a 'lasting' event,"[30] and "if genuine creativity is not the creation of something out of nothing, but a continuous transformation of that which is already there, the world as it now exists is the authentic manifestation of the cosmic process in its all-embracing fullness."[31] In further analysis, Tu also acknowledged that his view on *Tian*'s creativity originates in the cosmology of Zhang Zai (1022–1077) centering upon the all-pervasive cosmic vital-energies, which Zhang called the "Great Vacuity."[32]

Conceiving of *Tian* in this way, Tu also creatively reenvisions the role of humans as "cocreators." Tu says, "It is true that human nature is imparted from heaven, but human beings are not merely creatures and heaven alone does not exhaust the process of creativity.... Through reciprocity, humanity becomes interfused with the cosmic transformation and thus, as a co-creator, forms a trinity with Heaven and Earth."[33]

We can summarize Tu's view on the relationship between *Tian* and the world as follows: Before any concrete thing is brought into being, the world is a giant vacuity pervaded by the undifferentiated *Qi*, and there is a creative power intrinsic to *Qi*, the self-differentiation and self-perpetuation of which lead to the ceaseless emergence of things in the world. Finally, the entire cosmic process is encapsulated by one singular Chinese term, *Tian*. In comparison to his teacher, Mou Zongsan, and his contemporary, Liu Shu-hsien, Tu's articulation of *Tian* agrees with them on the transcendence of *Tian*'s creativity in the sense that the ceaseless cosmic creativity of *Tian* is taken to be the origin of things in the world. However, if questioned by Christian scholars concerning whether *Tian* can be understood to be ontologically prior to the de facto existence of the world, Tu's response is a denial, in contrast to Mou's reticence and Liu's uncertainty.

Nevertheless, how can *Tian*, which creates the world in its "all-embracing fullness," be instead in need of humans to cocreate? This challenging question implied by Tu's thought calls our attention to another confusion the transcendence debate might engender. As noted above, Ruist philosophers virtually all agree that *Tian* can be described as an all-encompassing, constantly creative power or field which is the origin of the world. However, Ru classics also delve into the concrete manifestations of *Tian*'s creativity in its cosmic unfoldings. In the *Xici*, we have *Taiji* as the highest ontological category which gives birth to everything, but we also have two modes (*yin-yang Qi* in later interpretations), four images (four seasons or five phases), and eight hexagrams (eight natural phenomena), the interaction of which explains how concrete cosmic realities change. In the text of *Zhong Yong*, we have *Tian* as the highest category, which refers to the origin of everything, but we also have heaven (read also as *Tian*), earth, and humans as three cocreative capacities within *Tian* to show how *Tian*'s all-creative power manifests itself in concrete terms.

In other words, we need to distinguish two meanings of *Tian* and two modes of metaphysical thinking that are equally endorsed by Ru classics: *Tian* means the all-encompassing ontological context mentioned above, but *Tian* also means heaven in relation to earth and human beings. The all-encompassing creative power of *Tian* enables us to set it in comparison to Christian ideas of God and to ask further whether *Tian* is transcendent in regard to its relationship to the created world. However, if we treat *Tian* as a minor, less-encompassing cosmological concept in parallel with earth and human beings, then *Tian* will be like the concepts of *yin/yang*, the four seasons, or the five phases, a cognitive tool alongside other cosmological concepts to explain concrete cosmic changes.

Although it is worthwhile to ask how these two modes of metaphysical thinking, that is, ontology and cosmology, relate to one another in Ruism, it is only legitimate to investigate the ontological understanding of *Tian* to clarify whether Ruism conceives of any reality with "ontological transcendence" comparable to the *creatio ex nihilo* of the Christian God.

WESTERN COMPARATIVISTS

The question of whether Ru cosmology involves a transcendent dimension has generated controversy among Western comparative scholars seeking impartial comparisons. Within these controversies, two contrasting stances emerge: On one side stands the "correlative thinking" school, which includes scholars such as Marcel Granet, Joseph Needham, A. C. Graham, David L. Hall, Roger T. Ames, and others.[34] On the other side are scholars like Robert Cummings Neville, Benjamin I. Schwartz,[35] Paul R. Goldin,[36] William Franke,[37] Joshua R. Brown and Alexus McLeod,[38] among others.

David Hall and Roger Ames are the most influential comparative philosophers in the contemporary expression of the "correlative thinking" school. They state:

> We shall continue to argue here, as we have in the past, that one of the most striking features of Chinese intellectual culture from the perspective of the Western interpreter is the absence, in any important sense, of transcendence in the articulation of its spiritual, moral, and political sensibilities.[39]

Here, "transcendence" is defined in a "strict" sense: "We characterize strict transcendence in the following way: A is transcendent with respect to B if the existence, meaning, or import of B cannot be fully accounted for without recourse to A, but the reverse is not true."[40] Hall and Ames further attribute this "strict transcendence" to the Christian understanding of God, which Ames describes as "Greek and Abrahamic interpretations of origins or beginnings."[41] In contrast, the Ruist idea of *Tian* is not "some ontologically independent order of Being," but is "defined as the 'day' and the 'skies' under which culture accumulates," and thus maintains a significant continuity with the human world. In this sense, "where the Judeo-Christian God, often referred to metonymically as 'Heaven,' creates the world, classical Chinese *Tian* is the world."[42] More specifically, Ames asserts that the Christian understanding of God champions the idea of *creatio ex nihilo*, which is contextless and ahistorical, and which emphasizes agency and originality, rather than situation and novelty. Chinese thought, on the other hand, pivots upon *creatio in situ*, which is context-based, historical, and cherishes situation and novelty.[43]

Interestingly enough, the way Hall and Ames formulated the definition of "strict transcendence" bears a striking resemblance to Aristotle's definition of "priority" regarding the "nature and being" of things: "those which can be without other things, while the others cannot be without them—a distinction which Plato used."[44] The intellectual history of *creatio ex nihilo* (which is a focus of chapter 5 of this book) indicates that this Aristotelian understanding of "priority of nature and being" speaks to one crucial concept—"ontological dependence"—which drives the Christian conception of divine creation as *creatio ex nihilo* from its earliest inchoate form in Plato's cosmology to its first systematic expression in Augustine of Hippo's thought. We also find that this idea of "ontological dependence" underlies Paulos Huang's conception of transcendence as "objective beyond the limits" and Hyo-Dong Lee's as "deeper ontological context unconditioned by that which depends on it." In other words, it will be necessary for scholars' further engagement with the transcendence debate to clarify whether there may be any idea of "ontological dependence" involved in Ruist conceptions of *Tian*. Although their contrastive comparisons between Chinese and Western thought have engendered controversies, we would have to accept the conclusion of Hall and Ames that there is no strict sense of transcendence in ancient Chinese thought if "correlative thinking" is what ancient Chinese thought is all about.

Though proposing powerful counterarguments to Hall and Ames's thought, the aforementioned scholars did not take the Christian-Ru interaction, as well as its transcendence debate, as the central focus of their scholarship. While directly responding to the school of correlative thinking's stance in the transcendence debate, Robert Cummings Neville's thought provides an impressive case.

Regarding Hall and Ames's strict definition of transcendence and their complete denial of any important sense of it in ancient Chinese thought,

Neville emphasizes the varieties of "transcendence" meant by different traditions.[45] He then suggests a "vague" definition of transcendence to bridge the distance between these variations and thus make their comparison available:

> Suppose we say that a general definition of transcendence is that to which reference can be made, in any sense of reference, only by denying that the referent lies within the boundaries of a specifiable domain, whatever else is supposed or said about the referent.[46]

Guided by this vague definition, Neville terms the highest metaphysical principles conceived by various philosophical and religious traditions as "ultimacy," which refers to any "finite-infinite contrast" marking something as transcendent.

From a comparative perspective, we find Neville's vague definition of "transcendence" still aligns with Aristotle's "priority of nature and being," Lee's "ontological unconditionality," Huang's "objective beyond the limits," and Ames and Hall's "strict transcendence." All these conceptions of transcendence resonate with the ancient Greek and Christian metaphysical tradition of creation pivoting upon the idea of ontological dependence. However, one crucial difference in Neville's definition leads to his different view in the transcendence debate.

For Neville, the transcendent "ultimacy" defined as such can be purely indeterminate. Its grounding ontological power is to specifically explain the origin of the existence of cosmic realities, but the investigation of what each cosmic reality is still considers the relationships among realities. In this sense, the creative power of "ultimacy" does not impose any extra or "imperial" order upon cosmic realities. Epistemologically, the de facto cosmic realities are instead the only conduit through which human beings could know anything about the ultimacy. In contrast, according to Huang's and Ames's understanding, the metaphysical principle on the highest end of the chain of ontological dependence must be determinate. It is either a "substance" (Huang) or an "independent order of being" (Ames) that not only accounts for the origin of the existence of the world, but also imposes some extra order upon the empirical one of cosmic realities. Surely, Huang and Ames are different from each other as well, in that Huang thinks the determinate, highest principle conceived as a supreme substance is commendably Christian, while Ames considers it as one deep root of the crisis of Western culture. Regardless, the highest ontological principle regarding creation is conceptualized by both as determinate. If measured by this standard, both of them would agree that there is no "transcendent" dimension in the Ru metaphysics.

In his reliance upon his unique conception that the transcendent is indeterminate, yet ontologically originating a determinate world, Neville maps out a lineage of ancient Chinese cosmologies rich with this sort of "transcendence": "In China it is the dominant tradition, illustrated by the opening lines of the *Daodejing*, by Wang Bi, and by the classic statement of Neo-Confucian cosmogony in Zhou Dunyi, among other sources."[47] This Chinese tradition does not typically conceive of ultimacy as a "determinate deity," and hence, according to his judgment that what is genuinely ultimate is indeterminate per se, Neville thinks the Chinese tradition did even better to represent the idea of "ontological unconditionality" implied by the traditional Christian doctrine of *creatio ex nihilo*.[48]

Summary

We have illustrated the major contentions in the transcendence debate during the three stages of Christian-Ru interaction. We find that the strikingly diverse stances regarding the key debated question largely depend upon what criteria of "transcendence" scholars hold and what materials they employ. In retrospect, there are four major implied definitions of transcendence.

What is transcendent in a philosophical and religious discourse can be defined as:

(1) Something determinate and ontologically unconditioned by the existing world.
(2) Something indeterminate and ontologically unconditioned by the existing world.
(3) Something constantly advancing beyond the existence of de facto realities in the world.
(4) Something beyond humans, which can be considered as the origin of both the existence and moral values of human life.

Informed by these definitions, we can use table 1 to summarize scholars' explicitly stated conceptions of transcendence when they debate each other. One caveat in reading the table is that since the first four Christian scholars listed there never directly used the term "transcendence"

TABLE 1: Definitions of transcendence

Categories	Names	Def. (1)	Def. (2)	Def. (3)	Def. (4)
Christian scholars in the first stage	Matteo Ricci	√			
	Julius Aleni and Alexandre de la Charme	√			
Christian scholar in the second stage	James Legge	√			
Christian scholars in the third stage	Julia Ching			√	√
	Hyo-Dong Lee	√			
	Paulos Huang	√		√	√
Ru scholars in the third stage	Mou Zongsan			√	√
	Liu Shu-hsien			√	√
	Tu Wei-ming			√	√
Independent Western comparativists	Roger Ames	√			
	Robert Neville		√		

during the historical debate, their understandings of transcendence are inferred from their conceptions of divine creation.

In addition, we can use table 2 to illustrate the major scholars' answers to the key question of whether the Ruist idea of *Tian*, or its metaphysically more accurate referent *Taiji*, is transcendent in comparison with Christian ideas of the Creator God. Understandably, these answers are

TABLE 2: Contentions in the transcendence debate

	Is the Ruist idea of *Tian* or *Taiji* transcendent?
Matteo Ricci	Yes, in the sense of (1), but only yes for "original Ruism," the metaphysics of which pivots upon an understanding of *Tian* as a personalistic "supreme deity."
James Legge	Yes, in the sense of (1), but only yes for "original Ruism," the metaphysics of which pivots upon an understanding of *Tian* as a personalistic "supreme deity."
Julia Ching	Yes, in the sense of (3) and (4). No, in the sense of (1).
Hyo-Dong Lee	Yes, in the sense of (1), but the "yes" case is not available to construct "Asian contextual theology."
Paulos Huang	Yes, in the sense of (1), (3), (4), but the sense of (1) only exists in "original Ruism." No, in the sense of (1) for other forms of Ruism.
Mou Zongsan	Yes, in the sense of (3) and (4).
Liu Shu-hsien	Yes, in the sense of (3) and (4); uncertain, in the sense of (1) or (2).
Tu Wei-ming	Yes, in the sense of (3) and (4); but no, in the sense of (1) or (2).
Roger Ames	No, in the sense of (1).
Robert Neville	Yes, in the sense of (2).

based upon scholars' varying definitions of transcendence, and therefore, when reading table 2, we need to bear table 1 in mind.

Proposed Method for Further Engagement in the Christian-Ruist Transcendence Debate

Given these astoundingly diverse stances regarding the transcendence debate, is there any hope that future scholars will be able to reach an agreement on certain aspects of the debate?

From the above analysis, we find three major reasons underlying such a diversity of views: First, scholars hold different understandings of "transcendence." However, if we look into tables 1 and 2, we find that scholars more often agree with one another regarding definitions (3) and (4) of transcendence and their applications to comparisons. That means, if "transcendence" is defined in the ways of (3) and (4), scholars within each category, that is, within the Christian, Ruist, or independent category, not only tend to agree with one another that Ruism has its transcendent dimension but also more easily reach agreement across the categorical border. For example, Julia Ching and Paulos Huang would have no disagreement with Mou Zongsan, Liu Shu-hsien, and Tu Wei-ming if the transcendent element of Ruism is defined in the sense of (3) and (4). However, the most contentious point of the transcendence debate focuses upon the definitions (1) and (2). That is, if "transcendence" is defined ontologically, not only do scholars in one category disagree with those in a different category, they also forcefully disagree with one another within the same category. For example, Hyo-Dong Lee's stance is rather different from that of every other Christian scholar, and even Mou Zongsan and Liu Shu-hsien are not entirely in line with Tu Wei-ming at this point. Therefore, the advancement of scholarship regarding the transcendence debate will crucially rest upon a clarification of whether the concept of "ontological dependence" is employable to characterize the Ruist idea of *Tian* or *Taiji*, and how Christianity and Ruism are comparable on this concept.

During the transcendence debate, the Christian understanding of divine creation as *creatio ex nihilo*, and the Ruist understanding of *Tian*, or *Taiji*'s creativity as *sheng sheng*, are the most frequently referenced ideas. However, we find the second major reason leading to scholars' disagreement is that they rely upon different sources from each tradition to present their understandings of creation. For example, Matteo Ricci's understanding of *creatio ex nihilo* is informed by Thomas Aquinas. Roger Ames and David Hall's version is modeled on this idea's first orthodox expression around the time of the Council of Nicaea. Robert Neville's version is more comprehensive in the sense that he does not only study different theories of *creatio ex nihilo* including its medieval and modern variations, but creates his own theory of *creatio ex nihilo*. It is also the case that some scholars presented the theory of *creatio ex nihilo* in general terms and thus didn't specify the source from which their presentations derive. The same situation could be found in scholars' understandings of *Taiji*'s creativity as well. For example, Ames and Hall rarely use materials in Song through Ming Ruism to present their understanding of *Tian* or *Taiji*. However, the major conclusions of Hyo-Dong Lee and Paulos Huang are based upon their analyses of key Song Ruist masters' works such as Zhou Dunyi's and Zhu Xi's. For early Christian missionaries, their affinity to the so-called original Ruism implied by major pre-Confucian classics rich with a personified understanding of *Tian*, and their corresponding critiques of Song through Ming Ruism, speak to a selective strategy fit for their Christian missions. Even Ruist scholars who use the same range of materials to evidence their understandings of *Taiji*'s creativity vary in their selections and emphases. For example, Tu Wei-ming is informed by Zhang Zai's cosmology, while Liu Shu-hien is more oriented toward Zhu Xi's.

Therefore, in order to conduct a more methodical comparison for the future development of the transcendence debate, two major strategies are suggested. First, comparativists must specify which parts of which traditions will be used for comparison, and accordingly, all their disputants must address the same parts. In other words, we need to constrain our comparative data to a well-defined range of materials for a more organized conversation between comparativists. Second, because the *creatio ex nihilo* of God and the *sheng sheng* of *Taiji* are the most frequently quoted ideas, and also because it is crucial for the advancement of the transcendence debate to clarify the logic of ontological dependence which is possibly shared by the two traditions, a second strategy is suggested according to the method of intellectual history. In other words, we need to trace the major historical stages for the development of the idea of *creatio ex nihilo* in Christianity, and that of *sheng sheng* in Ruism, in order to clarify how the logic of ontological dependence is continuously implemented by each of these traditions, and after this, we need to pursue a comparison between traditions, rather than between any specific figures or texts within each tradition.

In these two strategies, the strength of the first is its susceptibility of deep reading, while its defects can be anticipated as well: First, the constrained focus upon specific figures or texts may make scholars lose sight of the continuity of views on creation in each tradition. Second, since the figures and texts which scholars addressed in the transcendence debate have added up to an amount of data broad enough to indicate major traits of the compared traditions concerning creation, a further constrained focus on particular figures or texts will make it difficult for new comparative conclusions to remain relevant to disputants whose argumentative foci have hitherto been outside these selected figures or texts. In this case, scholars would be more likely to talk across, rather than to, each other. In other words, the contribution made via the first strategy to advancing the transcendence debate may turn out to be minimal.

The second strategy, since it addresses the continuity of each tradition concerning creation, can understandably rectify the defects of the first. However, its weakness is that a much broader range of comparative data will challenge scholars' accurate understanding of them. But this challenge can be met in two ways: First, focusing upon two particular ideas, *creatio ex nihilo* and *sheng sheng*, under the guidance of the logic of ontological dependence will significantly decrease the needed range of comparative data. For the sake of the comparison, I suggest paying attention to three constitutive moments of the compared ideas in their respective intellectual histories: their original seeds of thought, their classical systematic expressions, and their significant innovations following the classical expressions. If we can pin down these three crucial moments for the development of each compared idea and furthermore showcase their continuity using a method of intellectual history, we will have a well-defined, strong basis for comparison. Second, *creatio ex nihilo* and *sheng sheng* are studied abundantly by scholars in each tradition. What remains for comparativists to do is to canvass the continuity of the varying expressions of each idea and to compare them across traditions. In other words, established research by noncomparative specialists can be utilized to verify and correct a comparativist's reading of the selected figures and texts so as to check the accuracy of comparison.

After all these due considerations, I submit that the second strategy is preferable since it can engage various disputants in the transcendence debate and, if implemented methodically, demonstrate the disciplinary nature of comparative theology as a falsifiable, scientific endeavor. In particular, since I consider Ruist CT as a rooted and nonconfessional liberal art, the second strategy is favorable because it allows a Ruist comparativist to seek the most relevant sources within the entire tradition to respond to questions raised by the ongoing debate.

Last but not least, the unsettledness of the transcendence debate is also due to the fact that comparative methodologies affect scholars' approaches to comparative studies. Three points about this last reason are elaborated as follows. First, most of the discussed scholars are not major contributors to the methodological part of the emerging modern disciplines of comparative religion and comparative theology. This is particularly true for virtually all the aforementioned Christian and Ruist scholars.

Second, given the fact that most of the disputants have not yet been methodologically self-reflective, it would be no surprise that their disparate comparative motives lead to astoundingly diverse conclusions. For example, early Christian missionaries' comparative studies were mission driven. They chose portions of the Ru tradition which were thought of as the best fit for their missionary purpose, while jettisoning the others. David Hall and Roger Ames's comparison is oriented toward finding in Chinese thought a genuine alternative to Western thought.[49] Therefore, Hall and Ames's methodology would not be able to treat seriously those components of ancient Chinese thought which happen to be in line with their interpretation of mainstream Western thought.[50] Comparatively, we have to appreciate Hyo-dong Lee's candid statement that his purpose of constructing a postmodern Asian contextual theology means that the idea of "ontological transcendence" would not be interesting for him, although Lee did acknowledge the existence of this idea in Zhu Xi's thought. However, this refusal to have Zhu Xi's and other similar ideas in Ruism play a more significant role may undermine the progress of the transcendence debate. Third, even for scholars who try to maintain an objective stance regarding the debate, it is not universally the case that a comparative methodology is properly crafted so as to take the great cultural and linguistic gap between the two compared traditions into disciplined consideration.

In this regard, Neville's scholarship is an exception. Neville stands at the front and center of the contemporary methodological discussions for comparative religion, theology, and philosophy. As I will analyze in the next chapter, Neville's stance in the transcendence debate is also a result of his comparative methodology centering upon his Peircian pragmatist use of "vague category." So, is Neville's methodology the ultimate one for further scholarly engagement with the transcendence debate?

Before answering this question in the next chapter, I conclude here that in light of the discussed reasons of the unsettledness of the transcendence debate, the advancement of scholarship in the debate calls for developing a comparative methodology which is able to (1) be minimally prejudiced by one's starting comparative motives, (2) maximally address concerns voiced by disputants in the ongoing debate, and also (3) make comparative conclusions improvable so that further development of scholarship concerning transcendence can be expected on the basis of scholars' collective critical thinking.

4 Methodologies of Comparative Theology, Religion, and Philosophy for the Progress of the Transcendence Debate

At the end of the previous chapter, I proposed three strategic points for a further engagement with the transcendence debate. The third one is the most important, because only after being immersed in an appropriate comparative methodology can the concerns raised by the first two points be addressed. Therefore, to seek a methodology suitable for the comparison of the ideas of *creatio ex nihilo* and *sheng sheng* is our current task.

Framing Ruist comparative theology (CT) as a rooted, nonconfessional, and scientific liberal art challenges the semantic boundaries of theology, religion, and philosophy, for good reasons. Nevertheless, the current task requires me to reflect upon major methodological achievements in all three disciplines (CT, comparative religion, and comparative philosophy of religion) before devising my own. In the following, themes such as the conception of theology and the typology of CT will be revisited after their initial discussion in chapter 1. However, the discussion here will be conducted on the basis of new materials contributing to the stated task of this chapter.

Comparative Theology

For reasons articulated in chapter 1, my reflection on the methodology of CT will start from Francis X. Clooney. As discussed, theology, for Clooney, is a tradition of "faith seeking understanding" and is written for the need of a clearly bounded faith community. CT should stand within a home tradition, and then search for enriching elements from other traditions, while its ultimate goal through interreligious encounters shall be to enhance the truth within the home tradition. In contrast,

Clooney defines comparative religion as a "detached scholarly research," which tries to maintain neutrality in regard to where comparison leads.[1]

To Clooney's theorization on the nature of CT, Catherine Cornille adds much methodological sophistication through formulating an inclusive typology of comparative studies of religion.[2] Cornille differentiates CT from comparative religion by specifying that the former addresses issues of truth central to one's faith, and the latter does not. Furthermore, Cornille categorizes CT into its several subcategories. When holding one's home tradition of faith seeking understanding through comparison, a CT is "confessional." Meanwhile, scholars can compare multiple traditions for common issues, and the resulting solutions to those issues are thought of as being significant for all compared traditions. This is "meta-confessional" CT. An "inter-confessional" comparative theologian may focus on seeking a common ground among traditions while oscillating between the normativity of the traditions.[3]

In a more recent work, Cornille elaborates that confessional CT based in a home tradition "does not consider the possibility of discovering truth that would fundamentally exceed or clash with the contours of that tradition."[4] By emphasizing that a meta-confessional CT can define CT in terms of its subject matter, but not in terms of the antecedent theological commitment of a comparativist's, Cornille thinks meta-confessional CT "thus moves toward a philosophical, rather than a traditional, theological understanding of truth," and hence, can be barely distinguishable from comparative religion.[5] In light of my analysis in chapter 1, it is discernible that the uneasiness of Cornille's wording concerning the case of meta-confessional CT derives from the same reason as Paul Hedges's mischaracterization of Keith Ward's theology. I agree with Cornille that whether attending to issues of truth central to one's faith, as well as whether insisting on a normative pursuit of religious truth, is a significant difference between the existing scholarship respectively belonging to the disciplines of comparative theology and comparative religion. Nevertheless, the ineptness of Cornille's conceptual tool to characterize the meta-confessional CT consists in the term "confessional." Cornille's conception of confessional CT takes Clooney's works as its paradigm, and adopts the notion of "home tradition" implied by Clooney's conception of theology. This entails that Cornille's standard to differentiate one project of CT from others as "confessional" is to see whether that project takes a determinate set of expressions of divine revelation within a clearly bounded tradition as fixed and unalterable, as confirmed by the above quote. However, if this standard were to be executed consistently, the meta-confessional CT (also thought of by Cornille as being instantiated in Keith Ward's and Robert Neville's works) ought to be simply called "nonconfessional," since neither of these theologians holds Clooney's Scholastic understanding of theology.

In other words, Cornille's typology of comparative studies of religion did not encompass the more original Aristotelian pursuit of theology, and hence did not take it as a notable type of CT despite the fact that this type of CT is contemporarily pursued by Ward, Neville, and a Ruist scholar (me) as a rooted and nonconfessional theology. This being the case, those very fine methodological reflections on CT offered by Cornille's typology cannot furnish much support to the methodology of CT sought by my project.

Comparative Religion

The modern discipline of comparative religion can be seen as deriving from Max Müller, who initiated the project of world religions vis-à-vis the European discovery of non-Christian religions in a colonial era. Müller envisions the study of comparative religion with two objectives: first, to answer what religion is through objectively describing its varying forms; second, to explain the similarities and differences among religions using linguistic, historical, and sociological perspectives, among others. Müller likens these two goals to the distinction between kinematics and dynamics in modern physics, and asserts that his comparative study is a "science of religion."[6] However, the early development of comparative religion attends to similarities more than differences. Scholars following Müller's initiative could not easily avoid Christian biases, and they tended to conduct studies on religions in accordance with a standardized conception of religiosity drawn from the forms of Christianity with which they were most familiar. To Müller's critics, especially postmodernists around the middle of the last century, his comparative religion is little more than a delicate façade of Eurocentrism and social Darwinism.[7] In response, contemporary scholars of comparative religion defend its scientific nature by highlighting two methodological points, and I'll focus on Jonathan Z. Smith's thought in this regard as an example.

To the challenge about how to correctly describe compared traditions, Smith maintains that the impartiality of comparison does not derive from any transcendent view detached from research contexts. Instead, the objectivity of comparison can be achieved through an open-ended process of "description, comparison, re-description and rectification."[8] Inspired by Wittgenstein on "family resemblance," Smith notices the importance of comparative category, and advocates that "comparison would be based on a multiplicity of traits, not all of which might be possessed by any individual member of the class."[9] In other words, not all the traits of a category elicited from one tradition are able to be carried over by a comparativist to describe another one, and whether one can succeed in doing so rests upon the continual process of hypothesization and correction. This renders Smith's thought similar to Robert Neville's and Aaron Stalnaker's comparative methodologies, which I will analyze later. As for another challenge concerning how to conduct legitimate comparisons, Smith proposes his understanding of religion as a "situational thinking." He says: "Religion is not best understood as a disclosure that gives rise to a particular mode of experience. To the contrary, religion is the relentlessly human activity of thinking through a 'situation.'"[10] Hence, scholars of comparative religion enjoy their freedom to interpret or explain comparative data from any perspective, depending upon their interests and what scholarly "situation" they are tackling. However, scholarly perceptions of such contexts need to be exposed to a broader scholarly community so as to benefit from further critique and correction. If the first point of Smith's thought answers the "how" question for doing accurate comparison, the second addresses the "why" and "so what" questions. These two points correspond to the objectives that Müller initially set for the discipline of comparative religion and respond to postmodern criticisms through devising a more refined, properly chastened form of comparative methodology.

In light of Smith's methodological reflection, we find that what Smith has in mind is definitely not the "confessional" type of comparative theology as defined by Clooney and Cornille. Nonetheless, an intriguing question to ask is what if a comparative study aimed for an impartial description of compared traditions, but also tried to tackle a particular scholarly situation pertaining to the first-order, theological issue of religious truth? Per Smith's reflection, this study would be perfectly "comparative religion," but once again, we have witnessed the blurred boundary between "comparative religion" and "comparative theology" envisioned by Cornille, yet from the side of scholars of comparative religion such as Smith. In what follows, I will raise one example, Robert Neville's works,[11] to illustrate how this blurred boundary plays out concretely, with a further purpose of sorting out a comparative methodology fit for my project.

Regarding the purpose of theological dialogue, Neville believes that "we should not think that the work of theological dialogue is only to look good in a dialogue, or to make for cultural peace and mutual accommodation. Rather, it is for the sake of ascertaining the truth." Therefore, Neville continues, "in theological dialogue, the creed would be a matter of theological truth if and only if it could be communicated as an assertion about divine matters that other traditions recognize."[12] Hence, Neville refuses to understand theology as a given faith seeking understanding which must be constrained within a clearly bounded faith community. He also maintains that neither a sociological (i.e., to say something is true because my group believes it) nor a voluntaristic (i.e., to say something is true because of my commitment to its authority) approach to theological study is suitable for providing evidences to argue for religious truth.[13]

In a word, comparative theology of Neville's sort has its specific locus within the Christian tradition of "philosophical theology," which aims to search for truth about ultimate reality, and the obtained truth-claims are expected to have interreligious relevance and cross-cultural efficacy. For the enterprise, the comparative study of religion serves as both a resource and a test-field for Neville to formulate, rectify, and refine hypotheses about the first-order issue of truth.

Understood as such, Neville's comparative study of religion can be categorized as comparative religion, because Christianity and Ruism, albeit remaining constitutive of Neville's work, serve his comparison mainly as perspectival starting points, and theological claims need to be tested impartially by varying critiques by other traditions. However, Neville's comparison is deeply concerned with first-order issues of truth, and it can therefore be seen as comparative theology per Cornille. But is Neville's work readily thought of as a meta-confessional comparative theology? I once asked Neville this question, and he denied it. I think the major reason for the denial is that Neville's comparison is not premised upon Clooney and Cornille's definition of any "home tradition." Hence, it would be inappropriate to use terms centering on the adjective "confessional" to describe his scholarship, unless Cornille can provide a more nuanced definition of the adjective beyond what is conventional to the Catholic "faith seeking understanding" tradition.

So far as this chapter proceeds, I have investigated Clooney's and Cornille's taxonomies of comparative studies of religion, as well as Smith's self-description of comparative religion. I also analyzed Neville's works to show that there are certain cases for which it is difficult, if not impossible, to insist upon a rigid boundary between comparative theology and comparative religion. So, where should I locate the comparative study of this book?

As concluded above, Cornille's taxonomy of comparative studies of religion is not adequate to characterizing the meta-confessional theology instantiated in Ward's and Neville's works because it holds on to the understanding of theology, philosophy, and religion implied by the Scholastic model of theology as a given faith seeking understanding, and this model is not shared by the comparative theologians in question. Notably, the two comparative theologies hardly characterizable by Cornille's taxonomy all indicate a great affinity to "philosophy": Ward's case has been analyzed in chapter 1, and Neville argued the best category to depict his three-volume systematic theology is "philosophical theology."[14] Given the intense concerns of these theologians with first-order issues of religious truth and practical implications of these issues in daily human life, "philosophy" conceived by them is definitely not a purely intellectual endeavor. Instead, this type of philosophy maintains a great continuity with its earliest Greek form as a way of life that aims to transform people's whole personality in line with a comprehensive and well-argued worldview. In summation, the CT of Ward and Neville's type, as well as the one that I am pursuing from a Ruist starting perspective, is a uniquely new research phenomenon that cannot be adequately categorized by existing taxonomies of CT.

Notably, the impartial and universalist pursuit of religious truth does not preclude the addressed comparative theologians from being religiously identified with a certain tradition: Ward claims to be an Anglican Christian, and Neville is a Methodist Christian minister and proclaims his double religious identity as both a Christian and a Ru (Confucian). This furthermore verifies my conclusion in chapter 1 that depicts the CT of Ward's type as a rooted, nonconfessional, and impartial study of theology, since, as I argued, the nature of this theology does not exclude religious affiliations. We can now aver that that conclusion is applicable to Neville as well.

Nevertheless, although I put my project in the same category as these appreciable comparative theologians', it is distinctive in one particular aspect: As influenced by the grounding feature of the Ruist metaphysical and theological discourse upon social realities (as argued in chapter 2), the primary purpose of my project is not to construct a metatheory of ultimate reality purporting to be cross-culturally effective. Instead, unpacking the terms "creation" and "transcendence" in the two compared traditions (Christianity and Ruism) and thus advancing the progress of the transcendence debate is the main driving motif of my comparison. This will make my comparative methodology focus more on intellectual histories, and whenever philosophical construction is needed, it will be oriented to tackling controversies among disputing scholars. In other words, the "rooted" nature of the nonconfessional Ruist CT that I am pursuing is not only pertaining to my spiritual identity, but also referring to the unique situation of the subsisting transcendence debate to which I, as a Ruist comparative theologian, need to respond.

Even so, the nonconfessional and impartial commitment to the accuracy of comparison shared by all the three mentioned cases of CT speaks to the fact that we can learn quite a great deal from any methodology aiming to achieve similar goals. Having analyzed the case of comparative religion, I will now move on to the discipline of comparative religion with mainly a philosophical interest, or the one of comparative philosophy of religion.

Methodologies of Comparative Philosophy of Religion

Among contemporary comparativists who share a major interest in the comparison between Christianity and Ruism, there are two whose scholarship is exactly located within the category "comparative religion with a philosophical interest," or "comparative philosophy of religion." Thus, an investigation into their comparative methodologies will be of significance for parsing the most viable methodology for my comparative study. They are Robert Neville and Aaron Stalnaker.[15]

Neville's comparative methodology centers on the use of "vague category" deriving from Peirce's pragmatic semiotics. Robert Smid once summarized Peirce's thought as follows:

> For Peirce, . . . a sign is vague if it is capable of further specification in multiple ways, all of which are not necessarily compatible with another; Peirce contrasts this with a "general" sign, which is specified in the same way in every instance.[16]

While being applied for comparative purposes, a vague category is elicited when "a conception from some one tradition is extended, abstracted further, and purified of its particularities to serve as a vague ground for comparison."[17] This process is conducive to comparison because (1) a vague category enables us to find the similarity between two traditions so as to make a comparison possible; (2) the similarity can be rendered as vaguely as possible so that it allows comparativists to attend to the specificities of compared traditions, which makes it possible to minimize the carryover of bias from one tradition to another; and (3) hypotheses about the similarity and difference between compared traditions can be devised in such a way as to be susceptible of further rectification and reformulation. Comparison is therefore capable of being pursued in an open-ended, scientific process regarding the same or multiple comparative points of reference.

As for the criteria of successful comparison, Neville endorses that "if the category of comparison vaguely considered is indeed a common respect for comparison, if the specifications of the category are made with pains taken to avoid imposing biases, and if the point of comparison is legitimate, then the translations of the specifications into the language of the category can allow of genuine comparisons."[18] Among the three conditions, the third one of legitimacy speaks to the scholar's interests and personal situations that orient comparisons in a particular explanatory or interpretative direction. The first two indicate the proper use of vague categories to describe comparative data impartially and accurately.

Neville has a distinct metaphysical interest, so that the vague categories he selects for comparison are normally put into the further construction of his metaphysical system. However, this also puts Neville's comparative methodology in a quandary. The metaphysical system constructed by Neville with the help of comparative vague categories tends to be so abstract that it is hard for people within the compared traditions to find resonances with Neville's work.[19] In my view, a way to improve Neville's method is to add Jonathan Smith's situational thinking to Neville's comparative formula. It means that in order to account for the legitimacy of comparison, comparativists should seek comparative points among the entire histories and the contemporary situations of the compared traditions. When philosophical construction is needed, after an appropriate vague category is chosen and an impartial comparative description is aptly pursued, a comparativist's philosophical creativity can be exerted in the direction that the survey of situations in the compared traditions indicates. In short, the comparison undertaken by a combination of Neville's vague category and Smith's situational thinking could address simultaneously the concerns of whether a comparison is accurate and whether comparative points are legitimate and relevant.

Aaron Stalnaker's comparative method centers on the use of "bridge concepts":

> Bridge concepts are general ideas, such as "virtue" and "human nature," which can be given enough content to be meaningful and guide comparative inquiry yet are still open to greater specification in particular cases.... The process of selection and refinement is thus in an important sense inductive, and any broader applicability any given set might possess is essentially hypothetical and subject to further testing and revision in wider inquiries.[20]

Evidently, Stalnaker's basic insight of bridge concept is very similar to Neville's vague category. However, Stalnaker explicitly refuses to construct a grand ethical theory that might be construed as a universal deep structure for the compared traditions, as he clarifies: "Bridge concepts are not, then, hypotheses about transcultural universals that purport to bring a 'deep structure' of human religion or ethics to the surface; I am skeptical about all such deep structures or 'epistemes' that are supposed somehow to determine or explain thought and practice, whether for humanity as a whole, or merely within a single tradition or era."[21] In this way, Stalnaker's bridge concept is effectively halfway toward the metavagueness of vague category, which is employed by Neville for constructing grand metaphysical and ethical theories.

Due to the halfway nature of his method, the application of bridge concepts in Stalnaker's comparison is problematic. Stalnaker does not explain explicitly why he remains skeptical about the existence of any deeper ethical structure of human behaviors, and from the above quotation, we may surmise that this skepticism is mainly due to his realization that discourses of deep structures tend to "determine" or prejudice comparative inquiry in particular ways. However, in my view, as long as a comparative process is open-ended and hypotheses formulated through bridge concepts continue to be refined, a constructive endeavor that deepens into identifying more universal features of ethical traditions and addresses issues shared by all humanity will be more than helpful and certainly should not be ruled out in advance. Because Stalnaker asserts the impossibility of "transcultural universals," and thus preempts the elevation of the abstract level of comparative terms from bridge concept to Neville's sort of vague category, his work lacks the means to evaluate the metaphysical assumptions in thinkers such as Xunzi and Augustine. After comparison he concludes somewhat disappointingly: "It appears that there is no easy way to harmonize these two types of moral psychological pictures."[22] Although I am not so optimistic as to assert there is a way to harmonize them, I remain critical of Stalnaker's insistence on using bridge concepts solely within the realm of ethics and his preempting of the possibility of finding new comparative points and hence new opportunities to build mutual insight between the compared traditions.

In a nutshell, Neville and Stalnaker appear to have strong commonalities in their understandings about how to conduct impartial and accurate comparison. First, they both underscore the significance of the selection of appropriate comparative categories. Second, the selected categories must admit a certain degree of vagueness so that their application in comparison can be flexible and adaptable. Third, a scholarly community needs to contribute a joint effort to continually critique and refine comparative hypotheses. But they are not identical, and Neville's method occupies a unique niche. Compared with most of scholars in the field of comparative religion, Neville's comparative method accommodates studies of religion in more diverse disciplinary perspectives, including philosophy and theology. Compared with Stalnaker's method, Neville's comparative method of vague category embraces the ambition to explore more universal aspects of metaphysics, ethics, epistemology, and so on, free from the suspicion toward universality that often precludes such adventurous inquiry in comparative philosophy of religion. Since it does not conform to any preestablished disciplinary or subdisciplinary boundaries, Neville's comparative method can be responsive to varying scholarly interests, especially when it is assisted by Smith's situational thinking. And it enables the comparative study of religion to be conducted as a science broadly construed in a pragmatist sense, argued in chapter 2. In other words, any statement made by comparativists about religion is thought of as explorative, hypothetical, fallible, and formulated so as to be readily testable against reality in varying ways: If the statement is about compared traditions, then data gathered from these traditions will provide feedback for refining hypothetical statements; if it is about something else, then the statement is vulnerable to critique by scholars in relevant disciplines, no matter how abstract the hypothetical statement appears to be.

Conclusion

After considering a variety of comparative methodologies in the disciplines of comparative theology, comparative religion, and especially comparative philosophy of religion, I have to determine which one of them fits my project best.

Because I will compare Ruism and Christianity regarding a key metaphysical and theological concept of "creation" in a general framework of Ruist CT, articulated previously as a rooted, nonconfessional, and scientific liberal art, I believe a combination of Neville's pragmatical methodology of vague category and Jonathan Smith's situational thinking is the path forward. This combined methodology will adequately accommodate two central aspects of the Ruist CT: its rooted nature, which accounts for the situation and legitimacy of my comparison; and its scientific nature, which aims for impartial and accurate descriptions of compared tradition.

5 *Creatio ex Nihilo* from Plato to Augustine

Foreword to Chapter 5

From a historical and philosophical perspective, Christian conceptions of creaturehood are rooted in the Bible. An all-powerful God creates the world out of His gratuitous love and free will, and without God, any goodness, beauty, and order of the world would cease to exist. However, it was not until the late second century that the Christian doctrine of *creatio ex nihilo* was explicitly stated for the first time. This happened in the works of Theophilus of Antioch (ca. 120–190 CE) when he refuted Plato's cosmology in the *Timaeus*, highlighting the uniqueness of the Christian conception of creation. If we consider Augustine of Hippo (354–430 CE) as the decisive figure in Christian intellectual history who developed a cluster of Christian theses, including original sin, salvation, Christology, and theodicy, all of which hinge on the doctrine of *creatio ex nihilo*, it took nearly half a millennium after the common era for a full-fledged Christian doctrinal system of *creatio ex nihilo* to be constructed.

This prolonged period of philosophical reflection within Christianity is noteworthy. Although the Bible has always been the seminal text for Christian piety and the text of authority that Christian intellectuals continue to invoke to defend themselves against criticism from outside, it took time for the Bible to be canonized, and a distinct theory of *creatio ex nihilo* could only be formulated in an intellectual environment where various non-Christian philosophies and religions interacted with their Christian counterpart. This complex intellectual milieu contained key competitive and interactive elements such as Christian piety grounded in the biblical texts; Greco-Roman philosophy, particularly Plato's cosmology and its development in middle Platonism and Neoplatonism; and

Gnosticism with its various modifications within emerging religions like Manichaeism. Thus, only after understanding the nature of each of these elements and how they interacted with one another can we explain the historical emergence of the Christian doctrine of *creatio ex nihilo* and comprehend the doctrine's philosophical distinctiveness.

Creatio ex Nihilo in the Hebrew Bible

In this analysis of intellectual history, I will examine the feeling of Christian piety grounded in biblical texts, which is the first element in the aforementioned intellectual milieu. Among the Hebrew Bible passages, besides the Genesis, that resemble an explicit expression of *creatio ex nihilo* is one found in 2 Maccabees 7:28: "Consider everything you see there, and realize that God made it all from nothing, just as He made the human race."[1] Theophilus of Antioch and Origen, early Christian fathers, relied on this passage when formulating their theory of *creatio ex nihilo*.[2] However, Gerhard May questions whether it presents an unequivocal statement of *creatio ex nihilo* in its original context. May thinks that the text is not a theoretical disquisition on the nature of the creation process, but a paraenetic reference to God's creative power. In other words, the text implies that the world came into existence through the sovereign creative act of God, and that it was not there before. It is simply an unphilosophical everyday turn of phrase, which tells us that something new that was not there before comes into being. Whether this something new comes about through a change in something that was already there or whether it is something absolutely new is beside the point.[3]

N. Joseph Torchia shares May's doubts about the phrase "ἐξ οὐκ ὄντων" in 2 Maccabees 7:28, which is rather ambiguous and can be translated either as "from the nonexistent" or "from things which did not exist" (that is, preexisting amorphous matter).[4] The ambiguity of thought can be confirmed in another Hebrew Bible text, Wisdom 11:17: "And indeed your all-powerful hand which created the world from formless matter did not lack the means to unleash a horde of bears or savage lions . . . or unknown beasts."[5] This text is reminiscent of Plato's cosmology of world-formation in the *Timaeus*. Both 2 Maccabees 7:28 and Wisdom 11:17 were composed during Hellenistic Judaism, a period when Jewish minds were influenced by Greek philosophy that stimulated Jewish reflection on divine creation in an abstract and ontological way. However, the implications of these two statements seem to be diametrically opposite to each other if the "ἐξ οὐκ ὄντων" in 2 Maccabees 7:28 means what *creatio ex nihilo* does in Christian terms.

Even if a passable interpretation of *creatio ex nihilo* could be read into 2 Maccabees 7:28, the ambiguity of this interpretation is aggravated by the fact that there was, in fact, no solid expression of the doctrine of *creatio ex nihilo* in Hellenistic Judaism.[6] Based on these analyses, it can be concluded that a philosophically significant expression of *creatio ex nihilo* could not be achieved directly from a firsthand reading of the Bible. If a unique intellectual and religious milieu that demanded responses from believers of the Bible had not existed, they would have felt free to use any philosophical language to express their religious piety without much concern for the adequacy or coherency of the adopted philosophical concepts.

Early Christian fathers were faced with a unique demand: to frame and argue their Christian confession on realized religious truth in a distinctively philosophical and theological way. According to May, the Christian claim that truth has been realized by Christ brought unparalleled intensity to the debate between Christian and pagan thinkers.[7] To surmount the debate, they had to interpret Biblical texts on divine creation, such as the Genesis and other parts of the Hebrew Bible, in a way that would illuminate what was at stake in the competing theological interpretations leading to the full-fledged theory of *creatio ex nihilo* in Augustine's thought.

Two moments in Genesis 1:1–5 are particularly important to this illumination. First, the "formless void and darkness" of the earth in 1:2 may be read as the amorphous Platonic matter. If so, the creation of God would have unfolded exactly as Plato had conceived it: The spirit of God puts order into preexistent matter, and the world, comprising a myriad of things each with its distinctive form, is thereby created. However, if matter is formless and can be identified with chaos, what is the origin of the matter? Is it coeternal with God? Furthermore, if matter is formless and can be identified with chaos, in what sense can it be said to be "Good"?

Second, "the beginning" in 1:1 may be understood in two ways. Does it mean that the world as created by God has a temporal beginning? If so, how can any time be defined before the creation of God if God creates everything? If God's creation is eternal and nontemporal, what then does "creation" mean? After the initiation of the world in time, does God need to continue to sustain the world lest it cease to exist? Is there any purpose underlying the whole process of divine creation and world-formation? These sets of questions became a powerful engine that compelled early Christian intellectuals to provide a philosophically distinct and coherent theory of creation as they were forced to compete and interact with Greek philosophy and other religious views such as Gnosticism. The theory of *creatio ex nihilo* is the hard-won fruit of this engagement.

Plato's Philosophical Cosmology in the *Timaeus*
PLATONIC ONTOLOGY

Plato's argument on the causality of ontological dependence among cosmic realities, as crystallized in the *Timaeus*, had a decisive influence on early Christian thinking of *creatio ex nihilo*. However, to fully appreciate the significance of Plato's ideas, we must examine several other Platonic dialogues to capture key moments of his ontological thinking.

One major breakthrough Plato made in comparison with the pre-Socratic natural philosophers was that he explicitly explains in the *Phaedo* that his theory of Forms searches for causes that are of another type than "cosmological succession":

> If someone said that without bones and sinews and all such things, I should not be able to do what I decided, he would be right, but surely to say that they are the cause of what I do, and not that I have chosen the best course, even though I act with my mind, is to speak very lazily and carelessly. Imagine not being able to distinguish the real cause from that without which the cause would not be able to act as a cause. It is what the majority appears to do, like people groping in the dark; they call it a cause, thus giving it a name that does not belong to it. That is why one man surrounds the earth with a vortex to make the heavens keep it in place, another makes the air support it like a wide lid. As for their capacity of being in the best place they could possibly be put, this they do not look for, nor do they believe it to have any divine force, but they believe that they will some time discover a stronger and more immortal Atlas to hold everything together more, and they do not believe that the truly good and "binding" binds and holds them together.[8]

I consider this an "ontological" turning point that occurred in Plato's conception of causality.[9] According to Plato, previous natural philosophers cannot explain why things in the universe could be "in the best place they could possibly be"; neither do they believe "the truly good and 'binding' binds and holds them together." In other words, what Plato is searching for is the origin of the overall order of the entire universe. Understandably, if the focus of natural philosophers is to uncover the series of "cosmological succession" step by step regarding the temporal succession of cosmic events, they cannot provide answers to Plato's ontological inquiry. Instead, Plato explains his own approach to answering his questions as follows: "So I thought I must take refuge in discussions and investigate the truth of things by means of words. . . . I assume the existence of a Beautiful, itself by itself, of a Good and a Great and all the rest."[10]

In this way, in order to answer the ontological question about the overall order of the entire universe which comprises many things, Plato turns to words. His theory of Forms, understood from this perspective, is a philosophical discourse that probes the ontological causality of things in the universe by relying on a philosopher's knowledge of the most generic features of things signified by the logic of human words.

If my interpretation of the theory of Forms is correct, Plato must have a clear understanding of "ontology" as a science of "being" different from the more empirical work of earlier natural philosophers. This is indeed the case in dialogues such as the *Parmenides* 142b5–c5 and the *Philebus* 58a, which address the key question of "what is one" versus "whether one is." Plato deems the highest knowledge to pertain to both "being" and what is "self-same" among what is real. This indicates that Plato's thought gestures toward the distinction between "being" and "essence," which is of great significance to later Western metaphysical thinking.

With this conceptual distinction in mind, Plato's reasons for unpacking the overall order of cosmic events must account for both what an event is and where the being of that event comes from. As a systematic thinker, Plato is dedicated to finding a singular reason capable of providing both explanations. In the *Republic*, he states:

> The sun not only provides visible things with the power to be seen, but also with coming to be, growth, and nourishment, although it is not itself coming to be. Therefore, you should also say that not only do the objects of knowledge owe their being-known to the Good, but their being is also due to it, although the Good is not being, but superior to it in rank and power.[11]

This quoted statement can be viewed as the earliest philosophical precursor to the later Christian idea of *creatio ex nihilo*, as it posits that an ultimate cause, beyond and generative of being, accounts for both our knowledge of what a thing is and our inquiry into where it comes from. However, the statement does not specify how ultimate causality proceeds concretely.

To provide a concrete explanation in the *Timaeus*, Plato also poses a typical ontological question in the *Philebus*: What are the most generic features that a thing has as long as it is said to be? Plato's answer consists of four fundamental categories.[12] The "unlimited" of a thing is its quantifiable feature, such as the fact that a thing can be hotter or cooler, bigger or smaller, and there is no limit to these quantifiable traits. The "limit" of a thing is what structures and unifies these unlimitedly quantified features of the thing. For example, a healthy human body depends on a balance between the hot and cool elements within it and the proportionality among the sizes of its bones. "The mixture of limited and unlimited" is the process by which a thing comes to be, and correspondingly, "the cause of this mixture" is what produces a thing, similar to the efficient cause in Aristotle's thought.

What is of particular interest to us is that Plato believes there is an "all-encompassing wisdom" or an underlying cosmic soul that acts as what the fourth category, the cause of the mixture of limit and unlimited, requires.[13] This cosmic soul, being eternal and always self-same, generates the being of the universe and brings an overall order to it via a process of mixing the limit and the unlimited. During this process, all things are created and sustained by the cosmic soul, and they, including human beings, also live and become for the sake of the cosmic soul. In other words, the cosmic soul is the initiator, sustainer, and telos of the entire universe, a thesis to be echoed in more detail in the *Timaeus*.

THE *TIMAEUS*

During the period of late antiquity, Plato's *Timaeus* played a pivotal role in theological discussions concerning the origin of the universe. In keeping with the fundamentals of his ontological idealism, Plato introduces the principle of his philosophical cosmology at the beginning of the *Timaeus*: What becomes but never is lies in the realm of visible, tangible, and empirical realities, which entails unreasoning sense perceptions, while what always is and has no becoming marks the realm of ideas, forms, and models, which can only be grasped through understanding. As "everything that comes to be must of necessity come to be by the agency of some cause,"[14] the empirical world must have an ultimate cause. And this ultimate causation is conceived of as "a work of craft" by "the maker and father of this universe" in accordance with "that which is changeless and is grasped by a rational account, that is, by wisdom."[15] Plato distinguishes three aspects of this divine craft work.

First, an intelligible and immutable model of ideas and forms necessitates the presence of an invisible soul of the universe that brings order and harmony to the empirical world. As the most excellent of all the things begotten by the divine creator, which Plato calls the "Demiurge," the cosmic soul is considered the immediate fruit of divine creation, manifesting the divine nature.[16] The *Timaeus* further identifies the order and harmony of ideas and forms as the algebraic proportions, geometrical relationships, and musical rhythms that the movement of physical phenomena reveals, which can only be grasped by exceptional human understanding.

Second, the receptacle of all things that come to be is the amorphous matter, which is formless, invisible, and does not belong to the empirical world.[17] Together with the ideas and forms of the cosmic soul, the preexistent matter constitutes the eternal ingredients of divine creation, which takes place before the beginning of time. In short, the Demiurge, ideas, and matter are the three ontological principles that generate the entire empirical world. If expressed through the four categories in the *Philebus*, the divine creator can be viewed as the cause of the mixture, ideas as the limit, and matter as the unlimited. Divine creation is then seen as a mixture of the limit and the unlimited by the Demiurge.

Third, the empirical world, comprising things that come to be and imitate the intelligible and eternal model of ideas and forms, is our world. When the model with its harmonious mathematical proportions is cast upon the amorphous preexistent matter, fire, air, water, and earth are formed. Each of these basic elements possesses its unity with a measured relationship to the others, and a myriad of things are generated through the mixture and interaction of these elemental materials.[18] As an imitation of the intelligible model, the empirical world has the potential for order and harmony. However, because the underlying matter is amorphous and eternal, becoming things are susceptible to corruption and can deviate from their appropriate natures apportioned by divine creation. Once this deviation takes place, disorder, evil, and disaster follow.¹⁹ The *Timaeus* does not refer to any ultimate endpoint of the empirical world. Instead, the world keeps changing in ebb and flow, sometimes being more orderly while at other times not. The Demiurge creates the visible world and puts order into it because he wishes to manifest his own goodness and make everything as good as he is.²⁰ However, because the corrupting power of matter is coeternal with the divine creator, the Demiurge can only "produce a piece of work that would be as excellent and supreme as its nature would allow."²¹

The vulnerable nature of the empirical world also implicates the fate of human beings. As a mixture of body and soul, the changeable and the changeless, humans have an obligation to harmonize these two. If a person during the course of life consistently relies upon reason to control emotions stimulated by random sense perceptions, "he would at the end return to his dwelling place in his companion star, to live a life of happiness that agreed with his character." Nevertheless, if he continues to fail to do so, he will first be reborn as a woman and then as some wild animal that resembles the wicked character he has acquired. Accordingly, the salvation for human beings is "to learn the harmonies and revolutions of the universe, and so bring into conformity with its objects our faculty of understanding, as it was in its original condition."²²

CREATION IN PLATONISM AND EARLY CHRISTIANITY

In summary, there are four key points in Plato's philosophical cosmology that could either contradict or be consistent with Christian understandings of divine creation. First, the preexistent and eternal amorphous matter undermines the omnipotence of the Christian God. Although the intelligible model of ideas and forms is said to be begotten by the divine creator, the *Timaeus* maintains that the creator needs preexistent matter to accommodate ideas and forms for completing his creative craftwork. This assertion makes divine creation no different from human creativity, which always needs preexistent materials to receive human ideas. In other words, the divine creation in Plato's thought cannot bring anything entirely new, for it only alters the patterns by which the preexistent material is organized.

Second, divine creation in the *Timaeus* can make a visible world good only to the extent that its nature allows, as the amorphous matter always has the potential to corrupt any established order and harmony in the cosmos. Matter is evil, whereas idea is good; body is evil, whereas soul is good; and no principle dictates the triumph of one side over another. Here, the theme of Platonic dualism stands out, and it would provide impetus to another even more dualistic tradition in late antiquity, namely Gnosticism, which typically maintains that the visible world is created by a malevolent God to fight against the good God dwelling above, making the world an ongoing battlefield full of disorder and evil. Nonetheless, Christians believe in the Genesis narrative, which states that everything created by God is good. This belief commits Christians to monotheism, but it also raises the challenge of explaining the origin of evil, the thorny issue of theodicy.

Third, for Plato, divine creation as a craftwork of three moments (namely the divine creator, ideas, and matter) is a necessary process. The entailed necessity of the ideas and forms in the cosmic soul or divine intellect is determined to be embodied in the changing visible world. Thus, the world is pervaded with "nature," from which nothing, not even the gods, can be exempt.[23] This Greek notion of nature hardly aligns with the Christian belief in the absolute freedom of God in divine creation.

Last, for Plato, the origin of time coincides with the origin of the universe. They are both generated together by the same act of divine creation: "Time, then, came to be together with the universe so that just as they were begotten together, they might also be undone together, should there ever be undoing of them."[24] In other words, the creative act, depicted as the divine creator placing his ideas onto amorphous matter, occurs before the origin of both the universe and embedded time, and hence, it transpires eternally and nontemporally.[25] Plato further portrays time as a "moving image of eternity":

> So, as the model was itself an everlasting Living Thing,[26] he [the Demiurge] set himself to bringing this universe to completion in such a way that it, too, would have that character to the extent that was possible. Now it was the Living Thing's nature to be eternal, but it isn't possible to bestow eternity fully upon anything that is begotten. And so he began to think of making a moving image of eternity: at the same time as he brought order to the universe, he would make an eternal image, moving according to number, of eternity remaining in unity. This number, of course, is what we now call "time."
>
> For before the heavens came to be, there were no days or nights, no months or years. But now, at the same time as he framed the heavens, he devised their coming to be. These all are parts of time, and *was* and *will*

be are forms of time that have come to be. Such notions we unthinkingly but incorrectly apply to everlasting being. . . . These, rather, are forms of time that have come to be—time that imitates eternity and circles according to number.[27]

According to this image, the past, present, and future modes of time, regardless of how they change and evolve in the empirical world, are created altogether as an unsummed totality by the same divine creation. Consequently, it is conceivable that the world exists forever while still being created, or the world has a beginning but no end while still being created, or the world has no beginning but an end while still being created. It is also conceivable that the divine creator originates and sustains the existence of the visible world from below. In this way, the term "eternal" secures a uniquely ontological connotation: However long the visible world lasts, even perhaps forever, the divine creation conditions the being of the world without itself being conditioned in such a way, and hence, is eternal in a full ontological sense.

Middle Platonism

Middle Platonism refers to a group of Platonic philosophers who lived between the late first century BCE and the early third century CE. They formulated a theology that shared an affinity with Christian thinking. On one hand, they systematized the cosmology of the *Timaeus* into a discourse orchestrated by three ontological principles: God,[28] Ideas, and Matter, which were believed to be of equal rank. The eternity of matter, from which the world is made, was generally accepted. On the other hand, inspired by Jewish-Christian monotheistic thinking, middle Platonists sought a singular, universal ground of being, pressing toward the suppression of the three-principle scheme to provide a more transcendent expression of the first principle.[29]

Middle Platonists continued to contemplate the concept of time in the *Timaeus*, with Aristotle once critiquing Plato for the asymmetry of time concerning how a generated world could last forever: "For there are some who think it possible both for the ungenerated to be destroyed and for the generated to persist undestroyed. (This is held in the *Timaeus*, where Plato says that the heaven, though it was generated, will none the less exist for the rest of time.)"[30] In response, middle Platonic philosopher Calvenus Taurus (fl. ca. 145 CE) reflected on the word "create," stating that "the cosmos is said to be 'created' as being always in the process of generation" and that "One might also call it 'created' by virtue of the fact that it is dependent for its existence on an outside source, to wit, God, by whom it has been brought into order."[31] Therefore, it is reasonable to assert that the cosmos is always changing while still in need of a transcendent God to sustain its existence. Similarly, while positing an everlasting generation of the universe, Albinus (fl. ca. 145 CE) recognized the need for an unbegotten cause to sustain this ongoing process, stating that "since what is continually becoming cannot account for itself, it requires some external cause."[32]

Following this thread of philosophical thought, which elevated the status of divine creation from the horizontal cosmic dimension to a vertical and ontological one, Sallustius (fl. ca. 4th c. CE) differentiates two kinds of creation: creation by means of skill or natural process and creation by means of function. According to Sallustius's analysis, those who create by skill or natural process are prior to what they create; conversely, what they create is subsequent to the creator. Those who create by function, however, bring their creatures into being simultaneously with themselves. For Sallustius, God must create by means of function.[33]

Following Sallustius's argument, not only is it reasonable to assert the eternity and nontemporality of divine creation, but the synchronicity or simultaneity of divine creation with the ongoing generated world at each moment can also be acknowledged. In my view, Sallustius's understanding of time is a corollary to Plato's related theory. Because God creates the universe and its time altogether, and the world needs an ultimate cause to sustain its continuous existence, divine creation sustains its creatures eternally both above the totality of time and within the process of time. If we see into the creating process from the latter perspective, divine creation is simultaneous with each worldly moment; whereas if we see into it from a more transcendent perspective, divine creation is nontemporal. It is because of the ontological dependence of the entire world-process upon the divine creation that we can characterize it as both eternal and synchronic, both transcendental and immanent.

Not all middle Platonic philosophers held similar views. Nevertheless, Sallustius's interpretation of the *Timaeus* and his solution to the problem of time in the context of divine creation, as it had been prepared in Taurus's and Albinus's thought, became dominant in later middle Platonism.[34] I believe the main reason for its dominance was the capacity of Sallustius's ontological thinking to accommodate a variety of possible hypotheses on time informed by the progress of empirical knowledge of the world. Assuming that each mode of time in the visible world depends upon an ultimate cause in a vertical and ontological manner, philosophers could then focus on the construction of their systematic metaphysics. As indicated in the following, this philosophical thought on the ontological dependence of the created world upon God assisted both Christian intellectuals and Platonists in interpreting the "beginning" in Genesis 1:1 in a more delicate way.

The First Christian Philosophical Formulation of *Creatio ex Nihilo* by Theophilus

In the intellectual history of Christianity, Theophilus of Antioch was the first to articulate a philosophical conception of *creatio ex nihilo*. Theophilus formulated this conception while disputing various Platonic cosmologies rooted in the *Timaeus*. Against Platonism, Theophilus argued that if matter is unoriginated like God, then God cannot be thought of as the omnipotent creator in the fullest sense. If God had to create the cosmos based on preexisting matter, there would be no difference between God and a human craftsman who makes what they want from a given material.[35] Instead, Theophilus claimed that the divine creation as revealed in the biblical story can only be from God, who creates everything out of nothing through an absolutely free will. Nothing is coeternal with God. Even if the world could exist forever after its beginning, it would still exist in time created by God. As Theophilus put it, "God was himself space, was self-sufficient and was before all times."[36]

The first philosophical doctrine of *creatio ex nihilo* is based on the absolute unconditionality of divine creation and the absolute dependence of all cosmic realities upon it. The designation of "nothingness" does not refer to "something" or some status of being that existed before the beginning of cosmic time, if there was any beginning at all. Instead, "nothingness" indicates God's creative act as the ultimate condition of cosmic realities, which conditions all other realities while being itself unconditioned. Vertically, this Christian idea of *creatio ex nihilo* tries to grasp the ultimate ontological condition of all created beings in the world. Horizontally, it also attempts to encompass all determinate realities within the scope of created worldly phenomena.

A Potential Form of *Creatio ex Nihilo* in Plotinus's Neoplatonism

In the intellectual history of *creatio ex nihilo*, Neoplatonism in Plotinus's thought represents a significant philosophical development between Theophilus of Antioch, the first Christian theologian to formulate the philosophical idea of *creatio ex nihilo*, and Augustine of Hippo, the first theologian to systematize the idea into orthodox Christian theology. Plotinus used the key metaphor of "emanation," "flowing," or "overflowing" to describe the productive act of the One, rather than the term "creation." Nevertheless, Plotinus advanced Plato's ontology to explain the entirety of the world using one singular principle, thus adding momentum for the formation of the Christian doctrine of *creatio ex nihilo*.

CREATION OR EMANATION?

At first glance, Christian thinkers may question whether Plotinus's idea of "emanation" is truly about "creation," given that Plotinus maintains that the emanation of the world from the One is necessary, while creation should be based on the absolute freedom of divine will. Nevertheless, Plotinus consistently asserts that the One "exists of necessity"[37] and that the One's production of reality is "free," "independent," and "in accordance with its will."[38] This assertion implies the One's "self-determination,"[39] self-causation, and self-sufficiency. In other words, there is no external constraint determining the One's act, which is thus both necessary and free. Since "self-determination" is also a key element in the Christian concept of divine freedom, we cannot conclude that the emanation of realities from the One is not a form of creation based solely on Plotinus's emphasis on necessity.

On the other hand, the Christian tradition also includes the idea of "ontological contingency" of the entire created world, as we have seen in the case of Theophilus of Antioch. This means that since God creates the world in an absolutely free way, the world depends on God, not vice versa. Is this idea found in Plotinus's thought? Plotinus asserts that the One "does not need to move to something else, since the other things move to it and it has no need of anything."[40] He also affirms that since the One is the "generator of being," it is "beyond being"[41] and remains what it is even if we do not predicate anything about the existing things to it.[42] In other words, the many beings depend on the One, but the One can have no need of and be unrelated to any lower realities. Thus, the idea of "ontological contingency" of the entire produced world upon the One is present in Plotinus's thought. This conclusion is supported by the fact that Plotinus often uses words like "make," "produce," and "bring into existence" (more akin to "creation" than "emanation") to describe the causal relationship between the One and derived realities.

However, despite the similarities between Plotinus's and Christian thought, there are also elements of Plotinus's philosophy that are typically Greek and atypically Christian. One example is Plotinus's answer to the question of why the One overflows. As analyzed above, the productive act of the One can be considered both "necessary" and "free" in the sense that it is not constrained by anything outside of itself. However, freedom also implies the aspect of an act that it can be otherwise than it is, which is an idea later entertained by Christian theologians in the tradition of *creatio ex nihilo*. Yet, as corroborated by other texts in *Ennead* 4.2, Plotinus specifically stresses:

> How then could the most perfect, the first Good, remain in itself as if it grudged to give of itself or was impotent, when it is the productive power of all things? How would it then still be the Principle? Something must certainly come into being from it, if anything is to exist of the others which derive their being from it: *that it is from it that they come is absolutely necessary.*[43]

For Plotinus, the One overflows because it has to; it is the only way that the One, as the first and most perfect, can be what it is. In other words, the overflowing of the One is a result of its nature, and as the One, it cannot not overflow. This thought prevents Plotinus from envisioning the nonexistence of the produced world and a more radical idea of ontological contingency, which would imply that there can be no relationship between the two sides of divine creation at all, since the produced world would possibly be simply nonexistent.

Based on the above analysis of the similarities and differences between Plotinus's and Christian thought, I categorize Plotinus's ontological cosmogony centering upon the emanation of the One as being halfway between the Greek idea of nature and the Christian idea of radical ontological contingency.

PLOTINUS'S CONTINUITY WITH PLATO AND *CREATIO EX NIHILO*

Understood as such, exploring the continuity between Plotinus's and Plato's thought, and assessing to what degree the productive act of the One is interpretable as *creatio ex nihilo*, provides another perspective to deepen our understanding of Plotinus and his influence on Christianity.

Bearing a striking resemblance to Plato, who in *Phaedo* 99b–c distinguished himself from pre-Socratic natural philosophers (as discussed above), Plotinus in *Ennead* 6.8.14.25–32 suggests that the One furnishes the explanation for both why things fit together in the universe and where their "being" comes from. Accordingly, the essence and being of the One are also the same.[44] Plotinus's ontological cosmogony of the One can be seen as a continued endeavor after Plato to seek a singular principle to explain both what a thing is and why it exists. The Intellect, which consists of forms and logical possibilities, more directly explains the essence of a thing. However, because the Intellect is the first outcome of the overflowing One, the One in Plotinus's thought is still the singular reason for both the essence and the being of all realities.

The motive of employing a singular principle to account for the overall order and being of worldly realities drives Christian thought to the philosophical formulation of *creatio ex nihilo*. Since Plotinus's thought is driven by the same motive, we can anticipate finding similar thoughts on *creatio ex nihilo* in his work, although *emanatio ex nihilo* may be a more accurate phrase for Plotinus, given the analyzed distinction between creation and emanation.

As we anticipated, Plotinus posits that the One is self-caused, as it "[makes] itself from nothing (*oudenos*)."[45] He further expounds on this idea: "It is because there is nothing in it [the One] that all things come from it: in order that being may exist, the One is not being, but the generator of being. This, we may say, is the first act of generation: the One, perfect because it seeks nothing, has nothing, and needs nothing, overflows, as it were, and its superabundance makes something other than itself."[46] Plotinus denies that any causation above the level of Intellect in the hierarchical chain of being is "prior in time."[47] Thus, when Plotinus mentions "nothing" in this context, it is in line with Theophilus of Antioch's idea of *creatio ex nihilo*. In other words, the "nothingness" of the One is meant to convey the "ontological unconditionality" of its productive power in relation to all produced realities. Two other traits of *emanatio ex nihilo* are noteworthy for their influence on later Christian thought.

First, the nonreciprocal ontological dependence of derived realities on the One leads to Plotinus's mystical vision that the One cannot be characterized by anything present in the world of derived realities. The One is "formless," "shapeless,"[48] and "beyond being," even though it generates form, shape, and being. As Plotinus stresses, "we could find nothing to say which is applicable to it [the One] or even really about it; for all noble and majestic things come after it."[49]

Second, Plotinus also positively describes the One as an "activity," a "productive power,"[50] or a "generator of being." Even so, the normal concept of "making" something out of passive matter does not apply to the One's activity:

> What then are "all the things"? All things of which that One is the principle. But how is that One the principle of all things? Is it because as principle it keeps them in being, making each of them exist? Yes, and because it *brought them into existence*. But how did it so? By possessing them beforehand. But it has been said that in this way it will be a multiplicity. But it had them in such a way as not to be distinct: they are distinguished on the second level, in the rational form. For this is already actuality; but the One is the potency of all the things. But in what way is it the potency? Not in the way in which matter is said to be in potency, because it receives: for matter is passive; but *this [material] way of being a potency is at the opposite extreme to making*.[51]

Corroborated by previously quoted texts such as *Ennead* 5.2.1.5–10, this quotation evidences that the essential feature of the One's ultimate activity is "ontological unconditionality," which is the power to make everything out of nothing. To convey Plotinus's idea, I suggest the term "sheer making," which refers to the nontemporal process of making everything out of nothing.[52]

It is evident that much of Plotinus's thought anticipates key moments in the later intellectual history of *creatio ex nihilo*. Plotinus's characterization of the One as an "activity" is like Aquinas's view of God as "pure act to be," and "generator of being" is like Tillich's "ground of being." Plotinus's emphasis on the ineffability of the productive power of the One foreshadows the tradition of Christian mysticism. Finally, his exploration of "sheer making" implies a perennial debate within the tradition of *creatio ex nihilo* concerning the unconditional nature of divine creativity.

From the demonstrated continuity of thought between Plato, Plotinus, and the Christian tradition of *creatio ex nihilo*, I discern a condition for philosophers and theologians to fashion an idea of creation similar to the Greek/Christian case: They need an idea of "ontological dependence" or, using Aristotle's term, an idea of the "priority of nature and being." Aristotle characterized "the prior" in relation to "nature and being" as "those which can be without other things, while the others cannot be without them—a distinction which Plato used."[53]

In the thought of Plato and Plotinus, the priority of nature and being concerns a relation of nonreciprocal dependence in which, in a series of items, the posterior depends on the prior and cannot exist without the prior, whereas the prior exists independently of the posterior and remains after the elimination of the posterior.[54] Importantly, the relationship of dependence registers synchronically among the items in the series. Since the ultimate item conditions all other derived ones, the relationship of dependence can also be thought of as "eternal" or "nontemporal" in the sense that all temporal modes among conditioned terms are nonreciprocally dependent upon the ultimate. Therefore, it is easier to grasp the relationship between "transcendence" and "immanence" as it is implied by this series of the priority of nature and being. The conditioning power of the ultimate item in the series transcends all other terms in the sense that it is prior by nature to all of them, and thus, everything characteristic of the derived items cannot fully and adequately characterize the first. However, the ultimacy is immanent in all the derived items in that all these items are a manifestation of its ultimate conditioning power. Thus, we can still say something about the ultimacy by means of our knowledge of its consequences in the derived items. In other words, "transcendence" and "immanence" are mutually defined in such a series of the priority of nature and being or of ontological dependence. If there is no immanent manifestation of the ultimacy, there is no way for human knowledge to reach the primal principle, and thus, no way to differentiate what is transcendent from what is immanent. On the other hand, once we establish that derived realities are the immanent manifestation of the ultimate conditioning power, we are also certain of the transcendence of the ultimacy.

Emanatio ex Nihilo Not Quite *ex Nihilo*

Plotinus's thought, while sharing continuity with the Christian tradition of *creatio ex nihilo*, falls short of its radical version of ontological dependence. First, the unconditionality of divine creation, characterized by the absolute freedom and gratuitous love of the Creator God in Christian thought, has no parallel in Plotinus, since the One overflows necessarily as a result of its nature.

Second, although the One's productive act creates all derived realities from nothing, the Intellect, as an immediate outcome of this overflowing power, is a necessary conduit for the One to complete the making. The Intellect contains all forms and measures that entail the intelligibility of the produced world, and so the indispensable instrumentality of the Intellect implies that the overflowing of the One cannot be irrational and unintelligible.

I believe that Plotinus's statement that "as first existence it [the One] is not in the soulless and not in irrational life"[55] confuses the concepts of "irrationality" and "nonrationality." According to the relationship of the priority of nature and being, if the One is ontologically prior to the world of rational principles, it can be said to be "nonrational" because rational principles cannot exhaust its overflowing power. However, when Plotinus says that it is impossible for the One to be "not in the soulless and not in irrational life," he means that the One cannot generate other possible worlds different from the one conditioned by the rational principles of the Intellect or not generate anything at all. In this sense, the overflowing power of the One would not be as unconditioned as it ought to be, as implied by its ultimate position in the series of ontological dependence.

In the later history of *creatio ex nihilo*, the question of whether the intelligibility of the created world exists prior or posterior to divine creation remains a subject of controversy. A prevailing idea among most Christian theologians and philosophers, similar to that of Plotinus, is that divine creation is necessarily intelligible because God cannot create something beyond the limits of divine intelligence, which encompasses all forms, measures, and logical possibilities of the created world. However, as I will discuss in more detail later, this notion may undermine the unconditionality of divine creation as *creatio ex nihilo*.

Third, Plotinus falls short of the unconditionality of the overflowing power of the One, which is also evident in his view of matter. Unlike Plato's idea of preexisting eternal material, Plotinus considered matter to be a derived reality produced by the One. However, for Plotinus, matter is the residue of the productive power of the One and lacks any kind of form, making it "absolute evil" and merely a "nonexistent (or nonbeing)."[56] These notions raise questions about how the One, as the generator of being, could produce a nonbeing and how the utterly good and most perfect One could produce something purely evil. These questions challenge Plotinus's monistic intention to explain the world using one singular principle.[57] Later, Augustine addressed these remaining questions in Plotinus's system in a Christian way, as we will discuss later.

To conclude this section on Plotinus, it is hard to overestimate his influence on the Western intellectual history of *creatio ex nihilo*. His persistence in using a singular principle to explain the order and being of the existing world drove later Christian thought to continually refine the idea of *creatio ex nihilo*. His metaphysics of the chain of being provided a basic vocabulary for later theologians and philosophers to address various issues implicated by the idea of ontological dependence or the priority of nature and being. Finally, the potential incoherence and defects in Plotinus's thought demand responses from the Christian tradition of *creatio ex nihilo*, which maintains great intellectual continuity with *emanatio ex nihilo*.

Early Christian Polemics Against Gnosticism

When studying the intellectual history of early Christianity that led to Augustine's systematic account of *creatio ex nihilo*, it is crucial not to overlook the significant role of Gnosticism. Karen King's summary of traditional Western scholarship reveals that the term "Gnosticism" primarily served to construct Christian identity through the characterization of a religious other.[58] Early Christian polemicists used this term to argue for the legitimacy of their own purported Christian orthodoxy. This phenomenon, which began with the patristic fathers, has also influenced modern scholars' understanding of Gnosticism because of the lack of available material beyond the polemical works. However, the discovery of the Nag Hammadi codices in Egypt in 1945 has prompted recent Gnostic studies to reevaluate the biases of historical research and retrieve the historical realities of the tradition.

For the purposes of this study on the intellectual history of early Christianity leading to Augustine's systematic account of *creatio ex nihilo*, it is appropriate to focus on how early Christian polemicists refuted the "Gnosticism" they imagined. The goal is to understand how Gnostic ideas were received in the Christian tradition and contributed to the development of the idea of *creatio ex nihilo*. While traditional categories are inadequate to encompass the diverse worldviews represented by the Nag Hammadi texts, they are not entirely inaccurate. The Gnosticism refuted by the patristic fathers remains a significant portion of the Gnostic literature currently under investigation by scholars.

Two sources in modern scholarship concerning Gnosticism are relevant to my study. The first is a definition of the term "Gnosticism" that was endorsed by the 1966 international conference on Gnosticism.[59] The second is a summary of the major tenets of Gnosticism by a Christian church historian, Adolf von Harnack (1851–1930).[60] These sources provide insight into how Gnosticism was originally engaged by early Christian polemicists and by Neoplatonic philosophers such as Plotinus. I will rely on them to investigate the role of the Gnostic tradition in the intellectual history of *creatio ex nihilo* in early Christianity.

Resonating with its definition in the first source, Gnosticism is generalized by Harnack as containing eleven major features, among which the first to fifth remain the most relevant to our study:

> One, Gnostic thought distinguishes between the supreme God and the creator, and hence between redemption and creation. Two, the supreme God was separated from the God of the Old Testament, and hence at least some parts of it could no longer be accepted as revelation of the supreme God; the Old Testament did, however, give an essentially accurate portrait of the world creator. Three, matter was considered to be independent and eternal. Four, the created world was conceptualized either as the product of an evil being or intermediary acting out of hostility to the supreme God, or as a "fall of humanity." Five, evil was understood as a physical force, inherent in matter.[61]

The anti-cosmic dualism found in Gnosticism poses a significant challenge to the Christian intellectual history of *creatio ex nihilo*. The division between the supreme God and the world creator not only places Gnosticism in opposition to Christian theology, but also stands in contrast with the middle and Neoplatonic endeavors to seek a singular supreme principle of the universe. As such, Plotinus's thought on the One can be understood as a direct response to Gnostic dualism, while the Christian idea of *creatio ex nihilo* represents a monistic commitment to the singular supreme principle of divine creation and a refutation of the Gnostic view.

However, the Platonic idea of the independence and eternity of "matter" is in conflict with early Christian thought on *creatio ex nihilo*, which denies the existence of any being coeternal with God. Both Plato's *Timaeus* and Gnosticism, in terms of the ontological status of matter, stand in opposition to Christianity.

To address the problem of evil, both Platonic and Christian thinkers have grappled with the challenge of reconciling the existence of evil with a supreme and all-good creator. In response to Gnosticism's dualistic worldview, Plotinus viewed matter as a measureless, orderless, and inherently valueless byproduct of the One's overflowing power. While this view refutes the Gnostic perspective by asserting that matter can be recovered by the Soul and restored to goodness, Plotinus's frequent characterizations of matter as "absolute evil" or "nonbeing" raise doubts about whether his monistic commitment to the goodness of the One is sufficient to incorporate the intrinsically evil nature of matter.

In other words, the problem of theodicy is a challenging issue for any philosophical or theological enterprise that seeks to explain all aspects of the existing world using a single principle, since it raises the question of how a supremely good principle can produce plain evils in the world. This issue emerged in Plato's thought but was not resolved. Plotinus attempted to tackle it but inadequately, as his monistic commitment to the goodness of the One left it unclear how the intrinsically evil power of matter could be incorporated. In early Christianity, Augustine of Hippo systematically addressed this issue in an orthodox theology centered around *creatio ex nihilo*.

Augustine on *Creatio ex Nihilo*

After analyzing the disputes among Platonists, Gnostic thinkers, and patristic fathers on divine creation, Augustine presented his idea of *creatio ex nihilo* as a version of Christian theology in line with the orthodox beliefs established after the Council of Nicaea. This became the foundation for later developments in mainstream Christian theology on creation and was not significantly challenged until René Descartes. In my further study, I will focus on the Augustinian understanding of divine creation and explore its inheritance and transformation in the confluence of various intellectual trends. This will conclude my investigation of the intellectual history of *creatio ex nihilo*, from its Platonic and biblical origins to its Augustinian systemization.

AUGUSTINE AND HIS PREDECESSORS

Gnosticism, exemplified in Manichaeism in Augustine's case, presented a challenge to his Christian piety with its anti-cosmic dualism and denigration of the Creator God in the Old Testament. In response, Augustine carried on the tradition of his predecessors Irenaeus and Tertullian in refuting Gnosticism, while also sharing the Neoplatonic commitment to a metaphysical worldview grounded in a singular principle.

To counter Manichaeism's literal reading of the Bible and preserve the authority of the Old Testament, Augustine employed a less anthropomorphic interpretation of scripture that emphasized spiritual rather than literal meanings. For example, when the Bible states that "man is said to have been made to the image of God," Augustine argued that this does not imply God is corporeal; rather, he insisted that "it is said with reference to the interior man, where reason is to be found and intelligence."[62] However, this approach to biblical exegesis put Augustine's thought in an intricate relationship to Platonism. He needed a new philosophical vocabulary to aid his spiritual interpretation of scripture, which he found in the "books of the Platonists."[63] There were three key Platonic ideas that influenced Augustine's thinking on divine creation:

Augustine's model of divine creation is rooted in the Platonic threefold conception from the *Timaeus*, where God imposes forms onto amorphous matter to create things in the world. Augustine also incorporates the Neoplatonic idea of a "chain of being," which sees the universe as a hierarchical structure comprising beings of different ranks, from God and angels to corporeal beings. This concept emphasizes the graded harmony of created beings within the universe, enabling Augustine to appreciate the overall goodness of divine creation. Additionally, the Platonic concept of "ontological dependence" plays a crucial role in Augustine's thinking, as it allows him to interpret God as the creator of time and to assert that the process of divine creation is ultimately nontemporal, even though the Bible may reveal a concrete starting point of time from an empirical perspective. This concept enables Augustine to present a spiritual interpretation of Christian scripture and highlight the "invisible truth"[64] of created realities in refuting Gnosticism.[65]

108 *Creatio ex Nihilo from Plato to Augustine*

Therefore, Augustine's relationship with Platonists and Gnostics regarding divine creation can be understood as his use of Platonic philosophy to create a distinctively Christian understanding of divine creation, specifically to refute Manichaeism.

THE CHRISTIAN NATURE OF AUGUSTINE'S CONCEPTION OF CREATION

We must differentiate Augustine's conception of divine creation from those of the Platonists to understand its distinctively Christian character. First, both Augustine and his patristic predecessors reject the notion of amorphous matter as a precondition for divine creation. For Augustine, only the Son of God and the Holy Spirit can be coeternal with God, and matter, like all other created beings, is made by God from nothing.[66] Since earlier Christian thinkers had already demonstrated the dependence of matter on divine creation, and Plotinus had attempted to derive the existence of matter from one singular principle, Augustine's position on this point is more a reiteration than a novel development.

Second, Plotinus's idea of *emanatio ex nihilo* is incomplete as a Christian conception because the nature of the One determines that it must overflow, as implied by the term's Greek etymology. Augustine's *creatio ex nihilo* radically transforms this idea. Divine creation, he argues, is entirely free, not only because it is not constrained by external factors but also because the ultimate reason for God's creation is His will, which is unconstrained and can freely withdraw from the act of creation. Christian piety toward the free will of God radically alters the Greek, Platonic notion of nature, allowing Augustine to develop the more radical notion of *creatio ex nihilo*. This idea allows Augustine to envision not only the nonexistence of the created world but also the possibility of alternative worlds that God could have created.[67] The following quotes speak well to the originality of Augustine's thought in comparison to Greek philosophy:

> So then, if these people ever say, "why did it take God's fancy to make heaven and earth?" . . . You see, they are seeking to know the cause of God's will, when God's will is itself the cause of everything there is. After all, if God's will has a cause, there is something that is there before God's will and takes precedence over it, which it is impious to believe.[68]

> ... divine providence, while being in itself absolutely unchanging, nonetheless comes to the aid of changeable creatures in various ways ... in order to bring back from the malady which is the beginning of death, and from death itself, to their proper condition and state of being, and to strengthen them in it, the creatures that are failing, slipping, that is to say, into nothingness. But you say to me: "Why are they failing?" Because they are subject to change. "Why are they subject to change?" Because they do not have being in the supreme degree. "Why not?" Because they are inferior to the one by whom they were made. "Who is it that made them?" The One who *is* in the supreme degree. "Who is that?" God, the unchanging Trinity, since he both made them through his supreme Wisdom and preserves them through his supreme Kindness. "Why did he make them?" So that they might be. Just being, after all, in whatever degree, is good, because the supreme Good is being in the supreme degree. "What did he make them out of?" From nothing, since whatever is must have some kind of specific look, however minimal.[69]

In these dialogues, Augustine offers a distinctly Christian perspective on divine creation that addresses some major questions. One of these questions is why God creates. Augustine asserts that God creates out of love for what God wills freely, without any external motivation or constraint. The contingency of the created world on the voluntary act of divine creation is a radical notion in Augustine's thought. Another question is how God creates. Augustine's answer includes two key points: first, that God creates out of nothing, without reliance on any external factors; second, that divine creation is nontemporal and unchanging, shaped by the Trinity, although its effects are manifested in the changing creatures of the world. In contrast to Platonic thought, Augustine's Trinitarian conception of God attributes the role of imposing forms into matter to the Holy Spirit, rather than a Demiurge. The redemption of human consciousness and the salvation of humanity's original sin is achieved through reunion with the gratuitous love and supreme beauty of divine creation, which is made possible by the Son of God. As Augustine succinctly proclaims, "the creature, which is indeed good but unequal to the creator and subject to change, was made out of nothing by the Father through the Son in the goodness of the Holy Spirit, the Trinity, which remains always consubstantial, eternal, and immutable."[70] Overall, Augustine's distinctively Christian perspective on divine creation is firmly grounded in the Trinitarian orthodoxy that emerged after the Council of Nicaea.[71]

Nevertheless, Augustine's answer to the motive of God's creation contains a tension. In *De Genesis contra Manichaeos* 1.2.4, Augustine puts the final word on the motive upon divine will, while in *De vera religione* 17.34–18.35, the motive is restated as the goodness of the existence of created things in the world. In resonance with this restatement, Augustine also specifies that the goodness of the created world consists of the graded harmony and the "supreme measure, form and order" of creatures appreciated as a whole, all of which are manifestations of divine wisdom.[72] This tension raises the potential conflict between wisdom, which is derived from divine intelligence, and gratuitous love, which arises from divine will. If the former is considered the primary motive of divine creation, then the latter will be subordinated to it. In other words, if divine will necessarily wills the overall good order of the world, which is imparted by divine intelligence, it cannot be said to be entirely free and undetermined by anything beyond it.

To shed light on this potential conflict, a comparison with Plotinus's thought is useful. In Plotinus's system, the Intellect is the immediate outcome of the One's overflowing, and it contains forms and measures to account for the intelligibility of the world. The Intellect explains what a thing is in relation to its worldly context, while the One is the origin of being. The being of all forms and measures, in Plotinus's view, derives from the overflowing power of the One, so the answer to what a thing is is subordinated to the answer to where a thing comes from. This subordination does not necessarily create a conflict in Plotinus's system, as the overflowing power of the One naturally produces an ordered world. However, the Christian perspective complicates this issue for Augustine. Augustine refers to divine intellect as the answer to what a thing is, and divine will as the answer to where a thing comes from, while attributing the final cause of the world to divine will. He also believes divine will is totally free and undetermined by anything beyond it. If Augustine understands divine creation as a process of imposing forms and measures preconceived by divine intelligence onto amorphous matter, he must explain whether these forms and measures restrict divine will.

A textual analysis of Augustine's thought on this question yields ambiguous answers. In a context similar to Plotinus's discussion on the impossibility of irrationality in the emanation of the One (quoted above),

Augustine addresses whether Platonic "ideas" constrain divine creation in the following passage:

> For ideas are the principal forms or the fixed and unchangeable reasons of things that have themselves not been formed and consequently are eternal, always constituted in the same way and contained in the divine intelligence.... Who would dare to say that God made everything irrationally? ... If the reasons for all the things that will be created and that have been created are contained in the divine mind, and if there can be nothing in the divine mind that is not eternal and unchangeable, and if Plato refers to these principal reasons of things as ideas, then ideas not only exist but are themselves true because they are eternal and remain the same and unchangeable.[73]

The language stating that the Platonic ideas "have themselves not been formed" (*formatae non sunt*) is particularly striking, as it may suggest that these ideas are coeternal with God and thus not made by God like other creatures. However, in other passages, Augustine firmly asserts that "although the matter of heaven and earth is one thing and the form of heaven and earth another, you [God] nevertheless made both of them simultaneously,"[74] thereby conferring on the Platonic ideas the same degree of contingency upon divine creation.

In light of my previous discussion on Plotinus's thought regarding the rationality of the One's emanation, the conundrum Augustine faces here becomes clear. For Augustine, the Platonic ideas represent the measure, form, and order of the created world, which speaks to the intelligibility of creation. However, does the intelligibility of the created world exist before or after the free act of divine creation? If the world must be intelligible before it is created, then the divine will to create it is significantly limited. On the other hand, if the world can be unintelligible due to the absolutely free act of divine will, unrestricted by anything, then how can human beings understand divine creation at all?

In later medieval philosophy, theologians and philosophers may choose to emphasize either divine will or divine intelligence to address these contested questions, giving rise to the respective trends of thought known as "voluntarism" and "intellectualism."[75] Although Augustine is generally considered a precursor to "voluntarism" due to his explicit statement on the priority of divine will in creation, it would be more accurate to say that Augustine's work provides the initial rationale for the emergence of both trends. This is primarily because Augustine's writings raise the question of whether divine will is prior to the intelligibility of the created world without explicitly and systematically addressing it. For the tradition of *creatio ex nihilo*, these contested questions point to an even more pressing issue: the extent to which divine creation can be truly unconditional. This issue will be further investigated in chapter 6.

AUGUSTINE'S THEODICY

In addition to his views on the why and how of divine creation, theodicy is also a significant and related aspect of Augustine's thought on *creatio ex nihilo*. As previously discussed, the Platonic and Gnostic traditions posed challenges to early Christian thinkers in addressing the problem of evil. Plato's *Timaeus* regards matter as a corrupting force in the world, while Plotinus sees matter as intrinsically evil due to its perviousness to nonbeing. Gnosticism's dualism between an evil creator and a supreme good God presents an even greater challenge to theodicy. Given the belief in God as the singular reason for the existence of all things, early Christian thinkers had to grapple with the question of why a supremely good God would create both good and evil beings. Augustine's concept of *creatio ex nihilo* directly confronts this issue, though whether he succeeded in addressing it is still a matter of debate.

Augustine's solution to the issue of theodicy can be summarized as follows:[76]

God, as being itself, is unmovable and eternal, and being is good. Therefore, the created world, as the result of the supreme creative power of God, is also good, particularly manifested in the overall measure, form, and order of the universe. Matter, equally a creature of God, always has the potentiality of acting as the bearer of form and order and is intrinsically good as well. If one perceives evil in its various forms, it indicates the insufficiency of human intelligence to comprehend the overall goodness of the world.

For instance, from a localized perspective, there appear to be physical evils among nonhuman sentient beings, such as the suffering of animals. However, Augustine holds that God creates things in the world out of nothing. Creatures are not as perfect as God precisely because they are created from nothing, bear the privation of being, and thus are subject to change and corruption, leading to inevitable suffering and pain. Depending on how much being a creature possesses to occupy its niche within the created hierarchy, it may be more or less perfect, and its life may be better or worse in a relative sense. This is the price of having a harmonious whole with a diversity of beings. As Augustine avers, "it is precisely their inequality that makes it possible for them all to exist."[77]

Given the hierarchy of being and goodness in the world, God grants humans the will to freely pursue the highest and most comprehensive good over lesser ones, enabling them to live rightly and honorably—an experience unavailable to nonfree agents—ultimately leading to genuine wisdom and happiness. Therefore, free will is itself a great good, as "anyone who does not have a good will certainly lacks the very thing the will alone would provide through itself, something more excellent than all the goods not within our power [i.e., all earthly kingdoms and all bodily pleasures]"[78]

Nevertheless, the original nothingness that humans bear as creatures accounts for the corruptibility of free will as a natural good. This is primarily evident in the misuse of human free will to turn away from the highest good to lesser ones, resulting in various moral evils such as pride, envy, greed, and lust. Consequently, humans also endure physical afflictions—punishments that seem disconnected from the choices of free will—such as the loss of natural immortality and vulnerability to physical pain, disease, aging, bodily disorders, and sexual lust. In this way, the moral evils humans commit and the physical evils they suffer are deeply intertwined. Only through the grace of Jesus Christ can human beings be redeemed from original sin and restored to the pristine order of creation.

With Augustine's theodicy understood in this way, and considering the primary characteristics of *creatio ex nihilo* as it developed historically up to Augustine, it is worth asking: Does Augustine fully overcome Manichaean dualism to the extent that he can use a single principle to explain the diverse phenomena in the world, including the existence of both good and evil?

Before addressing this question, it is worth noting that in the context of theodicy, beyond connoting the unconditional nature of divine creation, the "nothing" (or "nonbeing") from which God creates is construed by Augustine in a very specific way: It is contrary to God as being itself, and the ultimate act of *creatio ex nihilo* is thus considered as consisting of two distinct components. Regarding the contrary nature of nothingness, Augustine maintains, "if you look for something contrary to God, there is absolutely nothing. For being does not have any contrary except nonbeing. There is, therefore, no nature contrary to God."[79] Additionally, for the separateness of "nothing" and "God" within *creatio ex nihilo*, Augustine specifies:

> For when one says "corruptible nature," one says not one but two things. So too, when one says, "God made from nothing," we hear not one but two things. Ascribe those individual terms to individual things, therefore, so that, when you hear "nature," it goes with "God" and when you hear "corruption," it goes with "nothing." Thus, though these corruptions do not come from God's handiwork, they are still to be placed in His power in accord with the order of reality and the merits of souls. And so we are correct to say that reward and punishment come from Him. For He did not make corruption, but He can deliver to corruption one who merits to suffer corruption, that is, one who has begun to corrupt himself by sinning, in order that against his will he may feel the corruption that torments him who willingly brought about the corruption that attracted him.[80]

Augustine's writings are a valuable resource for contemporary Manichaean studies, as he famously identified dualism as the core problem within the Manichaean worldview. This dualism is characterized by two coeternal principles: the realm of light ruled by God and the realm of darkness ruled by *hyle* (matter) or Satan, which together explain the cosmic struggle between good and evil.[81] Augustine attests, "this fellow [Mani] devised two principles different from and opposed to each other and said that they are eternal and coeternal, that is, always existing."[82] Simply based on Augustine's statements about the opposing and distinct nature of nothingness versus God in *creatio ex nihilo*, it is not entirely reasonable to speculate that Augustine's view on *creatio ex nihilo* is influenced by the Manichaean dualism he fervently opposed. Clearly, as defined in opposition to "being," nothing does not exist and, therefore, is not a coeternal principle like *hyle*, which "always exists" in the Manichaean universe. Ultimately, Augustine's key to the problem of theodicy lies in understanding evil as a privation of good and grounding this perception ontologically on the premise that nothingness is contrary to being. Consequently, God, as being itself, is responsible only for what is, not for what is not.

Nevertheless, despite Augustine's insistence that nothing does not exist, our questioning can probe a bit further to examine whether "nothing" or "nonbeing" plays a necessary role in explaining the existence of things in the created world, and, by extension, whether Augustine's

Creatio ex Nihilo from Plato to Augustine 115

thought might imply that nothingness shares some common quality of "existing" similar to "being." If we find reasons to affirm both of these questions, "nothing" may unwittingly be treated by Augustine as a principle, and our suspicion of a Manichaean dualism in Augustine's thought may be more substantiated. This further inquiry can be pursued in the following two phases.

First, Augustine sometimes measures the hierarchy of created beings by the degree of being each possesses against a backdrop of nonbeing, as follows:

> Now if you find some kind of creature other than (a) that which exists but does not live, (b) that which exists and lives but does not understand, or (c) that which exists and lives and understands—then venture to say that there is some good that is not from God! ... These two things, namely body and life, are counted among creatures at least—for "life" is said of the Creator Himself, and this is life in the highest degree. Hence, because these two creations, body and life, are "formable," and because if the form were completely lost they would lapse back into nothing, they reveal well enough that they maintain their existence from that form which always remains the same. Consequently, all good things whatsoever, no matter how great or small, can exist only from God. What can be greater in Creation than intelligent life? What can be less than body? However much these things deteriorate and thereby tend to nonbeing, some form nevertheless remains in them, so that they do exist in some way.[83]

Augustine presents a clear depiction of creation, wherein all ranks of creatures stand above the bottomless abyss of nonbeing, with each rank possessing a specific, unchangeable "form" that prescribes unique "laws of their own numbers"[84] to distinguish them from one another. Most significantly, lower ranks of beings are understood to lack certain forms of existence that are present in higher ranks, such as the being of unintelligent life, the being of intelligent life, and ultimately, the highest degree of life found in God as being itself.

Does nonbeing play a necessary role in explaining the existence of such a hierarchy of beings? Using an analogy drawn from traditional Chinese art modeled on the *yin/yang* cosmological framework, we can observe that in Augustine's depiction of creation, nonbeing or nothingness functions like the colorless, purely white background silk of a traditional Chinese painting, while God resembles a painter who applies dark ink in varying densities and shapes onto the white silk: the more darkness an object possesses, the more prominent it becomes in the painting, and by analogy, the better the created object. The painter may assert that he is solely responsible for everything dark that is visible and good in the picture. Nevertheless, from an external perspective, the white, colorless silk background remains an ineluctable element with which the painter must work. If the white background is interpreted as *yin* and the black ink as *yang*, the entire picture assumes a dualistic character since two distinct causes are required to explain the differentiation of each object within the composition.

Nevertheless, this analogical argument for the dualistic nature of Augustine's thought on *creatio ex nihilo* can only go so far. Augustine may counter that there is no silk-like state of nonbeing in his system; instead, the hierarchy is built from lifeless matter, with all other creatures being reconfigurations or reshaping of this lifeless matter according to varying forms. If a certain rank of creatures lacks a degree of being present in a higher rank, it is merely a comparison among beings, rather than between being and nonbeing. Augustine's quoted views on the physical suffering of nonhuman sentient beings already indicate that the evaluation of better or worse among creatures is relative. Taken as a whole, creation contains no genuine evil; everything is good when evaluated according to its own form and its relationship to the whole.

If the first phase of our further inquiry into the suspicious nature of Augustinian dualism yields no clear evidence, I will now transition to the second phase, moving from the natural hierarchy of beings to the specific problem of human free will.

Scholars have reached a virtual consensus that around the year 396, Augustine's view on free will underwent a significant shift. Prior to this, Augustine upheld a libertarian view of free will, asserting that the ultimate power of the human will to turn away from the highest, unchangeable good to the lower, changeable goods is not caused by external forces and thus resides within humans themselves. However, afterward, in the context of debates with the Pelagians, Augustine emphasized that it is divine grace alone that determines whether humans are able to will the pursuit of good, thereby denying the libertarian sense of free will.[85] Despite this shift, Augustine's ontological insight remained consistent: It is out of the nothingness from which God creates humans that the corruptibility of human nature arises, and thus, it is also this nothingness that conditions humans' moral capacity. Therefore, our second phase of inquiry can focus on whether nothingness plays any necessary role in explaining the (non)existence of free will.

The above quote from *De libero arbitrio* 1.12.26 indicates that, prior to 396, Augustine affirmed the existence and goodness of libertarian free will. Nevertheless, when inquiring why humans turn away from higher to lower goods and commit sin, Augustine states:

> Since the will is moved when it turns itself away from the unchangeable good towards the changeable good, where does this movement come from? . . . We admit that this movement is sin, since it is a defective movement, and every defect is from nothing. Be assured that this movement does not pertain to God! Yet this defective movement, since it is voluntary, is placed within our power.[86]

Since the existence of libertarian free will is predicated upon the human ability to "turn" in two directions—either from the unchangeable good, God, to changeable goods, or vice versa—nothingness becomes necessary to explain the existence of such an ability. This is because if nothingness did not exist, human nature would not be corruptible, and humans would be fixed solely upon the unchangeable good, leaving no room for choice. As the voluntary power within humans ultimately executes this turning, it can be inferred that, prior to 396, Augustine held that nothingness served as a necessary but not sufficient condition for the existence of libertarian free will.[87] Therefore, he had to—perhaps even unwittingly—acknowledge that nothingness in his ontological system shares the common attribute of existence with God as being itself.

Nevertheless, this pre-396 assessment of the role of the ontological principle of nothingness in human free will can only apply to Adam and Eve in Augustine's later anti-Pelagian writings. Augustine later held that after Adam and Eve freely committed original sin, this sin was passed down to human offspring as their inborn condition, leading to a perpetual struggle between the strong desires of flesh—namely, concupiscence—and the spirit. Consequently, humans must endure various seemingly gratuitous sufferings as divine punishment.[88] It is solely divine grace that predetermines whether humans can be saved from this struggle, as Augustine states: "In order that we will, then, God works without us; but when we will, and we will in such a way that we act, He works along with us. Yet without Him either (a) working that we will, or (b) working along when we will, we are powerless to accomplish good religious works."[89]

Since Augustine consistently maintains that it is from nothingness that the corruptibility of human nature arises, in the post-396 stage, he must acknowledge two positions:

(1) Reiterating the argument regarding his pre-396 stance on free will, nothingness must exist to explain the free choice made by Adam and Eve. Without the existence of nothingness, original sin could not have been freely committed, and thus divine punishment would not be justified.
(2) In the post-Fall state, for those not chosen by God to will good, nothingness becomes both a necessary and sufficient condition for humans' consent to concupiscence and various other forms of evil. Therefore, as long as concupiscence exists and endures within the human species, nothingness must exist.

Between these two points, Augustine could potentially mount a defense against the suspicion of Manichaean dualism by arguing that concupiscence exists merely as a privation of good such as genuine love and care for fellow humans, thereby lacking true ontological status as an evil. Consequently, "nothing" does not need to "exist" to explain the presence of concupiscence. However, this same defense becomes difficult to uphold based on position (1) and the related pre-396 position that affirms the goodness and existence of libertarian free will.

Therefore, our two-phase inquiry into the role of nothingness in creation tends to lead to this conclusion: If Augustine advocates for the existence of libertarian free will, upon which the idea of divine punishment is based—a stance he maintained throughout his theological career, though in varying degrees—then, according to his understanding of *creatio ex nihilo* where nothingness is viewed as both distinct from and contrary to God, he must acknowledge that nothingness also exists and thus functions as an ontological principle on par with God within the grand scheme of *creatio ex nihilo* to account for diverse worldly phenomena.

The question of whether and to what extent Augustine's thought inherits Manichaean influences was first raised by his contemporary, Julian of Aeclanum, and has been vigorously revisited by scholars in recent decades.[90] Julian, noting the role of nothingness in Augustine's later thought on original sin and concupiscence, remarked: "If evil arose because the condition of the preceding nothingness demanded it, then this nothingness, however, was eternal."⁹¹ For Julian, this would render Augustine's conceptual framework on original sin indistinguishable from Manichaean dualism.

Contemporary scholarly responses to Julian's critique vary. Kurt Rudolph finds the charge difficult to refute.⁹² A similar criticism was made by Ludwig Koenen, who stated that "he explains the existence of corruption and evil as due to God's creatio *de nihilo* ... Without Augustine's being aware of it, his *nihil* becomes an *aliquid* [something] and assumes the negative qualities of the Manichaean *hyle.*"⁹³ However, emphasizing a privationist understanding of evil, Mathijs Lamberigts argued that "to equate Augustine's view of the human being with that of Mani is simply incorrect. In contrast to the Manichaean *princeps tenebrarum* [principle of darkness], the devil is not assigned a role at the level of creation, whatever Julian wishes to imply."⁹⁴

There is an even larger body of scholarship dedicated to analyzing the generally dualistic tendencies in Augustine's thought, which extends beyond the ontological status of nonbeing to encompass dualisms such as corporeal versus spiritual and the City of God versus the earthly city of humans, among others.⁹⁵ Scholars have also extensively defended Augustine against these dualistic interpretations. For example, Simon Olivia emphasizes that for Augustine, worldly creatures, imbued with the *rationes seminales* implanted by God at creation, are guided by divine providence toward the fulfillment of the divine Word. In other words, God is both extrinsic and intrinsic, both transcendent and immanent to the created world, offering a fundamentally nondualistic and more processual view that resists the dualistic critique put forth by many contemporary interpreters.⁹⁶

This book does not intend to comprehensively survey the vast and dynamic body of scholarship concerning Augustine and Manichaean dualism. Given that this area of study continues to expand, I caution readers to consider my earlier inquiry into Augustine's theodicy not as a definitive critique, but as a contribution to the ongoing, evolving scholarship from a specific angle within Ruist comparative theology.

One final point I would like to emphasize, as suggested by this research angle, is that Augustine's construal of nothingness or nonbeing, out of which God creates, as both distinct from and contrary to God, is novel and unique in the intellectual history of *creatio ex nihilo* up to his time. Such novelty furnishes the privationist solution to the problem of evil, but, as demonstrated above, it has raised suspicions regarding the dualistic nature of Augustine's thought on *creatio ex nihilo*. If such suspicions were indeed substantiated, Augustine's construal would undermine the unconditionality of *creatio ex nihilo* as a singular creative origin. As will be discussed in chapter 6, Augustine's legacy in the development of *creatio ex nihilo* is vast and enduring. We will encounter genuine innovations of this idea both along the path Augustine pioneered and through different, alternative perspectives.[97]

6 *Creatio ex Nihilo* in Continuum: Aquinas, Descartes, Schleiermacher, and Tillich

Thomas Aquinas

Aquinas's theory of creation, detailed in *Summa theologiae* I, q.2, a.3 stems from his reexamination of Aristotle's argument for the "unmoved mover." This thought process is conventionally referred to as the cosmological proof of the existence of God, in contrast to Anselm of Canterbury's ontological proof, which involves a semantic analysis of the word "God." It is crucial to note, however, that Aquinas's argument is formulated precisely using the traditional Christian conception of God as the ultimate creative agent who generates a series of ontological dependence, through which all proximate realities are conditioned. In other words, the so-called cosmological proof pertains only to where the argument begins and not to the ontological logic by which the argument proceeds.

Aquinas's comprehension of the "nothing" from which God creates is a prime example in this realm. Initially, when Aquinas uses the phrase "from nothing," he simply intends that what is formed is not produced from anything preexisting. In other words, it is not derived from any kind of subject that existed before it.[1] Aquinas also identifies another meaning: "Nonexistence is prior to existence in a created thing in the sense that if the creature were simply left to itself without being caused by God, it would not exist."[2] Here, Aquinas clarifies that the priority involved in this usage is a priority of nature and being, rather than one of time.[3] The former point highlights Aquinas's disapproval of the Greek misunderstanding of preexisting matter, which is exemplified in Plato's *Timaeus*. The latter point underscores the nature of ontological dependence implied by *creatio ex nihilo*, and why Aquinas can criticize Plato in this regard.

In the following discussion, I will examine how Aquinas employed the conventional notion of *creatio ex nihilo* to develop his own creation theory. Specifically, I will focus on his analysis of several issues related to divine causation, which are vital for understanding various controversies in the transcendence debate.

AN EVERLASTING, ETERNAL WORLD

The distinction of Aquinas on divine creation can be best illustrated through two key themes: the possibility of an eternal world and creatures as causes of *esse* (being).

With regard to the question of whether the world has a temporal beginning, Aquinas offers two arguments. First, he argues that since God is "a cause that produces effect not through motion but instantaneously,"[4] it is not necessary for God to precede His effects in time. Second, while the preposition "ex" in *creatio ex nihilo* implies a definitive order of being after nonbeing, this "after" order may be understood in two ways: an "order of time" or an "order of nature." Since within *creatio ex nihilo*, nonbeing is prior to being by nature, rather than by time, there is no reason to hold that an eternal world is impossible. These arguments share the insight that since the world is ontologically dependent upon God in all its possible temporal modes, it is entirely compatible to hold the idea of either "an eternal world" (meaning "everlasting") or "a world with a beginning," while simultaneously asserting that the world is created by God from nothing.

Moreover, the condition of ontological dependence does not imply that the "nonbeing" from which God creates necessarily occurs at the same time as "being," whether the world has always existed or "at some time nothing exists,"[5] because the priority of nonbeing over being is not one of time. As Aquinas explains, "There is, therefore, no before and after in Him [God]; He does not have being after non-being, nor non-being after being, nor can any succession be found in His being. . . . God, therefore, is without beginning and end, having his whole being at once. In this consists the nature of eternity."[6] Notably, the term "eternity" here simply means "nontemporality," rather than "everlastingness."

Hence, I would like to emphasize that Aquinas's cosmological proof of the existence of God goes beyond a purely cosmological argument. This is because, in theory, an eternal, everlasting world is compatible with *creatio ex nihilo*, meaning that the chain of creatures as efficient causes in the way of "cosmological succession" can have infinite regress without undermining the ontological dependence of the entire cosmos. Aquinas argues that an infinite series of efficient causes, where each cause depends upon that which is prior to it, is not inherently contradictory when such causes are related to one another only *per accidens*. Thus, it is not impossible for one man to have been generated by another to infinity.[7] In other words, as long as the efficient cause exerted by creatures to each other is the "efficient cause *per accidens*" (which I will analyze shortly), it does not matter whether this series of creaturely efficient causes has a temporal beginning or not. Regardless, God, as the ultimate uncaused cause, always grounds the series ontologically.

CREATURES AS CAUSES

Aquinas's concern with the issue of creaturely causal power is rooted in his theological epistemology, which seeks to understand God through reason's investigation of the outcomes of God's creation. Since God lacks imperfection and bears no proportion to any creature, the knowledge of God can only be obtained through negation—understanding what God is not. However, even though God is infinitely different from the outcomes of His creation, He is the cause of these outcomes. Therefore, Aquinas believes that the language used by human reason to discuss both God and His creatures should not be univocal or equivocal. In other words, human reason can only know God through His outcomes analogically and by negation. Aquinas ultimately denies that human beings can arrive at quidditative knowledge of God during their lifetime.[8]

These epistemological insights align well with Aquinas's cosmological proof of the existence of God. He begins with the fact of creatures in the world and arrives at an ultimate cause that sufficiently explains their existence. However, creatures also cause effects, and human reason uses the causal relationship among creatures to explain new outcomes and determine whether an outcome is necessary or contingent. The relationship between these natural causes and the uncaused cause of divine creation therefore remains a question.

Since God's creation is the sole source of being, no creaturely cause can be considered as the proper creation of the world.[9] Aquinas employs several pairs of categories to highlight the distinction between creaturely causes and the divine cause. First, he distinguishes between "cause of becoming" and "cause of being." In the *De veritate*, Aquinas explains that some lower causes are causes of becoming, such as those that bring about a form from the potentiality of matter through a process of motion. For example, an artisan making a knife is a cause of becoming. In contrast, a cause of being is that upon which the being (*esse*) of an effect depends, such as how the existence of light in air depends on the sun. The cause of becoming and the cause of being are typically separate from each other in the realm of creatures. However, since divine creation is ontologically prior to any creaturely causation, the creaturely causes of becoming are a manifestation of the higher ontological cause of being brought about only through divine creation. Therefore, Aquinas views God as both a cause of becoming and a cause of being with respect to creatures.[10]

Second, Aquinas also distinguishes between "efficient cause *per accidens*" and "efficient cause *per se*." John Wippel's explanation of Aquinas's view in the *De potentia* sheds light on this distinction.[11] Empirically, a creaturely efficient cause can be discerned by human reason to explain the succession of the form of an effect from nonexistence to existence or from one way of existence to another. For example, a form of fire is set by another generating instance of fire, and the latter can be deemed as the efficient cause *per accidens* of the former. However, this empirical approach cannot explain where the form (the fire proper in our example) as a mode of being ultimately comes from. This latter question can only be answered sufficiently by divine creation as an efficient cause upon which the form of an effect depends *per se*.[12]

Third, Aquinas also distinguishes between "a cause of being in the unqualified sense" and "a cause of being this or that."[13] The distinction can be understood as follows: Regarding the sheer being (*esse*) of effects, creaturely causes can be considered as producing it under the condition that these causes act together as the manifestation of the creative power of the first uncaused cause. On the other hand, regarding the question of what concrete type of *esse* an effect has or why an effect has a mode of being this or that, the powers of creaturely causes can be used to provide perfections that determine and particularize the *esse* of their effects in a specific way.

In simpler terms, what a thing is, or its form of being, depends on its relationship with other things, whereas whether a thing is, or why there is something rather than nothing, depends entirely on God. However, given the unconditional ontological priority of divine creation, the distinction between the question of what a thing is and the question of whether a thing is ultimately becomes trivial since even the being of the form of a thing can only be sufficiently explained by recourse to the first uncaused cause.

In summary, creaturely causes, as a "cause of becoming," an "efficient cause *per accidens*," and a "cause of being this or that," answer the question of what a thing is and provide an empirical explanation for why a thing takes place in the series of cosmological succession. Divine creation, as a "cause of being," an "efficient cause *per se*," and a "cause of being in the unqualified sense," specifies the origin from which the form of an effect ultimately derives and answers the ultimate ontological question of why there is something, rather than nothing.

Aquinas's fine analysis of the concept of causation fulfills his ontological intention of ordering the generic traits of a thing in ranks. Causes in a lower ontological rank cannot explain the effect produced by a cause in a higher rank. Meanwhile, causation in a lower rank can be seen as the manifestation of the power of causes in a higher rank. This principle of thought enables Aquinas to view an effect as being produced from the "co-working" of all causes in all ranks, while also ascribing specific traits of an effect to certain causes.

NECESSARY AND CONTINGENT CAUSES

Taken together, the previous discussions suggest that *creatio ex nihilo* concerns the ontological dependence more than the cosmological succession among cosmic realities. Consequently, for the sake of "efficient cause" (which is largely what we mean by "cause" in modern science), *creatio ex nihilo* does not impose an extra order upon the empirical order of cosmological succession, nor does it change our knowledge of whether cosmic changes are necessary or contingent.

Aquinas maintains that whether an effect is necessary or contingent depends on its relationship with its proximate cause in a particular mode of time. However, in refining Augustine's original thought on this point,[14] Aquinas emphasizes that God's vision is eternal and beyond any mode of time. What is seen as future by a proximate cause is present in the vision of God as the First Cause. Therefore, God produces necessary or contingent effects through necessarily or contingently acting proximate causes, and free effects through freely acting proximate causes, such as human freedom.[15] In other words, by clarifying the ontological nature of divine causation in *creatio ex nihilo*, Aquinas provides a solution to the traditional conundrum of Christian theology: the apparent contradiction of God's omniscience and human freedom. From a theistic perspective, I think this solution is highly successful.

AQUINAS'S COMPROMISED VISION OF *CREATIO EX NIHILO*

After examining Aquinas's thought on themes such as "nothingness" in *creatio ex nihilo*, the possibility of an eternal world, creatures as causes of *esse*, and divine providence versus human freedom, it becomes clear that Aquinas adheres to the nature of the "ontological unconditionality" of *creatio ex nihilo*. This means that if God is ontologically the First Cause, His creation should not be conditioned by anything. However, this insight does not apply to all aspects of Aquinas's thought, particularly in his defense of the unrestricted freedom of divine creation.

God creates the world in an absolutely free way, and the world's continuous existence depends on God's unceasing conservation. According to Aquinas, God will not stop creating because the divine power and goodness are better manifested by the fact that He keeps things in existence.[16] But this raises the question of whether the manifestation of God's perfection through the creation of the world is a motive or end that necessarily constrains God's creation and limits His freedom. Aquinas argues that it does not, because "the divine goodness is not the kind of end that is produced or results from those things that are ordered to it. Rather, it is the kind of end by which those things which are ordered to it are themselves produced and perfected."[17] However, this leads to another question: If there is no necessity for God to produce the whole of the world, is there anything that causes God to will to create one being rather than another? Aquinas answers that a *ratio* (a reason or explanation) can be given for God's willing other things besides Himself, and that since God wills His own goodness as an end, He wills all other things as ordered to it. But this *ratio* is not a cause derived from created things that necessarily determines God's creativity.[18]

Even so, we find that Aquinas's use of the term *ratio* introduces limiting conditions to divine creation. Aquinas spells out different ways in which *ratio* may be assigned to God's willing as follows: "God wills man to have reason in order for man to exist. He wills man to exist in order for the universe to be complete. And he wills the good of the universe because this befits his own goodness."[19] In other words, a harmonious hierarchy of cosmic beings, each of which manifests a unique degree of perfection, is deemed to be an overall reason for divine creation, an idea clearly influenced by Augustine. What intrigues us most about this aspect of Aquinas's thought is that because the *ratio* of divine creation is manifested by forms in God's intelligence that are endowed with varying degrees of perfection, divine creation as such implicates the questionable relationship between God's intelligence and God's will. For Aquinas, if there is any necessity implied in divine creation, it is a necessity by supposition, not a necessity *per se*. For example, if God wills the existence of humankind, He must also will the existence of human reason, since without reason, humankind would not exist. However, this leads to the conclusion that God will not will what is incompatible with suppositional necessities, which means that God's will must abide by basic intellectual laws that exclude logical impossibility.[20]

Taken together, it seems that Aquinas's conception of divine creation is not far from Plato's theory of creation in the *Timaeus*. Turning the threefold model of divine creation from matter-form-Demiurge to being-essence-God, Aquinas posits that God possesses an infinite abundance of being, which He then limits, particularizes, and actualizes using reasons and forms that are diverse manifestations of divine perfection. However, while doing so, God cannot contradict basic intellectual laws. This view, expressed in traditional Christian theistic terms, undermines the philosophical rigor and theological power of the idea of *creatio ex nihilo*. If God creates by means of inviolable forms and reasons, it is difficult to say that He creates the world from nothing. Moreover, the harmonious hierarchy of cosmic beings which Aquinas views as God's reason for creation is noticeably anthropocentric. The concrete process by which Aquinas believes God creates such an anthropocentric world is also anthropomorphic. In Aristotelian terms, if Aquinas succeeded in not imposing order onto the de facto world from above in the realm of "efficient cause," he instead enforced a prejudiced anthropocentric and anthropomorphic order from the perspectives of "formal cause" and "final cause."[21]

Descartes's Theory of Created Eternal Truth

René Descartes made a groundbreaking contribution to the tradition of *creatio ex nihilo* following Aquinas. In the previous section, I concluded that Aquinas believed that God cannot will what is logically impossible, a position that was anticipated by the thought of Augustine. If God wills anything necessary, it must adhere to "suppositional necessity," which is subject to logical laws and strictly limited to the realm of logical possibilities. This view was shared by other medieval theologians, such as Duns Scotus, who believed that necessary truths and logical possibilities were naturally caused by the divine essence. Consequently, God could not fail to create these objects, as they had an essential relationship with divine essence.[22] I interpret this aspect of Aquinas's thought, with its anthropomorphic and anthropocentric implications, as a theistic compromise of the philosophical rigor of *creatio ex nihilo*. Divine will is thus conditioned by logical possibilities that are entailed by divine essence and envisioned by divine intellect. In this way, divine creation is viewed as a conditioned process in which God bestows existence upon preexisting logical possibilities and brings them to fruition in the created world.

In contrast to his medieval predecessors, Descartes had a more voluntaristic view. According to him, the so-called eternal truths, which initially referred to the intelligible world of forms and implied the diversity of perfections in Augustine's and Aquinas's thinking, are exemplified by mathematical truths. It is only from the perspective of human beings that these truths could be considered "necessary" or refer to what is "logically possible." In Descartes's view, these eternal truths are created by God, inscribed into the human mind as "innate ideas," and thus enable human beings to understand the essentials of the created world.[23] In other words, eternal truths are only eternal for the human mind, but not for God. According to Descartes, eternal truths, just like every other creature, are freely created by God.[24]

What is most important about Descartes's theory of creation is that there is no substantial division between divine intelligence and divine will.[25] Unlike the tripartite sequence of divine creation, as it was conceived by Plato, Augustine, and Aquinas, Descartes did not believe in eternal truths as preexisting objects that limit the capacity of divine will to create. For Descartes, eternal truths become true only because God wills them to be so. Divine intelligence does not understand eternal truths before divine will wills them. Rather, it is the opposite: God wills eternal truths to be eternally true for the world He creates, and then divine intelligence simultaneously understands them as truth so that, at the same time, they are created. Because Descartes conceived divine will to be unconditioned by any preexisting "reasons," he believed that if God willed it, He could create eternal truths that were entirely opposite to what humans currently understand. Furthermore, because God's creative power is infinite, human reason can never comprehend why God creates the eternal truths that are currently understood as such by human beings, rather than not creating them at all. Thus, the "incomprehensibility"[26] of divine creation becomes a central theme in Descartes's theory of created eternal truth.

Here, I will outline several points that illustrate my understanding of Descartes's theory and its trailblazing role in the development of the Christian tradition of *creatio ex nihilo*:

First, the period during which Descartes developed his theory of created eternal truth in his letters, which was around 1628–30, marked a transition in his thinking from epistemology to metaphysics. At the beginning of his philosophical career, Descartes was an epistemological foundationalist who sought to establish a secure foundation for the "new science" that was characterized by the mathematization of nature and a mechanistic model of scientific explanation. Prior to his transition to metaphysics, Descartes had found the foundation for human knowledge in two unmistakable faculties of the human mind: intuition and deduction.

According to Descartes, the role of deduction was to transmit the certainty of human knowledge achieved by intuition in an inferential series, and therefore deduction was premised upon intuition. As a result, the true foundation of human knowledge was intuition. In "intuition," Descartes believed that the human mind was so attentive to an object, and the resulting perception about the object was so clear and distinct, that there could be no doubt about what had been perceived. In other words, in "intuition," what had been perceived was identical to the way in which objects revealed themselves, and as a result, knowledge corresponded exactly to reality.[27] Thus, "intuition" was the birthplace of true knowledge.

However, by around 1628, Descartes no longer held this view, as he had come to understand the radical finitude of human consciousness. All human thoughts and deeds happened in time, and humans could only be attentive to a certain object within a limited span of time.[28] "Intuition" was thus temporal, volatile, and short-lived. If this faculty was ultimately noneternal, how could it be the foundation for eternal truths? Descartes then decided to search for the foundation of human knowledge within the ideas of "God" and "Self," which led to his theory of created eternal truth.

I believe that when Descartes turned to the idea of "God" to seek the foundation of human knowledge, he was likely aware of the solutions proposed by Aquinas or Scotus to similar issues. It is possible that he formulated a similar theory, which posited that eternal truths were implied by divine intelligence and were therefore necessarily intended by divine will to be eternally true. However, what prevented Descartes from returning to the intellectualist rut of medieval Scholasticism was his emphasis on the role of human will, particularly in the form of "attention," in the act of "intuition." He had asserted that this faculty might ground the certainty of knowledge. As a result, when he turned to metaphysics, Descartes became acutely aware of the distinction between divine will and human will. He believed that divine will was "eternal" and "immovable," and once God created mathematical and logical truths, he would not change them. Consequently, human beings perceived these truths as eternal truths.

Meanwhile, Descartes also believed in the "greatest perfections," the "great and inexhaustible power," and the unconditioned, absolute freedom of divine creation.[29] Therefore, in the final analysis, it was Descartes's commitment to both the unconditionality and immovability of divine will that ultimately led to the conclusion that divine creation was both absolutely free and ultimately incomprehensible. In this sense, Descartes's foundationalist epistemology, which investigated human cognition in a revolutionarily modern way, was one of the decisive factors in his innovative understanding of *creatio ex nihilo*.

Second, Descartes's theory of created eternal truth revolutionizes the relationship between divine intelligence and divine will and highlights its stark contrast with the relationship between human intelligence and human will. According to Descartes, human will is passive and can only judge, either approving or disapproving of the ideas that are presented to it by human intelligence. The role of human intelligence is to receive and examine ideas, whether they are innate within the human mind or acquired from external sources. In contrast, divine will is active and identical to divine intelligence. This means that, first and foremost, divine will does not merely will the objects presented by divine intelligence. Rather, God can will whatever He desires and then freely create whatever is actually created. Furthermore, the active nature of divine will implies that what divine intelligence perceives as true is solely a result of the free willing of divine will. What is necessarily true for the created world is not necessarily intended by God. Instead, only when God freely intends an idea or statement as necessary can it be considered an eternal truth.

In comparison, Aquinas and Scotus also held the belief that divine intelligence and divine will are identical. However, their ideas of the identity leaned toward divine intelligence rather than divine will. For them, divine will can only will what divine intelligence has understood. In contrast, for Descartes, divine intelligence can only understand what divine will has freely willed. This reversal of the order between divine will and divine intelligence has, in my view, the most important consequence of Descartes's theory of created eternal truth: the de-anthropomorphism and de-anthropocentrism of divine creation.

The de-anthropocentric consequence of Descartes's theory is evident. Descartes asserts that mathematical truths are only eternal for human beings. They are not necessarily intended by divine will, and therefore, what is logically possible cannot be solely and fully assessed by human intelligence.

The de-anthropomorphic consequence goes even further. As the relationship between divine intelligence and divine will is not analogous to the human case, we cannot conceive of divine creation as operating according to any logical sequence resembling the tripartite model found in Plato's *Timaeus*. Descartes believed that even God would not comprehend what He is going to create before freely willing what will actually be created. In other words, any logical possibility can only be understood by humans as possible after its realization through divine creation. There is no ultimate reason for God to create this rather than that, and consequently, the model of divine creation becomes a genuine act of "sheer making," a continuous emergence of novelty from the abysmal, incomprehensible power of divine creation. Simply put, aside from the de facto existence of creatures as the outcome of divine creation, we cannot understand anything about it. The act of divine creation becomes infinite (in the sense that all finite creatures are created), unconditional (in the sense that nothing preceding divine creation can be imagined), and singular (in the sense that no sequence can characterize divine creation), which, in my view, is a reasonable and groundbreaking development of the idea of *creatio ex nihilo*.

Finally, we must recognize that the de-anthropomorphic consequence of Descartes's theory of *created eternal truth* extends beyond his original intentions. While he sought to expel the Scholastic "teleological explanation" from natural science,[30] the incomprehensibility of divine creation that he emphasized connects him to a lineage of Greek and Christian mysticism. This tradition includes figures such as Plotinus in Neoplatonism, Pseudo-Dionysius and Meister Eckhart in medieval Christian mysticism, and Rudolf Otto and Paul Tillich in contemporary Christian mysticism.

One crucial point that I should emphasize is that within this mystical lineage of the Christian tradition, the incomprehensibility of divine creation is not anti-rational or irrational. Rather, it is nonrational and can even be interpreted as pro-rational. This is because, as Descartes understood, the nonrationality of divine creation speaks to the infinite, unconditional, and inexhaustible creative power of God. Human beings can only understand what has been created, and before divine creation delivers, there is no way to comprehend what is possible. Thus, the power of divine creation is ultimately beyond human grasp, and in this sense, it is nonrational. However, the only way for humans to understand divine creation is through its created outcomes, namely, creatures. The idea of divine creation as a singular, all-encompassing creative act can continually drive human beings to understand the created world as a whole. As such, the idea of *creatio ex nihilo* can be seen as an ideal for regulating the use of human reason in order to achieve the soundest and most complete understanding of the world. In this sense, the "incomprehensibility" of divine creation is pro-rational rather than anti-rational. As the father of modern rationalism, perhaps no other thinker than Descartes can better illustrate the fact that a mystical commitment to the incomprehensibility of divine creation can be humanistically pro-rational.

Despite the extensive analyses presented above, it is worth noting that the various insights into the concept of *creatio ex nihilo* are mostly implicit in Descartes's theory of created eternal truth. It is clear that Descartes did not completely depart from the traditional Christian theistic notion of God. Rather, this notion still played a significant role in his mature metaphysical reflections.

In his *Meditations*, Descartes shifts the basis of human knowledge certainty to the concept of God, in a way departing from his earlier theory of created eternal truth in the 1630s. He argues that the clear and distinct perceptions humans have of things outside their minds are the natural and only way to obtain objective knowledge. If humans were capable of making errors in this regard, it would imply that God created a flawed world and is therefore deceitful. Hence, the capacity for humans to acquire objective knowledge is a natural given that cannot be doubted.[31] However, this new development in Descartes's metaphysical thinking contrasts with the groundbreaking insight in his theory of created eternal truth. First, it is anthropocentric, as it posits that the conditions of things in the world correspond naturally to human perceptions. Descartes suggests that this is part of God's intention in creation. Second, it is anthropomorphic, as God is portrayed as a good creator who would not make mistakes in his creation, lest the creatures he created be inherently flawed and vulnerable. Descartes's idea that "God is not a deceiver" implies that divine creation has a good *telos* that humans can comprehend and rely on. This deviates significantly from his earlier endorsement of the incomprehensibility of divine creation in his theory of eternal created truth, which suggests that there can be no reason for God's creation that humans can fathom before divine creation takes place.

In conclusion, I must note that, as already indicated by my comparative methodology in chapters 2 and 4, I disagree with Descartes's epistemological approach, which I have labeled as "epistemological foundationalism." I believe that human beings can never be certain whether our perceptions of things in the world are clear and distinct enough to guarantee knowledge free from doubt. All knowledge is conditioned, and our cognitive abilities are fallible. Even the so-called eternal truths Descartes claims can be represented through mathematical knowledge are not necessarily eternal, as the development of non-Euclidean geometries has since challenged the once seemingly unshakable foundation of early modern science. This historical hindsight suggests that Descartes's attempt to ground the absolute certainty of mathematical truths on the clarity and distinctness of human perception, which in turn depends on the good intentionality of divine creation, may have been misguided from the very beginning.

Instead, I suggest that any future theorization of *creatio ex nihilo* should return to Descartes's original insight expressed in his theory of created eternal truth: that we can only understand the conditions of divine creation through its actual outcomes. Therefore, the nonrational and potentially pro-rational nature of the "incomprehensibility" of divine creation can be seen as a guiding ideal for scientific progress moving forward.

Friedrich Schleiermacher

As a trailblazer in modern theology, Friedrich Schleiermacher (1768–1834) achieved a unique reformulation of the traditional ontological argument of *creatio ex nihilo*, approaching it from an existential standpoint. His approach begins with a phenomenological depiction of human self-consciousness, which contains two crucial elements. First, it recognizes that human freedom exists but is limited by the social and natural orders of existence.[32] Thus, with regard to the relationship between human freedom and the world, humans are relatively dependent. Second, a more profound sense of absolute dependence emerges from the feeling of human freedom as being relatively dependent. This deeper feeling points beyond the human self and the world altogether, toward a transcendent source: "The self-consciousness accompanying our entire self-activity . . . which negates absolute freedom, is already in and of itself the awareness that the entirety of our free, self-active being comes from elsewhere."[33]

From the feeling of relative dependence to the feeling of absolute dependence, this represents a pivotal shift in Schleiermacher's thought. If the sensation of relative dependence indicates the activity of human freedom as a subjective force in the face of objective reality, the feeling of absolute dependence points to a completely different order of causality. The former arises from the natural order of realities (including humans as a limited agent) demonstrated by patterns of cosmological succession, while the latter is rooted in the ontological contingency of the entire created world, encompassing both human freedom and the nonhuman world encountered. The feeling of absolute dependence can thus be viewed as an existential rephrasing of the preexisting Christian insight that the entire world relies on the ontological creative act of *creatio ex nihilo*.

We can verify this when we examine Schleiermacher's thought on the relationship between God and the world in greater detail. In terms of the nature of divine causality, Schleiermacher asserts that "the divine causality is equal in scope to the finite only insofar as it is opposite in kind."[34] Likewise, with respect to the omnipotence of God, "the natural order comprehending all space and time is grounded in the divine causality, which as eternal and omnipresent is opposite in kind to all finite causality."[35]

Placed in the context of the intellectual history of *creatio ex nihilo*, especially as evidenced by Aquinas's thorough analysis of various types of causality, Schleiermacher's thoughts on divine causality become more understandable. He posits that divine causality implied by *creatio ex nihilo* is of a different order than the ordinary causality we can infer from the temporal regularities among cosmic entities. The former addresses the ultimate ontological question of the world's origin and whether something exists rather than nothing, while the latter answers the penultimate question of what a thing is in relation to other things in the existing world. Because divine causality operates on a higher ontological level, while it does not directly answer the penultimate question, every answer provided by ordinary causalities can be seen as a manifestation of divine causality. Thus, the concept of divine causality as *creatio ex nihilo* is fully compatible with any modal description of cosmic events. Whether a cosmic event is empirically contingent or necessary, it is always ontologically dependent upon *creatio ex nihilo*. The ontological unconditionality of divine creation does not add any extra determinations to the natural, empirical order that is demonstrated by sequences of cosmological succession.

A cluster of ideas in Schleiermacher's thought that were traditionally discussed together in relation to *creatio ex nihilo* are now more comprehensible. Schleiermacher reframes the contrast between divine causality and natural causality as a difference in quality versus quantity.[36] He also views eternity as the divine presence that transcends all moments of time.[37] Schleiermacher sees God's *creatio ex nihilo* as both immanent in and transcendent of the quantitatively infinite totality of cosmic realities.[38] His approach reflects a mystical feeling toward the ineffable, inexhaustible, and "formless" nature of divine creation.[39]

Given that various aspects of Schleiermacher's thought are fundamentally based on *creatio ex nihilo*, it is worth asking how thoroughly he understood the concept. As I have previously analyzed, the degree of thoroughness depends on how well a thinker maintains the idea of the "unconditionality" of divine creation implied by *creatio ex nihilo*. For instance, while Augustine and Aquinas both speak about *creatio ex nihilo*, their views on the existence of an intelligible world of forms, ideas, or logical possibilities prior to the actual act of divine creation weaken their commitment to the unconditionality of divine creation. In contrast, Descartes's theory of created eternal truth pushes the idea of unconditionality to its limit and can be considered a legitimate and more thorough development of the idea of *creatio ex nihilo*. However, even within Descartes's thought, his dogmatic assertion about the ultimate intelligibility and rationality of divine creation undermines the insight expressed by his theory of created eternal truth.

In comparison, Schleiermacher's thought can be considered among the most thorough of all the Christian philosophers and theologians discussed, as evidenced by the following analysis by Robert Williams:

Schleiermacher rejects the Platonic and Leibnizian image of God as an artificer who creates by surveying an infinitude of merely abstract possibles, selects the best set of compossibles, and actualizes them. Not only is the image of God anthropomorphic, it suggests that possibility is antecedent to or independent of God's power.... Schleiermacher objects that "the whole productive activity is assumed to be critical and selective, and therefore secondary." Further, for God to create by selection and choice is not to enhance but to limit the perfection of creation, because to choose is to negate, and negation means limitation, and this implies that God does not do all that he can. As *posse ipsum*, God is the ground of possibility and actuality; he produces everything that can be, without limitation. Thus the creation is good, because God is sovereign over his work: "The world, as the whole content of the divine formation and production, is so perfectly enclosed within the divine causality that there is nothing outside of the whole which can gain an influence on the whole" and undo God's work.[40]

Therefore, the thoroughness is particularly evident in Schleiermacher's rejection of the Platonic and Leibnizian image of God as an artificer who creates by selecting from an infinity of abstract possibilities. Instead, Schleiermacher holds that the world, as the complete content of divine formation and production, is so fully enclosed within divine causality that there is nothing outside the whole that can influence it. In other words, anything we can know about divine creation can only be derived from our knowledge of the world's de facto existence. Platonic ideas about "logical possibilities," as addressed in Augustine's, Aquinas's (as analyzed previously), and Leibniz's thought,[41] cannot be conditions of divine creation since we can assert nothing possible apart from the outcomes of that creation. As Descartes notes, the intelligibility of the world is also dependent, and Schleiermacher would likely agree.

In the end, Schleiermacher's concept of divine creation can be summarized as a "coincidence of opposites,"[42] with divine creation being both opposite in kind and equal in scope to the world. The relationship between God and the created world is distinctly asymmetrical: Ontologically, the world is dependent on God, while God does not depend on the world; epistemologically, however, all that we can know about the creator-creature relationship between God and the world is dependent on the de facto existence of the world.

Paul Tillich

THREE ROLES OF *CREATIO EX NIHILO*

In part 2 of his *Systematic Theology* I, Paul Tillich (1886–1965) provides a comprehensive and systematic exposition of his conception of God. In essence, Tillich's conception is grounded in the doctrine of *creatio ex nihilo*, which asserts that God created the world out of nothing. Tillich's interpretation of this doctrine can be summarized as follows: God's *creatio ex nihilo* creates the entire world and imparts existence to every creature, including time itself. God's creation of the world as a whole is eternal, while the world-process is intransigently oriented toward the future. Tillich identifies three distinct roles of *creatio ex nihilo*: initiation, preservation, and direction. The first role, initiation, means that every being ontologically depends upon God as the power of being. Therefore, God is the initiator of being itself. The second role, preservation, asserts that at every moment of the cosmic process, the grounding power of being continuously supports the being of the world. In this way, God becomes the preserving power of being. The third role, direction, involves the divine power of being moving the world from nonbeing to being. This inexhaustible power provides both an ideal for human creativity and a capacity for humans to realize this ideal.

THE CONCEPT OF "NONBEING"

Tillich's conception of *creatio ex nihilo*, as summarized above, appears at first glance to be quite traditional. However, upon closer analysis of Tillich's understanding of the meaning of "nonbeing," we can uncover the innovation he brings to the tradition.

Tillich offers a dual understanding of "nonbeing." The first meaning of nonbeing, derived from its Greek origin, is "*ouk on*." It refers to the absolute unconditionality of divine creation, indicating that every creature is ontologically dependent upon it, and thus, beyond divine creation, there can be no higher condition of realities. This *ouk on* type of nonbeing "has no relation at all to being"[43] because, as describing a characteristic of God as the power of being, the *ouk on* affirms nothing other than being and does not refer to any lack of being in comparison to some concrete status of being.

The second meaning of nonbeing is "*me on*," which, according to Tillich, can be explained using Platonic terms.[44] In Plato's *Timaeus*, divine creation is depicted as the casting of ideas and forms by the godly Demiurge upon amorphous material. This amorphous material, lacking the status of being any concrete creature, is a sort of nonbeing in contrast to being when placed in the sequence of creation. Accordingly, we can conceptualize this type of nonbeing as cosmological because *me on* refers to the lack of a concrete type of being when two cosmic entities are compared. In contrast, the first meaning of nonbeing is ontological because *ouk on* does not involve comparison at all. It just refers to the unconditionality of divine creation as fully being.

This *me on* type of nonbeing enables us to conceive of cosmic changes as a process from nonbeing to being. Cosmic beings are always in a state of process, and nonbeing in the cosmological sense can never be eliminated from the process, or else there would be no change at all. Therefore, Tillich claims that this *me on* type of nonbeing "has a dialectical relationship to being."[45]

Interestingly, according to the same passage from Tillich, both types of nonbeing are necessary to fully understand the concept and consequence of *creatio ex nihilo*, thereby shaping a specific type of religious anthropology. On the one hand, the empirical observation that humans are generated from nothing and return to nothing characterizes human existence as sharing a cosmological *me on* type of nothingness. However, once the process of human existence sharing *me on* is considered panoramically (i.e., together with all other creatures in the universe) and nontemporally as being conditioned by the unconditional *ouk on* nothingness of *creatio ex nihilo*, the cosmological nothingness acquires an ontological perspective as well. This perspective implies that nonbeing, as an indication of the de facto, limited existence of human beings, is reconceptualized as designating the essential trait of human nature as a finite being ultimately deriving from divine creation.

On the other hand, the essential status of the finitude of human existence leads to a moral observation: Tillich views that the nonbeing nature of human existence speaks to the resistance of human beings as finite beings against being, and this nonbeing is the ontological origin of sin.[46] Intriguingly, as Tillich's readers, we may be tempted to analogously conceive of the *ouk on* type of nonbeing in *creatio ex nihilo* as a resisting power against being as well. However, the difference between the nonbeing that belongs to finite beings and the nonbeing that pertains to *creatio ex nihilo* is that the latter type of nonbeing is exclusively *ouk on*, which entails that as the ground of being, *creatio ex nihilo* can never be overcome by nonbeing. As long as the world has existed, exists, or continues to exist, nonbeing can never prevail over being in the ultimate creative act of *creatio ex nihilo*, because the existence of the world is the starting point of an intellectual and existential inquiry to which *creatio ex nihilo* serves as the answer. The *ouk on* unconditionality of divine creation speaks exactly to the ultimate conditioning of the given existence of the world as a created outcome.

On the basis of this deeper ontological reflection, the human condition becomes clearer in Tillich's terms. Every finite human being strives for being while also consisting of nonbeing, with no guarantee of overcoming the latter. Only by participating in the ground of being, through what is traditionally termed "grace," can a person have the courage to be and preclude their being from being swallowed by nonbeing. The combination of the differentiated *ouk on* and *me on* types of nonbeing enables Tillich to see *creatio ex nihilo* as a monistic dynamic act by which being eternally overcomes nonbeing, while also envisioning finite human realities as a process in which being may or may not overcome nonbeing.[47]

This is an evident departure from Augustine's view, which did not distinguish between the *ouk on* and *me on* types of nonbeing. Tillich asserts:

> The *nihil* out of which God creates is *ouk on*, the undialectical negation of being.[48] Yet Christian theologians have had to face the dialectical problem of nonbeing at several points. When Augustine and many theologians and mystics who follow him called sin "nonbeing," they were perpetuating a remnant of the Platonic tradition. . . . They meant that sin has no positive ontological standing, while at the same time they interpreted nonbeing in terms of resistance against being and perversion of being.[49]

In other words, as discussed earlier, in chapter 5, Augustine construes nonbeing, out of which God creates, not only as the unconditionality of divine creation but also as distinct from and contrary to God as being. This further provides the basis for conceptualizing creaturely evil as the privation of good. In this way, Augustine posits an alienating power of nonbeing that resists the power of being in the grand scheme of *creatio ex nihilo* itself, incurring a dualistic suspicion.

However, for Tillich, the process of creaturely changes sharing the *me on* type of nonbeing is the very result of *creatio ex nihilo*, which is the unconditional *ouk on* origin of being. As located on varying ontological depths of reality, the concrete *me on* existence of finite beings does not undermine the *ouk on* unconditional power of being in divine creation. In other words, the ontological origin of sin in the finite status of human beings merely implies a *me on* type of nonbeing, and this *me on* nonbeing's overcoming power against being never reaches *creatio ex nihilo* as the ground of being. In this way, Tillich succeeds in decoupling the nothingness from which God creates from the nothingness in which creatures are immersed. For Tillich, there is simply no alienating power within the monistic act of *creatio ex nihilo*, and hence, no dualistic mindset registers.[50]

As I will analyze shortly, this crucial difference in ontology between Tillich's and Augustine's thought regarding *creatio ex nihilo* affords Tillich a greater apparatus to deal with theodicy.

FINITUDE AND INFINITUDE

Tillich's systematic analysis of the relationship between being and nonbeing extends to the relationship between the finite and the infinite, echoing the existential analysis of faith in the *Courage to Be*. According to Tillich, "infinity" is "the dynamic and free self-transcendence of finite being,"[51] while Being-itself is not a finite or infinite being but rather what makes being possible. Therefore, the endless self-transcendence of finite beings toward the infinite is made possible by Being-itself, even though remaining finite is still the final destiny of humans as finite beings.

From this, several significant theological points can be inferred. First, the infinite is always manifested in the self-transcendence of the finite, meaning that there is no rigid boundary between the secular and the sacred. Every secular element, insofar as it strives for self-affirmation and self-transcendence, is simultaneously sacred. Second, demonic power in this process consists of any form of reification of finite being as a pseudo-infinite one. If a finite being stops self-transcending and blocks the cosmic process into a stalemate, it becomes a demonic power. Third, a finite being lacks the self-transcending power toward the infinite. Only by being deeply united with the power of Being-itself, the grounding *creatio* of being *ex nihilo*, can a finite being fulfill its intrinsic telos of existence as an endless self-transcendence toward the infinite.

In Tillich's view, any concern that is not truly ultimate yields idolatry and releases demonic power in human history. Thus, a deep understanding of the relationship between being and nonbeing, finite and infinite, and the power of Being-itself is essential to comprehend Tillich's theological vision.

TIME

In his concluding remarks in the third volume of his systematic theology, Tillich's analysis of time and human history aims to summarize the insights from his previous volumes. His analysis of time begins by exploring the meaning of "*eskhatos*": "the 'last' in the temporal sense is not the 'final' in the eschatological sense."[52] Thus, the end of time is normatively defined as the "aim" of history, but Tillich emphasizes that the beginning and end of time, insofar as the aim of history remains unfulfilled, "belong essentially to historical time at every moment."[53] To fully grasp the depth of Tillich's statements, we must hearken back to *creatio ex nihilo*.

As we have previously analyzed, *creatio ex nihilo* as the ground of being is the initiative, preserving, and directing power of creation. It creates the past, present, and future types of time together, and the grounding power of *creatio ex nihilo* is thus made manifest at every moment. However, human beings as finite beings consist of both nonbeing and being, and their ability to continue to be is dependent upon their union with the ground of being and their ability to push forward despite the negative forces resisting the power of being. The union with *creatio ex nihilo* as the ultimate power of being is both the condition and the ideal for the processual existence of finite beings, and Tillich defines the aim of history as "reunion with the divine ground of being and meaning."[54] Nevertheless, Tillich emphasizes that a finite being can never fully realize the power of being per se, since the nonbeing element in the finite being can never be eliminated. Therefore, we can never empirically locate a concrete temporal point in human history where the infinite is fully realized as a being.

Tillich's view of eschaton has two important theological implications. First, he critiques political utopianism as idolatrous because it gives ultimate value to something preliminary.[55] Second, he reenvisions human conditions by taking *creatio ex nihilo* as a directing creative power that continuously transforms the finite world-process toward the infinite. Tillich posits that a human's courage to be is a condition for seeking this creative power in oneself, and he employs the term "essentialization" to describe the relationship between divine providence and human freedom. As Tillich puts it, "the new which has been actualized in time and space adds something to the essential being.... Participation in the eternal life depends on a creative synthesis of a being's essential nature with what has been made of it in its temporal existence."[56] Tillich further explains that "the eternal act of creation is driven by a love which finds fulfillment only through the other one who has the freedom to reject and accept love."[57] Thus, the fulfillment of *creatio ex nihilo* as the essential ground of being becomes human-dependent.

In comparison to the traditional Christian understanding that does not recognize human freedom as shaping divine providence (as analyzed at the beginning of chapter 5 regarding Aquinas's thought), Tillich's view on essentialization is a significant revision. It elevates the status of human beings and is committed to humanism. However, in my view, Tillich's claim that *creatio ex nihilo* depends, to some degree, on human freedom in the holistic perspective of the world-process is an overstatement. From a Ruist perspective, I argue that the fundamental ontological features of *creatio ex nihilo*, including the endless transformation of the world-process from nonbeing to being as Tillich conceives it, would remain unchanged even if human beings do not fulfill their freedom to assist in divine creation. The ontological unconditionality of *creatio ex nihilo* entails that, no matter what happens in the human world, the cosmic power of *creatio ex nihilo* remains or continues unabated. However, the realization of those ontological traits of *creatio ex nihilo* in the human world in a specific humane way indeed depends on human freedom. Thus, the divine creation can be considered human-dependent only in the human world and in the humane standard. Being neither good nor evil as judged by human standards, the divine creation naturally continues to create and transform the world-process from nonbeing to being. I will return to this comparative point in the concluding chapter of this book.

Conclusion

At the end of the last volume of his *Systematic Theology*, Tillich presents his theology as an "eschatological panentheism."[58] He uses a curve as an image of time: "I would suggest a curve which comes from above, moves down as well as ahead, reaches the deepest point which is the *nunc existentiale*, the 'existential now,' and returns in an analogous way to that from which it came, going ahead as well as going up."[59] This imagery that "comes from above" and "returns to that from which it came" captures the eschatological aspect of Tillich's theology, referring to the aim of history, which is the reunion with the divine ground of being and meaning. The "pan-" in panentheism denotes that divine creation works everywhere and at each moment, even during moments of anxiety and despair when human beings feel swallowed by the threat of nonbeing. This corresponds to the clause "reaches the deepest point which is the existential now." The "en-" refers to the manifestation of the power of being in finite beings, but that it cannot be contained by them. It continually breaks through any finite creative moment and advances the whole cosmic process into infinity, echoing the image of "moves ahead" and "going ahead." Tillich's theology is still "theism" because it affirms *creatio ex nihilo* as the ultimate reality, conditioning all other dimensions of reality without itself being thus conditioned. However, the "theo-" in Tillich's conception of God is radically different from traditional personalistic understandings of God in Christianity. God is not a being, let alone a supreme being, but rather the ground of being.[60]

One aspect of Tillich's concept of *creatio ex nihilo* worth noting is how it complements his approach to theodicy. Tillich emphasizes a monistic and dynamic understanding of *creatio ex nihilo* as a continuous process of being overcoming nonbeing. He also distinguishes between *ouk on* and *me on* types of nonbeing, allowing him to affirm that *creatio ex nihilo* never fails to overcome nonbeing, while the success of finite beings in doing so remains uncertain.

In this context, any instance of successful overcoming of nonbeing by a being, as a manifestation of the divine creative power, is considered good. However, if human beings, as the most significant manifestation of such power on earth, use their sacredly endowed power of being to negate themselves, it is still considered good from the perspective of divine creation, as the overcoming power of being over nonbeing for *creatio ex nihilo* is constant and nontemporal. Yet, this self-negation is clearly not good from the human perspective.

Thus, divine goodness, as an all-pervading feature of creation, is compatible with all possible cases of dependence in finite realities, whether these realities can continue to be or not. In particular, it is compatible with the morally evil capacity of human beings to negate themselves. From the all-encompassing scale of the created universe, such negation does not affect the essential feature of divine creation, which is the constant overcoming of being over nonbeing.

Here, we find a key to resolving the traditional Christian issue of theodicy. Its requirements are, first, giving up the conception of God as an all-caring, benevolent person with omniscient wisdom to issue rewards and punishments; second, understanding that divine creation is nondualistically good, with "good" measured ontologically as the sheer power of being; however, "good" understood dualistically and ambiguously is contrasted and intertwined with evil in the human realm; and third, understanding that whether humans are good or evil depends on how they receive the grace of the power of divine creation and thus on whether they conduct their lives well accordingly by themselves.

7 *Sheng Sheng* as *Generatio ex Nihilo* from Confucius to Wang Bi

Laozi and Confucius: A Divergence

In the face of the social and political turmoil brought about by the collapse of the late Zhou dynasty (ca. 1046–256 BCE), Laozi[1] and Confucius, purportedly the two most influential Chinese thinkers, took different approaches to address this shared social reality. Confucius believed that the turmoil was a result of a lack of civilization, and therefore, people should cultivate themselves to become more virtuous. This would enable them to restore the social and political order that was once prevalent in the early Zhou dynasty and maintained through a system of rituals (禮, *li*). For his part, Laozi believed that the tumults were caused by an *excess* of civilization. Thus, political leaders should abstain from governing, and the use of technologies ought to be restricted. In addition, education needed to be curtailed. In other words, Laozi held that humans should refrain from employing the means of civilization if they wished to revive the most primordial and energetic state of society where a pristine condition of human existence might still be preserved.

We can clearly observe this difference in Laozi's and Confucius's divergent social ideals. Laozi expressed his social ideals as follows:

> Let the state be small and the people few. Even if there be technologies replacing tens of hundreds of people's labor, they would not be used. Let the people look upon death as a grievous thing and renounce traveling afar. Though there be boats and carriages, yet nobody rides in them. Though there be armors and weapons, yet nobody takes them out. Let people go back to the old days when knots in ropes were still used. People relish their food, like their dresses, find ease in their homes, and are

happy with their customs and ways of life. People in neighboring settlements behold one another from afar. They can hear the barking of dogs and the crowing of cocks from the neighborhood. Yet they age to death without meeting or communicating with each other.[2]

Confucius's social ideals were very different:

> When the Great Way is followed intentionally, all under heaven is distributed appropriately. People with virtues and merits are selected for public office, trust is cherished, and courtesy is cultivated. The people not only love their own parents and children, they properly love other people's parents and children as well. The elderly are attended until death; adults are employed; children are raised. Concerning widowers, widows, orphans, the aged with no children, the disabled, and the ailing: they are all nourished. Males and females are bonded in marriage; their talents and jobs are matched. It is detestable for possessions and resources to be thrown away upon the ground. However, when gathering them, people would not store them solely for selfish use. It is detestable that people refrain from using their strength to fulfill their duties. However, when people do use their strength, it is not solely for personal gain. Therefore, intrigues and deceptions can gain no foothold. There are neither robbers nor thieves; neither is there any mob nor rebellious bandits. The doors of households appear to be closed, but they are never locked. This is a society of great harmony.[3]

According to Laozi, the most desirable society is one in which people require minimal social interaction and can find enjoyment in solitude. Conversely, Confucius believed that an ideal society involves appropriately sharing all of the achievements of human civilization through a well-coordinated social life. The divergence between these two thinkers becomes particularly apparent when considering their differing attitudes toward rituals.

Confucius believed that one of the most important ways to cultivate the cardinal virtue of humaneness (仁, *ren*) is to behave in accordance with ritual-propriety.[4] In contrast, chapter 38 of the *Dao De Jing* asserts, "Ritualization represents the scarcity of the human virtues of 'loyalty' and 'trustworthiness,' and it is actually the supreme reason for social disorder." *Li* (ritual), broadly defined, encompasses all civilized symbols or conventions, such as ceremonies, artifacts, etiquettes, and institutions. The Ru tradition regards *Li*[5] as a key element that distinguishes humans from nonhuman beings, and therefore views the appropriate performance of *Li* as a manifestation of human dignity. However, given that *Li* is fundamental to civilization, Laozi's skepticism toward *Li* reflects his distinct Daoist sentiment regarding human civilization in general.

In brief, based on their differing social ideals and attitudes toward ritual, we may conclude that Laozi and Confucius held distinct perspectives. Laozi can be viewed as a heroic/proto-Chinese thinker who valued human civilization and culture to a lesser degree, while Confucius can be viewed as a heroic/proto-Chinese thinker who aspired toward a long-lasting human civilization and culture.[6]

The thesis I aim to argue is that this fundamental difference between Laozi's and Confucius's thought is reflected in the cosmological tendencies of the traditions they shaped, namely Daoism and Ruism, respectively. By examining Laozi's cosmology in the *Dao De Jing* and the Ru cosmology in the *Xici* of the *Classic of Change*, I will illustrate the interconnectedness between cosmology and anthropology, which primarily encompasses political theory and ethics, in each of these two texts.

"Reversion Is the Action of *Dao*": Laozi's Cosmology in the *Dao De Jing*

THE "NONBEING" (無) ASPECTS OF THE *DAO*

The core concept of Laozi's cosmology is the *Dao* (道). The *Dao* generates and sustains the entire world, and the process of cosmic change recurs cyclically, as "reversion is the action of *Dao*" (chapter 14).

Laozi's *Dao*, however, is characterized by both "nonbeing" and "being" aspects. The accurate interpretation of these two terms and their relationship to each other is a significant challenge in understanding Laozi's thought. This issue arises immediately upon opening the book of *Dao De Jing*:

> The *Dao* that can be told of is not the genuine *Dao*; the name that can be given is not the genuine name. Nonbeing (無) is the name of the beginning of Heaven and Earth; being (有) is the name of the mother of all things. Therefore, I constantly use the name of nonbeing in order to see into the subtlety of the *Dao*. I constantly use the name of being in order to see into the manifestations of the *Dao*. These two (nonbeing and being) share the same origin but have different names. They may both be called the mystery. Reaching from mystery into deeper mystery is the gate to the secret of all subtleties. (Chapter 1)

The challenge in comprehending the concept of "nonbeing" is that, when viewed comparatively, it is unclear what the term 無 (nonbeing) signifies in the enigmatic opening chapter of *Dao De Jing*. The complexity arises as we consider the rich implications of "nonbeing" or "nothingness" in both the Greek-European Christian tradition of *creatio ex nihilo* and the subsequent developments in Chinese intellectual history.

The term "nonbeing" can be interpreted in various ways within a metaphysical context.[7] For example, it may refer to the formlessness of an undifferentiated whole of being that lacks determination, as in the cases of Spinoza and Hegel.[8] Alternatively, "nonbeing" could denote a cosmic state of pure emptiness that lacks any kind of being, but still holds a temporal position at the primeval stage of cosmic evolution. In this sense, it would be akin to a great vacuum. Furthermore, "nonbeing" could also have an ontological significance, such as the pattern-principles (理, *li*) that articulate how a set of cosmic realities dynamically and harmoniously fit together. These principles are devoid of empirical attributes found in tangible cosmic entities. Zhu Xi contends that these entities possess aspects of "nonbeing," which I will examine in the upcoming chapter. In the tradition of *creatio ex nihilo*, "nonbeing" can refer to the unconditionality of the ultimate ontological creative power that generates beings rather than being a kind of being.

Given the various interpretations of "nonbeing" in a metaphysical context, the relationship between "nonbeing" and "being" can also be puzzling. In the opening chapter of the *Dao De Jing*, this relationship can be understood cosmologically, wherein "nonbeing" and "being" alternate with each other and are located in different temporal points in the sequence of cosmic changes. However, these alternating cosmic statuses are all manifestations of the singular *Dao*'s creative and regulative power; as the text suggests, "These two [nonbeing and being] share the same origin but have different names." Another way to understand the relationship between "nonbeing" and "being" is ontological, where they are two aspects of the same thing and exist and function simultaneously. This view resonates with the *creatio ex nihilo* tradition, which views unconditionality as just one necessary aspect of divine creation and not dialectically counteracting the "being" aspect. A third possible understanding is ontologically less ultimate, where the "nonbeing" feature of *Dao* structures and regulates the empirical process of cosmic changes, similar to Zhu Xi's conception of pattern-principles. In both these latter two understandings, the relationship between "nonbeing" and "being" is synchronic and potentially nontemporal.

It is evident that relying solely on the first chapter of *Dao De Jing* will not answer all the aforementioned puzzles. The situation does not improve much even when we consider two further key cosmological chapters as references:

> Reversion is the action of *Dao*. Weakness is the function of *Dao*. The myriad things under heaven are generated from being (有) and being is generated from nonbeing (無). (Chapter 40)
>
> Out of *Dao*, One is generated. Out of One, Two is generated. Out of Two, Three is generated. Out of Three, the myriad things are generated. Each of the myriad things carries the *yin* at its back and holds the *yang* in its front. Through the mutual impact of the *yin/yang* vital-energies, harmony among the myriad things is generated. (Chapter 42)

These two quotations establish a sequence of creation between "nonbeing" and "being" and a sequence of creativity between "Dao" and a myriad of things, regardless of what "One," "Two," and "Three" refer to. However, it is still unclear whether the creative sequence mentioned here is one of ontological dependence or cosmological succession. If the latter, the relationship between "nonbeing" and "being" for the *Dao* is primarily cosmological. Hence, it would be inappropriate to interpret Laozi's cosmology as analogous to the Greek-European Christian tradition of *creatio ex nihilo*.

Nonetheless, it is evident from the analysis conducted thus far that time is a critical factor in understanding Laozi's cosmology. Extensive textual evidence in the *Dao De Jing* suggests that Laozi's cosmology is primarily focused on cosmological succession, rather than ontological dependence. This emphasis on succession is a central feature of Laozi's cosmology and is closely connected to his anthropology as well.

THE UNDIFFERENTIATED WHOLE OF BEING BEFORE THE CREATION OF HEAVEN AND EARTH

The four following quotations describe a stage in *Dao*'s cosmic action that bears a striking resemblance to Hegel's concept of "the undifferentiated whole of being," as noted above. By analyzing these texts, we can gain clarity on the meaning of the "One," "Two," and "Three" stages referenced in chapter 42.

> *Dao* is hollow, but its uses are inexhaustible. Abyssal, yet it is the forebear of all things. Almost obliterated, yet it seems to still exist. I don't know whose child it is. Instead, it seems to exist even before the birth of the supreme deity (帝). (Chapter 4)
>
> We look, but it cannot be seen. This is called the invisible. We listen, but it cannot be heard. This is called the inaudible. We grasp, but it cannot be touched. This is called the intangible. These three elude our inquiries, and hence, they blend and become one (混而為一). Nor in its upper regions, is there light. Nor in its lower regions, is there darkness. Winding and twisting, it cannot be named; it reverts again to the realm of no things (無物). This is why it is called the status that has no status, and the image of what is not a thing. This is called the fleeting and obscure (恍惚). Meet it and you do not see its face. Follow it and you do not see its back. Grasp the *Dao* of old days to guide the beings of today. Know the ancient beginning, and this is called the regulation of *Dao* (道紀). (Chapter 14)
>
> *Dao* as a thing is fleeting and obscure. Fleeting and obscure, yet latent in it are images. Obscure and fleeting, yet latent in it are things.... From the days of old till now, its name never disappears, by which I can view the father of all things. How can I know the status of the father of all things? Through this, "the *Dao*." (Chapter 21)
>
> Before heaven and earth existed, there was something that is a complete blend (混成). Silent, vast, yet it stands alone and undergoes no change. It moves in a circle, yet is inexhaustible. It is worthy to be the mother of all things. I do not know its name and address it as *Dao*. If forced to give it a name, I shall call it "Great." Being great implies extending out, extending out implies far-reaching, and far-reaching implies reversion to the original point. Therefore, *Dao* is great, heaven is great, the earth is great, and human beings are also great. These are the Great Four in the universe, and humans are one of them. Humans take earth as their law, the earth takes heaven as its law, heaven takes *Dao* as its law, and *Dao* takes what comes out spontaneously and naturally (自然)[9] as its law. (Chapter 25)

To begin my analysis of the subtleties of Laozi's cosmology in these quotations, it is important to highlight one of its distinctive features in comparison to the tradition of *creatio ex nihilo*. Chapters 4 and 25 of the

Dao De Jing state that *Dao* "exists even before the birth of the supreme deity" and follows "what comes out spontaneously and naturally as its law." This indicates that the ultimate reality in Laozi's cosmology is not anthropomorphic. Laozi sought to eliminate the influence of the Shang and Zhou dynasties' worship of the "supreme deity (上帝)," and his explanation of how the cosmos is created and evolves shares a naturalistic affinity with modern scientific cosmogony such as the Big Bang theory. The central theme of Laozi's cosmology is the spontaneous emergence of all things from an intelligible cosmic process. Interestingly, we will later find that this theme is also shared by the Ru cosmology in the *Xici*.

To understand Laozi's cosmology correctly as mainly a temporal one, concerned with the relationship of temporal succession among cosmic realities rather than ontological dependence among varying ontological ranks of cosmic realities, we can rely on key evidence from the quoted texts. For instance, Laozi attempts to articulate what happens to *Dao* before the creation of heaven and earth (chapter 25) and uses his knowledge of this primordial status of *Dao* to guide his contemporary human society (chapter 14).

Laozi's depiction of the ancient status of *Dao* before the creation of heaven and earth is reminiscent of Hegel's portrayal of the undifferentiated whole of being before any determination occurs: it is invisible, inaudible, intangible, and, in one word, formless.[10] Despite the lack of determination within this primeval state of *Dao*, all images, forms, and essences of things lie latent within it, as the entire cosmos will emerge from this primordial whole of being under the function of *Dao*. Most crucially, the power of *Dao* latent in this "everything-blended-together" state remains ever-present, and thus, *Dao* continues to function throughout the entire process of cosmic changes (chapter 25). In this sense, Dao is not only a generator/creator but also a sustainer.

The use of the term 物 (thing) can be a bit confusing, since in chapters 21 and 25 it is said that the *Dao* is a thing, while in chapter 14 it is said that when everything blends together, the *Dao* locates itself in the realm of "no things." However, I interpret the seeming conflict in this way: The undifferentiated whole of being before the creation of heaven and earth can be said to be a thing in the vaguest sense that something is there, and this "something" is the basic, undifferentiated stuff of being. However, compared with all the concrete things after heaven and earth have been generated, this primeval status of cosmic being cannot be said to be a thing since it has not yet garnered any other determination than being a formless "something."

Given this analysis, it is relatively straightforward to understand the concrete references to "One," "Two," and "Three" in the cosmological sequence of chapter 42. First, it is clear that the creative sequence described in chapter 42 is one of cosmological succession rather than ontological dependence, implying that there must be a concrete status of cosmogonic evolution corresponding to "One," "Two," or "Three." Second, as the primeval undifferentiated whole of being is described as "blending and becoming one" in chapter 14, it is reasonable to interpret "One" in chapter 42 as referring to this cosmic stage. "Two" can be understood as referring to the *yin* and *yang* vital-energies (chapter 4), or to "heaven" and "earth" (chapter 25) when the primeval whole of being receives its initial determination under the function of *Dao*. "Three" refers to "heaven," "earth," and "human beings," which are all referred to as "great" in chapter 25. Finally, the myriad things are further generated through the interaction between heaven, earth, and human beings.

So, the sequence of the generative succession among cosmic realities according to Laozi can be illustrated in the following diagram:

Dao → One (the undifferentiated whole of being) → Two (*yin/yang* Vital-Energies; or Heaven and Earth) → Three (Heaven, Earth, and Human Beings) → the Myriad Things.

To avoid any potential misunderstandings of this diagram, it is important to remember that *Dao* is not only the creator, but also the sustainer of the cosmos. As such, its creative power persists relentlessly throughout the stages of the cosmogonic process, including the generation of the One, Two, Three, and beyond.

LAOZI ON COSMOLOGY AND ANTHROPOLOGY

A final crucial question that must be addressed regarding the cosmological sequence described above is which part of the sequence can be considered "nonbeing" and which part is "being." Chapter 40 and chapter 42 can be read together to conclude that One is being and *Dao* is nonbeing, making it relatively easy to determine. So the entire cosmic sequence will look like this:

"Nonbeing" (*Dao*) ➡ One (the undifferentiated whole of "being") ➡ Two (*yin/yang* Vital-Energies; Heaven and Earth) ➡ Three (Heaven, Earth, and Human Beings) ➡ the Myriad Things.

There are two important clarifications to be made regarding the revised diagram of Laozi's cosmic sequence.

First, the function of *Dao* permeates all stages of the sequence, regardless of whether *Dao* is considered as "nonbeing." Even if we acknowledge the possibility of a status of "nonbeing" before the undifferentiated One, this would be a vacuum-like state that is capable of generating everything of being under the power of Dao. Hence, *Dao*'s function runs through the "nonbeing" stage, and there is no true absence of *Dao* in any part of the sequence.

Second, while the textual evidence is limited, the placement of a great vacuum before the One is not essential for understanding Laozi's cosmology. This is because the undifferentiated One, compared to Two and all later stages, is already formless and can be considered a kind of "nonbeing." In this way, chapter 40 can be interpreted as saying that the myriad things under heaven belong to the cosmic status of "being," corresponding to the stages of Two and Three, while these statuses can ultimately be traced back to the undifferentiated One as a sort of "nonbeing."

Nonetheless, whether the beginning stage of Laozi's cosmogony is the nonbeing of a great vacuum or the being of the undifferentiated One, the most crucial point for Laozi is that the stage of "nonbeing" is not only temporally prior to "being" in this cosmic process but also cyclic. To Laozi, the temporal priority of nonbeing over being demonstrates that the most powerful manifestation of *Dao*'s creativity is the stage of nonbeing, as it gives rise to the latter. The cyclic process of cosmic changes also proves that the constant creation of myriad things results from a perennial return to the original "nonbeing" root of *Dao*'s creative power. Thus, any renewal status of human society must follow the pattern indicated by this eternally cyclic and recursive process. In other words, the temporal priority of nonbeing over being and the cyclic feature of cosmic changes form a cosmological foundation for Laozi's anthropology, which is highly skeptical of the complexity of human civilization, as previously discussed. The following two quotations, in conjunction with chapter 40, illuminate further how Laozi envisions the cyclic nature of *Dao*'s creativity.

> What happens between heaven and earth is like a pair of bellows! Emptying, yet it continually gives a supply. The more it is worked, the more it brings forth. (Chapter 5)
>
> Attain the utmost vacuum (虛). Hold firm to the basis of quietude. The myriad things arise and become together, but I watch how they return. Things, like plants, luxuriantly grow, but they all return to their roots. To return to the root is quietude. And this is returning to one's destiny. (Chapter 16)

Understanding Laozi's cosmology sheds light on his social ideal expressed in chapter 80. Since human civilization arises only after the One and Two stages, it is not difficult to comprehend why Laozi encourages a return to the most primordial status of human society, where little sociality and almost no technology are present. For Laozi, this represents the status of human existence closest to the most powerful and sublime manifestation of *Dao* in its "nonbeing" stage of the cosmic process. This also explains Laozi's suspicion of ritual-propriety and other humanistic Ru virtues since they come *afterward*.

In conclusion, it is clear that one of the driving forces behind Laozi's cosmology and anthropology was the difficult social and political climate of the late Zhou dynasty. Laozi sought to address the problems of war and human suffering in a unique way. However, his suspicion of the humanistic virtues of the Ru tradition, which aim for the continued flourishing of human civilization, reinforces the idea that he was a heroic/proto-Chinese thinker who placed lesser value on human culture and civilization.

The Ruist Cosmology in the Xici of the Classic of Change

The *Xici* (繫辭, appended texts) of the *Classic of Change* is the most elaborate text on Ru cosmology during Ruism's classical period.[11] Its importance to the Ru metaphysical tradition is so profound that it serves as the foundation for an exceptionally extensive commentarial tradition on Ru cosmology, including Zhou Dunyi's *Diagram of Ultimate Limit*, and numerous other works of Song through Ming Ruism which will be analyzed in chapter 8.

As soon as we delve into the first chapter of *Xici*, we will instantly perceive the distinction between this cosmology and its Daoist equivalent, which I previously discussed in the case of Laozi. The opening chapter states,

> As heaven is noble and earth is humble, so [the statuses of] Qian and Kun are determined. As the high and the low places are displayed, so the dignified and the ignoble are positioned. As movement and repose are constant, so the firm and the mild are distinguished. As events are of different kinds, and things are classed in groups, so good and ill auspices are generated. As images are formed in heaven and shapes are formed on earth, so alternation and transformation appear.
>
> Thus, the firm and the mild affect each other, and the eight trigrams interact with one another: as thunder and lightning stimulate, wind and rain fertilize, sun and moon move in their courses, and after cold comes heat. The *Dao* of Qian forms maleness, and the *Dao* of Kun forms femaleness. Qian conceives the great beginning, and Kun brings things to completion.
>
> Qian can be known because of its easiness, and Kun is powerful because of its simplicity. Because it is easy, it is readily recognized. Because it is simple, it is readily followed. What is readily recognized is accepted, and what is readily followed brings effectivity. What is accepted can endure, and what brings effectivity can grow great. Endurance is the virtue of the worthy, while greatness is the enterprise of the worthy. Being easy and simple, the pattern-principles under heaven are grasped. Once the pattern-principles are grasped, success ensues.[12]

There are several key motifs that underlie the opening chapter of *Xici*, all of which are significant for us in understanding the nature of Ru cosmology.

First, the primary aim of the opening chapter of *Xici* is to establish the authenticity and truth value of the philosophy underlying the symbology and text of the *Zhou Book of Change* (周易, *Zhouyi*).[13] This is achieved through a series of verses, such as the first one, which states, "As heaven is noble and earth is humble, so (the status of) Qian and Kun are determined." Qian and Kun are the first two hexagrams of *Zhouyi*'s symbology, each of which is associated with a text conveying wisdom. By stating that the symbols and associated philosophy correspond to reality (i.e., "heaven" and "earth"), the verse affirms their authenticity. Other verses in the opening chapter serve a similar purpose, highlighting the correspondence between the text and reality.

Second, the opening chapter delves into the fundamental teachings of Ru cosmology. Unlike Laozi's Daoist cosmology, the Ru perspective focuses on the "pattern-principle (理, *li*)" that underlies the de facto conditions of cosmic realities, rather than questioning what occurred before the existence of heaven and earth. Several key tenets of this worldview can be generalized, the first being that it is a world of order. Natural phenomena, such as thunder, lightning, wind, and rain, have their specific classes, roles, and positions in the constantly changing cosmic process, as do heaven and earth. Furthermore, the Ru worldview recognizes this world as one of constant creation and change, driven by the interaction between what is firm (剛) and what is mild (柔). In reference to other chapters in the *Xici*, these refer to the *yang* and *yin* forms of vital-energy (氣, *qi*). The interaction of *yin* and *yang* vital-energies is further elaborated in this opening chapter as being manifested in the more intricate interactions among "the eight trigrams," which symbolize the power of eight natural phenomena. These interactions, along with the concrete cosmic realities they create, constantly run and operate in the everlasting periodic course of the four seasons. Finally, human beings are generated from this cosmic process and inherit the same two basic cosmic creative powers, the explorative Qian and the receptive Kun, which they manifest in the human world.

Third, this constantly changing and creating world with its due order is intelligible to human beings. The symbolic system of *Zhouyi* has grasped the pattern-principles of realities, making it easy and simple enough for human beings to study and understand such that its referred realities also become comprehensible. The chapter states, "Qian is known because of its easiness, and Kun is powerful because of its simplicity," suggesting confidence in the authenticity of the book of *Zhouyi* and a commitment to the intelligibility of the entire created world.

The third motif demonstrates how individuals ought to use the book of *Zhouyi*. The final quoted paragraph conveys the notion that by reading and contemplating the *Zhouyi*, one can comprehend the pattern-principles of cosmic changes. Consequently, individuals should cultivate their virtues and expand their human enterprises. This humanistic emphasis concludes the opening chapter, highlighting the significance of human flourishing within the context of the cosmos.

Among the three interconnected motifs presented, the second one holds the most significance for our comparative purpose. The Ru cosmology does not engage in speculation about the temporal origins of cosmic realities before the existence of heaven/earth and *yin/yang* vital-energies, setting it in sharp contrast with Laozi's cosmology in the *Dao De Jing*. However, other verses of the *Xici* teach that there is something called the Ultimate Limit, which "creates" or "generates" (生, *sheng*)[14] heaven/earth and *yin/yang* vital-energies. This suggests that the creative sequence of the *Xici* does not prioritize the temporal one emphasized in the *Dao De Jing*. Subsequently, I will cite other chapters of the *Xici* to elaborate on the salience of Ru cosmology, as well as its connection to anthropology.

"BIRTH BIRTH IS CALLED THE CHANGE (生生之謂易)"

The following quotation from chapter 12 of part 1 highlights that the *Xici* doesn't speculate on the temporal beginning (or end) of the cosmos. As stated in the text:

> What lies beyond shape is called the *Dao*, and what lies within shape is called the utensil-like things (形而上者謂之道, 形而下者謂之器). Transforming and trimming things is called alteration. Stimulating and implementing things is called going through. Taking and applying them to all people under heaven is called the enterprise.[15]

It's evident that the *Xici* doesn't focus on the temporal dimension of the cosmos "before" the existence of heaven and earth, but rather on what's "beyond" and "within shape." The *Xici*'s vision is a combination of a horizontal and temporal perspective supervised by a vertical and nontemporal one, as portrayed by the spatial prepositions "beyond" and "within." This newly quoted chapter defines what is within shape as a utensil-like thing. This is understandable because things, like utensils, have a distinct shape and form and can potentially serve a particular human purpose. However, the meaning of the "Dao" when referred to as being "beyond" shape isn't entirely clear from this chapter. We do know that the latter part of the chapter urges people to rely on their knowledge of both the "Dao" and the "utensil-like" things to "alter," "go through," and "apply" things to the human world to expand human enterprise. The *Xici*'s humanistic emphasis underpins its perspective, and therefore we should seek clues in other resonating chapters of the *Xici* to understand what the "Dao" means.

I will be quoting additional chapters from the *Xici*, namely chapters 4 and 5 of part 1, where we can find a more detailed explanation of the term "Dao" mentioned in the quotation above from chapter 12.

> One *yin* and one *yang*, this is called *Dao*. What continues the *Dao* is called goodness, and what the *Dao* forms is called nature. Humane (仁, *ren*) people see it and call it "being humane," while wise people see it and call it "being wise." Ordinary people use it daily, but don't know what it is. Hence, the *Dao* of the exemplary person is exceptional. It shows itself within the virtue of humaneness and hides itself within its functions. It brings the myriad things into being and becoming, but it doesn't share the same worries and anxieties as the sages. It has the sublime virtue and pursues the greatest enterprise.
>
> Being rich and all-encompassing, this is called great enterprise. Being renewed on a daily basis, this is called sublime virtue. Birth Birth, this is called the Change. Forming images, this is called Qian. Imitating laws, this is called Kun. Calculating the numbers up to their ultimate, and knowing accordingly the future, this is called divination. Penetrating into the alternations of things, this is called the management of affairs. What cannot be fathomed by *yin* and *yang* is numinous and wonderful.[16]

The first verse of this quotation, "One *yin* and one *yang* (一陰一陽), this is called *Dao*," is reminiscent of "sun and moon move in their courses and after cold comes heat (一寒一暑)" in chapter 1 of part 1 of *Xici*. As mentioned earlier, the opening chapter of *Xici* indicates that, from a human perspective, the cosmic realities proceed spatially between heaven and earth and temporally during the four seasons' ceaseless process. Moreover, within these changing realities, there are layers of "pattern-principles" that explain why and how these changes occur, including the interaction of *yin/yang* vital-energies and its more intricate manifestations in the interactions among eight natural phenomena. Among these pattern-principles, the *yin/yang* interaction is the most general, as there are no others that can characterize the determinations of cosmic realities. Therefore, it is reasonable to infer that "one *yin* and one *yang*, this is called *Dao*" refers to the most general pattern-principle that underlies the constantly creative cosmic realities. In other words, according to the Ru cosmology system described in *Xici*, the interaction of *yin/yang* vital-energies is the furthest that human intelligence can go to describe and explain the determinate changes that the "shaped" cosmic realities undergo.

Given the complexity of the conceptual subtleties and intricacies developed in later Ru intellectual history, which I will analyze later, I agree with Zhu Xi that the "Dao" mentioned in the *Xici* context refers to "pattern-principles (理)" that describe and explain how cosmic realities constantly change and create.

Chapters 4 and 5 in part 1 of *Xici* provide two additional insights that aid in our understanding of the distinctive character of Ru cosmology. First, Ru cosmology places greater emphasis on the vertical relationship between the *Dao* as pattern-principles and the *Dao*-governed utensil-like things, rather than the horizontal stages of cosmic changes. This distinguishes it from Daoist cosmology in the *Dao De Jing*. Relationally, there is a significant difference between the holistic feelings and insights conveyed by these two texts regarding the ever-changing cosmos. While Laozi's cosmology is undoubtedly processual, his belief that "reversion is the action of *Dao*" considers the universe's movement as a constant return to its root in "nonbeing." As mentioned earlier, this cyclical idea of cosmic changes justifies Laozi's approach to human self-cultivation and statecraft, which centers on the "attainment of vacuum and quietude (虛靜)" and "nonaction (無為)" in the most profound cosmological sense. In contrast, the Ru text's perception of the processual cosmos implies that the process is periodic, as the de facto conditions from a human perspective take place during the four seasons' endless course. However, the process is not cyclic; instead, it is an endless process of advancing into novelty. Rather than the idea that "reversion is the action of Dao," the Ru text proposes that "Birth Birth is called the Change," "Being renewed on a daily basis, this is called sublime virtue" (part 1, chapter 5), and "The great virtue of heaven and earth is creativity" (天地之大德曰生, part 2, chapter 1). Accordingly, the Ru text's ideal of human existence differs greatly from Laozi's ideal of "attainment of vacuum and quietude" and "nonaction." In the Ru text's view, since the entire cosmos is constantly creating, human beings should become "rich and all-encompassing" and "expand" their greatest "human enterprise." In other words, human society ought to flourish continually in its all-encompassing and harmonious way.

From a comparative perspective, it is difficult to determine which view regarding the processual cosmos presented by the *Dao De Jing* and the *Xici* is truer. A modern assessment of this would depend on the latest developments in scientific cosmology.[17] However, regarding the effectiveness of cosmological justification for humanistic values, I argue that the *Xici* is superior to the *Dao De Jing*. First, regardless of whether there is a temporal beginning of the cosmos or not, the further determination and proliferation of the cosmic process aligns well with the Ru conception of the cosmic process as an endless advance into novelty. Thus, the Ru cosmology is more inclusive than Laozi's because it allows for varying conceptions of the cosmos's beginning without undermining the key insight on the generic features of cosmic changes. The same cannot be said of the latter because the state of cosmic beginning and the constant return of the cosmos to it indicate the decisive nature of Laozi's cosmology, which remains incompatible with the Ruist perspective on the universe's ceaseless advancement into novelty. Second, in correspondence with the inclusive Ru cosmology, the Ru method of statecraft and human self-cultivation has greater potential for inclusion. For human civilization to prosper on its own terms, "refraining from government" in the style of Laozi's "nonaction" may be effective if some developments of the civilization exceed their due measure of harmonization and equilibrium with humans or nature. However, this approach can be viewed as a potential application of the more adaptable strategy of human collaboration to discover the best possible means for continued prosperity. The same cannot be said of Laozi's Daoist strategy, which once set as refraining from government, would be incapable of adopting another strategy urging humans to act and collaborate in changing situations. The *Xici* describes the more adaptive Ru strategy as "to be continually adjusted and adapted according to the changing situations" (唯變所適, part 2, chapter 8). The Ru text underpins a deep appreciation of the uniquely human endeavor leading to the sustainable prosperity of human civilization.[18]

The second additional point of interest in the quoted chapters 4 and 5 of part 1 of the *Xici* pertains to the relationship between the cosmos and humanity. In Laozi's case, the relationship is simple because the action of the *Dao* is continually reverting to the root of "nonbeing," which, due to its temporal priority over all following statuses of cosmic realities, is more potent than any form of "being." As a result, human beings should also abstain from governance and achieve the spiritual status of great vacuum and quietude. However, the Ruist conception of the relationship between the cosmic *Dao* and the human world is not as straightforward. On the one hand, the Ru text acknowledges that the "goodness" of human nature, summarized by the Ru tradition as the virtue of Humaneness (仁), is inherited (繼) from the constant creativity of the cosmic *Dao*. On the other hand, the relationship between the two requires some clarification:

First, the cosmic *Dao*'s power is so far beyond human power that during the process of constant cosmic creation that gives rise to all creatures, the *Dao* "does not share the same worries and anxieties of the sages." This implies that the *Dao*'s function, compared to human standards, is effortless. It lacks contrivance, speculation, and any human-like plan or purpose. In short, the cosmos is a natural process of spontaneous emergence under the operation of *Dao*, which, as the most sublime form of creativity, surpasses even that of the "sages," the personality model for the Ru idea of moral self-cultivation.

Second, although the cosmic *Dao*'s creativity exceeds that of human beings, it will not automatically come into existence in the human world in human form without further human efforts. In chapter 8 of part 1, the text states: "Sages could see all activities under heaven and after observing how they gather and run forward, the sages perform norms and rituals;" in chapter 8 of part 2, after similar emphasis on the importance of social norms and rituals, the text notes, "if not through human beings, the *Dao* cannot be carried over automatically (in the human world) (苟非其人, 道不虛行)."[19] In other words, despite the fact that the exceptional efforts of the sages, which contribute to the ongoing prosperity of human society, demand greater exertion than the power demonstrated by the cosmic *Dao* in creating and sustaining the entire universe, it remains crucial for the sages to harmonize human society while primarily considering a human viewpoint. Thus, what humans do in terms of inheriting and perpetuating the creativity of the cosmic *Dao* is to add uniquely human values to the nonhuman natural world and manifest the cosmic creativity of *Dao* in a particularly human, that is, humane, way.

Based on this analysis, I categorize the Ru conception of the relationship between the cosmic *Dao* and the human world as an escalated continuum and manifesting unity. "Escalated continuum" means that the conditions of the human world are continuous with the nonhuman natural world, but human beings aim to harmonize the needs of a thriving human society with its natural environment and add unique humanistic values to the nonhuman natural world. Additionally, the relationship is one of "manifesting unity" because the cosmic *Dao* functions in both the nonhuman natural and human worlds and must be manifested in the human world through human efforts. However, the cosmic *Dao*'s transcendent creative power can also be seen as an ideal that human efforts continually strive toward but can never fully realize.

The sophisticated Ru idea of the relationship between what is transcendent and what is immanent offers an immediate existential payoff in the realm of theodicy, which concerns the cosmic problem of evil. According to this idea, if human beings do well, the cosmic *Dao* will be manifested in the human world. On the other hand, if human beings do badly, the sublimity of the transcendent creative power of the cosmic *Dao* will not be affected, since the *Dao*'s creative power is always all-encompassing and does not revolve around human interests or comprehension. However, if human beings do poorly, this will cause the cosmic *Dao* to be poorly manifested in the human world. In comparison to the *creatio ex nihilo* tradition that the previous chapters of this study have explored, the *Xici* places less tension on the problem of evil. One reason for this is the conjunctive emphasis on the nontheism of the cosmic *Dao* and the proactive role of human efforts, namely, humanism. This point will be revisited in the final chapter of comparison in this book.

"ULTIMATE LIMIT CREATES TWO MODES (太極生兩儀)"

Now that we have explained the general nature of Ru cosmology and anthropology, we are better equipped to analyze a quintessential text of Ru metaphysics. Its influence on later Ru intellectual history cannot be overestimated. The text in question is chapters 10 and 11 in part 1 of the *Xici*:

> Thus, closing a door is called Kun and opening a door is called Qian. Closing and Opening is called alternation. Endless backing and forthing is called penetration. What can be perceived is called an image. Given shape it is called a utensil. Putting it into use is called imitation. Using this for all the people's sake whether they go outside or come inside is called what is numinous and wonderful.
>
> Thus, there is Ultimate Limit in the Change. Ultimate Limit creates two modes. Two modes create four images. Four images create eight trigrams. The eight trigrams define good and ill fortunes. Good and ill fortunes give rise to the great enterprise.
>
> Therefore, the image to imitate is no greater than heaven and earth. No alternation or penetration is greater than four seasons. No bright image in the sky is greater than the sun and moon. No honor or rank is greater than wealth and nobility. Preparing things for use, making utensils and techniques for the benefit of all under heaven, no one can achieve more about these than sages.[20]

The quoted chapters in my adapted translation resonate with the Ru cosmology indicated in the opening and other analyzed chapters. To provide further clarity, let us recapitulate the key aspects of Ru cosmology. It places great emphasis on the actual conditions of the cosmic realities that are perceived by humans to occur in the spatial realm between heaven and earth, and the temporal framework of the four seasons. These cosmic realities are constantly changing and creating, forging ahead into new novelties. The Ru cosmology attempts to identify layers of pattern-principle within these cosmic realities. This serves a threefold purpose: first, to describe and explain these cosmic processes; second, to ground humanistic ethical values in their cosmological foundation; and third, to discover and harmonize leveraging realities in order to bring about the realization of these humanistic values in the human world.

Drawing upon this overarching Ru cosmological perspective, it appears that the second paragraph in the above quotation—specifically chapter 11 in part 1—seeks to identify a singular pattern-principle within a cluster of cosmic pattern-principles, in order to achieve all the aforementioned goals simultaneously. This marks the culmination of the distinctively Ru endeavor to anchor humanistic moral values on their cosmological foundation.

To unravel the meaning of this enigmatic passage, we must first recognize that the term "change" used here, as in other similar cases in the *Xici*, carries a dual connotation. It refers not only to the symbolic system of the book of *Zhouyi* but also to the cosmic realities that this system seeks to represent. To emphasize this dual meaning, I have capitalized the letter "C." Zhu Xi further elucidated the symbolism conveyed in this passage using the following chart,[21] which I believe, supported by a long-standing commentary tradition on Ru metaphysics, provides us with a sufficient understanding of the original text.

By examining the chart, we can observe the creative sequence involving the Ultimate Limit, two modes, four images, and eight trigrams, as per the perspective of *Zhouyi*'s symbology. This sequence describes how the eight trigrams are generated from the *yin* and *yang* forms of the *yao* (爻), represented respectively by a broken and a solid line. Consequently, we understand that the relationships among these four layers of *Zhouyi*'s symbolism are fundamentally mathematical. The addition of the same geometric figure (either the broken or the solid line) in a different manner results in the formation of a new geometric figure. In other words,

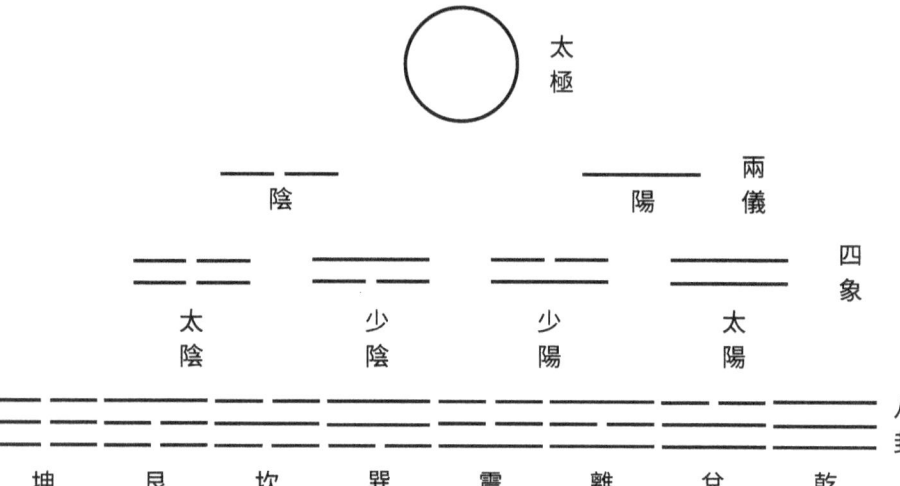

Trigrams formed from the Ultimate Limit and *yin/yang yao*

although creating the symbols requires time, their relationships are based on logic and are, therefore, nontemporal.

Given this understanding, it becomes intriguing to contemplate the ontological referents of these symbols. The "eight trigrams" allude to natural phenomena such as thunder, lightning, wind, rain, sun, moon, and so on. These eight fundamental elements are partially mentioned in the opening chapter of *Xici* and will be elaborated upon in another commentary titled "說卦" (Discourse on Trigrams) of the *Yijing*, which was likely composed during the same time period as the *Xici*. As suggested by the context, particularly the third paragraph of the passage quoted above, the "four images" most likely refer to the "four seasons," while the "two modes" signify heaven and earth, or more broadly, the *yin* and *yang* vital-energies.

An extremely important question to consider is what kind of creative relationship exists among the cosmic realities designated as *yin/yang* vital-energies, four seasons, and eight natural phenomena. Is it a relationship of cosmological succession, as emphasized in the *Dao De Jing*? The answer is no. First, cosmological succession is not among the primary concerns of Ru cosmology, as previously discussed. Second, the relationship among these pattern-principles of cosmic realities is synchronic, and therefore potentially nontemporal. This is evident since cosmic realities are perceived as de facto constantly occurring between heaven and earth, and within the course of four seasons. Accordingly, the relationship between "two modes" and "four images" is vertical rather than horizontal. The third crucial reason for this conclusion is that the *Zhouyi* symbols referring to the creative sequence among these layers of cosmic realities relate to each other mathematically, logically, and thus, nontemporally. This makes us more confident that the creative sequence among the ontological referents of these symbols also shares a similar relationship.

Drawing upon these considerations, I have concluded that the creative sequence among the pattern-principles of cosmic realities mentioned in this analyzed passage reflects ontological dependence rather than cosmological succession. This conclusion establishes a parallel between the Ru cosmology and the Greek-European Christian tradition on an ontological level. This tradition traces its roots to Plato's quest to understand the fundamental nature and order of the universe by delving into the logical structure of human "words," and is exemplified by the Neoplatonic concept of the "chain of being." Consequently, this conclusion provides a firm basis for comparing the Ru cosmological tradition with that of *creatio ex nihilo*. Moreover, it is important to note that the relationship of ontological dependence among these four layers of cosmic pattern-principles enhances our understanding of the enigmatic phrase "*sheng sheng* (birth birth)" mentioned in chapter 5 of part 1 of *Xici*. We now realize that this phrase conveys both its cosmological and ontological references: Cosmologically, the universe is a horizontal process of continual progress into novelty; ontologically, all cosmic realities depend on the creative power of cosmic pattern-principles, such that the process of cosmic creation can also be understood in a vertical sense.

To fully comprehend the Ru cosmology presented here, we must address a critical question: What is Ultimate Limit, and what is its ontological significance? Unfortunately, the *Xici* provides limited clues to the answers to these inquiries. The term "Ultimate Limit" is mentioned only once, with no further elaboration on its ontological reference. Nonetheless, based on my prior analyses, we can confidently assert two essential points regarding Ultimate Limit.

First, Ultimate Limit cannot be equated with the "formless thing" that blends everything together prior to the emergence of heaven and earth, as described in chapter 25 of the *Dao De Jing*. This is due to the nontemporal relationship between Ultimate Limit and the "two modes" (heaven/

earth or *yin/yang* vital-energies). Even after the creation of *yin/yang* vital-energies, the creative force of Ultimate Limit continues to operate within them. If Ultimate Limit were to be understood as a "formless thing," it would be challenging to affirm that this formless entity remains active after the formation of *yin/yang* vital-energies, which permeate the entire universe. Additionally, characterizing Ultimate Limit as originally "formless" has limited value for Ru anthropology. As previously analyzed, Ru anthropology does not espouse Laozi's renunciatory approach of "nonaction" without qualification.

Second, while the ontological referent of Ultimate Limit remains elusive in the text, we do know that the term encapsulates the distinct Ru effort to discern a singular pattern-principle amid the ever-changing cosmic realities. This effort aims to elucidate the origin and order of these realities. Furthermore, we understand that the relationship between Ultimate Limit and the cosmic realities is one of ontological dependence rather than cosmological succession. Consequently, while it is uncertain whether the Ru metaphysical tradition, which originated from this seminal Ru text, shares comparable insights into its *creatio ex nihilo* counterpart, we can anticipate that the Ru tradition offers some ontological considerations that align with the Western philosophical and theological traditions. Chapter 12 of part 1 provides an essential example of this comparability by addressing the issue of the asymmetrical relationship between ultimate reality and derived realities, a subject thoroughly examined in the *creatio ex nihilo* tradition:

> The Master said: "Writing does not fully convey speech. Speech does not fully convey meaning. Can we then not fully know the sages' meaning?" The Master said: "The sages established images to convey all meanings; set up hexagrams to convey truth and point out falsity; added texts to explain speeches; altered and penetrated into things in order to bring benefits; drummed and danced to convey what is numinous and wonderful."
>
> Qian and Kun, do they not constitute the core for the Change? When Qian and Kun form ranks, the Change stands in their midst, but if Qian and Kun were abolished, there would be no way that the Change could manifest itself. And if the Change could not manifest itself, this would mean that Qian and Kun might almost be at the point of extinction![22]

The first paragraph of this chapter addresses an epistemological concern regarding conveying truth and meaning. The second paragraph, building upon the ontological primacy of Ultimate Limit over "two modes," intriguingly suggests that epistemologically, the two modes of Qian and Kun take precedence over Ultimate Limit, the highest pattern-principle in the "Change." In essence, the relationship between Ultimate Limit and the two modes is doubly asymmetrical. On one hand, Ultimate Limit is ontologically superior to the two modes and other derived cosmic realities. On the other hand, our understanding of Ultimate Limit depends solely on our knowledge of the two modes and other determinants of derived cosmic realities.[23]

This understanding sheds light on my translation of the Chinese character 神 (*shen*). In chapter 5 of part 1, the *Xici* asserts that "what cannot be fathomed by *yin* and *yang* is 神," and in other places, it frequently depicts the inexhaustible and all-encompassing creative power of the cosmic *Dao* as 神 (for instance, in chapters 9 and 11 of part 1; chapter 5 of part 2). Drawing on the above analysis of the relationship among different pattern-principles, all of which are referred to as "Dao" by the *Xici* because they are "beyond shape" in some sense, I conclude that the reason the power of Ultimate Limit can be characterized as 神 is that its boundless creative potency surpasses what the fundamental human concepts of *yin* and *yang* can disclose about the ceaselessly generative cosmic process. Due to the ineffability and fecundity of Ultimate Limit as the preeminent Ru pattern-principle of cosmic creativity,[24] I have rendered 神 as "what is numinous and wonderful."

EXPLORING THE RELATIONSHIP BETWEEN ULTIMATE LIMIT AND *CREATIO EX NIHILO*

Based on the previous analyses, we may hypothesize that, with further consideration, Ultimate Limit could be interpreted by later commentators of the *Xici* as a version of *creatio ex nihilo* in the Ru cosmology. We will discover that this is, in fact, the case in the commentaries of Wang Bi and Hang Kangbo, which we will examine later. However, is there any indication that the character 無 (nonbeing), used in this Ru text, can convey a sense of "ontological unconditionality" similar to what "ex nihilo" denotes in the Greek-European Christian tradition?

In chapter 4 of part 1, the *Xici* states,

> What the *Book of Change* teaches comprehends all of heaven and earth's transformations, and it never errs. It fulfills the intricate courses of the

myriad things, without overlooking any of them. It fathoms the *Dao* of day and night with penetrative understanding. Therefore, what is numinous and wonderful is without locality (無方), and the Change has no shaped bodies (無體) to cling to.[25]

Here, the character 無 refers to the metaphysical, nonshaped feature of the cosmic *Dao* that the book of *Zhouyi* tries to grasp, and can be understood more specifically as connoting the abstract, yet all-inclusive effectivity of cosmic pattern-principles in contrast to concrete shaped cosmic realities that these pattern-principles regulate and harmonize.

In addition, chapter 9 of part 1 teaches:

> The *Book of Change* has neither thought (無思) nor contrived action (無為). It is tranquil and motionless. However, once affected, it penetrates all causes under heaven. If the *Book of Change* doesn't derive from what is utmost numinous and wonderful under heaven, what else can achieve this?[26]

This passage suggests that the 無 aspect of the book of *Zhouyi* signifies the attainment of a spiritual state by the author, who, through great intellectual and practical effort, has grasped the most significant pattern-principles of cosmic realities. This spiritual state enables the author to align perfectly with the workings of the cosmos and respond authentically to its realities without contrived or inauthentic thought or action. Therefore, the character 無 here can be interpreted as referring to the spiritual adeptness of a Ru virtuoso, who can respond spontaneously and appropriately to cosmic realities.

Based on these representative chapters in the *Xici* where 無 is mentioned, it is evident that, first, the character's usage differs from that of Laozi's as it is based on distinctively Ruist cosmological and anthropological insights. Second, none of these uses imply a meaning similar to the "ontological unconditionality" of *ex nihilo* in the Greek-European tradition of creation. It is clear that if the creativity of Ultimate Limit is to be construed as a form of *creatio ex nihilo*, the Ru tradition needs further reflection and more powerful conceptual tools. In the following sections of this chapter, I will attempt to illustrate how this process unfolds by interpreting a cluster of cosmological texts, such as *Huainanzi*, *The Weft Book of the Change* (緯書), Zheng Xuan's commentary on *The Weft Book of the Change*, Wang Bi's commentaries on the *Dao De Jing* and the *Yijing*, as well as Han Kangbo's commentary on the *Yijing*.

Converging Ruism into Daoism: Cosmology from *Zhuangzi* to *Huainanzi*

In the above analysis of Laozi's cosmology, I presented a generalized diagram of its cosmological sequence like this:

"Nonbeing" (*Dao*) ➡ One (the undifferentiated whole of "being") ➡ Two (*yin/yang* Vital-Energies; Heaven and Earth) ➡ Three (Heaven, Earth, and Human Beings) ➡ the Myriad Things.

We also specify that in this diagram, "nonbeing" could refer to a great vacuum that occupies space and time but lacks material substance to fill it. We can therefore adjust the diagram of the sequence this way:

Dao ➡ "Nonbeing" (great vacuum) ➡ One (the undifferentiated whole of "being") ➡ Two (*yin/yang* Vital-Energies; Heaven and Earth) ➡ Three (Heaven, Earth, and Human Beings) ➡ the Myriad Things.

The analysis of Laozi's cosmology above reveals that the function of *Dao* is present in each stage of the sequence, but its existence in the "nonbeing" and "undifferentiated whole" stages is considered more powerful and authentic. Additionally, Laozi believes that the cosmic *Dao* constantly returns to itself in a cyclic manner. Therefore, the proper approach to self-cultivation and statecraft in the human world, according to Laozi, is to retreat, to refrain, and ultimately, to return.

In a comparative fashion, I will demonstrate the Ru cosmology found in the *Xici* of the *Classic of Change*, which focuses on the ontological dependence between various levels of cosmic realities. Given its primarily vertical emphasis, the diagram needs to be reconfigured as the following:

Ultimate Limit
⬇
... ➡ Two Modes (*yin/yang* Vital-Energies, or Heaven and Earth) ➡ ...
⬇
... ➡ Four Images (Four Seasons) ➡ ...
⬇
... ➡ Eight Trigrams (Thunder, Lightning, Wind, Rain, Sun, Moon, etc.) ➡ ...

⬇

... ➡ Human Beings and the Myriad Things ➡ ...

The Ruist Ontological Cosmology in the *Xici* of *Yijing*

In this Ru cosmological diagram, everything below Ultimate Limit operates in a periodic and perpetual manner, like the changing of the four seasons. The upper four levels of cosmic realities are referred to as "pattern-principles" or "*Dao*," which are believed to provide structure and existence to concrete cosmic realities, including human beings and all other things. Unlike Laozi's cosmology, Ruist cosmology does not speculate on the temporal origin of the cosmos and does not view the function of the cosmic *Dao* as being constantly recursive. Instead, the most prominent feature is the perpetual evolution of cosmic realities toward novelty, with the primary goal of Ruism being to facilitate the continuous flourishing of human society on its own terms and in harmony with the surrounding cosmos, based on human understanding of these pattern-principles.

It is clear that when viewed as a holistic system that contains both cosmological and anthropological constituents, the *Dao De Jing* and the *Xici* of the *Classic of Change* have very different orientations. However, perhaps due to the abstract nature of its nontemporal and ontological features, the Ru cosmology in the *Xici* has not been fully understood until the interpretations of Wang Bi and Han Kangbo, who used their distinctive term "nonbeing (無)" to explain Ultimate Limit after the Han dynasty. As a result, the mainstream ancient Chinese cosmology from the *Xici* until Wang Bi was actually Daoist, although the influence of the *Classic of Change* and its Ruist commentary coexisted. During this mainly Daoist period, cosmologists attempted to merge the Ru discourse on Ultimate Limit into Laozi's cosmology, resulting in a variety of hybrid cosmologies. Ultimate Limit could be interpreted as one stage of Laozi's cosmological sequence or could be explained using terms from Laozi's text. In the following, I will use three texts as examples to illustrate this situation: *Zhuangzi*, the *Lü Annals of Spring and Autumn* (also known as the Annals of Lü Buwei), and *Huainanzi*.

Zhuangzi and the *Lü Annals of Spring and Autumn*

In the *Xici*, Ultimate Limit is regarded as the ultimate ontological foundation for all beings, which in the view of the Ru commentator (probably Confucius himself) exist and arise together in the spatial realm defined by heaven and earth, and in the temporal sphere defined by an endless periodic course of the four seasons. Since this cosmological view does not concern itself with the temporal origin of the cosmos, for those who struggle to reconcile this idea with an ontological mindset, Ultimate Limit may be seen as a placeholder term encompassing all realities between heaven and earth. From the perspective of the *Dao De Jing*, this means that Ultimate Limit cannot exist prior to the emergence of heaven and earth and can only be situated in a later stage of Laozi's aforementioned cosmological sequence.

This possible interpretation of Ultimate Limit is exemplified in the text of *Zhuangzi*:

> This is the *Dao*: it is true and reliable, yet it has neither action nor shape. Its manifestations may be handed down, but its essence cannot be received. Its manifestations may be apprehended, but its essence cannot be seen. It has its root and ground of existence in itself. Before there were heaven and earth, from of old, there It was, securely existing. From It came the mysterious existences of ghosts, from It came the mysterious existence of the supreme deity. It produced heaven; It produced earth. It was beyond (or before)[27] the Ultimate Limit (太極之先), and yet cannot be considered high; It was below the six directions of all space, and yet cannot be considered deep. It was produced before heaven and earth, and yet cannot be considered to have existed long; It was older than the highest antiquity, and yet cannot be considered old.[28]

In this quotation, "heaven and earth," as in the *Dao De Jing*, is believed to be produced later in time by the generative power of the cosmic *Dao*. Additionally, Ultimate Limit is mentioned alongside the "six directions of all space," and is also viewed as being under the productive power of the cosmic *Dao*. Clearly, Ultimate Limit is treated as a term that encapsulates all formed realities between heaven and earth, which are produced by the cosmic *Dao*. Thus, if we were to fit Zhuangzi's cosmological sequence into the original *Dao De Jing*'s sequence, it would be represented as follows:[29]

Dao ➡ Nonbeing (great vacuum) ➡ One (the undifferentiated whole of being-as-becoming) ➡ Ultimate Limit, which encapsulates the Two (*yin/yang* Vital-Energies; Heaven and Earth) ➡ Three (Heaven, Earth, and Human Beings) ➡ the Myriad Things.

Besides the *Zhuangzi*, an alternative way to interpret Ultimate Limit in *Dao De Jing*'s terms is represented by another text compiled in the late Warring States period (475–221 BCE), the *Lü Annals of Spring and Autumn*.

Two passages from the "Great Music (大樂)" chapter of this text describe the concept of the "Ultimate One (太一)":

> The origin of music lies in the distant past: it is born of measurement and founded by the Ultimate One. The Ultimate One brought forth the two modes; the two modes brought forth *yin* and *yang*. *Yin* and *yang* metamorphose and transform, the one rising, the other falling, and then, they join together in a perfect pattern. Spinning formlessly and pulsing shapelessly, if dispersed, they rejoin, and if joined, they disperse again. This is called the Constant of *Tian* (天常). Heaven and Earth turn like the wheel of a carriage. Reaching the end, they begin again; reaching their limit, they revert again, everything fitting the overall scheme. Sun, moon, planets, and constellations: some move fast, others slow, all in the completion of their movements. The four seasons alternately arise. Some hot, others cold; in some, the days are short; in others, long; sometimes they are soft, the other times hard. The myriad things that emerged were created by the Ultimate One and transformed by *yin* and *yang*. . . .
>
> Great Music brings delight, enjoyment, and pleasure to ruler and subjects, father and son, and old and young alike. Delight and enjoyment are born of equilibrium, and equilibrium is born of *Dao*. It is the nature of the *Dao* that when we look for it, it is invisible, and when we listen for it, it is inaudible, for it cannot be given form. Whoever is aware of the visible in the invisible, the audible in the inaudible, and the form of the formless almost knows it. The *Dao* is the supreme instance of the seminal essence, for it cannot be given shape or name. Forced to give it a name, I would call it "Ultimate One."[30]

This text clearly shows influences from both the *Dao De Jing* and the *Xici*. While it doesn't use the term "Ultimate Limit," the description of the "Ultimate One" as the generator of the "two modes" is reminiscent of the verses about Ultimate Limit in the *Xici*. Additionally, the words used to describe the "Ultimate One" are very similar to Laozi's depiction of the second stage of *Dao De Jing*'s cosmogony: Ultimate One is formless and shapeless (渾渾沌沌); even though it is invisible, inaudible, and without any status, there is still something there which contains its "essence (精)." This interpretation places Ultimate Limit one stage earlier than in

Zhuangzi's case. Therefore, if we use the *Dao De Jing*'s sequence as our basic framework, the cosmogony in the *Lü Annals of Spring and Autumn* can be represented as follows:

Dao ➡ One or Ultimate Limit as renamed by "Ultimate One" (the undifferentiated whole of being-as-becoming) ➡ Two (*yin/yang* Vital-Energies; Heaven and Earth) ➡ Three (Heaven, Earth, and Human Beings) ➡ the Myriad Things.

Given that Ultimate Limit is understood as the formless totality of being-as-becoming prior to any further determination, the *Lü Annals of Spring and Autumn* can be regarded as a precursor to the interpretation of Ultimate Limit in relation to "primordial vital-energy (元氣)," which will be extensively explored in the cosmologies of the Han dynasty.

After examining the interpretations of "Ultimate Limit" in the *Zhuangzi* and the *Lü Annals of Spring and Autumn*, I must conclude that neither aligns with the term's basic semantic orientation in the Ruist *Xici*. While the Ru text does not speculate about the cosmos's beginning before the existence of heaven and earth, the ontological priority of Ultimate Limit over all derived realities means it can be reconciled with any narrative about the cosmos's temporal beginning. Thus, it is ontologically incorrect for the *Zhuangzi* to treat Ultimate Limit as merely a cap name for all formed realities between heaven and earth and to suggest that there are cosmological stages temporally prior to Ultimate Limit.

On the other hand, I previously mentioned that the idea of the "formless thing" (possibly construed by the *Lü Annals* as the "primordial vital-energy"), as understood in *Dao De Jing*'s cosmology, is not suitable for Ru purposes. It cannot be viewed as a prior reality shared by all derived realities, nor does it offer moral benefits to Ruist ethics, which emphasizes the value of human efforts for manifesting cosmic creativity. As a result, the *Zhuangzi* and the *Lü Annals* attempt to merge some Ru elements, particularly the concept of Ultimate Limit, into the *Dao De Jing*'s Daoist cosmology, but they lose the distinct ontological feature of Ultimate Limit in the process.

Huainanzi

The *Huainanzi*, compiled early in the Han dynasty, elaborates on the theoretical tendency of the middle and late Warring States texts analyzed above. The cosmology of the *Huainanzi* is best illustrated in these two paragraphs:

> When Heaven and Earth were yet unformed, all was ascending and flying, diving and delving. Thus it is called the Grand Inception (太昭). *Dao* produced nebulous vacuum (虛廓). The nebulous vacuum produced space-time (宇宙); space-time produced vital-energy. A boundary divided the vital-energy. That which was pure and bright spread out to form Heaven; that which was heavy and turbid congealed to form Earth. It is easy for that which is pure and subtle to converge but difficult for the heavy and turbid to congeal. Therefore, Heaven was completed first; Earth was fixed afterward. The conjoined essences of Heaven and Earth produced *yin* and *yang*. The supersessive essences of *yin* and *yang* caused the four seasons. The scattered essences of the four seasons created the myriad things.[31]
>
> Of old, in the time before there was Heaven and Earth: there were only images without shape. All was obscure and dark, vague and unclear, shapeless and formless, and no one knows its gateway. There were two spirits, born in murkiness, one that establishes Heaven and the other that constructed Earth. So vast! No one knows where their ultimate end (終極) is. So broad, No one knows where they finally stop. Therefore, they differentiated into the *yin* and *yang* and separated into the eight cardinal directions (八極). The firm and the mild formed each other; the myriad things thereupon took shape. The turbid vital-energy became creatures; the refined vital-energy became humans.[32]

The stage preceding the existence of heaven and earth is referred to as the "Great Inception (太昭)," which includes three minor stages: nebulous vacuum, space-time, and the primordial vital-energy. The *Huainanzi*'s cosmological sequence is more explicit and organized than Laozi's ambiguous argument in chapters 40 and 42 of the *Dao De Jing*. Still, let's use a diagram to illustrate the *Huainanzi*'s sequence:

Dao ➡ Great Inception (Nebulous Vacuum) ➡ Space-Time ➡ Primordial Vital-Energy) ➡ Heaven/Earth and *yin/yang* Vital-Energies ➡ Four Seasons ➡ Human Beings and the Myriad Things.

What is the position of Ultimate Limit in this sequence? In another chapter, the *Huainanzi* says:

All resemble their forms and evoke responses according to their classes. The burning mirror takes fire from the sun; the square receptacle takes dew from the moon. Of all the things between Heaven and Earth, even a skilled astrologer cannot master all their techniques. Even a hand that can hold minutely tiny and indistinct things cannot grasp a beam of light. However, from what is within the palm of one's hand, one can trace (correlative) categories to beyond Ultimate Limit. Thus, the reason that one can set up (these implements) and produce water and fire is because of the mutually responsive movement of the same *yin* or *yang* vital-energy (陰陽同氣相動).[33]

In this chapter, a law of mutual resonance among all things in the world is presented. The text states that this law extends even to the realm of reality that is "beyond Ultimate Limit (太極之上)," immediately bringing to mind similar language used in the quoted passage from the *Zhuangzi*: "It (Dao) was beyond (or before) the Ultimate Limit, and yet could not be considered high; It was below the six directions of all space, and yet could not be considered deep." This suggests that Ultimate Limit is seen as a term encompassing all formed realities between Heaven and Earth, and according to the *Huainanzi*, the law of mutual resonance applies to anything within this realm of "Ultimate Limit."

Taking this into consideration, we can illustrate the *Huainanzi* cosmological sequence as follows, which is clearly similar to that of *Zhuangzi*:

Dao ➡ Great Inception (Nebulous Vacuum) ➡ Space-Time ➡ Primordial Vital-Energy) ➡ Ultimate Limit, which encapsulates Heaven/Earth and *yin/yang* Vital-Energies ➡ Four Seasons ➡ Human Beings and the Myriad Things.

We can further support the idea of Ultimate Limit in the *Zhuangzi* by examining the concept of the "No Limit" feature of "Nebulous Vacuum" in the *Huainanzi*. This confirms the similarity between the two texts in their understanding of Ultimate Limit:

Contrast these with the Perfected: they eat exactly what suits their bellies, they wear precisely what fits their forms. They roam by relaxing their bodies. They act by matching their genuine responses to the situation. Having left the empire, they do not covet it; if entrusted with the myriad things, they do not profit from it. They rest in the space of great vacuum (大廓之宇), roam in the field of No Limit (無極), ascend the constellation of Tai Huang, and ride the one of Tai Yi. They play with Heaven and Earth in the palms of their hands.[34]

Here, the *Huainanzi* characterizes the "space of great vacuum" as "No Limit," which corresponds to the "nebulous vacuum" and "space-time" stages in its cosmology, and is considered to be prior to the existence of Heaven and Earth. The "nebulous vacuum" is seen as without limit because it is formless. All realities between heaven and earth can be encapsulated as "Ultimate Limit" because they are all formed. Therefore, No Limit and Ultimate Limit correspond to successive stages of the *Huainanzi*'s cosmogony, which is essentially a *Dao De Jing* Daoist one. Interestingly, the passage uses the cosmological discourse on No Limit and Ultimate Limit to argue for the superiority of pro-Daoist views on human self-cultivation and statecraft over Ruist ones. This mode of argumentation also resonates with the use of "nonbeing" and "being" in the case of the *Dao De Jing*.

To conclude, the aforementioned texts such as *Zhuangzi*, *Lü Annals of Spring and Autumn*, and *Huainanzi* attempted to integrate the Ruist concept of Ultimate Limit into the Daoist cosmology of the *Dao De Jing*. Their interpretations either depict Ultimate Limit as the umbrella term for all formed realities between heaven and earth or as the formless entirety of primordial vital-energy. Regrettably, none of these interpretations did justice to the unique ontological trait of the Ruist Ultimate Limit.

The Transition by Zheng Xuan's Commentary of Qian Zao Du

After the *Huainanzi*, another significant text for understanding how the ancient Chinese cosmological tradition gradually shifted from the *Dao De Jing*'s emphasis on cosmological succession to the *Xici*'s emphasis on ontological dependence is the *Qian Zao Du* (乾鑿度, *An Investigation into the Hexagram of Qian*). In my opinion, it was Zheng Xuan (鄭玄, 127–200 CE) who paved the way for Wang Bi to anchor the interpretation of the *Xici*'s Ru cosmology in an ontological orientation through his commentary on this text and the *Xici*.[35]

THE COSMOLOGY OF THE *QIAN ZAO DU*

The *Qian Zao Du* is one of the "weft books (緯書)" that were likely compiled during the later period of the Han dynasty (25–220 CE). It belongs to a particular type of commentary on the *Classic of Change* that relies on the symbology, including numbers and images, to create an all-encompassing "correlative cosmology"[36] for divination and explanation purposes. Due to the magical nature of correlative cosmology, these "weft books" were generally not accepted as mainstream Ruist teachings by Ru scholars after the Han dynasty. However, for having addressed various scientific, geological, and astronomical issues specific to their time, they are a valuable resource for contemporary scholars studying ancient Chinese thought. The *Qian Zao Du*'s cosmological model is particularly significant for our purposes.

As the *Qian Zao Du* is a text based on the symbology of the *Classic of Change*, it comes as no surprise to see direct quotes from the *Xici* in the *Qian Zao Du*:

> Confucius said the Change begins from Ultimate Limit (易始於太極). Ultimate Limit is divided into two, and so heaven and earth are generated. Heaven and earth have their due measures in spring, autumn, winter and summer, so the four seasons are generated. Every season has its division of *yin* and *yang*, the firm and the mild, so eight trigrams are generated. After eight trigrams are in line, the images of thunder, wind, water, fire, mountain and marshlands are established. Now, the Way of heaven and earth is set. . . . The vital-energies in eight trigrams are completed, and then, . . . a myriad of things are generated according to their classes.[37]

We observe that this paragraph is a meticulous rephrasing of chapter 11 in part 1 of the *Xici*. Specifically, its ontological references to significant terms such as "two," "four," and "eight trigrams" align with what I have previously determined through an intratextual analysis of the *Xici*.

However, the distinct cosmological perspective of *Qian Zao Du* becomes apparent when the text raises the question of the temporal origin of Qian and Kun, a matter that is not addressed in the *Xici*. The *Qian Zao Du* asks the question this way:

> Of old, the sages followed *yin* and *yang*, investigated ebb and flow, and established Qian and Kun in order to regulate Heaven and Earth. Because

the shaped realities are generated from the shapeless, where do Qian and Kun come from?

And the *Qian Zao Du*'s answer is this:

> Therefore, there are (stages of) Great Change (太易), Great Initial (太初), Great Inception (太始), and Great Plainness (太素). In the stage of Great Change, no vital-energy is seen. In the stage of Great Initial, vital-energy begins. In the stage of Great Inception, shape (形) begins. In the stage of Great Plainness, matter (质) begins.
>
> Vital-energy, shape and matter are there, but are yet to be separated. Therefore, it is called the formless and shapeless (渾淪, *hunlun*). The term *Hunlun* means that the myriad things are blended together and thus are not yet to be distinguished. Look, but it is invisible; listen, but it is inaudible; search, but it is intangible. It is therefore called "the Change (易)." In the Change, there is neither shape nor boundary.
>
> One is the beginning of the formation of shapes. What is light and clear ascends to become heaven; what is turbid and heavy descends to become earth. Things have their beginning, maturation, and death, so three strokes form the trigram of Qian. Qian and Kun are always formed in tandem, and *yin* and *yang* are needed to generate things; therefore, the doubling of the three strokes (trigrams) generates six strokes, and they are all the hexagrams.[38]

It is fascinating to compare the quoted text with previous quotations. As we have seen, the opening words of the *Qian Zao Du* echo chapter 11 in part 1 of the *Xici*. However, while the *Xici* posits layers of pattern-principles to explain the existence and order of changing realities, the relationships among which are logical and nontemporal, the *Qian Zao Du* takes a different direction in interpreting this *Xici* chapter. According to the *Qian Zao Du*, the phrase "There is Ultimate Limit in the Change (易有太極)" means that there is a cosmological stage prior to the existence of heaven and earth. This stage is known as either "Change," Ultimate Limit, or "One," and is divided into three minor stages: Great Initial, Great Inception, and Great Plainness. In other words, the addition of these three minor stages is equivalent to the stage of "Change," Ultimate Limit, or "One," which is described as "formless and shapeless (渾淪, *hunlun*)." Before this stage of *Hunlun*, Change, Ultimate Limit, or One, there is another, more original stage called the "Great Change," which lacks any actual substance and can be envisioned as a vast vacuum situated at the beginning of the cosmos.

Still, let's use a diagram to illustrate this cosmological sequence:

Great Change ➡ Change, Ultimate Limit, *Hunlun*, or One: (Great Initial ➡ Great Inception ➡ Great Plainness) ➡ Heaven and Earth, *yin/yang* Vital-Energies ➡ Four Seasons ➡ Eight Trigrams ➡ Human Beings and the Myriad Things.

In comparison to the following cosmological sequence of the *Lü Annals of Spring and Autumn*,

Dao ➡ One or Ultimate Limit as renamed by "Ultimate One" (the undifferentiated whole of being-as-becoming) ➡ Two (*yin/yang* Vital-Energies; Heaven and Earth) ➡ Three (Heaven, Earth, and Human Beings) ➡ the Myriad Things,

the similarity with *Qian Zao Du* is that the *Qian Zao Du* equally interprets Ultimate Limit as the primordial vital-energy that exists before heaven and earth but has not yet obtained any separable determination.

Compared to the sequence presented in the *Huainanzi*,

Dao ➡ Great Inception (Nebulous Vacuum ➡ Space-Time ➡ Primordial Vital-Energy) ➡ Ultimate Limit, which encapsulates Heaven/Earth and *yin/yang* Vital-Energies ➡ Four Seasons ➡ Human Beings and the Myriad Things,

the *Qian Zao Du* places Ultimate Limit differently, as the *Huainanzi* has Ultimate Limit follow the stage of primordial vital-energy which is equivalent to *Hunlun* in the *Qian Zao Du*. However, the *Qian Zao Du* draws clear inspiration from the *Huainanzi*'s concepts of "Nebulous Vacuum" and "Space-Time" in two ways. First, it combines them into the "Great Change," which precedes the stage of "Change" and represents a cosmic stage where no basic material exists yet. Second, the *Qian Zao Du*'s elaboration on the idea of primordial vital-energy is more nuanced than that of the *Huainanzi*, as it includes three minor stages. This attention to both the "shape" and "matter" aspects of the cosmic vital-energy adds texture to the idea of basic cosmic material, and explains why this stage is called *Hunlun*, meaning "formless and shapeless."

Based on these comparisons, and given that the *Qian Zao Du* was compiled around the same time as the *Huainanzi*, it appears that while

180 Sheng Sheng *as* Generatio ex Nihilo

the *Qian Zao Du* is a commentary on the Ruist *Xici*, its cosmology remains fundamentally Daoist, emphasizing the sequence of cosmological succession among cosmic realities.

ZHENG XUAN'S COMMENTARY ON THE *QIAN ZAO DU* AND HIS UNDERSTANDING OF ULTIMATE LIMIT

Zheng Xuan was one of the most important commentators of the Ru tradition during the Han dynasty. In his commentary on the *Classic of Change*, Zheng made a major contribution by shifting the focus of the ancient Chinese cosmological tradition from Laozi's emphasis on cosmological succession to the ontological dependence of the *Xici*. However, it should be noted that Zheng's thought was still greatly influenced by Daoism. Therefore, Zheng can be considered a transitional figure between the Daoist cosmological tradition and the Ru ontology of Wang Bi and Han Kangbo.

One example of the transitional nature of Zheng Xuan's thought is his interpretation of Ultimate Limit, which is still evidently Daoist. In his commentary on chapter 11 in part 1 of the *Xici*, Zheng defines Ultimate Limit as "the vital-energy that is pure, harmonious, and yet to be divided."[39] Likewise, in his commentary on "Confucius said the Change begins from Ultimate Limit" in the *Qian Zao Du*, Zheng defines Ultimate Limit as "the time when images of vital-energy (氣象) have not yet been divided, which is the starting point for the derivation of heaven and earth."[40] Therefore, Zheng still interprets Ultimate Limit as undifferentiated primordial vital-energy, similarly to the *Lü Annals of Spring and Autumn* and the *Qian Zao Du*. However, when he comments on the minor stages listed in the *Qian Zao Du*, his thought begins to tilt toward the ontological Ru tradition rooted in the *Xici*, showing some distinctive features.

For "In the stage of the Great Change, no vital-energy is seen," Zheng Xuan says, "This is named 'Great Change' because there is nothing, and only total quiescence remains (寂然無物)."[41]

For "In the stage of Great Initial, this is the beginning of vital-energy," Zheng Xuan says, "'Great Initial' is where the primordial vital-energy (元氣) derives from. Since nothing exists and only total quiescence remains in the Great Change, how can it generate this Great Initial? The Great Initial actually generates of its own accord all of a sudden (忽然而自生)."[42]

For "it is called the formless and shapeless (*hunlun*)," Zheng Xuan says, "Although there are these three beginning stages, they are not yet distinguished from one another. This is what Laozi means by, 'Before heaven and earth existed, there was something that is a complete blend.'"[43]

For "Look, but it is invisible; listen, but it is inaudible; search, but it is intangible. It is therefore called the Change. In the Change, there is neither shape nor boundary," Zheng Xuan says, "This means, during the time of the shapeless Great Change, the universe is like being contained in a great vacuum (虛豁). It is silent and vast, and thus cannot be visible, audible or tangible. This is what the *Xici* means by, 'The Change has no shaped bodies (無體) to cling to.'"[44]

Obviously, Zheng Xuan still interpreted the stage of *Hunlun* mentioned in the *Qian Zao Du* according to Laozi's concept of "something that is a complete blend." However, concerning the relationship between the various stages before the existence of heaven and earth mentioned in the *Qian Zao Du*, we can discern some intriguing aspects of Zheng's thinking.

First, Zheng Xuan believed that the stage of Great Change, which is viewed as a vast vacuum existing before any cosmic substance is present, plays no role in generating the stage of Great Initial from which the primordial vital-energy is derived. According to Zheng, the stage of Great Initial, which refers to the actual existence of vital-energy as the fundamental cosmic substance from which all myriad things are formed, can generate "of its own accord," regardless of whether there is a temporally prior stage or not. This is evident from Zheng's response to the question of how Great Change can generate Great Initial, as seen in the second quotation above.

Second, in considering the significance of the term "Great Change" in generating cosmic stages, Zheng Xuan's repeated use of the term suggests that he still finds it to be meaningful. However, what is most intriguing about his usage is that he no longer treats Great Change as a vacuum that existed prior to the stage of *Hunlun*. Rather, he interprets "great vacuum" as a feature within *Hunlun* itself, which helps to explain the formless and shapeless nature of primordial vital-energy. Zheng's citation of the verse "Change has no shaped bodies to cling to" from the *Xici* underscores the relationship between Great Change and *Hunlun*. This suggests that Zheng no longer viewed the relationship between "non-being (無)" and "being (有)" as two distinct cosmic stages, as was the view of the *Dao De Jing*. Instead, he saw them as two different features within the same cosmic stage of *Hunlun*, which in turn give rise to a distinctive ontological relationship in accordance with the Ruist way of thinking.

Another commentary on the verse "The Change has no shaped bodies to cling to" in the *Xici* confirms Zheng Xuan's ontological interpretation of the relationship between "nonbeing" and "being" in accordance with Ruist philosophy:

> *Dao* has no locality (無方), while *yin/yang* vital-energies have their localities (有方). *Dao* has no shaped body (無體), and yet *yin/yang* vital-energies have their bodies (有體). Because it has no locality, the *Dao* generates things and can be counted as what is numinous and wonderful (神). Because it has no body, it can use numbers to make changes. What has locality is fixed in an upper or lower place, what has a shaped body is greater or smaller, and these are just things (物). However, what is called *Dao* does not stay away from things. This is because there is no thing which is not a manifestation of *Dao* (物無乎非道). Therefore, *Dao* is not *yin/yang* (非即陰陽), while it is not distant from *yin/yang* either (非離陰陽). The *Dao* is that by which the myriad things are generated during the constant succession of *yin* and *yang* vital-energies. To imitate heaven but not earth, to imitate *yin* but not *yang*, this is not the way that the myriad things will follow.[45]

This interpretation of the relationship between *Dao* and concrete things is strictly ontological, according to Zheng Xuan's understanding. Cosmic changes occur through the succession of *yin* and *yang* vital-energies, which are a manifestation of *Dao*'s generative power. However, this generative power transcends any concrete cosmic changes and can therefore be characterized as a form of "nonbeing," since, ontologically speaking, *Dao* exists prior to any posterior realities.

In this way, Zheng's conception of *Dao* aligns with the Ruist *Xici* tradition, which sees *Dao* as the cosmic pattern-principle that brings order and existence to cosmic realities. Its relationship with derived realities is logical, ontological, and vertical rather than temporal, cosmological, and horizontal.

Given this understanding of Zheng Xuan's thought, it is worth considering what led him to shift from Laozi's cosmology toward the ontology of *Xici*. Specifically, what motivated him to move from a focus on cosmic processes to an emphasis on ontology? The key question that seems to have triggered Zheng's transition was how the Great Change, which is characterized by the absence of anything, could generate the Great Initial, which is the beginning of all things. Zheng found it difficult to explain how cosmic stuff could emerge from a vacuum where nothing yet existed. In my view, the answer to this question reflects Zheng's fundamental rethinking of Laozi's cosmology under the influence of *Xici* ontology.

Laozi's cosmological sequence was diagramed above as such:

Dao ➡ "Nonbeing" (great vacuum) ➡ One (the undifferentiated whole of "being") ➡ Two (*yin/yang* Vital-Energies; Heaven and Earth) ➡ Three (Heaven, Earth, and Human Beings) ➡ the Myriad Things.

As I noted earlier, while the cosmic sequence may begin with a stage of "nonbeing," in which nothing can be found, the function of *Dao* permeates all stages, maintaining consistency and persistence throughout. In other words, it is *Dao*, rather than the stage of nonbeing itself, that creates all the cosmic stages. Simply positing a stage of pure nothing as the first cosmic stage does not provide a sufficient explanation for the *Dao*'s inexhaustible generative power. This is especially true since, regardless of whether the cosmos has a temporal beginning or not, the *Dao* is always generating.

Despite the challenges posed by positing a stage of nonbeing, we can understand why Laozi includes this stage as well as that of the formless One. Laozi's purported cosmic pattern of "reversion is the action of *Dao*" suggests that the cosmic process is cyclical and constantly returns to its root in nonbeing before moving forward again. This cycle provides the ultimate cosmological justification for Laozi's anthropological ideas, which emphasize the renunciative method of human self-cultivation and minimalist governance in the statecraft.

The *Xici* provides a Ruist perspective that offers several reasons to reject certain key ideas in the *Dao De Jing*. First, merely positing a beginning cosmic stage of pure nothing does not sufficiently demonstrate the eternally generative power of *Dao*. Even from Laozi's perspective, regardless of whether the cosmos has a temporal beginning or not, the de facto existing cosmic realities are always dependent upon the power of *Dao*. Thus, it is a discernible pattern of human thought that any philosophical discourse on the creative power of ultimate reality will ultimately rest upon the idea of "ontological dependence," rather than "cosmological succession." The former idea contains a greater variety of possibilities for the latter and, in this sense, conditions it, making itself more ultimate. This is evidenced by the intellectual history of *creatio ex nihilo*, and we can find similar evidence in the cosmological traditions of ancient Chinese thought. Zheng Xuan's suspension of the generative power of the stage of "Great Change" is an impressive case in point.

Second, positing a beginning cosmic stage of pure nothing and assuming a corresponding cyclic cosmic process may seem dogmatic if Laozi's propositions are meant to capture the general principle of cosmic changes beyond what empirical study of the cosmos can tell us. Even modern science struggles to investigate whether there was any cosmic status before the Big Bang based on empirical evidence. Therefore, it is more reasonable to explore the pattern-principles within existing cosmic realities based on their de facto conditions, as the *Xici* does, rather than to speculate philosophically about the beginning cosmic status in the way Laozi did.

The ontological orientation of the *Xici* thus offers greater potential for formulating a philosophical cosmology that is compatible with what scientific cosmology tells us. This inclusive capacity of an ontological way of thinking is evidenced by multiple philosophers and theologians in the *creatio ex nihilo* tradition, such as Aquinas, Descartes, Schleiermacher, and Tillich. Accordingly, we can expect the ontological tradition implied by the Ruist *Xici* to be no less inclusive.

Third, as I noted earlier, the concepts of a temporal beginning of pure nothing and formless vital-energy are not particularly useful for Ruist anthropology. This is yet another reason why these ideas can be rejected from a Ruist perspective.

Given these three major considerations, it seems reasonable to assume that Zheng Xuan would have initiated the transition that we have been discussing. However, it is important to note that we have limited textual evidence from Zheng's works to support these considerations, and they remain a hypothetical interpretation of his thought. That being said, we can continue to hypothesize on how this transition might have been further developed in the thought of Zheng's followers:

First, from a Ruist perspective, it is necessary to reject the concept of primordial *Qi* (vital-energy) according to Laozi's orientation. This is because the relationship between primordial *Qi* and the subsequently divided *yin/yang Qi* can only be temporal. Once *Qi* is divided, its primordial state no longer exists in subsequent cosmic stages. However, the ontological relationship between Ultimate Limit and the Two Modes mentioned in the *Xici* implies that the creative power of Ultimate Limit must always be present and operative upon the *yin/yang* modes. Therefore, a more authentic interpretation of *Xici* would not allow the use of Laozian primordial *Qi* as a way of construing Ultimate Limit in conjunction with the use of *yin/yang Qi* as a way of construing Two Modes.

Second, the relationship between "nonbeing" and "being" must be understood in an ontological way. They should be treated as two features of the same existing cosmic realities, with the temporal priority of "nonbeing" over "being" no longer being emphasized.

In the following, we will see that these two possible developments of Zheng Xuan's thought are precisely the case in the works of Wang Bi and Han Kangbo. As such, my hypothetical considerations about the reasons behind Zheng's transition can be significantly supported.

The Ruist Idea of *Generatio ex Nihilo* in Wang Bi and Han Kangbo

WANG BI'S COMMENTARY ON THE *DAO DE JING*

Wang Bi and his follower Han Kangbo were successful in returning the interpretation of the *Xici* to its original ontological track. Wang accomplished this by creatively cross-reading the Daoist *Dao De Jing* and the Ruist *Xici*. As a general hermeneutical strategy, Wang annotated *Dao De Jing*'s verses with the logic of ontological dependence to construe the sequence of cosmological succession. Wang's commentary can be regarded as a significant ontological turning point in the exegetical history of *Dao De Jing*.[46]

For example, in commenting on chapter 42 of the *Dao De Jing*, "Out of *Dao*, One is generated. Out of One, Two is generated. Out of Two, Three is generated. Out of Three, the myriad things are generated . . . ," Wang Bi says:

> What the myriad things go back to is the One. How can we attain the One? Through "nonbeing." Because from "nonbeing" we can attain the One, the One can be called "nonbeing." Since there is already something that is called the One, can it still be called "nonbeing" (已謂之一, 豈得無言乎)? Since there is the One and there is also the calling of the One (as either nonbeing or being), doesn't this imply the Two (有言有一, 非二如何)? Since there are already the One and the Two, then the Three comes

up. During the process from nonbeing to being, these are the numbers that can be used up. Anything beyond this is not consequential to *Dao*. Therefore, I know the origin for the generation of the myriad of things.[47]

Unlike his predecessors, most of whom interpreted the One, Two, and Three in the *Dao De Jing* as temporally referring to various stages of cosmic creation, Wang Bi believes that these numbers describe different aspects of the origin of all things. From his perspective, the myriad things are generated from a singular origin, which he calls the One. Since the One generates the myriad things without being conditioned by anything, it can be described as having "nonbeing." However, since it is still responsible for the creation of all things, it can also be described as "being." The Three is introduced to represent the countless results of the One's creativity. When commenting on this important chapter of the *Dao De Jing*, Wang Bi emphasizes the ontological dependence of all things on the *Dao* as the One, rather than the cosmological succession of creation stages.

Another example concerns the text "The myriad things under heaven are generated from being (有), and being is generated from nonbeing (无)" in chapter 40 of the *Dao De Jing*. Wang Bi says:

> The myriad things under heaven are generated during the process of "being." However, the beginning of "being" is rooted in "nonbeing." This is because if we want to embrace "being" as a whole, we must return to "nonbeing" (將欲全有, 必反於無).[48]

Wang emphasizes that regardless of whether the universe has a temporal beginning or not, any explanation for the emergence of a concrete thing must rely on a process of successive realities that come before it. However, the generation of all beings as a whole ontologically rests upon an ultimate creative power, which is the *Dao*. The *Dao*'s creativity is unconditional, and in this way, the process of all beings is rooted in nonbeing.

The aforementioned examples indicate that Wang Bi's interpretation of the *Dao De Jing* is shaped by the ontological significance of Ultimate Limit in the Ruist *Xici*. This claim is further supported by Wang Bi's commentary on chapter 6 of the *Dao De Jing*: "The spirit of the valley does not die. I call it 'Mysterious Female.' The door of the Mysterious Female is called the root of Heaven and Earth. It is intangible, yet still exists. Its function is inexhaustible." Wang Bi explains, "The door is where the work of the Mysterious Female comes from. As the foundation of the Mysterious Female, it shares one body with Ultimate Limit (與太極同體), and therefore it is referred to as the root of Heaven and Earth."[49]

The *Dao De Jing* employs the metaphor of "the spirit of the valley" and "the door of the Mysterious Female" to describe the ultimate creative power of *Dao*. According to the *Dao De Jing*, the generative power of Dao is manifested in several cosmogonic stages that begin with a form of non-being and lead to the emergence of a myriad of things. Due to Laozi's influence, the ancient Chinese cosmological tradition before Wang Bi emphasized the idea of cosmological succession. Thus, whenever the Ruist idea of Ultimate Limit was combined with Laozi's cosmology, Ultimate Limit was either treated as the stage of *Hunlun*, the undifferentiated whole of being-as-becoming, or as a general name encompassing the existence of the myriad of things between heaven and earth. Ultimate Limit was never equated with *Dao*.

However, Wang Bi directly equates the *Dao* of the *Dao De Jing* with the Ultimate Limit of the *Xici*. This suggests that Wang's interpretation of the *Dao De Jing* was consistent with the Ruist emphasis on ontological dependence among layers of cosmic pattern-principles in the *Xici*. Thus, we can conclude that Wang employed a uniform strategy to interpret the *Dao De Jing*, based on the Ruist terms emphasized in the *Xici*.

Taking this into consideration, it would be intriguing to explore how Wang Bi interpreted the stage of the undifferentiated whole of being-as-becoming in Laozi's cosmogony. While commenting on chapter 21 of the *Dao De Jing*, "Dao, as a thing, is fleeting and obscure. Fleeting and obscure, yet latent in it are images. Obscure and fleeting, yet latent in it are things," Wang Bi says:

> *Dao* has no shape, is fleeting and obscure. This means *Dao* doesn't cling [to anything]. *Dao* starts to generate things in a way of no-shape. It doesn't cling to any created things (不繫成物). However, it is in reliance upon the *Dao* that the myriad things are generated and completed. We don't know exactly the process [by which the things are generated] (不知其所以然), and therefore, we say "fleeting and obscure, yet latent in it are images."[50]

As per our previous analysis, when Laozi describes a cosmogonic stage that is fleeting and obscure, he is referring to it literally. At this stage, the undifferentiated whole of being-as-becoming, which was later interpreted as the stage of primordial *Qi* or *Hunlun*, has not yet attained any determination. According to Laozi's perspective, it is pointless to stress that the creative power of *Dao* is not attached to any created thing at this stage, as nothing has yet been generated. However, for Wang Bi, the statement that the *Dao* "doesn't cling to created things" is a general statement, which implies that even after things are generated, the creative power of *Dao* is not limited by having done so, and therefore, it "doesn't cling to created things."

In light of Wang Bi's equating of *Dao* with Ultimate Limit, the unlimited creative power of *Dao* for Wang refers to the ontological dependence of created things upon it. Only in this sense can we understand Wang's subsequent statement that the "fleeting and obscure" aspects of the *Dao* mean that how the *Dao* created the myriad things remains unknown. This is because, although the *Dao* ontologically conditions all created things, since it is the *Dao* which generates them, we can only know the *Dao* through these created things. In other words, how the *Dao* creates the myriad things in the ultimate ontological sense can never be known by human beings since everything humans can know about this process derives from created things. Hence, the knowledge itself can address only the created, rather than the creating process. This speaks to an essential nature of the idea of an unconditional ontological creative power: its twofold asymmetry. *Dao* is prior to things ontologically, but things are prior to *Dao* epistemologically. In short, because of Wang's innovative reinterpretation of the *Dao De Jing* using the *Xici*'s terms, Laozi's idea of the undifferentiated whole of being-as-becoming becomes unavailable for Wang Bi's understanding of *Dao*. The fleeting and obscure designates instead the epistemological ineffability of *Dao*'s creativity, and it accordingly loses its original cosmogonical reference in the *Dao De Jing*.

FURTHER CONFIRMATION: WANG BI'S CRITIQUE
OF THE *DAO DE JING*

Rendering each cosmogonical verse in the *Dao De Jing* in an ontological fashion constitutes a hermeneutical change that should not be underestimated. However, focusing solely on these verses, it is not impossible to interpret its sophisticated metaphysical terms, such as "nonbeing (無)" and "being (有)," in an ontological way, as I have previously analyzed. Laozi presented a cosmology that gravitated toward speculation about the temporal beginning of the universe to justify renunciative human self-cultivation and minimalist statecraft. Given the holistic nature of Laozi's thought, it is even more surprising to witness how Wang Bi drastically reinterprets the *Dao De Jing*. This prompts me to consider the thought process that Wang Bi may have undergone. First, Wang Bi was likely aware of the difference between his interpretation of the *Dao De Jing* and the original cosmological emphasis. Second, his anthropology may have been somewhat congruent with Ruism, suggesting that his hermeneutics on the *Dao De Jing* may not have solely derived from metaphysical speculations. In the following, I will provide two pieces of evidence that suggest that Wang's thought as a whole is indeed infused with Ruist insights.

The first quotation concerns Wang Bi's criticism of Laozi:

> Sages can feel and probe "nonbeing." However, "nonbeing" per se cannot be explained, and hence a sage would not say anything about "nonbeing." Laozi was a person who endorsed "being"; nevertheless, he always talked of "nonbeing." This speaks to a deficiency of his thought.[51]

Regarding Zheng Xuan's transitional understanding of Ultimate Limit, I previously noted that his rejection of the generative role of "great vacuum" reveals a potential inconsistency in Laozi's thought. Laozi treats *Dao* as the ultimate generator of all beings, so why does he need to posit a temporal beginning of "nonbeing" (understood as a great vacuum) or an undifferentiated whole of being (understood as primordial *Qi*) to explain the ultimate origin of the universe? From a cosmological, horizontal perspective, regardless of whether the universe has a temporal beginning, humans will always seek to identify a cosmic state as an *explanans* prior to things as an *explanandum*. The extent to which a cosmological explanation of existing things can proceed is ultimately an empirical matter. However, from a vertical perspective, or as long as we acknowledge the necessity of an ontological explanation (as the major ancient Chinese texts and thinkers discussed so far, such as the *Dao De Jing*, the *Xici*, Zheng Xuan, and Wang Bi, do), there must be an ultimate creative power on which all horizontally emerging cosmic realities depend. In this Ru lineage of ontological thinking pioneered by Zheng, Wang Bi's criticism of Laozi is highly relevant. According to Laozi, *Dao*'s creativity always exists, meaning it is always the foundation of "being." Thus, why do we need to posit "nonbeing" as its temporal beginning point? Wang argues that this postulate is ontologically unnecessary.

Second, Wang Bi supports the Ruist thesis, "Sages have emotions (聖人有情)," to counter another Daoist thesis, "Sages have no emotions (聖人無情)":

> Sages are more excellent than ordinary human beings because of their wondrous awareness (神明). Sages are the same as ordinary human beings because of their five emotions. Their wondrous awareness is more excellent, so sages can feel the interaction and harmonization of vital-energies so as to be aware of nonbeing (通無). Their five emotions are the same, so sages cannot respond to things without sadness or joy. However, the truth about the emotions of sages is that they respond to things but would not be wearied by things (應物而無累於物者).[52]

Wang Bi's belief that sages have emotions is reflected in chapter 5 of part 1 of the *Xici*, which describes sages as anxious and concerned about society during moments of crisis. However, the view that Wang challenges, which is that "sages have no emotions," was held by thinkers such as He Yan (何晏, ca. 195–249 CE), who was influenced by the *Dao De Jing*'s teachings (such as chapters 49, 57 and 64) on sages having neither desires nor human-like thoughts. Wang Bi, to the contrary, argues from a Ruist perspective that no human emotion is inherently detestable, and emotions can appropriately respond to external stimuli without being existentially perturbed. This positive view toward emotions is grounded in Wang's conception of Ultimate Limit. As the relationship between Ultimate Limit and cosmic realities is vertical, human emotions are a manifestation of Ultimate Limit's creative power. Therefore, no human emotions are inherently bad, but humans need to refine their emotions to manifest Ultimate Limit's creativity in a humane way. However, if we consider the *Dao*, as described in the *Dao De Jing*, as being at its most powerful during the cosmogonical stage of nonbeing, which is either a great vacuum or primordial *Qi*, the complexity of human emotions, along with everything else in human civilization, needs to be restrained in terms of human self-cultivation.

It is important to note that the two quotations from Wang Bi serve to support his general approach to interpreting the *Dao De Jing*, rather than to establish a strict dichotomy between Ruism and Daoism, implying that Wang is exclusively a Ru thinker with no connection to Daoism. In fact, it is difficult to draw a definitive boundary between the two traditions, particularly during and immediately after the Han dynasty when the textual foundation of both was being established in a mutually influential manner. Moreover, an understanding of either tradition without the other is likely to lead to misunderstanding, as scholars of apparently Ruist or Daoist texts during this period were often innovative interlocutors whose ongoing questioning and defense of their respective positions were essential for the further development of each tradition. Therefore, my interpretation of the differences between the *Dao De Jing* and the *Xici*, as well as my analysis of Wang Bi's interpretation of these texts, should be viewed as heuristic rather than prescriptive.[53]

WANG BI'S IDEA OF ULTIMATE LIMIT IN HIS COMMENTARY ON THE *CLASSIC OF CHANGE*

With the confirmation of the overall Ruist character of Wang Bi's metaphysics, it becomes clear that his interpretation of the "being generates from nonbeing" verse from the *Dao De Jing* is heavily influenced by his interpretation of the "Ultimate Limit creates two modes" verse in the *Xici*. This creative cross-reading of two very different texts leads to a groundbreaking achievement in ancient Chinese cosmology. Wang Bi assigns a new meaning, "ontological unconditionality," to the character 無 (nonbeing) and uses it to interpret key verses in the *Xici*. In doing so, he reveals the implicit ontological meaning of the *Xici*, which had not been articulated by the text or its commentators prior to Wang.

For instance, when Wang Bi commented on chapter 8 of part 1 of the *Xici* (which explains the operational process of using yarrow sticks for divination), separately from the *Dao De Jing*, Wang says:

> The number that is used to deduce all changes between heaven and earth is 50. We use 49, and leave 1 for nonuse. Although we do not use it, its use is penetrative. Although we do not enumerate it, all numbers are completed by it. This is what the Ultimate Limit in the *Change* refers to. 49 is the utmost among numbers. Nonbeing cannot be nonilluminated, and its illumination relies upon being (無不可以無明, 必因於有). Therefore, it is because we extend the being of things to their utmost (有物之極) that we can understand where they originated.[54]

Wang Bi's concept of Ultimate Limit clearly aligns with his commentary on chapters 6 and 42 of the *Dao De Jing*. For him, Ultimate Limit is the source of being and represents the highest level of existence to which we can aspire. While Ultimate Limit is characterized as "nonbeing" from a perspective beyond which nothing can be said or exists, it is also considered the originator of being, since all things derive from it. In this sense, being and nonbeing are two complementary aspects of the same ultimate reality.

Another instance is Wang Bi's explanation of "one *yin* and one *yang*, this is called *Dao*" in the *Xici*:

> "One *yin* and one *yang*" means [*Dao*] can be called *yin*, or can be called *yang*, but it has no fixed name. If a thing is *yin*, it cannot be *yang*; if a thing is mild, it cannot be firm. Only when something is neither *yin* nor *yang* can it be the origin of *yin* and *yang*; only when something is neither firm nor mild can it be the master of firmness and mildness. Therefore, only when something has neither boundaries nor shaped bodies (無方無體), and is neither *yin* nor *yang* (非陰非陽), can it then be called the *Dao*, and can it then be called what is numinous and wonderful (神).[55]

In this passage, the equation of *Dao* with Ultimate Limit is implicit in Wang's interpretation, and his understanding of the relationship between *yin/yang* and *Dao* is informed by his understanding of the relationship between *yin/yang* and Ultimate Limit. This also brings to mind Zheng Xuan's commentary on the *Xici*'s verse "the Change has no shaped bodies to cling to" that was analyzed earlier. The ontological dependence implied by the original *Xici* verses on Ultimate Limit suggests that it is Ultimate Limit that creates *yin/yang*, and thus *yin/yang* vital-energies depend ontologically upon Ultimate Limit, which implies that Ultimate Limit's creativity cannot be exhausted by *yin/yang*. As *yin/yang* is the most basic pair of categories in ancient Chinese thought used to account for any possible determination of cosmic realities, the inexhaustibility of Ultimate Limit's creativity by *yin/yang* implies a dimension within Ultimate Limit that is utterly beyond human understanding. In other words, the creativity of Ultimate Limit itself is indeterminate, and its creativity can be described as what is numinous. However, the cosmos continues to evolve and advance into novelty without cease, as described in the *Xici*. Therefore, humans would be awed by the fact that the utterly inscrutable, indeterminate creative power of Ultimate Limit is also inexhaustibly fertile. This is the major reason why Wang Bi can describe the ultimate creative power of Ultimate Limit, the *Dao*, as being both without boundary or shaped bodies and numinous and wonderful.

HAN KANGBO'S COMMENTARY ON THE *XICI*

Wang Bi did not leave a completed commentary on the *Xici*, likely because of his early death. However, his style was continued by Han Kangbo (332–380 CE), who completed the commentary during the Eastern Jin period. Later, Han's commentary on the *Xici* was combined with Wang's commentary on other texts of the *Classic of Change* and compiled into the *Correct Meanings of the Zhou Book of Change* (周易正義) by Kong Yingda during the Tang dynasty (618–907 CE). This compilation became an official textbook for the civil examination in imperial China and has had an enduring influence, particularly on later Song through Ming Ruism. To appreciate the metaphysical groundbreaking point which Wang was making, it is critically important to read Han Kangbo's commentary in tandem with Wang Bi's thought.

In commenting on the term Ultimate Limit, Han says:

> Being necessarily has its origin in nonbeing. Thus, Ultimate Limit generates the two modes. Ultimate Limit is the term for that for which no term is possible. As we cannot lay hold of it and name it, we think of it in terms of the ultimate point to which we can extend being (取有之所極) and regard this as equivalent to Ultimate Limit.[56]

In other words, "nonbeing" means the ontological unconditionality of Ultimate Limit's creative power, which is the generator of all beings under heaven.

In commenting on "one *yin* and one *yang*, this is called *Dao*," Han says:

> Although *yin* and *yang* are different, "nonbeing" as the One treats them equally (無一以待之). When *Dao* is in *yin*, *Dao* is not *yin*; however, it is *Dao* that generates *yin*. When *Dao* is in *yang*, *Dao* is not *yang*; however, it is *Dao* that generates *yang*, and therefore we say "one *yin* and one *yang*."[57]

The ultimate creative power of Ultimate Limit, also known as the *Dao*, is believed to be both manifested in and transcendent of the *yin/yang* cosmic realities that result from Ultimate Limit's creativity.

In commenting on the verse, "What cannot be fathomed by *yin* and *yang* is numinous and wonderful," Han Kongbo says:

> Actually, how could there ever be an agent that causes the movement of the two modes *yin* and *yang* and the activity of the myriad things to happen as they do! Absolutely each thing just undergoes transformation in

the great void, and all of a sudden, comes into existence of its own accord. It is not things themselves that bring about their own existence; rather, the pattern-principle here responds to the mysterious. There is no master that transforms them; the fate here operates via the working of the dark. We do not understand why all this is so, so we characterize it as the numinous! It is for this reason that in order to clarify the two modes of *yin* and *yang*, we take Ultimate Limit as their initiator, and in addressing changes and transformations, the term "numinous and wonderful" is the utmost we can say.[58]

Han Kangbo beautifully encapsulated the ontological wisdom of the Ruist commentators on the *Xici* prior to him with the words quoted above. Horizontally, things in the cosmos emerge spontaneously, without the need for a divine agent to explain their existence. Vertically, however, things do not bring about their own existence. Rather, there is an ultimate "mysterious" and "dark" pattern-principle, which surely refers to Ultimate Limit, that brings the myriad things into being. Because our knowledge of this mysterious pattern-principle must derive from the existing things themselves, we cannot see through the process by which the ultimate pattern-principle creates the myriad things. The epistemological priority of existing things renders the process of their ontological creation by Ultimate Limit utterly unknowable.

On the one hand, we are certain that Ultimate Limit is the initiator, but on the other hand, terms other than "numinous and wonderful" will not be sufficient to describe the initiator's abysmal depth and inexhaustible fertility. The term "great void (大虛)" in the quoted passage therefore refers to the unconditionality of the indeterminate creativity of Ultimate Limit, rather than a physical "great vacuum" as in Laozi's case. Furthermore, the vertical unknowability and indeterminacy of Ultimate Limit construed by Han implies leniency to the spontaneous nature of things' coming to be, since no determinate order is imposed from above by Ultimate Limit to dictate how things should emerge from the cosmos of their own accord.

A Brief Comparison with the Tradition of *Creatio ex Nihilo*

Inspired by the thoughts of Wang Bi and Han Kangbo, we can revise the diagram of "The Ruist Ontological Cosmology in the *Xici* of *Yijing*" as follows:

The Ruist Ontological Cosmology in the *Xici* as Interpreted by Wang Bi and Han Kangbo

In this revised diagram, "Nonbeing" is placed at the top, but it is not separate from Ultimate Limit. The ontological creative power of Ultimate Limit is unconditional, and thus "nonbeing" is just one aspect of its ultimate creativity. The vertical line, rather than an arrow, connecting Nonbeing and Ultimate Limit represents their bond.

This new diagram suggests that owing to the interpretations of Wang Bi and Han Kangbo, the Chinese Ru tradition developed a clearer concept of the ontological creativity of ultimate reality, which can be compared to the concept of *creatio ex nihilo* in the Greek-European Christian tradition. As we move forward to explore the metaphysical works of Song through Ming Ruist masters, it is worth noting the preliminary similarities between the Ru tradition and the Greek-European Christian tradition concerning the idea of creation:

First, the Ru tradition of ontology was driven by the symbology found in the *Classic of Change* (*Yijing*), which led to the emergence of a concept similar to *creatio ex nihilo*. In the *Xici*, ontological relationships among cosmic realities are parsed based on the logical and nontemporal relationship among *Yijing*'s symbols (such as those in the chart of "Trigrams formed from the Ultimate Limit and *yin/yang yao*"). This approach is very similar to the basic drive behind the entire Greek-European Christian tradition of *creatio ex nihilo*. Plato, dissatisfied with the natural philosophers' use of causality that relied on the perception of cosmological succession to explain cosmic events, instead turned to "words" such as the ideas of "Beauty" and "Good" themselves, as well as the ultimate causation as "a work of craft." He used these words to parse the ontological relationships among ranks of cosmic realities, which accounted for the overall order and existence of the universe. The logical and nontemporal relationship among symbols and words serves as an inspirational fountain of ontology for both traditions.

Second, both the Ru tradition of Ultimate Limit and the Greek-European Christian tradition of *creatio ex nihilo* embody the idea of the "ontological dependence" of all cosmic realities on the unconditional creative power of ultimate reality, even though they use different terms for ultimate reality—one uses God and *creatio ex nihilo*, while the other uses Ultimate Limit or *Dao* and *sheng sheng* (生生, birth birth). Due to this shared ontological idea, it is legitimate to define Ultimate Limit's creativity as "transcendent" if God is considered "transcendent" according to the concept of "ontological unconditionality."

Third, both the Ru tradition of *sheng sheng* and the Greek-European Christian tradition of *creatio ex nihilo* demonstrate their inclusiveness toward various cosmogonical views regarding the possible temporal beginnings of the cosmos. Aquinas stated that *creatio ex nihilo* maintains its ontological value, whether the cosmos has a beginning or not. Similarly, the Ru metaphysical tradition investigates the ontological pattern-principles that bring order and existence to cosmic realities based on the de facto conditions of these realities. In this sense, Laozi's cosmogonical speculation about the beginning of the cosmos can be included in the Ru discourse as a possible beginning narrative. Zheng Xuan's reinterpretation of the Great Change in the *Qian Zao Du*, which is a Laozian idea of great vacuum, is the best evidence for the inclusiveness of Ru metaphysics among all the texts and thinkers analyzed. For Zheng, the stage of Great Change has no generative power, but to explain how things emerge in the horizontal cosmic process, we need only conceptualize that a thing "generates of its own accord all of a sudden" and then turn our minds vertically to the ontological pattern-principles that regulate cosmic changes in a de facto way. In the contemporary context, we can legitimately expect that the Ru idea of *sheng sheng* and the Greek-European Christian idea of *creatio ex nihilo* are among the most resilient metaphysical/religious ideas to encapsulate possible advances in modern science without limiting their spiritual potency.

Fourth, both traditions demonstrate an awareness of the "ontological priority" of the ultimate reality, regardless of its name, in relation to the "epistemological priority" of derived realities. This common understanding leads to a mystical commitment to the ineffability and inexhaustibility of ultimate reality in both traditions.

Even so, there are significant differences between these two traditions:

First, inspired by Plato's ideas in the *Timaeus*, Christian theologians conceive of the process by which God creates the world as one in which a divine agent puts forms into a formless preexisting state of being, despite their insistence that the Platonic "matter" does not fit the unconditional creative power of God. This raises the question of whether the world of forms exists prior to or posterior to the de facto existence of created realities. If it exists prior, divine creativity will not sound as unconditional as the idea of *creatio ex nihilo* suggests.

However, in the Chinese Ru tradition, Ultimate Limit is typically seen as an ultimate creative act without an actor or creator standing behind the scenes. The changing process of cosmic realities is viewed as one of spontaneous emergence, where no plan, purpose, or telos issued from a divine agency can be detected. As a result, probing the pattern-principles of cosmic realities, such as their *yin/yang* aspects, becomes a purely empirical commitment: Ru thinkers summarize the most generic features of cosmic realities based upon their de facto conditions, and the intelligibility of the entire world therefore does not exist prior to the world, but instead arrives afterward.

This nontheistic idea of Ultimate Limit makes the Ru theological tradition comparable to the de-anthropomorphic minor tradition within the major theistic Greek-European Christian tradition of *creatio ex nihilo*, defined by thinkers such as Plotinus, Descartes, Schleiermacher, and Tillich, who conceive of God as the "generator of being" or the "ground of being," rather than as the most powerful being. If we need a contrasting phrase to highlight the nontheistic nature of Ultimate Limit's creativity, "generatio ex nihilo" would be more appropriate than "creatio ex nihilo," as the latter term implies a creator standing behind the scenes because of the mainstream theistic idea of divine creation in the Christian tradition. However, the use of "generatio ex nihilo" is only for heuristic purposes since, in the minor tradition of *creatio ex nihilo*, "creation" is still vaguely used and does not necessarily imply an all-powerful God as the Creator standing behind the scenes.[59]

Ultimately, if we view the transcendence of ultimate reality as the ontological unconditionality of ultimate creativity, according to the logic of ontological dependence shared by both the Ru and Christian traditions, the Ruist nontheistic idea of Ultimate Limit is more transcendent than the mainstream Christian theistic idea of God.

Second, as mentioned earlier, the Greek-European Christian tradition of *creatio ex nihilo* uses "form" and "matter" as a basic pair of categories to explain the most generic traits of cosmic realities. "Form," "matter," and related concepts belong to the second tier of ontological categories in the *creatio ex nihilo* tradition, which are ultimately understood as a manifestation of God's creative power, but are used specifically to explain the order rather than the existence of the world. In comparison, the *Xici* employs many categories to describe the generic features of cosmic realities, such as 變 (change), 化 (transformation), 位 (position), 道 (way), 器 (utensil), 理 (pattern-principle), 氣 (vital-energy), and others. In the commentarial tradition of *Xici*, 形 (shape) and 質 (matter) are also used to explain the formation of things in the dynamic matrix of pervasive vital-energies. However, the task of thematizing the most generic traits of cosmic realities in an overall processual worldview and thus formulating a more sophisticated metaphysical system had not yet been prioritized by Ru thinkers in the commentarial tradition of *Xici* until the time of Wang Bi and Han Kangbo. With historical hindsight, we find that in Song through Ming Ruism (which we will discuss shortly), especially in Zhu Xi's cosmology, the Ru tradition achieves a systematic employment of the basic pair of categories, 理 (pattern-principle) and 氣 (vital-energy), the significances of which are more comparable to form and matter in the West.

8 *Generatio ex Nihilo* in Continuum: Zhou Dunyi, Zhu Xi, Cao Duan, and Luo Qinshun

Zhou Dunyi on Ultimate Limit

It is not an overstatement to suggest that the role played by the works of Zhou Dunyi (1017–1073 CE)—his *Diagram of Ultimate Limit* (太極圖), along with its related *Explanation of the Diagram of Ultimate Limit* (太極圖說, abbreviated as EDUL), and the *Book of Penetration* (通書, abbreviated as BP)—in the ethical-metaphysical tradition of Song through Ming Ruism was comparable to that of Plato's *Timaeus* in the Greek-European Christian tradition of *creatio ex nihilo*. However, the terse and abstruse nature of Zhou Dunyi's seminal texts has made it challenging for Ru scholars to reach a consensus on their interpretation. To address this hermeneutical difficulty, I propose two approaches.

The first approach involves recognizing Zhou Dunyi's philosophy as the precursor to the medieval revival of Ruist ethical-metaphysical thought, which was embedded in the commentarial tradition of the *Xici* of the *Classic of Change*, established during the Han through Tang dynasties. To understand Zhou's thought in its own right, particularly his concepts of Ultimate Limit (太極, *Taiji*) and Non-Limit (無極, *Wuji*), it is necessary to explore this preexisting commentarial tradition and consider which lineage of thought Zhou's ideas most likely followed. The second approach involves examining EDUL in conjunction with Zhou's own words in the BP. An intratextual analysis of Zhou's thought can enhance the coherence of our interpretation of it.

TWO LINEAGES OF THE INTERPRETATION OF ULTIMATE LIMIT IN THE COMMENTARIAL TRADITION OF *YIJING*

As detailed in chapter 7, during the Han dynasty (when the text of *Yijing* was transmitted and its commentarial tradition began) and up until the Tang dynasty, there were two significant lineages of interpretive thought regarding the pivotal sentence to Ru cosmology in the *Xici*: "Ultimate Limit creates two modes." Since the commentarial philosophers almost unanimously interpreted "two modes" as symbolizing the *yin/yang* vital-energies, the controversy centered on how to comprehend Ultimate Limit. One lineage of interpretation, primarily represented by Wang Bi and Han Kangbo, employed the idea of "nonbeing (無)," understood as "ontological unconditionality," to interpret Ultimate Limit. The other lineage viewed Ultimate Limit as the primordial *Qi* (vital-energy) that has not yet obtained any determination.

Regarding the first lineage, it has been previously discussed that Wang's and Han's shared notion of Ultimate Limit is akin to the concept of *creatio ex nihilo*. In this case, "nonbeing," as the farthest point to which "being" can extend, is not distinct from Ultimate Limit. Instead, it is a characteristic of Ultimate Limit, indicating that nothing can be said beyond the ultimate point. Wang and Han also alluded to the double asymmetrical nature of Ultimate Limit, comparable to that of *creatio ex nihilo*: Ultimate Limit is ontologically prior, such that all realities are conditioned by it. However, epistemologically, cosmic realities come first, since humans can only know anything about Ultimate Limit through them, as Wang's previously quoted words explain: "Nonbeing cannot be nonilluminated, and its illumination relies upon being."

The second lineage posited that Ultimate Limit pertains to the primordial vital-energy that (1) exists as the initial stage of cosmic evolution and (2) has not yet acquired any determination aside from being the primordial vital-energy. Several cosmological texts and thinkers subsequent to the *Xici* but prior to Wang Bi and Han Kangbo, which I analyzed in chapter 7, belong to this lineage. My analysis further indicates that the *Dao De Jing*'s Daoist cosmology had a significant influence here. During the Tang dynasty, the understanding of Ultimate Limit as primordial *Qi* was evident in *The Correct Meanings of the Zhou Book of Change* (周易正義) by Kong Yingda (574–648 CE), a significant work summarizing the prior commentarial tradition of the *Yijing*. Kong says,

Ultimate Limit refers to the primordial vital-energy (元氣) which was a formless whole before the division between heaven and earth. It is also called the "ultimate initiation (太初)," or "ultimate oneness (太一)." Therefore, Laozi says: "*Dao* creates One," and this One is Ultimate Limit. As a result, after the one formless whole is divided, then heaven and earth are created. Therefore, "Ultimate Limit creates two modes" actually refers to Laozi's idea that "One creates Two."[1]

Ultimate Limit is interpreted here as the one-formless-whole of primordial vital-energy, and "Ultimate Limit creates two modes" is understood as the self-determination of this formless whole into the two fundamental forms of cosmic reality: *yang* vital-energy (also represented by "heaven") and *yin* vital-energy (also represented by "earth").

When viewed comparatively within the Chinese tradition, the cosmogony of Wang Bi and Han Kangbo originates from nonbeing, namely the unconditionality of the creative power of Ultimate Limit as the generator of being, while the cosmogony of the second lineage begins with the being of Ultimate Limit as the formless whole of primordial vital-energy. In comparison to Western thought, the first lineage is more akin to the *creatio ex nihilo* tradition, while the second is more comparable to Spinoza's and Hegel's understandings of divine creation. The being of the world as a whole is presumed, and therefore metaphysicians of the second category focused on explaining the process of the self-determination of the world as a given whole of being to provide accounts for concrete things.

Interestingly, when Kong Yingda created his commentary on the *Xici*, he drew on the two lineages as antecedents and attempted to discover a synthetic approach to merge the notion of "nonbeing" with primordial vital-energy. Kong says,

> "One *yin* and one *yang*, this is called *Dao*." One is nonbeing, and the *Dao* has the status of neither *yin* nor *yang*. The reason why the One is nonbeing is that nonbeing is a vacuum of nothing, and a vacuum of nothing is the great vacuum. It has not yet been differentiated, and thus only the One remains. In this way, the One can be thought of as nonbeing (以一為無). In the sphere of beings, things have forms and shapes in contrast with one another, and thus there will be two, three, etc., and in this way, the One doesn't exist anymore.[2]

In this approach, the one-formless-whole of primordial vital-energy (which is equal to Kong's Ultimate Limit) was also seen as sharing the nature of nonbeing. Its nonbeing is exactly what the original Han commentarial tradition's term 混 or 渾 (formless, amorphous, or chaotic) seeks to express: that the primordial vital-energy has no form. As something both without form and with being, the entire primordial vital-energy can be identified further as a great vacuum, which is reminiscent of Zheng Yuan's similar interpretation of *Hunlun* (渾淪). Nonetheless, via this synthesizing interpretation, Kong Yingda renders 無 more as "nothingness" rather than the ontologically unconditional "nonbeing." For Wang Bi and Han Kangbo, the nonbeing of Ultimate Limit suggests the unconditionality of its creative power. Any form of being, whether formless or not, is created by Ultimate Limit. Wang and Han did not claim that there is any intermediary stage (such as the formless whole of primordial vital-energy) between the unconditional generative power of Ultimate Limit and the *yang/yin* vital-energies. This is because the alleged intermediary concept, if shaped by Laozi's understanding of cosmological succession, is both ontologically inappropriate and anthropologically inconsistent with Wang Bi's Ru ethical-metaphysical ideas inspired by the *Xici*. However, even if there were such an intermediary stage, according to Wang and Han's insistence on the logic of ontological dependence this stage would still have to be positioned at a lower ontological level than Ultimate Limit and would actually have been created by it. In short, Kong's apparently synthetic commentary did not yet make clear the distinction between "nonbeing (無)," namely the unconditionality of Wang and Han's concept of Ultimate Limit as the generator of being, and "nothingness (無)," namely the formlessness of the other lineage's idea of Ultimate Limit as the being of primordial vital-energy.

WHICH LINEAGE DOES ZHOU DUNYI BELONG TO?

Given that this was the intellectual legacy from Han through Tang that influenced the development of Zhou Dunyi's thought, a crucial question for us to consider is: Which lineage does Zhou belong to? While many scholars argue that Zhou belongs to the second lineage that interprets Ultimate Limit as the primordial vital-energy, I disagree with this view for several reasons. First, one of the most significant interpreters of Zhou Dunyi's thought, Zhu Xi, did not believe that Zhou belonged to the second lineage. Second, Zhou's own texts as a whole support a coherent interpretation of Ultimate Limit in the style of Wang Bi and Han Kangbo. Third, difficulties arise if we understand Ultimate Limit as primordial vital-energy, which makes it challenging to understand Zhou's thought coherently according to the second lineage. Fourth, in addition to these cosmological considerations, interpreting the "nonbeing" of Ultimate Limit as the unconditionality of its creative power, rather than interpreting the "formlessness" of Ultimate Limit as the amorphous primordial cosmic material, is more consistent with Zhou's Ruist goal of grounding ethics in its cosmological foundation.

Of course, these reasons do not make it entirely impossible to interpret Zhou Dunyi's thought according to the second lineage. In the end, it will be up to the readers of this book to decide whether these reasons are persuasive enough to support the argument I will present in the following sections.

ZHOU DUNYI'S CONCEPT OF ULTIMATE LIMIT

The most important texts for my analysis of Zhou Dunyi's thought on Ultimate Limit are respectively from his *Explanation of the Diagram of Ultimate Limit* (EDUL) and the *Book of Penetration* (BP), which are quoted as follows:

> Non-Limit and yet Ultimate Limit (無極而太極)! The Ultimate Limit in activity creates *yang*; yet at the limit of activity it is still. In stillness it creates *yin*; yet at the limit of stillness it is active again. Activity and stillness alternate; each is the basis for the other. In distinguishing *yin* and *yang*, the Two Modes are thereby established.
>
> The alternation and combination of *yang* and *yin* create water, fire, wood, metal, and earth. With these five [phases of] *Qi* harmoniously arranged; the Four seasons proceed through them. The Five Phases are what *yin* and *yang* unite; *yin* and *yang* are what Ultimate Limit unites; Ultimate Limit is fundamentally Non-Limit (太極本無極). [Yet] in the creation of the Five Phases, each one has its nature.
>
> The reality of Non-Limit and the essence of the Two Modes and Five Phases mysteriously combine and coalesce. "The Way of Qian becomes the male; the Way of Kun becomes the female"; the two *Qi* affect each other, transforming and creating the myriad things. The myriad things generate and regenerate (生生), alternating and transforming without limit.[3]
>
> That which has no stillness in activity and no activity in stillness is a thing (物). That which has no activity in activity, and no stillness in

stillness, is what is numinous (神). It is not the case that the numinous, having no activity in activity and having no stillness in stillness, can neither activate nor become still. Things, then, are not penetrating. The numinous renders the generative process of things subtle.

The *yin* of water is based in *yang*; the *yang* of fire is based in *yin*. The Five Phases are *yin* and *yang*. *Yin* and *yang* are the Ultimate Limit. The Four Seasons revolve; the myriad things end and begin [again]. The process mingles and opens up. How limitless it is![4]

To correctly understand these two quotations, it is important to keep in mind three points. First, the first quotation is Zhou's interpretation of the words in the *Xici* that were analyzed in the preceding chapter: "Ultimate Limit creates two modes, two modes create four images, and four images create eight hexagrams." These stages of cosmic creation grounded in Ultimate Limit are illustrated in the various layers of Zhou's Diagram of Ultimate Limit.[5] Second, Zhou explains what the "active" and "still" aspects of Ultimate Limit mean when it is said to create *yin Qi* and *yang Qi*, which is what the second quotation is about. Third, the reality of time emerges only after the creation of "five phases" and "four seasons." Once created, the entire process of cosmic change is depicted as "limitless," without any specific form of beginning or ending. In this way, Zhou's diagram and thought on Ultimate Limit's cosmic creation align with what the Greek-European Christian metaphysical tradition of "chain of being," starting with Plotinus's Neoplatonism, tries to convey. The *Xici* refers to this type of Ru metaphysical thought as pondering the Dao of "what lies beyond shape."

We can now interpret Zhou Dunyi's thought by probing the two aforementioned lineages: one espoused by Wang Bi and Han Kangbo and the other that interprets Ultimate Limit as primordial *Qi*. Using the first approach would lead to a straightforward and coherent reading of Zhou's thought:

Non-Limit is not an entity distinct from Ultimate Limit; rather, it is a feature of Ultimate Limit. Ultimate Limit can only be predicated as the generator of the entire world. Therefore, two significant aspects of Zhou's conception of Ultimate Limit can be inferred: First, the term "Non-Limit" in conjunction with "Ultimate Limit" does not suggest that Non-Limit is a positive force of nonbeing that opposes Ultimate Limit. As stated in the above quotation, Non-Limit is seen as having the reality to produce things in the world. In an interpretation similar to Wang Bi's and Han

Kangbo's understanding of "nonbeing," Zhou takes the nonbeing aspect of Ultimate Limit as referring to the ontological unconditionality of its creative power, which cannot be described further.

Second, the "activity" or "stillness" of Ultimate Limit in producing *yin* and *yang* is a means for humans to analogically conceive what happens with this ultimate creative power. Our knowledge of "activity" or "stillness" in general is derived from the existence of created things, and therefore, we can only analogically conceive the causal process through which Ultimate Limit generates and makes things movable or still. We cannot know whether Ultimate Limit activates or stills itself. However, because Ultimate Limit's creative act does bring activity and stillness of things into being, we cannot conclude that Ultimate Limit does not move or keep still either. Ultimate Limit neither moves nor unmoves, and is neither still nor non-still. Its creative power is singular and nondual, and thus, cannot be captured by dualistic human words. According to the logic of ontological dependence, which is emphasized by Wang and Han and shared by Zhou, the nondual nature of Ultimate Limit is derived from its position at the highest ontological rank of cosmic realities. Thus, anything pertaining to lower ranks can only depict, but not fully describe, Ultimate Limit.

Furthermore, this understanding of the Non-Limit feature of Ultimate Limit aligns well with Zhou Dunyi's metaphysical ethics. In the latter part of EDUL and in other sections of BP, Zhou discusses how humans are created during the same process of cosmic creation by Ultimate Limit, and thus human beings are endowed with an idiosyncratic ethical nature. Major Ru ethical virtues are firmly rooted in this cosmological framework: The virtues of Centrality (中), Uprightness (正), Humanness (仁), and Righteousness (義) are the means by which the *yin/yang* vital-energies and five phases are harmonized in the human world. Because these virtues are considered as moral criteria for being human, Zhou refers to them as "Human Limit (人極)." Since the Non-Limit feature of Ultimate Limit connotes the existence of the unconditional origin of cosmic realities, and the cherished Ru virtues, that is, the Limit of being human, are grounded in the most generic features of cosmic realities, a sort of ethical realism runs consistently through Zhou's thought, which is also a distinctive characteristic of Ru ethics in general.

Alternatively, let us consider using the second traditional approach to interpret Zhou Dunyi's thought and compare it to the first approach. According to the second lineage, Ultimate Limit must be understood as primordial *Qi*, and its Non-Limit feature refers to the formlessness of this primordial *Qi* as a single undivided whole. However, this interpretation presents significant challenges, which are explained as follows:

First, there is no mention of the concept of primordial *Qi* at all in any of Zhou's texts.

Second, the concept of primordial *Qi*, as understood in Laozi's cosmogony, namely a chaotic and formless whole of being-as-becoming that has not yet received any determination and exists temporally before *yin/yang* vital-energies or heaven and earth, must have been excluded from Zhou's diagram. This is because Zhou's diagram expresses an ontological tendency akin to the Neoplatonic "chain of being," and as such, relationships among different levels of cosmic reality are considered nontemporal. This suggests that the characteristics of a higher cosmic reality level are shared by the lower ones, as Zhou's own explanation of the diagram in EDUL clearly demonstrates. However, Laozi's concept of primordial *Qi* can no longer exist within *yin/yang* vital-energies after it has been divided and formalized. The fact that Wang Bi and Han Kangbo completely abandoned this "primordial *Qi*" idea indicates that it is not well suited for ontological thinking.

Nonetheless, for ancient Chinese cosmologists who are sympathetic to the idea of the Ultimate Limit as primordial *Qi*, as proposed by the aforementioned second lineage, primordial *Qi* can be understood in a different sense. It can be interpreted as "*Qi* in general."[6] The primary distinction between "primordial *Qi*" as per Laozi's conception and "*Qi* in general" is that the latter can, to some extent, align with an ontological "chain of being" mode of thinking. This is because characteristics of *Qi* in general can be shared by the two distinct *yin/yang Qi*. As a result, it is reasonable for us to hypothesize that perhaps the Ultimate Limit, when understood as primordial *Qi* defined as *Qi* in general, presents a viable option for interpreting Zhou. The following analysis on the third point of interpretive difficulties generated by the second lineage will be based on this alternative understanding of the Ultimate Limit as primordial *Qi* defined as *Qi* in general.

Third, if the Ultimate Limit is the formless whole of primordial *Qi* understood as *Qi* in general, interpreting the second aforementioned quotation regarding the activity and stillness of the Ultimate Limit becomes more complex. According to this quotation, the creative power of the numinous cannot be fully grasped by human knowledge, which is based on "things" that are visible, tangible, and therefore, entities with forms.

Following this line of thought, a corollary would be that the Ultimate Limit is the formless whole of undivided *Qi* in general, and after the function of the numinous, it differentiates into two basic forms: *yin* and *yang Qi*. This suggests that the existence and essence of *yin/yang Qi* must be explained by distinct principles. Their existence is derived from the being of *Qi* in general, which is always present. Meanwhile, their essence originates from the numinous, which brings the fundamental determinations of *Qi* into existence. In other words, the numinous does not clarify the origin of the being of *Qi* in general, and ultimately, it appears as a separate principle from *Qi* in general since their explanatory powers are dissimilar.[7] It is evident that the monistic commitment to the Ultimate Limit as the sole principle explaining both the existence and order of the entire created world in Zhou Dunyi's *Diagram* does not support this dualistic interpretation.

However, there are two possible approaches to addressing this challenge to the dualistic understanding of Ultimate Limit. First, we can assert that the numinous, which is used to explain what a thing is, is a power inherent to *Qi* in general. In other words, *Qi* in general not only is always present but also possesses the power of self-determination by integrating the two basic forms of *Qi* into itself. Nonetheless, this introduces further problems: (1) It still leaves the question of the origin of *Qi* in general unanswered. (2) A primordial formless whole of being now has a positive power within itself to determine itself further. This aspect of *Qi* in general cannot be considered entirely formless since it contains a basic differentiation of "principle of being" and "principle of essence" within itself. (3) As hinted above, if Ultimate Limit is such a primordial *Qi*, Non-Limit must be understood as the formless nature of *Qi* in general. Consequently, Non-Limit cannot be confirmed as one type of reality, as Zhou describes in his EDUL, since it is literally "formless," that is, without a solid mode of being. Similarly, such a concept of Non-Limit is not suitable for establishing the Ru ethical realism.

Another way to address the dualistic challenge is to propose that the numinous is for explaining not only what a thing is but also where its being originates. In other words, the numinous creates both the being of *Qi* in general and imparts basic determinations to it. In the EDUL, the term Non-Limit appears before Ultimate Limit. Accordingly, the numinous is synonymous with Non-Limit, and it both generates the Ultimate Limit as *Qi* in general and introduces basic *yin/yang* determinations into

Ultimate Limit. In this line of thought, the highest principle would be Non-Limit, rather than Ultimate Limit.[8]

However, difficulties arise from this approach as well. First, the entire BP does not mention Non-Limit. If Non-Limit is the highest principle of Zhou Dunyi's thought, it becomes inexplicable why the term is not mentioned at all in his most crucial writing, which supposedly explains the EDUL. Second, if Non-Limit is considered the highest principle that produces both *Qi* in general (Ultimate Limit) and its determination, then that which generates *yin/yang* vital-energies cannot be the Ultimate Limit but must be the Non-Limit. This is directly contrary to what the two quoted passages state about the activity and stillness of the Ultimate Limit producing *yin* and *yang* vital-energies. In fact, if we consider Non-Limit as both the creator of the entire world's being and the principle that explains what a thing is in relation to other things, its role would be precisely the same as the Ultimate Limit construed in the manner of Wang Bi and Han Kangbo.

As previously mentioned, it is possible for us to posit an intermediary stage, called "primordial *Qi*" defined as "*Qi* in general," between the ultimate ontological creative power (regardless of whether we call it Non-Limit or Ultimate Limit) and *yin/yang* vital-energies in accordance with Wang's and Han's interpretation of Ru metaphysics. However, if we use "Non-Limit" to name this ultimate ontological creative power, first, according to Wang and Han, we will need another name to refer to its unconditional feature. This would render the metaphysical terms unnecessarily redundant. Second, for interpreting Zhou's thought, this would make the verses about the creation of *yin* and *yang* by the Ultimate Limit incomprehensible. Additionally, naming an ultimate principle of reality "Non-Limit" instead of "Ultimate Limit" would make the Ru ethical realism seem peculiar.

In summary, there are numerous difficulties associated with the interpretive strategy of understanding Zhou Dunyi's idea of Ultimate Limit as primordial *Qi*, whether in Laozi's cosmological sense or in the ontological sense of *Qi* in general, and these difficulties are not easily resolved. Alternatively, positioning Zhou within the lineage of Wang Bi and Han Kangbo, and consequently interpreting Zhou's idea of Ultimate Limit as an unconditional ontological creative act that gives rise to both the existence and order of *yin/yang* vital-energies, presents a more straightforward and coherent reading of Zhou's thought. As a result, I conclude that Zhou Dunyi belongs to the tradition of Wang and Han, and his ideas on ethical metaphysics are comparable to those of the Greek-European Christian tradition of *creatio ex nihilo*, with the caveat that Zhou is part of the distinct Ruist tradition, which conceptualizes the Ultimate Limit's creativity as *generatio ex nihilo*.

Zhu Xi on Ultimate Limit and the Relationship of Li and Qi

To comprehend Zhu Xi, a highly systematic thinker in the Ru tradition's perspective on the *sheng sheng* of the Ultimate Limit, we must maintain a persistent focus on its "ontological" nature. Following his predecessor Cheng Yi (1033–1107 CE) and the Ruist commentarial tradition of the *Xici*, Zhu Xi consistently supports the idea that, from a temporal standpoint, cosmic changes have neither a beginning nor an end:

> If (cosmic changes) are pushed to their uttermost front, no beginning (始) can be seen. If they are pulled to their uttermost back, no end (終) can be perceived. Therefore, Master Cheng said: "There is no limitation to the alternation of movement and stillness. Neither is there any beginning for the one of *yin* and *yang*."[9]

Nevertheless, even if everything in the universe is continuously changing, there exists an order of *Li* (理) that allows Zhu Xi to discern a similarly Aristotelian "priority of nature and being" among ranks of cosmic realities. Zhu interprets the seminal sentence, "Ultimate Limit creates two modes," from the *Xici* in a distinctively ontological manner:

> For the teaching, "there is Ultimate Limit in the Change, and it creates two modes," the priority here is being considered from the perspective of solid pattern-principle (實理). If the coming-into-being of Ultimate Limit and two modes [of *yin/yang* vital-energies] is being discussed, these two come into being at the same time, and Ultimate Limit is within *yin* and *yang*. However, if the sequence of dependence is being addressed, we must acknowledge that the solid pattern-principle comes first, and then *yin* and *yang* come second. Their [*yin* and *yang*'s] pattern-principle is one. From what can be observed from things, *yin* and *yang* imply Ultimate Limit (陰陽函太極). However, if we probe their origin, we have to say that it is Ultimate Limit which creates *yin* and *yang* (太極生陰陽).[10]

It is evident here that Zhu Xi interprets the creative sequence between Ultimate Limit, the two modes (*yin/yang* vital-energies), and the four images (the five phases and the flow of vital-energy during the four seasons), mentioned in both the *Xici* and Zhou Dunyi's *Explanation of the Diagram of Ultimate Limit* (EDUL), as one of ontological dependence rather than cosmological succession. In Zhu's own terms, it is an order of "solid pattern-principle (實理)" rather than one of "observed things (見在)."

Similarly, the *sheng sheng* in the *Xici*, which was typically regarded by many of Zhu Xi's contemporary Ru interpreters as solely concerning the constant succession of changing realities, is perceived by Zhu Xi as also addressing the ontological creative sequence initiated by Ultimate Limit. Zhu says,

> The creativity of Ultimate Limit is like a tree. It branches, and again, from the branches flowers and leaves are generated. The process of *sheng sheng* is therefore endless. When fruits are formed, there is a principle of "endless *sheng sheng* (生生不窮)" within them. These principles start to give further birth. An infinite number of Ultimate Limit (無限太極) is therefore generated, forever and ever.[11]

In conclusion, it is fair to characterize Zhu Xi's ethical metaphysics as a combination of two dimensions: one horizontal/cosmological and the other vertical/ontological. However, Zhu Xi's view of the creativity of Ultimate Limit evolved during his lifetime. Specifically, regarding the question of how to employ the basic dyad of categories—*Li* (理, pattern-principle) and *Qi* (氣, vital-energy)—to explain the creative sequence of Ultimate Limit and other cosmic realities, Zhu's thought underwent several stages of development. By investigating the intellectual dynamics that led to these changes, and particularly by analyzing the advantages and disadvantages of Zhu's thought as manifested in this developmental process, we will have greater resources to determine the most reasonable form of Ru metaphysics in its contemporary and comparative context.

THE TRANSLATION OF *LI* (理)

An issue of translation regarding *Li* must be addressed before delving into Zhu Xi's intellectual biography. *Li* and *Qi* are notably the fundamental dyad of categories in Zhu's metaphysics. When making an initial comparison to the conceptual pair of matter and form in ancient Greek philosophy, *Qi* can be seen as the basic cosmic substance, while *Li* is the principle governing how that substance is organized. *Qi* addresses the question of a thing's origin, while *Li* answers the question of what a thing is in contrast to other things. However, because the Chinese cosmological outlook is typically process-oriented, *Qi* and *Li* possess a distinctly dynamic feature not always equally emphasized by their Greek counterparts, matter and form. It is more accurate to say that *Qi* answers the question of where the energy for a thing's becoming originates, while *Li* explains how a thing comes to be in a harmonizing process with other emerging entities.

Inspired by Stephen Angle's discussion in his book *Sagehood: The Contemporary Significance of Neo-Confucian Philosophy* (2009), I define *Li* as the dynamic and harmonious way in which a set of cosmic realities fit together. This act of "fitting-together" can occur spontaneously, which is consistent with how most natural phenomena emerge. In the human world, *Li* must be realized through human efforts. Overall, the key ideal of Ruism is to have the entire human society fit together both within itself and with the surrounding cosmos.

The benefits of understanding the Ruist concept of *Li* in this manner are evident. First, this definition of *Li* applies to both cosmological and anthropological domains, staying true to the original holistic concern of Ruism.

Second, it does not deny individuality. This is because each thing is a collection of realities, and only when these realities dynamically and harmoniously fit together to a certain degree can the thing maintain its individuality without falling apart. The Song through Ming Ruism, in particular, emphasized "nature (性)" to counter the Buddhist discourse of "no self-nature (無自性)." As a result, it was significant for Ruism to anchor its philosophical discourse on individuality in such an understanding of *Li*.

Third, this understanding of *Li* asserts that a self-harmonized form of individuality cannot be achieved unless the individual fits together with other sets of cosmic realities in their environment. As a result, the concept of "relationship" is also grounded. As evidenced in chapters 3 and 7, some Western interpreters tend to overemphasize the "correlative" aspect of ancient Chinese thought. While their interpretations may be controversial, I believe their relational view can find resonance with my understanding of *Li* here as well.

Fourth, this "fitting-together" language is particularly apt for interpreting Zhu Xi's thought. This is because, for Zhu, *Li* refers not only to the intelligible features that a set of cosmic matter—the vital-energy—displays, but also to the highest ontological principle, Ultimate Limit. As I will analyze in more detail, the *Xici*'s sentence, "Ultimate Limit creates two modes," is interpreted by Zhu to mean "*Li* creates *Qi* (理生氣)." In the Ruist metaphysics exemplified by Zhu's vision, the entire universe can accordingly be seen as "fitting together" from the perspective of Ultimate Limit, since Ultimate Limit is the singular ontological principle that creates and grounds all. Therefore, if we extrapolate by extending the term "set of cosmic realities" to include all possible cosmic realities, Ultimate Limit, as the supreme *Li* for Zhu, can have these realities "fit together" in the most abstract sense.

With connotations of *Li* understood in this way, we can discuss a bit more about its English translation, which has been a key issue in comparative philosophy within English scholarship for decades.

According to *To Explain and Analyze Characters* (說文解字), the origin of the character 理 refers to the action of "ordering jade (治玉)," specifically, following the pattern of veins and figures on an uncarved piece of jade to polish the jade and remove its impure parts.[12] In classical Ruism, 理 could refer either to patterns of phenomena in the entire world, as the verse "(A great person) discerns and institutes the great *Li*, and the entire cosmos is encompassed therein (治割大理而宇宙裡矣)"[13] in the *Xunzi* indicates, or specifically to moral principles in accordance with which the Ruist rituals were invented and maintained, as the verse "The *raison d'être* of ritual is *Li* (禮者, 理也)"[14] in the *Book of Rites* implies. Note that the impressive use of 理 in the opening chapter of the *Xici*, which I cited in chapter 7, refers to both meanings. For a Western audience, the greatest difficulty in translating 理 is that *Li*, for Ru thinkers, is both descriptive and prescriptive, or perhaps more accurately, both natural and moral. To illuminate this point, let's remind ourselves of the above definition of *Li* as the dynamic and harmonious way in which a set of cosmic realities fit together.

If we seek *Li* in the natural world, we may initially take the *Li* of things to refer to instrumental values to be utilized in human endeavors. In other words, we can try to have human behaviors fit into the *Li* of the surrounding environment and thereby realize greater human-related harmonies. However, what is more important is that by pondering how the all-inclusive set of cosmic realities, that is, the universe or *Tian*, fit together, the heartmind of a Ru can be aesthetically galvanized such that they grasp the values of objective natural entities, and then seek to accommodate them in the human world. In essence, the being of *Li* ought to be treated as a holistic world consisting of a value-laden anthropocosmic continuum.

Based on these features of *Li*, many of its traditional English translations falter. If we try to maintain its etymology and translate it as "pattern," then its prescriptive meaning is undermined.[15] If we try to emphasize its intelligible characteristic and interpret it as "principle," *Li*'s aesthetic connotation is lost, because when the English word "principle" is used to describe natural phenomena, it carries a Platonic undertone and will mostly sound as though it is describing a scientific theorem. Stephen Angle's translation, "coherence," does not quite fit either. The main problem with "coherence" is that it smooths out the Ru worldview too much. Natural disasters, like floods and earthquakes, and unavoidable human predicaments, such as disease and gratuitous suffering, have their *Li*, but these *Li* are hardly to be depicted as "coherent" unless we have a very abstract understanding of coherence.[16] This is also the reason why I insist on using vague terms such as "the dynamic and harmonious way in which a set of cosmic realities fit together" to define *Li* per se. From the all-inclusive and most abstract perspective of Ultimate Limit, the "dynamic harmony" that enables all cosmic realities to fit together can then be appreciated in the loosest sense that all realities exist and evolve together in the unsummed whole of the cosmic process. However, this does not imply that realities are necessarily coherent (or do not conflict) with one another, anyway.

In summary, just like other Ruist concepts such as 氣 (vital-energy), 儒 (civilized human), and 士 (scholar-official), in the case of 理, we cannot find a single English word or phrase that perfectly matches its original Ru meaning across varying contexts. Instead, I follow the main trend in current English scholarship, translating *Li* either as "pattern-principle" or "principle." I will include the original Chinese character in my translation if the ideas conveyed in the Chinese sentences cannot be fully illuminated otherwise.

DUALISM OF *LI* AND *QI*

I follow Chen Lai in dividing Zhu Xi's thought into three stages concerning *Li* and *Qi* in relation to Zhu's understanding of Ultimate Limit, though my view of the core features of Zhu Xi's thought at each stage differs from Chen's.[17] The first stage is manifested in Zhu's commentary on

Zhou Dunyi's works, including his commentaries on the *Diagram of Ultimate Limit*, the EDUL, and the BP. I summarize this stage of Zhu's thought as an ontological dualism of *Li* and *Qi* because Zhu Xi didn't believe *Li* was capable of creating *Qi*. He also didn't think that *Li* was ontologically prior to and thus able to be independent from *Qi*. My argument is as follows:

In interpreting the opening sentence in Zhou Dunyi's EDUL, Zhu Xi says,

> [The upper circle in the *Diagram of Ultimate Limit*] represents "Non-Limit and yet Ultimate Limit," which is the fundamental state (本體) from which *yang* arises from activity and *yin* from stillness. However, it cannot be separated from *yin* and *yang*; it is precisely *yin* and *yang* that indicate the fundamental state (即陰陽而指其本體). It is only for the sake of speech that it is distinguished from *yin* and *yang*.[18]

Here, what Zhu Xi means by "fundamental state" is not entirely clear. But it is evident that, as the fundamental state of the *yin/yang* vital-energies, the Non-Limit Ultimate Limit is understood to be inseparable from them. In other words, the actual movement of *yin/yang* vital-energies is always present, and the Non-Limit Ultimate Limit is merely what is used to explain how such a movement proceeds.

Two additional commentarial verses from the same source by Zhu Xi may further support this interpretation:

> Thus, Ultimate Limit is what is wonderful about the fundamental state (本然之妙); what is moving and still is the "occasion" on which it [Ultimate Limit] rides and thus manifests itself (所乘之機). Ultimate Limit is the *Dao* beyond shape, while *yin* and *yang* are the utensil-like things within shape. Observing from what is evident, one can see that while activity and stillness are not simultaneous, and *yin* and *yang* are not the same, nevertheless there is nowhere that Ultimate Limit does not exist in them. Observed from what is subtle, despite being shapeless and invisible, the pattern-principles (*Li*) of activity/stillness and *yin/yang* are completely contained in it [Ultimate Limit].[19]
>
> It is certain that Ultimate Limit and *yin/yang* are not two principles (*Li*). However, since Ultimate Limit has no image while *yin/yang* have their vital-energies (太極無象而陰陽有氣), how can we not differentiate between them what is beyond [shape] and what is within [shape]? This is the reason that there is a differentiation between *Dao* and utensil-like

things. Therefore, Master Cheng says: "*Dao* is beyond shape, and utensil-like things are within shape. We just must say this. However, we must also know that *Dao* is utensil-like things and utensil-like things are also *Dao*."[20]

I will cite another statement from Zhu Xi's letter, written during the same period, before presenting my final analysis of his initial stage of thought:

> Ultimate Limit means the utmost point of *Li* (理之極致). *Li* implies the existence of things, and there is no order of priority between them. Therefore, the verse in the *Xici*, "there is Ultimate Limit in the Change," means that Ultimate Limit is within *yin/yang* and thus is not outside *yin/yang*.... The existence of *Li* entails the existence of *Qi*, and *Qi* always has two forms. Therefore, the *Xici* says that "Ultimate Limit creates two modes."[21]

From these quotations, we can see that the "fundamental state" mentioned in the first quotation is actually the *Li* of *yin/yang* vital-energies. Ultimate Limit is *Li*, and it is thus the reason that *yang* becomes active and *yin* becomes still, leading to the differentiation of *yin/yang* vital-energies from each other. However, at this stage of Zhu Xi's thought, *Li* cannot be said to create *Qi* yet, since *Li* is always within *Qi* and cannot be separated from *Qi*. *Li* remains at the same ontological rank as *Qi*, as they are not considered to be two separate principles.

Following my previous analysis of Zhou Dunyi, we see that Zhu Xi explicitly denies the existence of any intermediary stage of primordial *Qi* between Ultimate Limit and *yin/yang* vital-energy. Any form of vital-energy must be either *yin* or *yang*, and they have their explanatory principles within Ultimate Limit. Since Zhu does not believe it is *Li* that creates *yin/yang* vital-energy, and instead views Ultimate Limit as the supreme *Li*, which explains how *yin* and *yang* move and are distinguished from each other, I will summarize his thought at this stage as an ontological dualism.

In this stage, Zhu Xi takes the existence of *yin/yang* vital-energies, the two most basic forms of cosmic realities, for granted. He does not intend to probe the ultimate reason for the origin of *yin/yang* vital-energies. The principle of Ultimate Limit, as the *Li* of vital-energy which is always present, is mainly used for explaining what *yin/yang* vital-energies are, rather than where they come from. Correspondingly, the Non-Limit feature of Ultimate Limit, at this stage of Zhu Xi's thought, is more aptly seen as a description of the non-*Qi* feature of *Li*, rather than the unconditionality of Ultimate Limit's creative power which brings either form of *Qi* into being. In other words, since vital-energy is always within shape as "utensil-like things," the non-*Qi* feature of *Li* is typically construed by Zhu Xi as beyond shape and "without sound, without smell (無聲無臭)."[22]

It is understandable that principles, which are used to explain the movement of shaped realities, cannot be said to have the same shape anymore. Just as in the Platonic theory of forms, the form of redness cannot be said to have the same visible features as a concrete mode of redness that a flower, for instance, has. However, Zhu Xi's thought has not yet delved into the sequence of ontological dependence between Ultimate Limit and the two modes, which is explicitly addressed by both the text of *Xici* and Zhou Dunyi's EDUL.

THE ONTOLOGICAL PRIORITY OF *LI* OVER *QI*

The first stage of Zhu Xi's thought contains an intrinsic difficulty because both the *Xici*'s and Zhou Dunyi's texts explicitly articulate the notion that it is Ultimate Limit which creates *yin/yang*. If we follow Zhu's interpretation and understand Ultimate Limit to be the *Li* of vital-energy, while simultaneously claiming that *Li* is always within *Qi* and can't be separated from it, it will be very difficult to establish the fact that it is Ultimate Limit, *Li*, which creates *Qi*, and thus is ontologically prior to *Qi*.

It was through a series of letter exchanges with other eminent Ru thinkers that Zhu Xi finally developed his more refined idea: *Li* is not only within *Qi*, but also ontologically prior to *Qi*. Among these exchanges, the debate between Zhu Xi and the Lu brothers, Lu Zimei (陆子美, 1128–1205) and Lu Zijing (陆子静, 1139–1193), played a crucial role. My analysis of the second stage of Zhu's metaphysical thought will therefore pivot upon this debate.

There are three major points upon which the Lu brothers (mainly Lu Zijing, also known as Lu Jiuyuan 陆九渊, a pioneering Ru thinker in the lineage of the learning of heartmind [心學] in Song through Ming Ruism) disagree with Zhu Xi: First, although both Lu brothers and Zhu Xi agree that Ultimate Limit is the root of all changes in the world, for the Lu brothers, in order to articulate the foundational role of the creative power of Ultimate Limit, there is no need to add another phrase, "Non-Limit," before it. They think this is redundant and will make the distinctive Ru cosmology, which is founded in "solid principle (实理)" rather than "vacuous principle (虚理)," sound too Daoist.

Second, Zhu Xi construes the meaning of the character 極 in 太極 (Ultimate Limit) as "the utmost point" or "ultimacy (致极)." For Zhu, because Ultimate Limit is the ultimate creative power beyond which nothing can be said, we need another phrase of "Non-Limit" to characterize its unconditionality. However, Lu Zijing, the younger brother, thinks 極 should be construed as "centrality (中)," meaning that Ultimate Limit is the root of all cosmic changes, and thus stands in the center of the entire universe. In Lu Zijing's view, accordingly, people can take the ontological features of Ultimate Limit's creative power to refer to the ultimate moral standards for human deeds. There is no need to add the phrase "Non-Limit" to Ultimate Limit since this will make human beings lose their moral standards and thus become morally disoriented and "non-centered."

Third, Zhu Xi understands that anything said about *yin/yang* is up to *yin/yang* vital-energy, and therefore, that those sayings belong to the discourse about "what lies within shape." However, Lu Zijing thinks, according to the *Xici* verses "one *yin* and one *yang*, this is called *Dao*" and "What lies beyond shape is called *Dao*," that *yin/yang* is already *Dao*, and thus, that sayings about *yin/yang* really pertain to "what lies beyond shape."

We can see that the first two points are interrelated. As for the third, it concerns how to correctly understand the ontological rank of the categorical dyad of *yin/yang*. Correspondingly, Zhu Xi's answers to the first two challenges are also interconnected, and for us, they are the most important since they reveal Zhu's further understanding of the creative sequence between Ultimate Limit and *yin/yang* in the second stage of his metaphysical thought. In the following, I will quote and analyze Zhu Xi's responses to the first two points, and then state my own view in regard to the Zhu-Lu controversy over the third point.

When asked by Lu Zimei whether "Non-Limit" should be added before "Ultimate Limit," Zhu Xi responds:

> If Non-Limit is not mentioned, Ultimate Limit will be understood as equal to a thing and cannot qualify as the root of all changes in the world. If Ultimate Limit is not mentioned, Non-Limit will degenerate into pure emptiness and quiescence, and cannot qualify as the root of all changes in the world either.[23]

Zhu Xi's response implies that the first sentence of Zhou Dunyi's EDUL, "Non-Limit and yet Ultimate Limit," describes two intimately interrelated aspects of Ultimate Limit as the foundational ontological creative power. Non-Limit connotes its unconditionality, but this does not mean that Ultimate Limit does not function. Non-Limit is not an opposing positive power to Ultimate Limit. Instead, considering Non-Limit as Ultimate Limit implies that the ontological creative power of Ultimate Limit is not conditioned by anything and is therefore not any created thing. In a comparative perspective, Zhu Xi's understanding of Ultimate Limit, as indicated by the exchanged letter, achieves the same ontological depth as Plotinus's idea of the One as the "generator of being" and Paul Tillich's idea of God as the "ground of being." This places Zhu Xi within the Ruist metaphysical tradition of *generatio ex nihilo*, which is defined by the *Xici* and by Wang Bi and Han Kangbo, as explained in chapter 7.

In answering a similar doubt from Lu Zijing, the younger brother, Zhu Xi further explained his understanding of the Non-Limit feature of Ultimate Limit:

> Master Zhou characterizes Ultimate Limit as Non-Limit because it has neither position nor shape. Ultimate Limit is able to exist before no thing exists, while simultaneously, it still establishes itself after things are generated. It is able to exist outside *yin* and *yang*, while simultaneously, it still functions within *yin* and *yang* (以為在陰陽之外而未嘗不行乎陰陽之中). It is omnipresent and thus runs throughout the entire universe; but originally, neither sound, smell, nor any kind of influence can be found in it. Now if you think the phrase "Non-Limit" is unnecessary [for depicting this nature of Ultimate Limit], then you actually take Ultimate Limit as something with shape and with position.[24]

It can be seen from this answer how Zhu Xi's metaphysical thought evolved from what it was in its first stage. In the first stage, Zhu Xi thought that "Ultimate Limit is within *yin/yang* and thus, is not outside *yin/yang*." However, here, Zhu Xi said that Ultimate Limit "is able to exist outside *yin* and *yang*, while simultaneously, it still functions within *yin* and *yang*." It is legitimate for us to claim that here, Zhu Xi finally grasps the exact meaning of ontological dependence connotated by the original *Xici*'s sentence, "Ultimate Limit creates two modes." Ultimate Limit is ontologically prior to the two modes, while the two modes and other concrete forms of cosmic realities are all manifestations of Ultimate Limit. On one hand, it can be said that Ultimate Limit exists even before no thing exists, since it is Ultimate Limit that creates everything. On the other hand, Ultimate Limit still "establishes itself" or "functions" when things in the universe are changing, since concrete cosmic realities are all manifestations of the ultimate ontological creative power. We need to keep in mind that no sequence of priority mentioned in this quotation is temporal. Ultimate Limit is able to exist "before (之前)" anything exists, with "before" here referring to ontological priority. By the same token, Ultimate Limit exists "outside" yin and yang, with "outside" also meaning the ontological independence of Ultimate Limit from its created outcomes since it is ontologically prior.

With Zhu Xi's following answer to Lu Zijing's challenge about how to construe the meaning of 極 (ji), we will be able to understand the reason why Zhu Xi could have reached this exact idea of ontological dependence at this second stage:

> What is the Ultimate Limit mentioned by the *Xici*? It is the principle of two modes, four images, and eight trigrams; that principle exists before them, while simultaneously being embodied within them (具於三者之先而蘊於三者之內者). It extends thoroughly to the ultimate point [of beings]. There is no name able to name it. Therefore, the sage called it "Ultimate Limit." ... The meaning of *ji* (極) is ultimacy (致極).[25]

In Zhu Xi's further explanation, "centrality" mentioned by Lu Zijing can be considered to be an outcome of the primary meaning of *Ji* as ultimacy. Only because the creativity of Ultimate Limit is ultimate, human deeds are conditioned by it and thus can refer to it as the ultimate moral standard. However, the most significant point for us about this quotation is that it indicates the intellectual origin of Zhu's thought. It is clear that Zhu's idea of ontological dependence comes from the operational process for how the two modes, four images and eight trigrams in the *Yijing* symbology derive from each other and ultimately from Ultimate Limit. As I discussed in Zhou Dunyi's case, Zhou's *Diagram of Ultimate Limit* also intends to illustrate an ontological cosmogony, or "chain of being," which corresponds to this *Yijing* operational process. In a word, this seminal *Yijing* text has a foundational role for the ontological thinking in Ruism. Zhou Dunyi and Zhu Xi are eminent representatives of this type of thinking in Song through Ming Ruism. And their predecessors can be identified in Wang Bi's and Han Kangbo's commentaries on the same text. This is because Zhu's words, "extends to the ultimate point (of beings)" and "no name able to name it" are so reminiscent of Wang's and Han's words that I quoted in chapter 7. I conclude that Wang Bi, Han Kangbo, Zhou Dunyi, and Zhu Xi belong to the same lineage of Chinese Ru metaphysics, the one of *generatio ex nihilo*, which is comparable to the one of *creatio ex nihilo* in the West.

Through such exchanges of letters with the Lu brothers, Zhu Xi fully grasped the idea of the "ontological priority" of Ultimate Limit over *yin/yang* vital-energies. Using the same character *Li* but with a new understanding of its role in Ru cosmology, Zhu further paraphrased the ontological priority of Ultimate Limit over *yin/yang* vital-energies as the ontological priority of *Li* over *Qi*. Therefore, in this stage of Zhu's thought, we can find similar expressions such as:

> Ultimate Limit creates *yin* and *yang*. This means *Li* creates *Qi* (理生氣). After *yin* and *yang* are created, Ultimate Limit is within them, and thus *Li* is also within *Qi*.[6]
>
> [Ultimate Limit] moves and then *yang* is created, it stills and then *yin* is created. The creative power referred to by the word "create" (生) is from Ultimate Limit. . . . Non-Limit and yet Ultimate Limit: This means nonbeing can create being (无能生有).[27]
>
> Although *Qi* is created by *Li*, . . . [28]

Compared with the first stage of Zhu Xi's metaphysics, which I characterized as an ontological dualism of *Li* and *Qi*, there are two new features for this second stage: First, the radical expression, "nonbeing can create being," refers to the ontological dependence of the entire world upon Ultimate Limit, and thus, Zhu was not taking the being of *yin/yang* vital-energies for granted and instead was trying to answer where the world ultimately came from. Among all philosophical statements on ultimate creativity in the Ru tradition we have surveyed in this book, Zhu Xi's "nonbeing can create being (無能生有)" turns out to be literally the closest to *creatio ex nihilo*. Second, it is no longer the case that *Li* is thought of as a parallel principle to *Qi*, and purports to explain what a thing is rather than where the thing comes from. Instead, Ultimate Limit was still considered by Zhu to be *Li*, but because of its ontological priority over all other derived cosmic realities, Zhu thought *Li*, as a singular principle, can explain both where the world is from and how the beings within the world continue to be diversified on a daily new basis. At this second stage, Zhu's understanding of *Li* has achieved the same unconditionality, singularity, and thus, nonduality of the Good for Plato, of the One for Plotinus, or of God in the Christian *creatio ex nihilo* tradition. In this sense, we can characterize this stage of Zhu Xi's metaphysics as an ontological monism of *Li*.

THE CONFUSING USE OF THE TERM OF *LI* BY ZHU XI

After Zhu Xi gained insight into the ontological priority of *Li* over *Qi*, his metaphysical thought progressed to its third and final stage. In this stage, the newly developed meanings of the conceptual pair *Li* and *Qi* were employed to address various issues related to metaphysics, epistemology, ethics, and psychology, among others. As I briefly discussed earlier, in Zhu's case, *Li* can be generally defined as the dynamic and harmonious way in which a set of cosmic realities (which can encompass the entire universe) fit together. However, when viewed from the perspective of the created realm of beings, *Li* and *Qi* should be considered as existing at the same ontological level. *Qi* explains the source of a thing's energy for becoming, while *Li* explains how a thing comes to be in a harmonious relationship with other things. From either a cosmologically temporal perspective or an ontologically nontemporal one, there is no priority or posteriority between the realities that these two terms refer to. This ontological dualism was indicated in the first stage of Zhu Xi's metaphysical thought. However, when Zhu Xi considered *Li* as ontologically prior to *Qi* in his second stage of thought, and named Ultimate Limit itself as *Li*, doing so increased the potential for confusion regarding either the use of terms or the philosopher's thought itself. I will illustrate the consequences of Zhu Xi's incautious use of terms with two examples from his writings.

In one of Zhu Xi's letters in response to Liu Shuyi, he discusses the relationship between *Li* and *Qi* as follows:

> *Li* and *Qi* are absolutely two distinct entities. However, when viewed from the perspective of concrete things, the two are intertwined and inseparable. This doesn't negate the fact that they are originally two distinct entities. If viewed from the perspective of *Li*, a thing's principle already exists even when the thing does not exist yet (雖未有物而已有物之理). However, in this case, only *Li* exists, and the thing has not come into solid existence.[29]

In my view, this statement is quite confusing. From a de facto empirical perspective, neither the *Li* nor the *Qi* of any concrete thing should be considered prior to the other. Instead, they are equal and indispensable to each other concerning their roles in explaining concrete cosmic entities. Zhu Xi's metaphysical thought in its first stage supports this interpretation. Only if *Li* is interpreted as Ultimate Limit, the singular principle (which is ontologically prior to any concrete principles) to explain both where a thing comes from and what it is, can we safely assert that even if a thing does not exist, its *Li* is able to be there. However, if we confuse these two very different meanings of *Li* and say, as Zhu Xi did in that quotation, that even if things don't exist, their *Li* are already there, this will closely resemble the idealism of Plato or Hegel, who envision the entire cosmos as the unfolding of a preexisting intelligible world of ideas or absolute spirit. With Zhu's thought interpreted as such, the creation of Ultimate Limit could not have been qualified as "Non-Limit" or unconditional since its creativity would unfold in compliance with a preexisting world of *Li*.

The second example is from two discussions between Zhu Xi and his correspondents about whether *Li* moves or remains still:

> It is acceptable to say Ultimate Limit contains movement and stillness (含動靜) [this is from the perspective of its role as the fundamental state (本體). Comment by Zhu Xi himself]. It is also acceptable to say Ultimate Limit has movement and stillness (有動靜) [this is from the perspective of its running and performing function (流行). Comment by Zhu Xi himself]. However, if it is said that Ultimate Limit is the movement and the stillness (是動靜), then this assertion confuses the two domains of discourse—the one about what is beyond shape and the one about what is within shape. In this case, the *Yijing* sentence, "There is Ultimate Limit in the Change" will become redundant.[30]
>
> Someone asked about the teaching, "*Li* is prior to *Qi*." Zhu Xi answered: "There is no need to say this. So far, who knows whether it is *Li* prior to *Qi* or *Qi* prior to *Li*? No alternative can be made clear. However, according to my assessment, it should be the case that *Qi* runs according to *Li*, and when *Qi* gathers, *Li* is also within it. This is because *Qi* can come together, produce, and make things up, while *Li* has no emotions, no intentions, no calculations, and thus, it cannot produce and make things up (氣則能凝結造作, 理卻無情意無計度無造作)."[31]

Zhu Xi's thought in the first quotation is very clear, and it refers to the verse of Zhou Dunyi's EDUL about how Ultimate Limit produces *yin* and *yang* through its movement and stillness. In Zhu's mind, Ultimate Limit is the reason *yin* and *yang* are produced, such that the movement and stillness of *yin* and *yang* are manifestations of the creative power of Ultimate Limit. Therefore, it can be said that Ultimate Limit contains the principle for the way in which *yin* and *yang* change, and that Ultimate Limit is manifested in the form of the changes of *yin* and *yang*. However, it is inappropriate to characterize Ultimate Limit *per se* as the movement and stillness of *yin* and *yang*. This improper characterization of Ultimate Limit tends to confuse the cosmological and ontological, or the physical and metaphysical features of cosmic changes, and thus makes the original teaching in the *Xici* ambiguous and redundant.

Zhu Xi's thought in the second quotation is also clear. From the point of view of the created world, *Qi* explains where the dynamics of things (which are in the perpetual process of becoming) ultimately come from, and *Li* explains how things in this process of becoming relate to other becoming things. In this sense, *Li* is merely the trait the process of a thing's becoming presents, and hence, we can construe *Li* as the intelligible principle underlying the dynamics of *Qi* to explain how *Qi* operates. It is therefore entirely legitimate for Zhu to say that it is *Qi* that produces and creates things, while *Li* is simply the way in which this generative process appears to be organized.

However, if we read these two quotations together, considerable confusion will undoubtedly arise. Because Zhu Xi also refers to Ultimate Limit per se as *Li*, it is hardly legitimate for him to say that, in general, *Li* does not produce and create things.

In summary, I believe that the likely fault in Zhu Xi's unclear thinking and wording about the relationship between *Li* and *Qi* stems from his ambiguous use of the term *Li*. When comparing these ideas with the Greek-European Christian tradition of *creatio ex nihilo*, philosophers in that tradition typically use one term to refer to the singular supreme principle and another term to distinguish it from the principle used for explaining what a thing is. For Plato, these are Demiurge and Form. For Plotinus, they are Oneness and Intellect. For medieval Christian thinkers, they are God and divine intellect. Although this Western tradition has its own inherent difficulties to overcome, none of them arises from the confusing use of terms, as in Zhu's case. Therefore, to enhance Zhu Xi's systematic metaphysics, I would suggest not using the term *Li* to designate Ultimate Limit per se. It is Ultimate Limit that creates both *Qi* and *Li*, and thus *Qi* and *Li* belong to the same ontological rank and are equally applicable for explaining concrete cosmic entities. In this way, the cognitive process for a Ru in probing how a cosmic entity changes will become entirely empirical, as it will not be constrained by any potentially preexisting idea of *Li*, and correspondingly, the creativity of Ultimate Limit will be secured as genuinely unconditional. As will be demonstrated in the following, some later versions of Ru cosmology in Song through Ming Ruism after Zhu Xi were actually oriented toward my suggestion.

ZHU XI'S VIEW OF LAOZI

The final aspect I need to reflect on regarding Zhu Xi's metaphysics is his view toward Laozi and the related Daoist cosmology.

As per my analysis in chapter 7, Laozi's and other Daoist or pro-Daoist philosophical cosmologies played a significant role in the formation of corresponding thought in Ruism. It was Wang Bi who interpreted the distinctively Daoist phrase, "being comes from nonbeing" (有生于無, *Dao De Jing*, chapter 40), and construed it to refer to the unconditionality of the ultimate ontological creative power of the *Dao* (which is equivalent to Ultimate Limit for Wang) proposed in the text of *Xici*. Following Wang Bi and Han Kangbo's thought, the Ru commentarial tradition on the *Yijing* ultimately reached the idea of Ultimate Limit as *generatio ex nihilo*. According to the current chapter, their way of interpreting the *Yijing* was followed by Zhou Dunyi and Zhu Xi. I have already analyzed the fundamental difference between Laozi's *Dao De Jing* and Confucius's *Xici* in chapter 7. Following this analysis, it will be valuable for us to investigate how Zhu Xi understood the Daoist founding text, and hence, to verify my interpretation of Zhu's metaphysics.

The following two quotations are from the first stage of Zhu Xi's metaphysical thought:

> The essence of [Zhou Dunyi's] *Diagram*, which illustrates the lost meaning of the *Yijing*, is different from Laozi. Laozi believes things are created from being, and being is created from nonbeing. He proposes a literal beginning and an end for cosmic changes (以造化為真有始終者), and this view is opposite to the *Diagram*.[32]
>
> The existence of *Li* implies that of *Qi*, and *Qi* always has two forms (氣則無不兩); therefore, the *Yijing* says Ultimate Limit creates two modes. In comparison, Laozi says *Dao* creates One at first, and then One creates Two. Laozi's insight is therefore not refined.[33]

Previously, I characterized Zhu Xi's metaphysics in its first stage as an ontological dualism of *Li* and *Qi*. Although he had not yet reached the idea of the ontological priority of *Li* over *Qi*, Zhu understands the creative relationship between Ultimate Limit, the two modes, and four images, which are portrayed in the *Xici*, as definitively nontemporal. In contrast, he perceives Laozi's cosmological sequence of *Dao*'s creation, which starts from the nothingness of *Dao*, or a giant vacuum, and then to the being of Oneness, Two, etc., as temporal. This highlights the ontological nature of Zhu's metaphysics, and such a nature characterizes the entirety of Zhu's thought consistently. In other words, Zhu Xi has a clear intention to differentiate temporal cosmological thinking from nontemporal ontological thinking in his work.

In the second stage of Zhu Xi's metaphysics, Lu Jiuyuan once accused Zhu of being too Daoist for following Zhou Dunyi to use "Non-Limit" to interpret Ultimate Limit. Zhu's first response was that Ruism is a progressively evolving tradition, and thus, although there were no prior Ru who had talked about the Non-Limit feature of Ultimate Limit, this doesn't mean that later Ru cannot discuss it. Neither does it mean that this new term of Non-Limit cannot capture the truth about the ultimate creative power of Ultimate Limit.[34] In addition, we find two other points within Zhu Xi's responding letters that attempt to differentiate his thought from Daoism:

> I [Zhu Xi] think that when Laozi talks of being and non-being, he considers these as two separate things. However, when Master Zhou talks of being and non-being, they are the same thing (以有無為一). Their thoughts are opposite to each other like north is to south and fire is to water.[35]
>
> When Laozi says "to return to Non-Limit," "Non-Limit" here means indefiniteness (無窮). It is like saying, "Pupil Zhuang enters into the door of indefiniteness, and thus travels in a wild field of Non-Limit." This is not what Master Zhou meant [by Non-Limit].[36]

The first quotation reemphasizes Zhu Xi's insight shared in the first and second stages of his metaphysical thought: Non-Limit is one feature of Ultimate Limit, and thus it is none other than Ultimate Limit. Instead, Laozi's thought was viewed by Zhu as understanding nonbeing to be separated from and temporarily prior to being. In Zhu's view, Laozi's thought has no real foundation to compare with its Ru counterpart, notwithstanding that both of them use the same Chinese characters in philosophizing related topics of metaphysics.

The most interesting point for our purpose is from the second quotation. Here, while quoting the *Dao De Jing* and the *Zhuangzi*, Zhu Xi denies that "Non-Limit" could mean the "indefiniteness" of a wild field. When I examined Zhou Dunyi's thought, I differentiated the interpretative thought of Ultimate Limit before the Tang dynasty into two lineages. One belonging to Wang Bi and Han Kangbo uses the unconditional "nonbeing" to explain Ultimate Limit, and thus is comparable to the Western tradition of *creatio ex nihilo*. The other understands Ultimate Limit to be an undifferentiated whole of primordial vital-energy, and "nonbeing" in this lineage means the formless nature of this primordial whole. In denying that Non-Limit connotes the indefiniteness of a wild field, Zhu clearly separates himself from the second lineage, which separation can also be confirmed by Zhu's frequent assertion in his aforementioned writings and dialogues that he does not believe in the existence of the kind of vital-energy which can be without *yin/yang* determinations.

In summary, Zhu Xi's view toward Laozi and the related Daoist cosmology is similar to my own, which I expressed in chapter 7. I must confess to my readers that my reading of Laozi took place much earlier than my reading of Zhu, so the similarity was a coincidence, although from a logical perspective, these similar thoughts are implied by our understanding of the logic respectively internal to the *Dao De Jing* and the *Xici*. One significant conclusion we can reach is that Zhu Xi's Ru metaphysics, pivoting on Ultimate Limit, follows the tradition of Wang Bi, Han Kangbo, and Zhou Dunyi, and is thus comparable to the Western tradition of *creatio ex nihilo*.

A Minor Challenge by Cao Duan to Zhu Xi's Understanding of Ultimate Limit

As exemplified by the orthodox status that Zhu Xi's Ru learning achieved in the Yuan dynasty (1271–1368 CE), his metaphysical thought was not significantly challenged during the remaining time of Song through Ming Ruism after his death.[37] However, as my analysis shows, Zhu's final achievement in Ru metaphysics is not flawless. His use of the term "principle (理)" is confusing, leading to a potentially unclear conception of Ultimate Limit. It seems that what later Ru metaphysicians need to do in order to improve Zhu's system is to "chip off" and then "bind back up." In other words, they need to remove the unnecessary confusion resulting from Zhu's less than clearly defined use of terms, and then reconstruct the Ru metaphysics surrounding the central idea of Ultimate Limit in a more coherent way. However, whether they can succeed in doing so is certainly open to debate. To illustrate this process, I will examine Cao Duan and Luo Qinshun as two exemplary Ru metaphysicians during the period of Ming Ruism.

CAO DUAN'S UNDERSTANDING OF ULTIMATE LIMIT AND PRINCIPLE

Cao Duan (曹端, 1376–1434 CE) was once praised by later Ruist intellectual historians as "the crown of the learning of *Li* at the beginning of the Ming dynasty (明初理學之冠)."[38] This phrase highlights the close connection between Cao Duan's thought and Zhu Xi's, and accordingly, Cao Duan's understanding of Ultimate Limit also largely follows Zhu's. Cao said:

> Ultimate Limit is another name for *Li*. It is where the Way of *Tian* is established, and how the solid *Li* acts. This is the origin of the learning of *Li* and rooted in *Tian*.[39]
>
> "Limit" means "the utmost point (至極)," and this is another name for *Li*. "Ultimate (太)" implies nothing greater can be added (大無以加). As for *Li*, it has no image, thus invisible; no sound nor vital-energy, and thus inaudible. It has no boundary or location to be pointed out, while its function pervades heaven and earth, penetrates the ancient and contemporary. Hence, since *Li* is so all-encompassing, how can we add anything [to it]?[40]

As for the relationship between *Li* (pattern-principle) and *Qi* (vital-energy), Cao Duan's ideas are also similar to Zhu Xi's:

> *Qi* is created by *Li*, and *Li* becomes solid because of *Qi*. There is no separation between them.
>
> Ultimate Limit is the *Li*. Yin and yang are the *Qi*. The existence of *Li* implies that of *Qi*. Where *Qi* is, *Li* is, and how can *Li* be separated from *Qi* (理豈離乎氣)?
>
> Although *Li* is within *Qi*, *Li* is not mixed with *Qi*. That is why Master Zhou describes *Li* within the movement and stillness of *yin* and *yang*, but also highlights it as being beyond them. This is because *Li* cannot be mixed with *Qi* (理氣之不相雜).[41]

It is not surprising that Cao Duan's thoughts about the relationship between *Li* and *Qi* continue the same ambiguity as Zhu Xi's since they both use *Li* to refer to two ontologically disparate things: Ultimate Limit, and the pattern-principle according to which a thing comes to be in a harmonizing relationship with other things in a de facto way. In my view, only when *Li* is referring to Ultimate Limit can it be said that *Li* creates vital-energy and can't be mixed with it ontologically. And only when *Li* is referring to the latter can it be said that there is no ontological split between *Li* and *Qi*. The confusion of these two referents will lead to ambiguous metaphysical thought evidenced by the above quotations.

CAO DUAN'S CHALLENGE TO ZHU XI

Though sharing many similar ideas, Cao Duan still challenged Zhu Xi on one crucial point: whether Ultimate Limit moves or not. Cao Duan says:

> Master Zhou says, "Ultimate Limit moves and then generates *yang*," and "Ultimate Limit stills and then generates *yin*." This means that the generation of *yin* and *yang* results from the movement and stillness of Ultimate Limit. Master Zhu's interpretation [of these words] is also very clear. Master Zhu says: "The division of the two modes is because of the movement and stillness of Ultimate Limit; the generation of the five phases is because of the alternation and congealing of *yin* and *yang* vital-energy." This is not different from Master Zhou. However, when I read his recorded dialogues, I find that Master Zhu says: "Ultimate Limit cannot move or be still by itself. It rides on the movement and stillness of *yin/yang* vital-energy and then it can move and be still." Then, Master Zhu says: "The way *Li* rides on *Qi* is like a human riding on horse. Because the horse goes outside and inside, the human also goes outside and inside." This is a metaphor for describing that, due to the movement and stillness of *Qi*, *Li* also moves and stills. If this is the case, the human [riding on the horse] is a dead one, and then cannot be qualified to be the most spiritual among the myriad things (萬物之靈); the *Li* [riding on the vital-energy] is a dead *Li*, and cannot qualify to be the origin of all changes. If this is the case, is there still anything about *Li* that will be revered and anything about humans that will be valued? Now I would say the person riding on the horse is alive. In this sense, the outside-and-inside, slow-and-fast running of the horse is entirely governed by human beings. A *Li* that is alive (活理) should also be like this.[42]

Cao Duan's doubt about Zhu Xi is that if *Li*'s movement and stillness are due to the movement and stillness of vital-energy, it can hardly be said that Ultimate Limit, as the supreme *Li*, is the creative origin of all under heaven. Hence, Cao would like to change the metaphor of "dead rider" to "alive rider" in order to illustrate that Ultimate Limit is a lively principle.

Nevertheless, I don't think Zhu Xi's thought necessarily fell into the defect that Cao Duan was challenging. Zhu's insight quoted previously[43] resonates with Zhou Dunyi when Zhou explains in what sense Ultimate Limit can be portrayed as moving or stilling: It is only from the results that it creates that Ultimate Limit can be seen as moving or not. However, because Ultimate Limit's creativity is prior to all derived observable realities, there is no way for human beings to know how Ultimate Limit creates all these realities in a moving or still way. Ultimate Limit is alive, but the way it creates *yin* and *yang* is beyond the observed duality of movement or stillness of any set of cosmic vital-energies.

However, Zhu Xi employed the term *Li* to refer to both Ultimate Limit itself and the pattern-principle through which a set of cosmic realities become organized in a de facto manner. This type of *Li*, namely the pattern-principle, is ontologically inferior to Ultimate Limit. Consequently, Zhu Xi can use the latter reference of *Li* to emphasize that *Qi* provides the origin of things' becoming, while *Li* itself does not move or become still. This is the primary reason that Zhu's ideas were challenged by Cao Duan: If the latter reference of "*Li*" coincides with Ultimate Limit itself, then the statement that *Li* does not move or create is evidently contradictory to Zhu's thoughts on Ultimate Limit.

In a word, Cao Duan did not contribute much novelty to the discussion, as his seemingly reformative point was already encompassed in Zhu Xi's thought, and he made no effort to clarify Zhu's confusing use of terms. However, Cao's challenge does draw our attention to an issue that should be addressed by subsequent interpreters of Zhu's thought: We ought to refine the references to "*Li*", thereby avoiding the confusion caused by Zhu's various formulations regarding Ultimate Limit and *Li*. We will find that this conundrum in Zhu Xi's metaphysics is also reflected in the thinking of Luo Qinshun (羅欽順, 1465–1547 CE).

"Principle as the Pattern of Vital-Energy"— Luo Qinshun on Ultimate Limit

The development of Song through Ming Ruist thought, within the lineage of Cheng Yi and Zhu Xi, commonly referred to as the "learning of principle (理學)," underwent a significant transformation led by Luo Qinshun during the Ming Dynasty. In chapter 2, I previously utilized the case of Luo Qinshun's argument with Wang Yangming to highlight the scientific nature of Ru metaphysical debates. Here, I will continue to elaborate on Luo's metaphysics to demonstrate the further development of Zhu Xi's metaphysics within Ming Ruism.

We are already aware of the challenge posed by Cao Duan to Zhu Xi's metaphysics in the early Ming dynasty. The challenge was that if *Li* refers only to the intelligible way in which a body of vital-energy structures itself and relates to other entities in a de facto manner, the "alive" and creative aspect of Ultimate Limit would be dismissed. Based on this point, Cao Duan argued that we should assert that *Li* is also alive.

Interestingly, Luo Qinshun's critical reflection on Zhu Xi's thought is actually based on what can be inferred from Zhu's metaphysics when we accept the basic assumption that *Li* is indeed only the intelligible way in which a body of vital-energy structures itself and relates to others in a de facto manner. In other words, Luo's metaphysics is predicated on the de facto and eternal existence of vital-energy as the fundamental "stuff" that fills the entire cosmos. Considering the immense influence of Luo's *Qi*-rooted cosmology on later Ruist thought, I will conclude chapter 8 with my interpretation of Luo Qinshun to demonstrate how the Ru metaphysical tradition of *generatio ex nihilo* reached its historical conclusion during the period of Song through Ming Ruism.

LI AS THE PATTERN OF VITAL-ENERGY

In the section where I discussed Zhu Xi's ideas, we saw that *Li* can be translated into English in multiple ways. This discussion is particularly relevant to Luo Qinshun's thought because, in his case, *Li* is more appropriately translated as "pattern" than as "principle." This is because the English word "principle" can, among other meanings, convey something similar to the Platonic idea of "form." These forms are independent entities that exist in an intelligible world. However, for Luo, all *Li* is the *Li* of vital-energy, and therefore it is impossible to imagine a world of "principles" that are independent of the empirical world. That being said, in order to maintain consistency in terms of translation, I will continue to use the term "principle" or "pattern-principle" instead of "pattern" throughout the remainder of this section.

We can observe Luo Qinshun's understanding of *Li* in the following two quotations:

> Principle is all about principles of vital-energy (理只是氣之理), and we should recognize the principle from where vital-energy turns and twists (於氣之轉折處觀之). Leaving and then coming, coming and then leaving, this is where vital-energy turns and twists. What leaves cannot fail to come again. What comes cannot fail to leave again. We don't know why this happens, but we do know it indeed happens. It seems to us that there is one thing dominating this coming-and-leaving process, and this thing makes the entire process happen. This is why "principle" gets its name.[44]
>
> I think that when vital-energy gathers, this is the principle for gathering. When vital-energy disperses, that is the principle for dispersing. Because vital-energy can gather and disperse, principle gets its *raison d'être*.[45]

According to Luo's view, the ontological realm of *Li* perfectly overlaps with that of *Qi*. *Li* is simply the pattern in which *Qi* moves back and forth, and humans can understand these patterns in a purely empirical way. In this sense, *Li* is one aspect of *Qi*. Epistemologically, we can differentiate them as two concepts: one representing the substance comprising any evolving cosmic reality, and the other referring to how that substance changes. However, ontologically, they belong to the same reality. This ontological insight is further encapsulated eloquently by Luo in this sentence, "I always think that principle and vital-energy are one thing."[46]

LUO QINSHUN'S VIEW OF ULTIMATE LIMIT

Because, as stated by Luo Qinshun, *Li* is considered ontologically identical to *Qi*, Zhu Xi's original insight that "*Li* creates *Qi*" is consequently abandoned. This leads us to an innovative understanding of Ultimate Limit. The following passage is a lengthy quotation, but we can dissect it step by step afterward:

> When Confucius commented on the *Classic of Change*, the topic "to thoroughly investigate principles (窮理)" began to be addressed. What is this "principle"? Between Heaven and Earth, from ancient times to the present, there is only one vital-energy. This vital-energy is singular, and it moves and becomes still, departs and returns, opens and closes, ascends and descends. It operates in cycles and is endless. Its function

becomes explicit due to the accumulation of implicit elements. Then, its function turns implicit again after becoming explicit. This is exemplified in the warmth, coolness, cold, and heat of the four seasons, the birth, growth, fruition, and dormancy of myriad things, the daily life and relationships of people, and the successes, failures, achievements, and mistakes in human affairs.

These things are intricately intertwined in countless ways, yet ultimately, they are not in disarray. It seems that we may not know the reasons for why they come to be so, but we do know they come to be so; thus, the term "principle" is coined (有莫知其所以然而然, 是即所謂理也). Therefore, the principle is not originally a separate entity that establishes itself alongside vital-energy and attaches to it. Some scholars, due to the verse "There is Ultimate Limit in the Change," believe that a single entity governs the change of *yin/yang* vital-energy. In reality, they are mistaken. The truth is that the Change is the collective name for two modes, four images, and eight trigrams, while the Ultimate Limit is the comprehensive term for all principles (太極則眾理之總名). "There is Ultimate Limit in the Change" signifies that all particular things originate from a single source; from here, we can deduce the order of the *sheng sheng* (生生) process and understand how the single origin is dispersed among all particular things. The verse's meaning concerning the Ultimate Limit refers to the driving engine of nature (自然之機). It governs in a non-dominant way, and how can we possibly depict it with shapes or traces?

Among Ru masters, Cheng Hao's understanding and formulation of this point is the most refined, and I suspect that what Cheng Yi and Zhu Xi taught might not be entirely accurate. The reason I say Cheng Yi is not completely correct is that Liu Yuan once recorded Cheng Yi's teaching as, "Dao is the reason yin and yang arise (所以陰陽者道)," and "Dao is the reason the open-and-close process arises." I believe the two characters used by Cheng Yi, "suo yi (所以, the reason that something happens)," refer to something beyond shape, but it still sounds as though two separate entities are involved. According to Cheng Hao's words, "What arises is just this Dao (隻此是道)," I recognize the completeness and wonder of the entire process of cosmic change and see no need to include "suo yi" within the sentence. The reason I think Zhu Xi is not completely correct is that he once said, "principle and vital-energy are indeed two things." Zhu Xi also made many similar statements, such as "the vital-energy is strong and the principle is weak," and "if there is no vital-energy, how and where can we locate the principle?" among others."[47]

Several key points in this quotation require explanation in order to understand Luo Qinshun's stance concerning Ultimate Limit:

First, since the principle is only about patterns of vital-energy, Luo cannot embrace an idea similar to Zhu Xi's, which posits that it is the principle that creates vital-energy. Instead, the Ultimate Limit, as the supreme "principle" in Zhu's case, is understood by Luo to be the collective name for all pattern-principles that can possibly be found among cosmic realities. In other words, there is no "creating-created" relationship between Ultimate Limit and all the pattern-principles; the former is simply a "name" for the latter.

Second, for Luo Qinshun, the most fundamental patterns indicated by the movement and stillness of vital-energy are *yin* and *yang*. All other patterns can be seen as further complexities and combinations of these two basic ones. When Luo identifies Ultimate Limit as the collective name for all pattern-principles, and when he further asserts that Ultimate Limit is the "engine" (機) of nature, his view is that the all-pervasive vital-energy, with *yin* and *yang* as its foundational patterns, is the origin of cosmic creation. In this sense, the movement and stillness of vital-energy are considered the primary driver of cosmic changes, and the entire changing cosmos can thus be seen as a process of self-determination of the same all-pervasive vital-energy.

Third, since the creative role of Ultimate Limit described in the original *Xici* verse, "Ultimate Limit creates two modes," has been rejected by Luo Qinshun, the dominant role of the Ultimate Limit over the entire cosmos is reinterpreted in a nondominant manner. This means that the entire cosmos is generated by the interaction of *yin/yang* vital-energy, and this is a natural process in its own right. Since Luo identifies Ultimate Limit as merely an overarching name for the *yin/yang* principles, which are themselves just descriptors of how vital-energy moves and becomes still, its dominant role as claimed in the *Xici* verse is also nominal. Thus, the Ultimate Limit governs in a nongoverning way.

Fourth, the comparison Luo Qinshun makes between Cheng Hao, on one hand, and Cheng Yi and Zhu Xi, on the other, is insightful. According to Luo, only Cheng Hao grasps the idea that *Li* and *Qi* are actually the same thing, just as the Way and the utensil-like things are also the same. For Luo, both Cheng Yi and Zhu Xi tend to view *Li* as something separate from *Qi*, and the primary reason for this tendency is that they ask the question about "suo yi (所以, the reason that something arises)" and attempt to answer it. For contemporary readers,

Luo's argument skillfully highlights the key difference between him and Cheng Yi and Zhu Xi. In the case of Cheng Yi and Zhu Xi, *Li* not only refers to the pattern according to which vital-energy organizes itself but also connotes the origin of vital-energy. However, Luo does not believe the latter question is necessary; instead, he takes the existence of the one all-pervasive vital-energy for granted and then analyzes its patterns.

Interestingly enough, Luo also classifies Zhou Dunyi as belonging to the same group of Ru scholars as Cheng Yi and Zhu Xi, and he further believes that Zhu Xi's tendency to adopt a dualistic view about *Li* and *Qi* is rooted in Zhu's interpretation of Zhou Dunyi:

> Regarding Master Zhou's *Explanation of the Diagram of Ultimate Limit*, when I read its verse, "The reality of Non-Limit and the essence of the Two Modes and Five Phases mysteriously combine and coalesce," I feel doubtful. There must be two things for them to be considered "combined (合)." However, are Ultimate Limit and *yin/yang* truly two separate entities? If they indeed are two separate entities, where are they when not yet combined? Throughout Zhu Xi's entire life, he recognizes principle and vital-energy as two distinct things (認理氣為二物), and the reason stems from this verse.[48]

From the ontological perspective represented by Zhou Dunyi and Zhu Xi, the creative power of Ultimate Limit and that of *yin/yang* vital-energy can be seen as "combined" because the latter is an incomplete manifestation of the former. As a result, when examining the creative origin of any concrete thing in the cosmos, one cannot avoid mentioning both. However, for Luo Qinshun, Ultimate Limit is not distinct from *yin/yang* vital-energy, making it unnecessary to assert that they can be combined in any sense.

Quite evidently, Luo's metaphysical thought does not belong to the group of Ru philosophers that I previously characterized as forming the tradition of *generatio ex nihilo*. He does not question the origin of vital-energy, which is the fundamental substance filling the entire cosmos. Moreover, he does not even believe the question about the origin needs to be asked. From the perspective of Ru philosophers leaning toward *generatio ex nihilo*, I will address Luo's concerns with the following points:

First, Luo's thought does not answer the question of where the being of vital-energy comes from, and in this sense, his metaphysics is incomplete.

Second, Luo's interpretation of Ultimate Limit dismisses the creative relationship originally articulated by the text of the *Xici*, and in this sense, his interpretation is misplaced.

Third, one major reason Luo does not endorse the "Non-Limit" interpretation of Ultimate Limit following the Ru lineage of *generatio ex nihilo* is that he believes the priority his metaphysics grants to the existence of vital-energy makes Ruist ethical teaching more realistic than its alternative. This is because Ru ethics would then be grounded in the patterns of the ever-present vital-energies. This point was made earlier by Lu Jiuyuan and was reiterated in a more elaborate way by Luo.[49] However, I have already presented my opinion on the debate between Zhu Xi and Lu Jiuyuan: The Non-Limit feature of Ultimate Limit signifies the unconditionality of its creative power. Quite contrary to Lu's claim that Zhu's metaphysics is Daoist, the recognition of the Non-Limit feature of Ultimate Limit makes its creative power more real than any derived realities since all other realities stem from it.

Despite the apparent weak points in Luo Qinshun's metaphysics, we must acknowledge one strong aspect in his system that Zhu Xi's metaphysics has not yet incorporated: the consistency in the use of terms, and as a natural consequence, the consistency of thought. Luo can now be seen as the Ru metaphysician who has pushed Zhu's metaphysics into its complete and consistent form, based on a revised assumption that *Li* is solely the *Li* of *Qi*, rather than a separate creative force beyond *Qi*. Although this innovative interpretation does not do justice to Zhu's metaphysics or the Ru lineage of *generatio ex nihilo* in general, its advantage of consistency allowed Luo's thought to decisively influence the development of Ru metaphysics in the late Ming period. After Luo, important Ru metaphysical thinkers were predominantly influenced by *Qi*-monism, making it difficult, if not entirely impossible, to find a single metaphysician in this period who attempted to revive Zhu's thought along the lineage of *generatio ex nihilo*.

Based on these considerations, I propose the following revision of Zhu Xi's metaphysics to refine the Ru tradition of *generatio ex nihilo*:

If *Li* is only understood as the patterns of vital-energy, then Ultimate Limit is neither *Li* nor *Qi*. Instead, Ultimate Limit is the ultimate creative power that generates all possible vital-energies and their pattern-principles. As this ultimate creative power is unconditional, the only way we know it is through its creative outcomes, manifested as the de facto conditions of cosmic realities typically termed in Ruism as "the myriad things under heaven." In other words, we must acknowledge both the ontological priority of Ultimate Limit and the epistemological priority of derived cosmic realities.

If *Li* is understood to be Ultimate Limit per se, we must adopt a cautious approach when using the term *Li* to describe cosmic realities. We need to carefully explain the significant difference between *Li* as Ultimate Limit and *Li* as patterns of vital-energy so that neither the ontological commitment to the unconditionality of Ultimate Limit nor the epistemological commitment to Ruism's empirical approach to the investigation of things is compromised.

Conclusion: Comparative Reflections on the Transcendence Debate

After surveying the two intellectual histories of *creatio ex nihilo* of God in the Greek-European Christian tradition and of *sheng sheng* of Ultimate Limit as *generatio ex nihilo* in the Chinese Ru tradition, it is now possible to present final comparative reflections on the transcendence debate, which was the initial motive of this comparative project.

We have to conclude that the ideas of *creatio ex nihilo* and *sheng sheng*, as illustrated by key moments in their respective intellectual history, share a philosophical conception of transcendence as ultimate reality which lacks any ontological conditions vis-à-vis ontologically dependent proximate realities. No matter how diversely the two traditions conceive of the realities themselves, the logic of the relationship between the realities emerges as comparable when interpreted in the context of their philosophical and religious thought. Therefore, we need to propose an affirmative answer to the debate under consideration that, though expressed in vastly different languages and cultural symbols far from those of Christianity, the Ruist idea of *sheng sheng* can be understood to contain a transcendent dimension which specifies ontological relationships among cosmic realities in a Ruist way.

Considering the entire spectrum of thought illustrated with diverse cases within their own respective intellectual histories, we find that the most comparable point between *creatio ex nihilo* and *sheng sheng* converges into two sets of thinkers: On the side of Christianity, we have René Descartes's voluntaristic understanding of divine creation, which is followed by the de-anthropomorphic understandings of divine creation in Schleiermacher's and Tillich's thought. On the side of Ruism, we have Wang Bi's understanding of Ultimate Limit's creativity as "being is generated from nonbeing," which is followed by Zhou Dunyi's cryptic verse

"Non-Limit and yet Ultimate Limit," which is itself further interpreted by Zhu Xi. For these two sets of thinkers, the *creatio ex nihilo* of the Christian God and the *sheng sheng* of the Ruist Ultimate Limit are both conceived of as an ultimate and *indeterminate* creative power conditioning all existing realities in the world without itself being thus conditioned. In this sense, although we cannot affirm that, for these two sets of thinkers, the Christian God and the Ruist Ultimate Limit are referring to exactly the same entity, we can at least conclude that according to the logic of ontological dependence, which specifies ontological relationships among cosmic realities, *creatio ex nihilo* and *sheng sheng* are, for these thinkers, located on the same supreme tier of these relationships, and hence share a cluster of ontological features unique to the reality of entities on this tier. For example, they share the following insights on the characteristics of ultimate reality: One, there is a difference between cosmological/temporal and ontological/nontemporal orders among cosmic realities, and the transcendence of ultimate reality is defined according to the second, rather than the first, order. Two, ultimate reality is indeterminate in the sense that human intelligence cannot give any account of it except through the effects of its creating. In other words, although the ontologically grounding power of ultimate reality can be made certain, what is behind the power per se is utterly beyond the full grasp of human intelligence. Human intelligence is a result of ultimate reality's creativity, and hence, cannot gaze through it. Three, as a result, a mystical commitment to the unfathomable fecundity of ultimate reality's creativity is expressed.

However, chapters 3 and 4 of this book provided answers concerning "why" and "how" this comparative project should be pursued. The two intellectual histories that followed have surveyed the continuity of these two lineages of thought. This entails the recognition that what we are able to compare regarding the two central ideas concerning transcendence amounts to much more than we have just concluded. First, the comparative methodology proposed in chapter 4 requires the use of vague categories, such as creation or ontological dependence, in order to understand the two different traditions across boundaries, and then, the furnished interpretations must succumb to a continuous back-and-forth reinterpretative process regarding multiple themes of common interest to the concerned scholarly community. This will open our final comparisons to scholars' unrestricted reflections and discussions. Second, the comparative methodology proposed in chapter 3 requires a reply to major contentions in the transcendence debate. This second point also speaks to the direct relevance of this comparative project to its targeted audience: Christian scholars, Ru scholars, and independent comparativists who are interested in the transcendence debate. Third, the comparative methodology detailed in chapters 3 and 4 is ensconced within a larger framework of pursuing comparative theology as a liberal art and science, and one major component of this framework is to envision a Ru theology of religions as a "seeded open inclusivism" and accordingly to pursue comparative Ru metaphysics as a scientific endeavor. Therefore, comparative conclusions to draw from chapters 3 to 8 will be consequential to my reconsidering of the larger framework, and this reconsideration will surely expand our vision on the "so what" significance this comparative project may generate.

Therefore, in the remaining sections of this final chapter, I will furnish a reply to major contentions in the transcendence debate, and then compare *creatio ex nihilo* and *sheng sheng*, immersing them in multiple themes in order to bring out the rich implications of these two ideas. Since at certain points of this book, such as chapter 3 and the end of chapter 7, I have addressed to a certain extent what I intend to demonstrate here, the following will be a further refinement of my preliminary reflections. These conclusive reflections will bear on the larger framework of Ru comparative theology as a liberal art and science, and hence, while carefully responding to contentions in the transcendence debate, I will also present my own constructive theological thought to address concerns raised in chapters 1 and 2.

Last but not least, comparative reflections on the content of the transcendence debate also drive us to provide additional reflections on the form of it. I will therefore evaluate whether my comparison fully complies with the comparative methodology which I mainly devised in chapter 4, and offer some reflections as to future directions for scholars who may wish to engage in this comparative study.

Reflections on the Transcendence Debate

While affirming that the Ruist conception of Ultimate Limit in Ruism's classical period (i.e., from Confucius to Wang Bi) to the Song period implies an idea of "ontological dependence," and that the creativity of Ultimate Limit can be understood to be transcendent in the sense of "ontological unconditionality," my comparative conclusion stands in line with Hyo-Dong Lee and Robert Neville. While affirming that the Ruist understanding of the transcendence of Ultimate Limit's creativity in Ruism's classical and Song periods refers to what chapter 3 defines as "something indeterminate and ontologically unconditioned by the existing world," my comparative conclusion stands with Neville.

However, in line with this basic orientation of my comparative conclusion, a reply to each contention in the transcendence debate including Hyo-Dong Lee's and Robert Neville's will be undertaken as follows. A caveat for readers: Key quotations from disputants and thinkers in the following sections are drawn from previous chapters and will not be referenced again.

MATTEO RICCI AND HIS FOLLOWERS

When Matteo Ricci went to China and attempted to accommodate his Christian message within the Chinese cultural soil in the late Ming dynasty, Ruism's metaphysics had already been significantly influenced by Luo Qinshun's theory of "vital-energy only" (氣本論, translated alternatively as "*Qi*-rooted cosmology" in chapter 8). Therefore, it will come as no surprise that Ricci understood Ultimate Limit as the overall name for all kinds of pattern-principles such as the musical forms played by instruments or the geometrical figures embodied by furniture, and thus it cannot sustain itself. We find that this conception of Ultimate Limit implies Luo's.

Further, when Ricci's followers, such as Julius Aleni and Alexandre de la Charme, likened Thomas Aquinas's idea of "plenitude of being" to Ultimate Limit, and then construed Ultimate Limit as "primary material" or "primordial vital-energy," we can now see that their understanding of Ultimate Limit still followed Luo Qinshun's. In the larger perspective of ancient Chinese cosmology, Luo's "vital-energy only" interpretation of Ultimate Limit followed the lineage of cosmological thought in pre-Song periods, which had construed Ultimate Limit as "formless primordial vital-energy" or "an overall name for existing things in the world." In the sections that discussed Wang Bi's and Zhou Dunyi's thought, I also argued that this lineage of cosmological thought was influenced by Laozi's cosmology, which emphasized the relationship of cosmological succession over that of ontological dependence among cosmic realities. However, in Ruist cases such as in Zhang Zai's and Luo

Qinshun's thoughts, Ultimate Limit as primeval vital-energy can also be thought of ontologically. It can be taken to be a foundational cosmic material pervading the entire cosmos, that is, *Qi* in general, followed by its further self-differentiation as *yin/yang* alternation and combination which gives rise to the myriad things. The changes and transformations of things are typically thought of as having neither beginning nor end in the temporal sequence of cosmological succession.

In other words, Luo's understanding of Ultimate Limit belongs to a lineage of ancient Chinese cosmology different from the one that is represented by Wang Bi, Han Kangbo, Zhou Dunyi, and Zhu Xi. In Luo's lineage of thought, the existence of the world as a self-diversifying, unfolding process from an originally inchoate and formless status is taken for granted. There is no further motif in this lineage that insists on inquiring into where this original status of the world comes from. Seen from this perspective, it is no surprise for us to witness Julius Aleni and Alexandre de la Charme finding this sort of Ultimate Limit to be ontologically inferior to the idea of divine creation in Thomas Aquinas's thought, since Aquinas's idea of divine creation as *creatio ex nihilo* addressed the radical question about the origin of anything and everything in the universe. In conclusion, if Ultimate Limit is understood according to the lineage of ancient Chinese cosmology congenial to Luo's thought, and if we abide by the definition of transcendence as the unconditionality of something's ontological status, we have to admit that Ricci and his followers were correct to affirm that the Ruist Ultimate Limit cannot be regarded as the origin of the world, and thus is less transcendent than the Christian idea of *creatio ex nihilo*, as construed by Aquinas.

However, if we switch our understanding of Ultimate Limit from Luo Qinshun's explanation to the alternate lineage of cosmology in the Ruist tradition, we will have to tell a different story. Ultimate Limit, as construed by Wang Bi, Han Kangbo, Zhou Dunyi, and the second stage of Zhu Xi's metaphysical thought, is the singular principle that explains the ontological origin of the existence of the world. It is neither *Qi* nor *Li* if *Li* is understood as the patterns of the existing and changing *Qi*. In particular, this singular ontological principle of Ultimate Limit is thought of by this lineage of Ru cosmology to be indeterminate per se. In Wang Bi's thought, the process by means of which things are created by Ultimate Limit remains unknowable. Han Kongbo described attempts to account for the process of Ultimate Limit's generativity thus: "We do not understand why all this is so, so we characterize it as the numinous." Similarly, Zhu Xi described Ultimate Limit's creativity as "without sound, without smell," not "a thing," with no "shape" or "position." In other words, for this alternative lineage of Ruist cosmology, Ultimate Limit's unconditioned creating power is affirmed, even while the nature of Ultimate Limit per se is typically conceived of as indeterminate. In conclusion, if the idea of transcendence is understood according to definition (2) presented in chapter 3 as "something indeterminate and ontologically unconditioned by the existing world," this lineage of Ru thinkers' understanding of Ultimate Limit is transcendent par excellence. Because the constantly creative power of Ultimate Limit's *sheng sheng* is understood in this way, I then proposed in chapter 7 that the power could be rendered as a sort of *generatio ex nihilo*, if we need an alternative term for "creation" in order to show the indeterminate feature of Ultimate Limit's creativity.

However, in our final analysis, Thomas Aquinas's understanding of divine creation as *creatio ex nihilo* is not indeterminate. I concluded at the beginning of chapter 6 that although Aquinas's thought in his analysis of causality and the relationship between divine knowledge and human freedom abides quite well by the logic of ontological dependence championed by the earlier tradition of *creatio ex nihilo*, his thought on the "process" of divine creation is not so ontologically unconditioned as it is supposed to be. In Aquinas's thought, the process of divine creation is one of divine will intending ideas of divine intelligence, and then putting these ideas into the divine abundance of being so that a variety of concrete cosmic beings is created. The resultant cosmos comprises a harmonious hierarchy of beings, which cannot be said to be deficient in any anthropocentric or anthropomorphic motif. Since the world is created according to a divine plan, and the divine plan is intelligible even before the plan is implemented, Aquinas's conception of divine creation cannot be thought of as ontologically unconditioned.

In other words, we can compare the Ruist tradition of conceiving Ultimate Limit's creativity as *generatio ex nihilo* with Aquinas's conception of *creatio ex nihilo*, but since Aquinas's conception has not yet achieved a similar idea of "ontological unconditionality" as in the Ruist case, we have to conclude that Aquinas's understanding of ultimate reality is less transcendent than the Ruist one. As a result, Ricci and his followers should have radically changed their way of looking into their own Catholic understanding of divine creation while comparing it with the Ruist understanding of Ultimate Limit's creativity.

The last sentence also makes it highly understandable why counter-arguments from Ruist literati in Ricci's time emphasized the grounding power of Ultimate Limit's creativity and its ontologically transcending status over both *Li* as patterns and *Qi* as vital-energies.

JAMES LEGGE

With historical hindsight, I am startled by James Legge's ambiguous, sometimes incoherent analysis of whether the Ruist cosmology in the *Xici* intends to answer the question of whether *Qi* "is eternal or created." This is especially surprising because we find that Legge mentioned Wang Bi, Kong Yingda, and Zhu Xi in his commentary on key cosmological verses of the *Xici*, while simultaneously asserting that "neither creation nor cosmogony was before the mind of the author whose work I am analyzing." According to my analysis in chapters 7 and 8, one primary motive of the cosmogonical thought rooted in the *Xici* and elaborated by Wang Bi and Zhu Xi is to furnish a singular supreme principle to account for the existence and order of the entire world. The contrast between this tradition of ancient Ruist cosmology and Legge's presentation of it is more than stunning.

However, in Legge's discussion of "original Ruism," he furnished an answer to the question of where vital-energy comes from, an answer he thought came from Confucius's own thought and refers exactly to the same God of Christianity. In other words, Legge doubted, if he didn't utterly deny, every nontheistic answer given by the later Ru cosmological tradition to the same question. Instead, he thought "the numinous and wonderful" mentioned in the *Xici* must be the Christian God who creates the entire world, including the all-pervasive vital-energy, from nothing. Although no words in the *Xici* can even slightly support Legge's interpretation, Legge's misplacement of the Christian God's ontological creativity into his interpretation of the corresponding verses of the *Xici* speaks to the argumentative power of *ontology* intrinsic to those verses. As I concluded at the end of chapter 7 and at the section on Zhu Xi's thought in chapter 8, the ontological power intrinsic to *Xici*'s verses is the foundation for the Ruist cosmogonical tradition conceptualizing the *sheng sheng* power of Ultimate Limit as *generatio ex nihilo*.

JULIA CHING

When Julia Ching affirms that "Confucianism has not developed any doctrine of creation" and "the Confucian tradition has never developed a theory of creation *ex nihilo*," she mainly meant that Ruism doesn't question the origin of the existing world. In this sense, Ching's understanding of the Ruist *Tian* is congenial to Ricci and his followers' understanding of Ultimate Limit. As analyzed above, Ricci and his followers' comparative insights landed in ancient Chinese cosmological thoughts which were not in the lineage of *generatio ex nihilo*. Julia Ching, Ricci, and his followers all therefore lost the opportunity to find a point within the Ruist cosmological tradition more comparable to the Christian one of *creatio ex nihilo*.

HYO-DONG LEE

Regarding Hyo-Dong Lee's central motive of constructing an Asian contextual theology, we have to emphasize that not all metaphysical systems that are centered on the priority of "Oneness" represent an imperial order from the "empire." In parts of the Christian tradition of *creatio ex nihilo* and the Ru tradition of *generatio ex nihilo*, the theme of the all-interconnectedness of cosmic events can be readily related to that of the ontological priority of God's or Ultimate Limit's creativity, such that the ontological priority of One does not bring extra order to the de facto order among cosmic entities.

Aquinas and Friedrich Schleiermacher are the best examples of thinkers who exemplify this stream of thought within the tradition of *creatio ex nihilo*. As explained in chapter 6, divine omniscience does not contradict human freedom for Aquinas. This is because whether cosmic events are contingent or necessary depends upon their mutual relationship in the order of "proximate cause," which itself hinges upon the relationship of cosmological succession among these events. However, regardless of whether an event was caused contingently or necessarily by another event, each event will still be ontologically caused by the "first cause" of divine creation. In other words, the primary function of the first cause of divine creation is to explain the origin of the entire universe, while the order of created cosmic events is more directly explained by another set of categories (such as forms, ideas, and measures in Aquinas's case), which are ultimately treated as the manifestation of the creative power of the first cause. Therefore, the primary ontological causal power of the "Oneness" of *creatio ex nihilo* and the secondary cosmological order shown by mutual relationships among "many" cosmic events go hand in hand in Aquinas's thought.

This point of Aquinas's was nicely recapitulated in Schleiermacher's thought. Schleiermacher used the term "coincidence of opposites" to describe the relationship between God and the world, because he thought of the range of divine causality as "opposite in kind and equal in scope to the world." It implies that God does not disrupt the unity of the natural order, and thus, the idea of *creatio ex nihilo* can accommodate whatever natural scientists want to say about the world based upon their empirical studies. Because of this, I also believe that *creatio ex nihilo* is among the most promising religious ideas that still hold their value in the contemporary context.

In comparison, the earliest point for the Ru tradition of *generatio ex nihilo* to clearly articulate its awareness of the difference between the order of cosmological succession and the order of ontological dependence appeared in Zheng Xuan's commentary on the *Qian Zao Du*, analyzed in chapter 7. Zheng thought that the stage of Great Change in the *Qian Zao Du*'s cosmology, construed in the text as a great vacuum existing before any cosmic stuff filled it, has no role whatsoever in generating the stage of Great Initial from which the primordial vital-energy was derived. Instead, Zheng thought Great Change was just one feature that was intrinsic to, rather than prior to, the stage of *Hunlun*, and hence he transformed this quintessentially cosmological concept in the *Qian Zao Du* into an ontological one. While doing so, Zheng Xuan used the words, "The Great Initial actually generates of its own accord all of a sudden," to explain the origin of the Great Initial, an inchoate form of any existing cosmic event. If we take into consideration Zheng's account of the ontological relationship between *Dao* and cosmic events which I quoted and analyzed in chapter 7, we will gain a further understanding of Zheng's thought regarding our current concerns about Hyo-Dong Lee's thought: The capability of "self-generation" of cosmic events acknowledged in Zheng's thought speaks to a distinct Ruist awareness of the intimate interconnectedness of two cosmic orders. On the one hand, the ultimate ontological origin of cosmic events is *Dao*, fecund yet without any determinate feature in itself. On the other hand, the sequence and order among the continually emerging cosmic events have their de facto cosmological reasons that can be explained in a purely empirical way.

In a word, the fecundity of *Dao* does not impose any extra order on the de facto order of the spontaneously emerging cosmic events, although this fecund ontological principle is indispensable to a complete explanation of why and how cosmic events come about.

This idea of Zheng Xuan's was reaffirmed in Wang Bi's and Han Kangbo's thoughts in a more articulate way. For Wang Bi, the myriad things under heaven are generated "during the process of 'being,'" but when considered as a whole, this process of being is rooted in the fecundity of *Dao*, or Ultimate Limit (which, in Wang Bi's terms, is equal to *Dao*), which itself does not cling to any fixed shape or boundary, and thus must be named "nonbeing." Han Kangbo clearly explains that things themselves cannot bring about their own existence. However, the Ultimate Limit grounding their existences is not a "Master" to "transform" them; thus, the only legitimate way to describe how things come about is that everything, "all of a sudden, comes into existence of its own accord." Clearly, an awareness of the close combination of an indeterminate ontological creative power and an empirically traceable de facto cosmic sequence among cosmic realities underlies all these Ruist philosophers' thinking. Given the high repetitiveness of some of those words quoted above in Zhou Dunyi's and Zhu Xi's writings, we have to conclude that similar thoughts are also sustained by later Ru thinkers in the Ru tradition of *generatio ex nihilo*.

With this understanding of two cosmic orders, we find that it is not totally legitimate for Hyo-Dong Lee to worry that metaphysical talk about "Oneness" will inevitably undermine the democratic power of "many" cosmic events, and thus build an unjust order into the Eurocentric theological "empire." For the Christian tradition of *creatio ex nihilo*, we found that the counterexamples come from Thomas Aquinas when he talked about the relationship between divine knowledge and human freedom, from Schleiermacher when he discussed the relationship between God and the world, and from Paul Tillich when he insisted that the *creatio ex nihilo* of God renders God the "ground of being," rather than a supreme being. Within this lineage of Christian thought, the ontological priority of *creatio ex nihilo* does not compromise the natural order of the world.

By the same token, it is not legitimate, either, for Hyo-Dong Lee to worry that the admission of the idea of ontological hierarchy into Zhu Xi's thought will bring a concern of ontological imperialism similar to the Christian case. If we focus on the second stage of Zhu Xi's ontological thinking about Ultimate Limit and *Li*, we will find that Zhu Xi's thought follows Wang Bi and Han Kangbo quite closely regarding the relationship between Ultimate Limit and the world. Since the creativity of Ultimate Limit is indeterminate, there is no justification for worrying that an affirmation of the ontological priority of Ultimate Limit will bring any extra order to the de facto order among created cosmic realities.

However, Hyo-Dong Lee's "imperialist worry," so to speak, is not entirely ungrounded, since not every major thinker in the tradition of *creatio ex nihilo* or of *generatio ex nihilo* thoroughly abides by the principle of ultimate reality's indeterminacy. In the Greek-European Christian tradition of *creatio ex nihilo*, virtually every major thinker we have examined prior to René Descartes holds a similar conception of the process of divine creation in the form of a supreme agent putting intelligible ideas and forms into an abundant yet inchoate form of being so as to create concrete things in the world. I frequently noted in my previous chapters that in this way the logic of "ontological unconditionality," implied by the original philosophical and theological impetus of the idea of *creatio ex nihilo*, has not been adhered to. In other words, if God had a plan before the world was created and the resulting world is thereby conceived of as manifesting this preexisting divine plan, then the power of divine creativity per se cannot be thought of as indeterminate, and thus this now determinate divine power indeed brings extra order to the de facto order among created cosmic realities, one which is discoverable in a purely empirical way. Hyo-Dong Lee's contextual Asian theology, which centers on the democratic power of the Ruist idea of an all-pervading vital-energy, will have many things to say about this sort of determinate conception of divine creation.

Similarly, in the third stage of Zhu Xi's metaphysical thought, the confusing use of the term *Li* made Zhu Xi sometimes entertain the thought that even before a thing is created, its *Li* already existed. This made Zhu Xi's thought similar to Plato's idealism by affirming that things exist for the sake of a preexisting reason or model. This is easily translated into the idea of "divine plan" in the Christian tradition. In this sense, Zhu Xi's thought indeed raises a legitimate alarm for Hyo-Dong Lee that the affirmation of the ontological priority of Ultimate Limit, also a sort of *Li* in Zhu Xi's thought, brings an extra imperial order to the de facto democratic order among cosmic realities.

However, chapter 8 also revealed that Zhu Xi does not necessarily need to confuse his metaphysical thinking with an unwarranted use of the same term *Li* to refer to different sorts of cosmic realities. In comparison, since the Ru tradition of *generatio ex nihilo* is nontheistic from its very beginning, it is easier for this Ru tradition to avoid Hyo-Dong Lee's criticism so that the ontological priority of the supreme One principle and the cosmological diversity among Many cosmic realities can be simultaneously acknowledged without contradiction.

Last but not least, after considering both the *creatio ex nihilo* and the *generatio ex nihilo* arguments along with Hyo-Dong Lee's criticism, we can conclude that the understanding of the transcendence of ultimate reality as "something indeterminate and ontologically unconditioned by the existing world" is among the most promising conceptions with which contemporary metaphysicians can maintain a good balance between the supreme priority of One and the fecund diversity of Many.

PAULOS HUANG

In comparison with his Christian predecessors in the history of transcendence debate, Paulos Huang has noticed the agential role of *Taiji* (Ultimate Limit) in "producing" the world. However, his view that "when *Taiji* is considered as the source of all things in the world, the producer and the world are of the same substance, bearing no distinction between the world and the producer" still does an injustice to the Ru tradition of *generatio ex nihilo*.

For Zheng Xuan, Wang Bi, Han Kangbo, Zhou Dunyi, and Zhu Xi, the ultimate creative power of *Taiji* is not bounded by any concrete thing in the world, yet it is still being manifested in the world. The relationship between *Taiji* and the world maintains a subtle balance with a two-dimensional asymmetry: *Taiji* is ontologically prior to the world, yet epistemologically posterior to the world. In this sense, it is not correct, as Paulos Huang claims, that *Taiji* produces the world, but is of the same substance as the world. On the contrary, these thinkers of *generatio ex nihilo* frequently expressed similar mystic insights that anything we know about the world cannot exhaust the unfathomable fecundity of *Taiji*'s creativity.

However, Paulos Huang's differentiated use of "creation" and "production" indeed does raise a worthwhile question concerning in what sense the creative powers of God as *creatio ex nihilo* and of *Taiji* as *sheng sheng* can both be described as "creation." Huang insists that "'creating' implies that the creator of the world has personality, and that the creator and the world are of different substances," and according to his understanding of *Taiji* as "producing" the world, and being of the same substance as the world, he further submits that *Taiji*'s productive power cannot be described as "creation" proper. To this view of Huang's, I have the following responses:

First, it is unfair to the Christian tradition of *creatio ex nihilo* to assert such a strict understanding of "creation." Among the Christian theologians under analysis, Huang's view of "creation" can only be applicable to Augustine of Hippo and Thomas Aquinas, who thought of God as a supreme person freely willing a world of ideas and forms in the divine intelligence such that the divine abundance of being can be differentiated and thereby create a variety of things in the world. In contrast, for Descartes, Schleiermacher, and Paul Tillich, the act of divine creation is singular, with no process, and cannot be thought of as a determinate "personal" deed describable in anthropomorphic languages. If we take into consideration the Hellenistic root of the Christian tradition of *creatio ex nihilo*, Plotinus's language of "sheer making," which refers to the fact that something determinate derives from something ultimately indeterminate and unknowable, is the best way to describe God's "creation" for this minor de-anthropomorphic tradition of *creatio ex nihilo*.

Second, if we follow Plotinus's understanding of ultimate reality's creativity as "sheer making," isn't it fair to describe the generative power of Ultimate Limit (as conceived in the Ru tradition of *generatio ex nihilo*) as just as much a "creation"? I think the answer is yes. For Zheng Xuan, Wang Bi, Han Kangbo, Zhou Dunyi, and Zhu Xi, the power of *sheng sheng* of Ultimate Limit can be construed in two different dimensions. In the first dimension, *sheng sheng* means that a determinate cosmic reality, with its determinate set of *yin/yang* and spatial/temporal features, spontaneously emerges from another determinate cosmic reality with its own determinate set of *yin/yang* and spatial/temporal features. In the second dimension, it also means that determinate cosmic realities, among which *yin/yang* is the most generic feature, spontaneously emerge from something indeterminate and ultimately unfathomable, the so-called *Dao* or Ultimate Limit. I conclude that the second sense of *sheng* overlaps nicely with Plotinus's and the aforementioned three Christian thinkers' understanding of divine creation as "sheer making," and in this sense, the "sheer making" capacity of God's *creatio ex nihilo* and Ultimate Limit's *sheng sheng* can be equally described as "creation."

Third, my final response to Paulos Huang's argument leads to reflections upon a crucial point of my methodology of comparative theology.

"Creation," understood as a process of "sheer making" where something determinate ontologically derives from something indeterminate, is the "vague category" or "bridge concept" that links our understanding of the vastly different metaphysical systems of the Christian *creatio ex nihilo* and the Ru *generatio ex nihilo*. As partially explained at the end of chapter 7, the ultimate reason that we are able to find this vague category is that the Christian tradition of *creatio ex nihilo* and the Ru tradition of *generatio ex nihilo* share the same logic of ontological dependence when they strive to use a singular principle to explain the order and existence of the existing world. In the Greek-European Christian tradition, the initiating moment for this logic is Plato's ontological shift from the pre-Socratic natural philosophers to a search for the nontemporal foundation of the existing world. In the Ru tradition, it is the symbology of the *Yijing* that lies at the root of later ontological reasonings.

I still cannot claim that the "sheer making" powers of God's *creatio ex nihilo* and Ultimate Limit's *sheng sheng* refer to exactly the same thing. This is so because such a claim would be so strong as to potentially collapse any substantial difference in languages and thinking between the two compared traditions. However, as bridged by the vague category of creation, which is implied by the logic of ontological dependence, the Christian idea of God's *creatio ex nihilo* and the Ru idea of Ultimate Limit's *sheng sheng* are comparable. If we correctly choose representative thinkers from these two traditions, that is, the ones mentioned above as following the minor, de-anthropomorphic Christian tradition of *creatio ex nihilo* and the Ru tradition of *generatio ex nihilo*, we can even confidently affirm that the aforementioned two ideas are not only comparable, but extremely similar.

MOU ZONGSAN AND LIU SHU-HSIEN

It is regrettable that Mou Zongsan and Liu Shu-hsien did not discuss the transcendence of *Tian* in comparison with the Christian idea of *creatio ex nihilo*, and thus neither of them directly responded to scholars' concerns about the presence of the idea of ontological transcendence in Ru metaphysics.

Liu is closer than Mou to recognizing the ontological idea in Ru metaphysics, since his frequent insistence that *Tian* "is not a thing, but it is the origin of all things" reminds us of similar insights of major figures in the Ru metaphysical tradition who are identified here as having proposed the idea of *generatio ex nihilo*. Nevertheless, I submit that Liu's limited knowledge of the variety of Christian understandings of divine creation may have been responsible for his lack of more precise conceptual tools with which to present the idea of ontological transcendence in the Ru tradition more explicitly. Liu's limited knowledge of the Christian cases was made clear by his sweeping judgment about "the pure transcendence of the Christian faith in a supreme God who created, but is not part of, the world." According to my analysis of the Greek-European Christian tradition of *creatio ex nihilo*, the world is in general thought of as what manifests the ultimately unfathomable creative power of God, and hence, it is inappropriate for Liu to make that judgment.

However, when commenting on Mou Zongsan's and Liu Shu-hsien's thoughts in chapter 3, I noted that their ideas addressed an epistemological question of whether humans have a cognitive capacity sufficient to fully grasp *Tian*'s all-encompassing creativity. On that occasion, I raised a caveat that while engaging in the transcendence debate, scholars should distinguish two kinds of "priority": *Tian* may be ontologically prior to the world, yet epistemologically posterior to it. After pursuing the necessary survey of the intellectual histories of *creatio ex nihilo* and *generatio ex nihilo*, I conclude that the relationship between ultimate reality and derived realities is commonly thought by these two traditions to be maintaining a very subtle two-dimensional asymmetry: Ontologically, God's *creatio ex nihilo* and Ultimate Limit's *sheng sheng* are both prior to the created world, and yet, epistemologically, humans can only rely on their knowledge of the created world in saying anything of God's or Ultimate Limit's creativity.

This comparative point is worthy of mention here because Mou and Liu both realize the limitations of human cognition in the face of the all-encompassing creative power of *Tian*. Even so, in looking more carefully into their words expressing this point, we find that the limitations of human cognition that they recognized actually only address "empirical experience" or "sense perceptions." They don't address human intelligence in general. This is particularly true for Mou, because he identifies *Tian*'s all-encompassing creative power with "the infinite awakening heartmind," which seems to suggest that humans have a supreme cognitive capacity to fully grasp *Tian*'s all-encompassing creativity. We also know that Mou's thought derived mainly from Wang Yangming's Ruist epistemology, and that scholars have used the term "epistemological optimism" to describe this tendency of ancient Chinese epistemology to affirm the sufficiency of human intelligence to fully understand the world.¹

A legitimate comparative question therefore needs to be raised: Since both the Christian tradition of *creatio ex nihilo* and the Ru tradition of *generatio ex nihilo* maintain a twofold asymmetrical understanding of the relationship between ultimate reality and derived realities, which leads to the two traditions' common commitment to the mystery of ultimate reality's creativity, how thoroughly is this commitment enacted in the thought of the major figures from each tradition?

In the tradition of *creatio ex nihilo*, although thinkers vary in their degree of thoroughness in sticking to the idea of "ontological unconditionality" when they articulate their understandings of divine creation, they all express views at certain moments about the utter limitedness of human intelligence in grasping ultimate reality's creative power. For example, Plotinus insists that nothing about lesser things can be fully applicable to the Oneness. Augustine of Hippo envisions the possibility of other worlds radically different from the current one because of his commitment to the utter freedom of divine creation. Thomas Aquinas denies that humans, during their lifetimes, can ever arrive at quidditative knowledge of God and, furthermore, supports the idea that the knowledge of God can only be obtained through negating what is affirmed of created things. The incomprehensibility of divine creation is a pivotal theme in Descartes's theory of created eternal truth. Schleiermacher says that the transcendent Whence of the human feeling of utter dependence "exceeds the limits of imagination."² For Paul Tillich, God's creativity as the ground of being, or as Being-itself, "lies beyond the polarity of finitude and infinite self-transcendence."³ Each of these examples is illustrative of how committed these exemplary thinkers in the tradition of *creatio ex nihilo* were to the mystery of ultimate reality's creativity.

In comparison, the first moment in which the Ru tradition of *generatio ex nihilo* realized the twofold asymmetrical relationship occurred in Confucius's purported discussion of the relationship between the Change and the hexagrams Qian and Kun in chapter 12 of part I of the *Xici*. Because *yin* and *yang*, the most generic categories to depict concrete cosmic realities, cannot be used to fully understand Ultimate Limit, or *Dao*'s creativity, the text also uses the cryptic verse, "what cannot be fathomed by *yin* and *yang* is numinous and wonderful" to characterize the twofold asymmetrical relationship. Echoing Zheng Xuan's view of the relationship between *Dao* and things, Wang Bi was very explicit that because *Dao* is ontologically prior to any created thing, including human knowledge, humans "don't know exactly the process (by which the things are generated)." Also, because of the indeterminate features of *Dao*, Wang Bi depicts the *Dao* per se mainly through a way of negating, saying that *Dao* "has neither boundaries nor shaped bodies, and is neither *yin* nor *yang*," and therefore "it can be called what is numinous and wonderful." The same insight was understood by Han Kangbo, when he described the process by which Ultimate Limit creates the world, using words such as, "Thus we do not understand why all this is so, so we characterize it as the numinous." Notably, when Wang Bi and Han Kangbo pointed out that humans cannot understand how *Dao* creates the entire world, they referred to human intelligence in general. This is different from Mou Zongsan and Liu Shu-hsien because Mou and Liu only addressed the limit of the empirical or sensible dimension of human intelligence in comprehending *Tian*'s creative power. By comparison, I conclude that Wang Bi and Han Kangbo's insight is more in line with the logic of the twofold asymmetrical relationship between Ultimate Limit and derived realities indicated by the Ru tradition of *generatio ex nihilo*.

Wang Bi and Han Kangbo's thought was also adopted by Zhou Dunyi and Zhu Xi. In my interpretation, Zhou's seemingly inscrutable words about the stillness and activity of Ultimate Limit can be understood when we place Zhou's thought in the tradition of *generatio ex nihilo*. The reason that we cannot use "stillness" or "activity" to accurately depict Ultimate Limit's creativity is that it refers to the same feature identified by Wang and Han: Humans cannot fully comprehend how Ultimate Limit creates. By the same token, in the second stage of Zhu Xi's metaphysical thoughts, he paraphrased many of Wang's and Han's words in describing the indeterminacy of Ultimate Limit's creativity, such as that "neither sound, smell, nor any kind of influence can be found about it"; that Ultimate Limit is without "shape" or "position"; that "there is no name able to name it (*Taiji*)," and so on. In this way, Zhu Xi also aligns with predecessors in the Ru tradition of *generatio ex nihilo* in affirming the radical finitude of human intelligence in being able to grasp Ultimate Limit's creativity.

However, my analysis of Zhu Xi's thought indicates that he didn't always thoroughly carry through with the ontological acumen that he had achieved in the second stage of his metaphysical thought. Instead, when he used similar words "without sound, without smell" to depict Ultimate Limit's creativity, he may just have meant *Li*, that is, the non-*Qi*, abstract feature of Ultimate Limit. This wouldn't have expressed any mystical commitment to the ultimate unfathomability of Ultimate Limit's creativity. At the third stage of Zhu's metaphysics, he sometimes alluded to the possible existence of a world of pattern-principles even before anything had been generated. Also, while commentating on the steps for "Attaining One's Knowledge" in his *Collected Commentary on the Great Learning* (大學章句集注), Zhu famously affirms that by means of an accumulative process of "investigations of things," humans can reach a comprehensive and thorough understanding of every pattern-principle in the world. Therefore, we cannot say that Zhu Xi's thought was fully exempted from the epistemological optimism that scholars have charged the Ru tradition with.

By comparison, we find that the Greek-European Christian tradition of *creatio ex nihilo* quite thoroughly abides by the twofold asymmetrical relationship between ultimate reality and derived realities and its implied principle of the radical finitude of human intelligence in grasping the mystery of divine creation. This speaks to a virtue of "epistemological humbleness," so to speak, that I think humanity should embrace when faced with the ever changing and transforming created world. However, in the Ruist tradition of *generatio ex nihilo*, only when the logic of the twofold asymmetry had been thoroughly complied with did thinkers and texts in the tradition express a similar commitment to the unfathomable mystery of Ultimate Limit's creativity. If we take into consideration the fact that the tradition of *generatio ex nihilo* is just one among many traditions in ancient Chinese metaphysics, we are obliged to admit that the virtue of epistemological humbleness was indeed practiced less impressively by Chinese thinkers than by their counterparts in the Greek-European Christian tradition of *creatio ex nihilo*.

TU WEI-MING

The reason why Tu Wei-ming denies any similarity between *creatio ex nihilo* and the Ru conception of *Tian* is that he chose an unfit candidate from the Ru metaphysical tradition with which to pursue his comparison. Tu's understanding of *Tian* hinges upon Zhang Zai's metaphysics, which, despite not being a major element in my comparative project, is congenial to Luo Quinshun's thought. In this lineage of Ru metaphysics, the world begins from an inchoate form (i.e., the all-pervading vital-energy in general) and the things in the world derive from a process of self-differentiation of *Qi* in general. There is no further ontological impulse for questioning the radical origin of *Qi*, and thus this branch of Ru metaphysics takes the existence of the world for granted. In comparison to Western metaphysical views, Zhang Zai's and Luo Qinshun's perspectives are more comparable to those of Aristotle, Spinoza, and Hegel, whose thought also takes the existence of the world for granted and hence stands outside the tradition of *creatio ex nihilo*.

When commenting on Tu's comparative insights in chapter 3, I said that the confusing use of the same term *Tian* to refer to two fundamentally different things makes Tu's argument compromise the difference between cosmology and ontology in Ru metaphysics. However, Tu's case does indeed raise a legitimate comparative question concerning how the relationship between a time-based, cosmological mode of thinking and a separate logic-based, nontemporal, and ontological mode of thinking is treated by the tradition of *creatio ex nihilo* and by that of *generatio ex nihilo*.

In the Ru tradition of *generatio ex nihilo*, the temporal elements arise in its vision of the *sheng sheng* process of Ultimate Limit only when the *yin/yang* vital-energies are manifested in the perpetual movement of the four seasons, which is typically conceived of as being without a beginning or an end. This is shown in the diagram of "The Ruist Ontological Cosmology in the *Xici* as interpreted by Wang Bi and Han Kangbo" in chapter 7; and the mapped thought also influenced Zhou Dunyi's *Diagram of Ultimate Limit* and Zhu Xi's interpretation of the *Diagram*. Whether items listed in the diagram are cosmological, temporal elements or ontological, nontemporal elements depends upon one's perspective. If we see them horizontally, then all of them have their cosmological consequences: The ultimate creative power of the Non-Limit Ultimate Limit is manifested in changes and transformations of cosmic realities in the lower ranks of the chart, and all concepts lower than Ultimate Limit can be used to explain how cosmic changes take place in their concrete terms. However, if we see the diagram vertically, then all the involved concepts speak to a set of generic features of cosmic realities from a holistic perspective, and thus can be thought of as nontemporal and ontological. For example, *yin* and *yang* are among the most generic features of cosmic realities if we see the cosmic changes as a whole. Evidently, the cosmological and ontological thinking in the Ru metaphysical tradition of *generatio ex nihilo* are so intertwined with each other that it will be legitimate for us to characterize this Ruist type of metaphysics as a "cosmontology."

The relationship between cosmology and ontology in the Greek-European Christian tradition of *creatio ex nihilo* can also be potentially understood in the same way. When the doctrine of *creatio ex nihilo* was first stated by Theophilus of Antioch, he kept the ontologically driven Platonic idea of time in mind: What *creatio ex nihilo* furnishes is different from, though perhaps compatible with, the thought of the pre-Socratic philosophers of nature which pivots upon a cosmological explanation of events in a temporal sequence. As particularly attested to by Aquinas's argument concerning the possibility of the eternity of the world, and Schleiermacher's scientific consciousness that *creatio ex nihilo* does not undermine the natural order of the world, we can further confirm that the idea of *creatio ex nihilo* is potentially compatible with any empirically approached account of the cosmos. Regarding the compatibility of an ontology for the "one" principle with an open cosmology of "many" cosmic events, there is no difference between the Ruist tradition of *generatio ex nihilo* and the Christian one of *creatio ex nihilo*.

However, two significant differences do need to be brought to the fore. First, open cosmology is quite often envisioned by the *creatio ex nihilo* thinkers (such as Augustine and Descartes) as an idea of "other possible worlds" that have a completely different set of intelligible rules and patterns. However, in the Ru tradition of *generatio ex nihilo*, we seldom find any such idea. From the grounding moment of this tradition in the *Xici*, rules and patterns of the world are thought of as functioning within the de facto existing things of this world as seen from a human perspective, that is, one including heaven, earth, and human beings. Accordingly, the ontological relationship is also conceptualized among tiers of rules and patterns in this world, and hence open cosmology is not primarily envisioned by Ru thinkers as the existence of other possible worlds. Rather, it is envisioned as the possible existence of radical novelty that may exist in the ever-changing-and-evolving realm of reality. In chapter 7, I translated the Chinese term "神 (*shen*)" as "what is numinous and wonderful." This meant that even *yin* and *yang*, the most generic cognitive tools used by Ru thinkers to capture the rules and patterns of cosmic reality, may come up short of the ultimately unfathomable fecundity of Ultimate Limit.

We can say, however, that the idea of "open cosmology" is shared by both traditions, though with differing expressions. In the Christian tradition of *creatio ex nihilo*, this idea is mainly embodied in a mode of thinking called "cosmologies + ontology," since different cosmologies may be needed to account for different possible worlds that are each ultimately created by the same singular creative act of *creatio ex nihilo*. In the Ruist tradition of *generatio ex nihilo*, open cosmology is embodied in a "cosmontology" mode of thinking, since the world seen from a human perspective potentially extends to all realms of reality, and all these realities are thought of as being generated from the singular creative power of *sheng sheng* of Ultimate Limit. Ultimately, it makes no difference whether we view the fecundity of ultimate reality's creativity in the form of a possible new world or in the form of possible new phenomena in the entire realm of reality, since both visions can point to an utterly new set of rules and patterns that have not yet been made available to human preconception.

Second, as discussed above regarding Hyo-Dong Lee, the overall theistic tradition of *creatio ex nihilo* cannot easily accommodate the aforementioned compatibility. If thinkers insist that divine intelligence has a preexisting plan to implement in the world even before any world has been created, an empirically approached cosmology may be in contradiction to it. This would make the cosmologies conceived by the tradition of *creatio ex nihilo* less open. By comparison, in the mainly nontheistic Ruist tradition of *generatio ex nihilo* it is easier to get rid of this preconceived idea of divine creation that is potentially at odds with the empirical sciences.

ROGER AMES AND DAVID HALL

Several major points in my comparative conclusion disagree with Roger Ames and David Hall's.

First, if we define transcendence as what is indeterminate, ontologically unconditioned by the existing world, we find that the de-anthropomorphic minor tradition of *creatio ex nihilo* and the Ru tradition of *generatio ex nihilo* are not only comparable, but share the same idea of an indeterminate, ontologically unconditioned ultimate reality. Hence, Ames and Hall's definition of "strict transcendence" is not refined enough to bridge our understanding of these two comparable metaphysical traditions.

Second, the two types of cosmologies termed by Ames as *creatio ex nihilo* and *creatio in situ* are, under an appropriate analysis, actually compatible with one another. This is because the idea of *creatio ex nihilo* is primarily used by the Christian tradition to explain the origin of the being of the existing world, while *creatio in situ*, as presented by Ames, describes the way ancient Chinese cosmologies used processual concepts to present the order of evolving cosmic entities in an all-interconnected world. According to my earlier reflections on the relationship between One and Many in Hyo-Dong Lee's thought and on the relationship between ontology and cosmology in Tu Wei-ming's thought, *creatio ex nihilo* and *creatio in situ* can coexist in the same metaphysical system as that presented in the Ru tradition of *generatio ex nihilo*, which was characterized above as a "cosmontology."

Third, Ames and Hall's comparative methodology for trying to find a genuine Chinese alternative to Western thought is also different from mine. With the general framework of a Ru comparative theology as a rooted, nonconfessional theology as a liberal art, I attempted to find controversial points in the transcendence debate, conducted a survey of two intellectual histories, and then employed "vague categories" pragmatically to reach comparative conclusions in order to examine the aforementioned points. This entailed striving to maintain an impartial stance before beginning my comparative work and attending to both the similarities and the differences between the two compared traditions. The strength of Ames and Hall's method is to highlight the distinctive feature of Chinese thought in comparison to some fragments of Western thought. Regarding the transcendence debate, however, it may not be a good idea to use their method as a way of pursuing an accurate comparison.

ROBERT C. NEVILLE

Two major points in my comparative conclusion agree with Neville:

First, if we define transcendence as the feature of something indeterminate and ontologically unconditioned by the existing world, then the Ruist tradition has such a feature. Moreover, according to the strict logic of ontological unconditionality, the Ruist concept of transcendence, as presented in the tradition of *generatio ex nihilo*, is even more transcendent than the idea of *creatio ex nihilo* in the mainstream theistic Christian tradition.

Second, Wang Bi and Zhou Dunyi are those Chinese Ruist thinkers whose views on *Dao*, or Ultimate Limit, share the characteristic described in the first point.

I suggest two major improvements to Neville's comparative project concerning the transcendence debate:

First, I would not include Lao Zi's *Dao De Jing* in the Ruist tradition of *generatio ex nihilo*. As examined in chapter 7, only under the interpretation of Wang Bi can key verses in the *Dao De Jing* be understood to be compatible with the ontological mode of thought in the *Xici* of the *Classic of Change*. Prior to Wang Bi, the tradition of ancient Chinese cosmology was more Daoist than Ruist, and focused on the idea of cosmological succession rather than on ontological dependence. I also include Han Kangbo and the second stage of Zhu Xi's metaphysical thought in this Ruist lineage of *generatio ex nihilo*, which expands the Ruist tradition beyond what Neville originally conceived to envision a more transcendent idea of ultimate reality than its Western counterpart.

Second, my comparative methodology begins with a situational study of the motive of my comparative project, that of engaging the transcendence debate. Although I am significantly indebted to Neville's pragmatist comparative methodology of "vague category," this situational thinking provides my comparative project with the additional advantages that I have elaborated in chapter 4.

General Comparative Points
SUMMARY OF THE POINTS ALREADY MADE

After briefly summarizing the completed comparative points as follows, we'll open our inquiry and address comparative issues that have not yet been addressed by my responses to scholars in the transcendence debate.

Regarding the Greek-European Christian tradition that conceives of God's creation as *creatio ex nihilo* and the Chinese Ruist tradition that conceives of Ultimate Limit's power of *sheng sheng* as *generatio ex nihilo*, I have made the following further comparative points beyond my comparative conclusion stated at the beginning of this final chapter:

(1) In comparing the two traditions, according to the logic of "ontological unconditionality," we have discovered which thinkers' views on ultimate reality are the more transcendent.
(2) The central philosophical motifs, those which ground the beginning of each tradition, provide ontological explanations of the overall existence and order of the existing world: Plato's turn toward "words"

and the author(s) of *Yijing*'s reflections on the references of and the relationship between the *Yijing* symbols.
(3) For each tradition, whether a unifying commitment to the principle of One undermines the de facto empirical order among Many depends upon whether the logic of "ontological unconditionality" is thoroughly followed.
(4) We have discussed in what sense the *creatio ex nihilo* of God and the *sheng sheng* of Ultimate Limit can be commonly described as "creation."
(5) The two-dimensional asymmetrical relationship between ultimate reality and derived reality is present in both traditions.
(6) We addressed an epistemological question: How thoroughly did the two traditions commit themselves to the mystery of ultimate reality's creativity? In other words, how was the virtue of epistemological humbleness embodied in each tradition?
(7) We discussed the relationship between cosmology and ontology, and the compatibility between "open cosmology" and the One principle of ultimate reality as it is presented in each tradition.

DIVERSITY WITHIN EACH TRADITION

The eighth insight resulting from our comparison is this:

We can differentiate at least three major or minor traditions or lineages of thought regarding the issue of "creation" in Western intellectual history. The first is the Greek-European Christian tradition, which conceives of divine creation as *creatio ex nihilo*. The second is the tradition represented by Aristotle, Spinoza, and Hegel. These philosophers take the existence of the existing world and its original inchoate form for granted, and do not inquire further into its radical beginning. The first tradition can be further divided into two subtraditions, one mainstream and the other minor: The mainstream tradition of *creatio ex nihilo* is represented in Plato, and received its first systematic Christian elaboration in the thought of Augustine of Hippo, and then was further strengthened by the thought of Thomas Aquinas. This tradition typically conceives of God as a supreme deity who created the world by putting intelligible ideas and forms into either a formless matter or the divine abundance of being. Its minor tradition was earlier illuminated in Plotinus's thought, and later articulated by modern figures such as Descartes, Schleiermacher, and Paul Tillich. Rather than envisioning divine creation as originating from a supreme deity, this minor tradition of *creatio ex nihilo* would like to think of God or ultimate reality as the "ground of being," or the "initiator of being," rather than as a being. At certain moments in this minor tradition, such as in Descartes's theory of created eternal truth and Schleiermacher's reflection on the relationship between God and the world, God is even thought of as being something indeterminate and ontologically unconditioned by the world.

By the same token, we can analyze at least three traditions of ancient Chinese cosmology regarding the creativity of *Dao* or Ultimate Limit. First, we have a Daoist tradition extending from the text of the *Dao De Jing* to that of *Qian Zao Du*. This tradition tends to view the creativity of *Dao* as being mainly manifested in a sequence of cosmologic succession where the abundance of diversities within cosmic realities derives from a self-differentiating and self-generating process beginning from an inchoate form of the cosmos. Under the influence of the Ruist cosmology that is centered on the generative power of Ultimate Limit, this tradition tends to categorize Ultimate Limit into one stage of a cosmological sequence, referring to it as either a stage of formless primordial vital-energy or a general name encapsulating all concrete things after these things acquire a form during a later cosmological sequence.

The second tradition is a Ruist tradition which prioritizes the relationship of "ontological dependence" over that of "cosmological succession" among cosmic realities, drawing inspiration from the ontological mode of thinking in the *Xici* of the *Classic of Change*. This second tradition can be further divided into two subtraditions. One subtradition is defined by Wang Bi, Han Kangbo, Zhou Dunyi, and the second stage of Zhu Xi's metaphysics. This tradition examines the radical origin of the existing world, and therefore construes the *sheng sheng* power of Ultimate Limit as *generatio ex nihilo*. However, another subtradition incorporates the Daoist idea of "primordial vital-energy" but interprets it in a Ruist ontological fashion. This subtradition typically believes that the ontological primary tier of cosmic realities is the pervading vital-energy in general, after which the self-differentiation of *Qi* in general leads to the endless changing and transforming of cosmic realities in time. As hinted in my previous chapters, this Ruist subtradition can be found in the thought of Dong Zhongshu, Zhang Zai, and Luo Qinshun. It is hard to determine which subtradition might be considered mainstream in the Ruist history of cosmologies. But when the Jesuits came to China and tried to figure out what the Ruists meant by Ultimate Limit, it was definitely Luo Qinshun's thought and its repercussions that were on the rise.

Therefore, an additional major comparative conclusion we can reach here is that the diversity of ideas and theories within each compared tradition is undeniable, which makes it extremely challenging, if not impossible, to essentialize the "Western" or "Chinese" thought. More important, these major and minor traditions have been discovered by my research only under a unique set of enabling preconditions. In other words, it is due to the purpose of engaging the transcendence debate and thus becoming intensely aware of the problem of "creation" that I have discovered and studied these traditions. I believe that if we shift our original perspectival focus, we will find even more diversities among thinkers for each of the compared traditions.

THEODICY

The additional comparative point we need to address concerns theodicy, the problem of evil.

We find that the problem of evil takes a prominent position in the intellectual history of the Greek-European Christian tradition of *creatio ex nihilo*. Before Augustine of Hippo, we witnessed a dualistic worldview among thinkers, even though some of them were trying to find a single principle that would account for everything in the world. For Plato, "matter" is the reason that changes in cosmic realities tend to deviate from orders and measures, causing the actual cosmic process to succumb to a constant cycle of decay and recovery. For Plotinus, matter is the last remnant issued from the emanation of the One. Because it lacks any kind of order or measure, Plotinus sometimes termed matter as "absolute evil." If we add to this list the Gnostic view of acosmism, we find that before Augustine, the way to account for the existence of evil under a purportedly absolutely good One principle was a great challenge for thinkers in the tradition of *creatio ex nihilo*.

Notably, based on my analysis in chapter 5, Augustine's thought represents the first systematic resolution of the problem of evil within the *creatio ex nihilo* tradition. In summary, Augustine's solution has generated debate on two major points. First, it undermines the principle of "ontological unconditionality" by affirming that there is a divine plan for God's creation, suggesting that the apparent existence of evil could be considered good if it aligns with the overarching plan conceived by divine intelligence. Second, in relation to the first point, Augustine ascribes the ontological cause of creaturely evil, which deviates locally from the grand plan of perfect divine creation, to the nonbeing out of which God creates, and hence, introduces a potentially dualistic mindset into the apparently monistic commitment to *creatio ex nihilo*.

Nevertheless, there are alternative approaches within the Christian tradition to address the problem of evil. First, the notion of God as a supreme deity implementing a divine plan designed prior to the creation of the world may need to be reconsidered. Second, the distinction between metaphysical and moral evils warrants further reflection. These two perspectives were introduced by Paul Tillich.

First, Tillich's conception of God as the "ground of being," rather than as a supreme being, represents the de-anthropomorphic tradition of *creatio ex nihilo*. This perspective makes Tillich reject the traditional idea of a divine plan, one consequence of which is that Tillich doesn't think of "eschaton" in the temporal sense. Instead, Tillich renders "eschaton" as the "aim of history" that humans ought to strive to realize at any moment of history. In this updated vision of history, the existence of evil in the human world is not to be thought of as becoming good again in the overall perspective of a divine plan. Rather, evil exists because of the failure of human beings to realize the aim of history at various historical moments, and this failure does not affect the validity of the claim that history has an aim, and that the aim is worth fighting for.

Second, the differentiation between the "*ouk on*" and "*me on*" types of "nonbeing" in *creatio ex nihilo* is a crucial step by which Paul Tillich reaches an awareness of the distinction between metaphysical and moral evils. On the one hand, according to my analysis in chapter 6, the "*ouk on*" type of nonbeing implies the unconditionality of divine creation. More important, when seen from the holistic perspective of the entire created realm of cosmic realities, the unconditionality of divine creation as the ground of being enables us to think of none of the cosmic realities as evil from the standpoint of God. In other words, metaphysically, there is no evil. Even gratuitous sufferings and inevitable limitations experienced by living beings, which are not caused by the perverted use of human free will, do not represent a punitive absence of perfection from a divine perspective. They can only be seen as evil if human agents fail to take care of them as per a human standard.

On the other hand, the "*me on*" type of nonbeing speaks to the intrinsic finitude of every concrete cosmic reality. In the case of human beings, the "*me on*" type of nonbeing implies that humanity always ought to strive to become good and then better in order to overcome a particular mode of human finitude in particular moments of human history. If we combine the two types of understanding of nonbeing in Tillich's worldview, which pivots on a conception of divine creation as *creatio ex nihilo*, we can say that metaphysically there is nothing that is evil. However, morally, the evilness of human behavior consists in whether it can accept the all-encompassing, unconditional divine creation as its ideal, and thus strive to realize this ideal in the human world. Here, the problem of evil is more adequately addressed in that, first, no alienating power of nonbeing against being is posited within the ultimate act of *creatio ex nihilo* itself, thereby ensuring the monistic nature of divine creation; second, the existence of moral evil does not diminish the all-encompassing metaphysical goodness of divine creation; and third, this resolution establishes criteria for distinguishing good and evil in human behavior and provides a rationale for moral efforts to become good. Regarding the final point, Tillich's thought also offers a solid metaphysical foundation for ethics.

However, as I also examined in chapter 6, I do not think Tillich's resolution of the problem of evil is entirely satisfactory, because the use of the dyad of categories, "essence" and "existence," and its related theory of "essentialization" prevented Tillich from treating this distinction between metaphysical and moral evils in a more consistent way. In revising his thought, I would prefer that Tillich's theodicy not rely on "essentialization," so that we can conclude something like this: Whether humanity succeeds in realizing the ideal of divine creation or not in the human realm utterly depends upon the freedom of human beings; that is, it depends on human effort. This way, the freedom would not impinge upon the all-pervading metaphysical goodness of the "eternal act of creation."

By comparison, I think the Ru metaphysical tradition is better equipped with conceptual tools for resolving the problem of evil from its very beginning. Based upon my reading of the *Xici* of the *Classic of Change*, I earlier characterized the Ruist understanding of the relationship between the cosmic *Dao* and the human world as one of "escalated continuum" and "manifesting unity." If we summarize the major points of this understanding, we find that they contain all the aforementioned conditions which lead to a more adequate resolution of the problem of evil in the Christian tradition: First, Ultimate Limit is not a personal deity. There is no divine plan, neither in the anthropomorphic nor the anthropocentric sense, for the creativity of Ultimate Limit. Second, Ultimate Limit's creativity is so all-encompassing and sublime that it can be taken to be an ideal for human enterprises; accordingly, any manifesting human enterprise can be defined as good or bad, better or worse. Third, compared with the nonhuman nature, human enterprises which manifest Ultimate Limit's creativity are to add unique humanistic values to the nonhuman natural world, such that the coevolving world of a human-nature continuum can be harmonized by human efforts. In this sense, the moral and metaphysical senses of evil are also firmly distinguished: No matter what happens to the human world, the cosmic *Dao* is still creating spontaneously and constantly. Nevertheless, bad things that happen to the human world are simply bad from a human perspective. From a human point of view, humans have the obligation to constantly overcome those bad things in order to realize an all-encompassing cosmic harmony in the human world.[4]

By comparison, this Ruist understanding of the problem of evil is very similar to my revised version of Tillich's thought concerning the same problem. I earlier stated the following conclusion regarding the comparability of two traditions: The Ruist tradition of *generatio ex nihilo* is most similar to the minor de-anthropomorphic tradition of *creatio ex nihilo*. In these two traditions, we also find a very similar case for resolving the problem of evil under the shared commitment to the absolute metaphysical goodness of ultimate reality's creativity: One is Paul Tillich's thought, and the other is implied by the earliest text in the Ruist metaphysical tradition of *generatio ex nihilo*.

WHEN RUISM MEETS PLATONISM

While considering all major comparative conclusions I have reached so far, I will present, preliminarily, my own Ruist systematic theology as follows, which also serves the Ru theology of religions argued previously as a seeded open inclusivism.

The normal state of human existence is deeply ambiguous. Good behaviors may be conducted with complicated intentions, while ominous demeanors could lead to unexpected lucky consequences. Using the words of Wang Yangming (1472–1529 CE), we can say that "humans are both good and bad when our intentions are in action (有善有恶是意之动)."[5] However, no matter how complex the realized, daily state of human existence is, all human beings, as long as we can be distinguished from other beings on the earth, have an inherent potential for striving to be good. The goodness here implies an ability of harmonization, that is, a human contribution to the co-thriving of beings involved in varying and gradually expanding social and natural contexts such as family, community, state, civilization, nature, and so on. This process of human harmonization will never end, and can never be fully accomplished. In this way, the finite modes of human harmonization take the spontaneous harmonization of *Tian* as an ideal. The words used by Ruist thinkers to characterize the most generic features of *Tian*'s creativity derive from the *Classic of Change*: 元 (initiation), 亨 (permeation), 利 (harmonization), and 貞 (integration).[6] "Initiation" means that without *Tian*, there would be nothing in the world, so *Tian* is the greatest initiator. Ultimate Limit or *Taiji*, as the highest ontological principle of *Tian*, denotes more specifically the singular creative power of *Tian* which generates the unfolding world in a mode of *generatio ex nihilo*, a topic central to our comparative project. Furthermore, *Tian*'s creativity permeates all things in the world because the evolution of *Tian* gives rise to everything. While endowing each changing being with a determinate nature, *Tian*'s all-encompassing creativity makes it possible for humans to perceive all cosmic beings as an integrated whole, because all beings change, interact, and coexist in the eternal cosmic scene comprising all possible temporal modes of past, present, and future. With these four generic traits being understood as such, the overall endlessly harmonizing process of *Tian* is depicted as *sheng sheng*, and can be taken as an ideal of human harmonization because (1) *Tian* is not a deity, and thus, *Tian* has no intention or plan prior to the actual act of creation. In this way, the harmonization of *Tian* is achieved constantly, instantaneously, and spontaneously, which is far superior to human harmonization, since the latter always involves ready-to-fail intentions, plans, and contriving. (2) *Tian* succeeds in harmonizing all created beings because it allows the coexistence and co-becoming of all beings in the broadest temporal scale of eternity. However, none of humans' harmonizing efforts can reach this far and succeed this completely: Humans, as finite beings, can manage to empower the co-thriving of beings involved in a certain context and to a certain extent, with many consequences and repercussions of the efforts impossible to foresee and control.

Despite the contrast between *Tian*'s and humans' harmonization, there are extraordinary human beings who succeeded in realizing *Tian*'s harmonization in the human world in varying contexts and to a significant extent. In particular, these human exemplars are lucidly aware of and able to reconcile with the finitude of human conditions, and thus, they never give up the efforts of harmonizing despite constant failures. If a human manages to cultivate in themselves these stable character traits needed for continual harmonization, they will be seen as a sage (聖), a role model to imitate and follow. Regarding the relationship of the everyday human existence, its ideal and ultimate reality, we can turn to Zhou Dunyi's words for a concise account of it: "A sage strives for being *Tian*-like, a worthy strives for being a sage, and a beginning learner strives for being a worthy."[7]

Under Ultimate Limit, its creative power of *sheng sheng*, and the most generic features of this creative power (initiation, permeation, harmonization, and integration), there are a variety of cosmic or human pattern-principles (理) discerned traditionally by Ru thinkers to manifest the *sheng sheng* of Ultimate Limit, and to explain how a set of cosmic or human realities dynamically and harmoniously fit together in concrete terms, such as the *yin/yang* vital-energies, the five phases, the four seasons, the reciprocal Ru virtues, and so on. Nevertheless, in a contemporary context, all empirical knowledge derived from the progress of modern sciences also contributes to a Ru theologian's knowledge of pattern-principle, and thus ought to be included as a necessary component of Ru learning.

However, as argued in chapter 2, Platonism played a crucial role in the birth of modern science in early modern Europe. As a comprehensive metaphysical and ethical system or lineage of thought, the principles of Platonism can extend beyond the concrete results of modern science, including contemporary scientific advancements, as evidenced by the work of Karl Popper. More important, as discussed in chapters 5 and 6, Platonism is deeply intertwined with the Christian tradition of *creatio ex nihilo*. Since, at the beginning of this book, I advocated for thoughtfully incorporating ideas from the Christian tradition to develop a Ruist theology of religions as a seeded open inclusivism, it follows that a Ru comparative theologian must acknowledge the significance of Platonism in this conclusion. Thus, how can Ruism integrate Platonism in its new era of global harmonization? While answering this question, we also need to keep all the ambiguities of Platonism in mind which are manifested in a variety of issues analyzed by our comparative project, such as the one where a Platonic commitment to the superior ontological status of the intelligible world contributes to the Christian idea of divine plan, and significantly undermines the ontological unconditionality of *creatio ex nihilo*. Such undermining is critiqued by philosophers and theologians (such as Roger T. Ames and Hyo-Dong Lee) as constituting a major cause of the imperialism and colonialism of Western metaphysics. In other words, while including Platonism into Ruism, a Ru systematic theology needs to avoid its historically evidenced faults.

Four major sources can help Ruism to achieve this: Descartes's theory of created eternal truth, the Ru concept of *Qi* (vital-energy) as an all-pervading cosmic stuff, the first stage of Zhu Xi's metaphysics which understands *Li* (pattern-principle) as the *Li* of *Qi*, and the broad Ru understanding of "ritual (禮)" as civilizational conventions including symbols. Per Descartes's theory, mathematical and logical theorems, as instances of the Platonic intelligible world, are also created. Hence, these intelligible items share the de facto status of creatures just as much as any other more materialized cosmic beings. Their de facto status implies that when it encounters these theorems, the human mind "discovers" rather than "invents" them just as empirically as it discovers other scientific truths, in spite of the fact that the initial symbols employed by the human mind to explore a set of mathematical or logical realities are human made. Since the Platonic intelligible world is ultimately also an empirical world, the Ru concept of the all-pervading cosmic *Qi* can be used to characterize the ontological state of this world: As belonging to the most refined forms of cosmic vital-energies, the Platonic intelligible world comprising mathematical and logical theorems is also part of *Tian*, pervaded by *Qi*, and hence, these theorems can be taken as a special kind of pattern-principle which indicates how mathematical and logical realities, as part of cosmic realities, dynamically and harmoniously fit together. However, as indicated by the first stage of Zhu Xi's metaphysical thought, all pattern-principles are *Li* of *Qi*. Although they can be studied alone for their own sake, the ways in which these Platonic pattern-principles harmonize with other pattern-principles pertaining to more materialized aspects of cosmic realities need to be studied case by case. This implies that the modern scientific methodology of hypothesis, deduction, and verification (or falsification) can be reinterpreted as a Ruist process of investigation of things aiming for ritualization, rectification, and harmonization. In other words, a Ru scientist would devise symbols, which are "rituals (禮)" understood broadly in the Ruist sense, to explore a set of mathematical, logical, or material realities as part of the cosmic *Qi*-reality created ultimately by Ultimate Limit. While deducing falsifiable consequences from the explorative, symbolized hypotheses, the Ru scientist would "rectify" inappropriate ones so as to "harmonize" the pattern-principles indicated by both the more intelligible and the more material aspects of cosmic realities.

Needless to say, such a systematic Ru theology is in a very inchoate form, and many of its details remain to be developed. Nevertheless, I intend to use this preliminary form of my constructive theology as a final comparative conclusion to respond to the transcendence debate.

Methodological Reflection

While articulating the criteria of "genuine comparisons," Neville furnished three criteria quoted in chapter 4. Since the major facets of my comparative methodology are in line with Neville and pivot upon the pragmatist use of vague category, we can use these three criteria to gauge whether I have reached a warranted comparison.

First, we find that the major vague categories used by our project to bridge our understanding of the vastly different metaphysical traditions, such as "ontology," "ontological dependence," "ontological unconditionality," "creation," and "transcendence," all derive from an endeavor to carefully read the two intellectual histories from a nonconfessional and impartial point of view. Using a scientific method of the back-and-forth reading, hypothesis, and rereading discussed in the beginning chapters, I have tried to show that the logic of "ontology," as well as its implied conception of the relationship of "ontological dependence" among cosmic realities leading to a conception of "transcendence" as something indeterminate and ontologically unconditioned by the existing world, is intrinsic to each compared tradition. In this sense, I made efforts to show that the categories vaguely considered have "indeed a common respect for comparison."

Second, my awareness of avoiding the imposition of biases when I introduced the specification of each selected vague category into each compared tradition is manifested by my efforts to find the most comparable subtraditions. As concluded above, the de-anthropomorphic minor tradition of *creatio ex nihilo* is the most comparable to the Ruist one of *generatio ex nihilo*. We therefore knew which thinkers and texts should be addressed first and foremost in serving as the apt options for comparing the Christian and the Ruist metaphysical traditions without imposing biases.

Third, my major comparative conclusions are intended to respond to controversies in the transcendence debate. So far as this comparative project contributes to a lasting, yet unsettled, scholarly debate which is of concern to a variety of participants and audience, it is legitimate.

Last but not least, the concrete comparative methodology devised by chapter 4 is embedded in a larger framework of comparative theology as a liberal art and science. So far as it aims for, and, per my fallible self-assessment, succeeds in meeting the aforementioned three criteria of genuine comparison, this comparative project also fits into this larger framework. As for how my comparative conclusions contribute to the Ru theology of religions as a seeded open inclucivism, I have laid out my constructive efforts, and thus, there is no need to repeat them here.

Future Directions of Comparative Studies

How future scholars continue to pursue comparative studies inspired by my project obviously remains a wide-open question. However, I do hope scholars will now be generally more equipped when they have to answer the question of whether there is anything transcendent in ancient Chinese thought, particularly in the case of Ruism. In addition, a modest suggestion for future scholars may be ritually appropriate before ending my book.

As indicated by point 8 in our comparative conclusions, we find that the Western metaphysical tradition represented by Aristotle, Spinoza, and Hegel is very similar to the Ru one represented by Dong Zhongshu, Zhang Zai, and Luo Qinshun. Both of these traditions are located outside the traditions compared in this project. Neither of them therefore questions the radical beginning of the existing world. Perhaps a future comparative project considering these two traditions is needed in order to help us better understand the unfathomable fecundity of the intellectual histories of so-called Chinese and Western thought.

ACKNOWLEDGMENTS

Given the story that I recount in the introduction, detailing how the ideas for this project were conceived and evolved over many years, it is crucial to extend my heartfelt acknowledgments to the individuals, organizations, and events that played a pivotal role in bringing this book to fruition. I feel truly blessed to finally organize these ideas into a publishable form. If I inadvertently omit mentioning any direct contributors to this project, it is less a reflection of faulty memory than a recognition of the transcendent force that connects all things and all people.

I am grateful to Pan Xiaohui and her colleagues at the Department of Philosophy at FUJEN Catholic University in Taiwan for inviting me to study medieval Scholasticism in 2010. I also extend my thanks to the Daofeng Institute of Sino-Christian Studies in Hong Kong for inviting me to engage in Christian-Confucian dialogue in 2011. These two visiting experiences nurtured the initial seeds of my academic interest in comparing transcendence.

I am grateful to the Harvard-Yenching Institute for supporting my visiting study of religious experience in classical Chinese philosophies during 2011–13. Li Ruohong and her colleagues at the institute provided a remarkable platform for scholars in Asian studies to exchange ideas and engage in dialogue, prompting me to explore and translate my thoughts on transcendence into a communicable form in English.

I would like to express my deepest gratitude to Master Juezhen, who served as my Buddhist teacher from 2010 until his passing. My decision to continue graduate studies in theology and religious studies, following my initial focus on philosophy, was not made lightly. Master Juezhen was among the very few who supported this path wholeheartedly, providing both financial and spiritual guidance until his final moments.

Unfortunately, I was unable to return to Hong Kong to visit him before his passing.

Master Juezhen's photograph remains atop my bookshelf, bearing witness to the entire revision process of this manuscript, from its initial submission to its completion. This book is uniquely dedicated to Master Juezhen, whom I believe genuinely embodied the *bodhisattva* virtue of compassion. I hope that he can smile upon reading this message from another world.

Intellectually, the impact of Robert C. Neville on the major arguments of this book is unparalleled. I have maintained a vivid connection with Bob even after completing my PhD under his guidance. If there is a spiritual lineage of Boston Confucianism in the US, scholars would undoubtedly agree that this lineage began with Bob. Similar to the traditions of ancient East Asia, this lineage has been established and transmitted academically. There was once a student who studied briefly with Cheng Hao (1032–1085), the Neo-Confucian master also known as Master Elder Cheng, and described the experience as akin to sitting amid spring breezes for over a month. I had the privilege of learning in person with Bob for more than five years, and given our ongoing connection, I can truly say that the spring breeze emanating from him has nurtured and sustained me for far longer.

In connection with Bob, I would also like to extend my gratitude to the late John H. Berthrong (1946–2022), Stephen C. Angle, and Anna Sun. John guided my transition from China to the US, immersing me in the American tradition of intellectual history in the study of Confucian materials. Steve, as the primary reader on Chinese materials, reviewed my 2018 dissertation, from which this book initially stemmed, and has since continued to support and collaborate with me on multiple projects. Anna, an undisputed leading sociologist of Confucianism, has provided crucial support for the development of this tradition in the US, including multiple collaborative projects that have contributed momentum to the formation of this book. All three of these scholars exemplify a genuine love for Confucian thought and ancient Chinese culture, and I hope their style of research will continue to flourish in American academia.

I also wish to thank Wesley J. Widman, Catherine Cornille, Kimberley C. Patton, and Francis X. Clooney. I believe the light of Wesley's friendship with Bob shines through in this book. The other three scholars mentioned have been instrumental in fostering cohorts of young scholars in the field of comparative theology based in Boston. The definition of theology and the methodology of comparative theology presented in this book owe their origins to the thought-provoking conversations I had with these scholars.

I am also deeply grateful to the two anonymous reviewers of this book manuscript, whose invaluable feedback motivated my continuous revisions and significantly strengthened the work. I thank them with the utmost sincerity.

The series editors of Comparative Theology: Thinking Across Traditions, John J. Thatamanil and Loye Ashton, guided me steadfastly through crucial moments during the revision of this manuscript. The acquisitions editor at Fordham University Press, John Garza, provided much-needed support, particularly in assisting me with responses to peer reviewers and pacing my work toward its final approval by the faculty board. To him, together with his colleagues at the press, I extend my sincere gratitude.

A previous version of chapter 1 was published in the *Journal of Interreligious Studies*. I extend my gratitude to the journal for granting permission to republish it here.

My colleagues in the Department of Philosophy and Religion at Washington College consistently supported my teaching and research endeavors. In particular, I have consulted Peter Weigel for the translation of Latin texts and sought his advice on publication-related matters. I thank Peter and my other colleagues at the college for their support.

Finally, though no words can adequately express my gratitude, I thank my wife Kiki and my daughter Maggie for their companionship and soul-deep connection throughout my entire scholarly career in the US. Even if no one knows who I am while I work, their presence continues to motivate me to work and live well.

GLOSSARY

本體	Benti: fundamental or original state
道	Dao: the Way
大虛	Daxu: great vacuum
君子	Junzi: exemplary person
禮	Li: ritual, rite, ritual-propriety, civilized symbol, or civilizational convention
理	Li: principle, pattern, or pattern-principle
良知	Liangzhi: conscientious knowing
氣	Qi: vital-energy, or psychophysical energy
器	Qi: utensil-like things
仁	Ren: humanity, or humaneness
儒	Ru: civilized human
上帝	Shangdi: supreme deity, or the Lord on High
神	Shen: numinous and wonderful
聖	Sheng: sage
生生	Sheng sheng: birth birth
太極	Taiji: Ultimate Limit
天	Tian: heaven, cosmos, or the universe
無極	Wuji: Non-Limit, No Limit, or the Limitless
無為	Wuwei: nonaction
繫辭	Xici: the *Appended Texts,* or the *Great Commentary*
心	Xin: heartmind
爻	Yao: A single line among the six that comprise a hexagram in the *Classic of Change*.
易經	Yijing: the *Classic of Change*
陰陽	Yin/Yang: two interdependent and co-generative aspects of cosmic processes or entities. They originally refer to the shady and sunny sides of a hill, respectively, but are symbolically associated with a wide range of complementary or contrasting qualities—such as darkness and light, cold and heat, receptivity and assertiveness, and more.
元氣	Yuanqi: primordial vital-energy
中庸	Zhongyong: centrality and commonality

| 周易 | Zhouyi: the *Zhou Book of Change* |
| 自然 | Ziran: what is as it is of its own accord, or what comes out spontaneously and naturally |

NOTES

Introduction

1. Following the reflective scholarly trend regarding the nomenclature, I will write "Confucianism" as "Ruism" or the Ru tradition, and "Confucian" or "Confucianist" as "Ru" or "Ruist" in this book. When used as a noun, the plural of "Ru" or "Ruist" is "Ru" or "Ruists." Accordingly, I will write "Neo-Confucianism," which normally designates new developments within Ruism during the Song through Ming dynasties (960–1644 CE), as Ruism in the concerned period of time. However, I'll respect the original use of "Confucianism" in quotations. For instance, I will still use "Boston Confucianism," and keep "Confucianism" whenever it appears in a direct quote. A detailed explanation of the nomenclacture via the disciplinary approach of religious studies can be found at Swain Tony, *Confucianism in China: An Introduction* (Bloomsbury Academic, 2017), 3–22, and Anna Sun, *Confucianism as a World Religion: Contested Histories and Contemporary Realities* (Princeton University Press, 2013), 45–76. From the perspective of philosophical historiography, please refer to Selusi Ambrogio, *Chinese and Indian Ways of Thinking in Early Modern European Philosophy: The Reception and the Exclusion* (Bloomsbury Academic, 2020), 110. At the outset of this book, I also refrained from delving into the debate over whether Ruism should be considered a religion, a longstanding question in religious studies. My intention is for readers to ponder this question themselves following my comprehensive argument throughout the book on the existence of a genuinely transcendent aspect within Ruist discourse.
2. Readers may get a glimpse into the description of my religious experiences in Jeremy Bendik-Keymer, "On Flight: Bin Song (Part I)" and "Practical Enlightenment: Bin Song (Part II)," in *Blog of the APA* (American Philosophical Association), February 19, 2021, and March 19, 2021, https://blog.apaonline.org/2021/02/19/on-flight/, and https://blog.apaonline.org/2021/03/19/practical-enlightenment/, as well as Bin Song, "The Abundant Diversity of Religious Experience," *Bin Song: A Lover's Garden of Ru and Confucianism*, April 18, 2021, https://binsong.live/2021/04/18/the-abundant-diversity-of-religious-experience/, accessed July 6, 2024.
3. "Greek-European" refers to the geographical basis of the intellectual tradition of *creatio ex nihilo* that chapters 5 and 6 are concerned with. Using the conventional nomenclature of Christian denominations, this tradition will include major thinkers in

"Catholicism" and "Protestantism," although it is not entirely fit to use these denominational terms to describe Greek philosophers and some of the early patristic fathers.

1. Comparative Theology as a Liberal Art

1. Clooney's general idea of comparative theology analyzed by this paragraph refers to Francis Xavier Clooney, *Comparative Theology: Deep Learning Across Religious Borders* (Wiley-Blackwell, 2010), especially 7–9, and 61.
2. Clooney specifies "intensification" rather than "progress" as the goal of his comparison in Francis X. Clooney, "La théologie comparée en question," in *La théologie comparée: Vers un dialogue interreligieux et interculturel renouvelé?*, ed. Christophe Chalamet, Elio Jaillet, and Gabriele Palasciano (Labor et Fides, 2021), 119.
3. Francis X. Clooney, "Strong Walls for an Open Faith," in *Theology Without Walls: The Trans-Religious Imperative*, ed. Jerry L. Martin (Routledge, 2019), 219–20. About the role of "creeds" in the formation of the Scholastic concept of "theology" and Clooney's concept of "comparative theology," see Bin Song, "Is There or Shall We Need a 'Home' for Comparative Theologies? A Ru (Confucian) Response to Francis X. Clooney," in *The Wiley Blackwell Companion to Comparative Theology: A Festschrift in Honor of Francis X. Clooney, SJ*, ed. Axel M. Oaks Takacs and Joseph L. Kimmel (Wiley-Blackwell, 2023), 491–500. In this recent article of mine, I assess the strengths and weaknesses of Clooney's approach to comparative theology in more detail, in light of a historical survey of the "confessional" attitude toward faith. I also investigate three definitions of "theology" in Western intellectual history: Aristotelian theology integral to philosophy as a way of life, Scholastic theology as faith seeking understanding, and the Protestant conception of theology exemplified by theologians such as Schleiermacher and Tillich. I argue that, in comparison, the Aristotelian type of theology is the most conducive to studies of comparative theology with non-Western traditions such as Ruism and Hinduism. Overall, although this article does not add new components to my core argument in this book, it provides extra support to my arguments in chapters 1 and 4.
4. A similar analysis of Clooney's CT can be found in Catherine Cornille, *Meaning and Method in Comparative Theology* (Wiley-Blackwell, 2020), 16.
5. Keith Ward, *Religion and Revelation: A Theology of Revelation in the World's Religions* (Oxford University Press, 1994), 46.
6. Quoted words from Ward, *Religion and Revelation*, 48–49.
7. Ward, *Religion and Revelation*, 24, 30–34.
8. A "radical revision" (xi) that Ward made to traditional Christian doctrines of Trinity in light of his interreligious studies and what humanity nowadays knows about the universe is in Keith Ward, *Christ and the Cosmos: A Reformulation of Trinitarian Doctrine* (Cambridge University Press, 2015). Such a reformulation, according to Ward, is "in no way a rejection of Christian faith as stated in the Nicene Creed or the formulae of the Council of Chalcedon" (xv), but a restatement of these doctrines in a new post-Enlightenment and postmodern context.
9. Paul Hedges, *Comparative Theology: A Critical and Methodological Perspective* (Brill, 2017), 24, 19.

10. Ward, *Religion and Revelation*, 40.
11. Hedges, *Comparative Theology*, 11.
12. See Pierre Hadot, *Philosophy as a Way of Life: Spiritual Exercises from Socrates to Foucault*, ed. Arnold Davidson (Wiley-Blackwell, 1995); Pierre Hadot, *What Is Ancient Philosophy?*, trans. Michael Chase (Belknap, 2004).
13. See Wilfred Cantwell Smith, *The Meaning and End of Religion* (First Fortress, 1991).
14. Hadot's thesis of ancient philosophy as a way of life is contested by John M. Cooper, *Pursuits of Wisdom: Six Ways of Life in Ancient Philosophy from Socrates to Plotinus* (Princeton University Press, 2012). In contrast with Hadot's thesis that the ancient philosophical "spiritual exercises" include but are not limited to philosophical discourse, Cooper articulates three ancient assumptions about reason that are pivotal to the conception of philosophy as a way of life: that reason motivates action (11), that philosophy brings perfection to reason (12), and that the perfection of reason secures success in action (14). In other words, in Cooper's reading of ancient philosophy, reasoning alone is sufficient for living a good way of life, whereas, for Hadot, such sufficiency is dismissed. I find limited evidence to support Cooper's sufficiency thesis and agree with scholars' analyses of this controversy, such as Trung Ngo, "Cooper vs Hadot: On the Nature of Hellenistic Therapeutic Philosophy," *Noesis Undergraduate Journal of Philosophy* 19, no. 1 (2018): 24–32; and Rachana Kamtekar's review of Cooper's book at *Notre Dame Philosophical Reviews*, February 20, 2014, https://ndpr.nd.edu/reviews/pursuits-of-wisdom-six-ways-of-life-in-ancient-philosophy-from-socrates-to-plotinus/. In the context of chapter 1, which clarifies the concept of theology for my comparative project, my agreement with Hadot is particularly meaningful because philosophical discourse, in the form of rigorous reasoning and logical argumentation, as per Hadot's understanding, plays a distinctive rather than contrasting role in our understanding of "philosophy" vs. "religion" in the ancient Western world. As my following analysis shows, reasoning may distinguish philosophy from religion regarding their varying means to achieve a similar goal, but this distinction by no means prohibits philosophers from participating in religious rituals and incorporating such participations into their spiritual exercises. If we follow Cooper's overspecified role of reasoning in philosophy, such mutual penetration of philosophy and religion in the ancient world would be unimaginable. About how philosophers participated in and philosophized religious rituals in ancient Greece, refer to Andrej Petrovic and Ivana Petrovic, *Inner Purity and Pollution in Greek Religion*, vol. 1, *Early Greek Religion* (Oxford University Press, 2016), particularly "Introduction" (65–66), "Heraclitus on Purification" (73–77), "Empedocles on Inner Pollution and Purity" (96–99), and "Xenophanes on Good Thinking and Drinking" (107). I thank Anonymous Reviewer 2 for prompting me to make this clarification.
15. Hadot, *Ancient Philosophy*, 64.
16. J. P. Migne, ed., *Patrologiae cursus completus*, vol. 8, col. 126 (Paris, 1861), which is translated and quoted by Smith, *Meaning and End of Religion*, 212.
17. The word appears in Aristotle, *Metaphysics* 6.1026a33. English translations of Aristotle's works discussed in this book are from Jonathan Barnes, ed., *The Complete Works of Aristotle* (Princeton University Press, 1991). A detailed analysis of the term "theology" can be found at Stephen Menn, "Aristotle's Theology," in *The Oxford Handbook of Aristotle*, ed. Christopher Shields (Oxford University Press, 2012), 1–45.

18. About Aristotle's God as Nous, please refer to Stephen Menn, "Aristotle and Plato on God as Nous and as the Good," *Review of Metaphysics* 45, no. 3 (March 1992): 543–73.
19. Aristotle's mystical tendency and mysticisms in ancient Greek philosophy are analyzed in Hadot, *Ancient Philosophy*, 88, 157–63.
20. For Aristotle on liberal arts, see Wayne Willis, "Liberating the Liberal Arts: An Interpretation of Aristotle," *Journal of General Education* 39, no. 4 (1988): 193–205.
21. For Aristotle and his antecedent theologians, see John A. Palmer, "Aristotle on the Ancient Theologians," *Apeiron* 33, no. 3 (2000): 181–205.
22. An advocacy on the religious significance of Aristotle's philosophy refers to Theo Gerard Sinnige, "Cosmic Religion in Aristotle," *Greek, Roman and Byzantine Studies* 14, no. 1 (1973): 15–34.
23. See Stephanie Corigliano, "Theologizing for the Yoga Community? Commitment and Hybridity in Comparative Theology," in *How to Do Comparative Theology*, ed. Francis X. Clooney and Klaus von Stosch (Fordham University Press, 2018), 324–50, and in particular, Mara Brecht and Reid B. Locklin, eds., *Comparative Theology in the Millennial Classroom: Hybrid Identities, Negotiated Boundaries* (Routledge, 2016).
24. The same can be said of Neville and Raimundo Panikkar, and their methodologies will be analyzed in chapter 4.
25. Aristotle, *Politics* 1137b22, trans. Benjamin Jowett, in Barnes, *Aristotle*, 166. The term *banausos* (mechanical) could also be translated as "vulgar."
26. Confucius, *Analects* 2:12. Translation adapted from multiple sources. The notation of verses refers to Peimin Ni, *Understanding the Analects of Confucius: A New Translation of Lunyu with Annotations* (State University of New York Press, 2017).
27. The received standard version of *Yijing* was compiled by Ru scholars around East Han (25–220 CE), among whom Fei Zhi (?), Zheng Xuan (127–200 CE), and Wang Bi (226–249 CE) did the most significant work. It consists of the original divination book of *Zhouyi* (*The Zhou Book of Change*), and ten later commentaries called "Ten Wings." Among the ten wings, the *Appended Texts* (繫辭, *Xici*, also called the "Great Commentary") was considered as philosophically the most significant by later Ruists. Although contemporary scholars continually debate the exact authorship of the *Xici*, it was traditionally ascribed to Confucius. The philosophical affinity between the *Xici* and Confucius's thought is conspicuous, and we will provide detailed analysis of this text in chapter 7. The received version of *Yijing* refers to Wang Bi 王弼, Han Kangbo 韩康伯, and Kong Yingda 孔颖达, *The Correct Meanings of the Zhou Book of Change* 周易正义, in *Commentaries on the Thirteen Classics* 十三经注疏, ed. Li Xueqin 李学勤 (北京大学出版社, 1999).
28. Wang et al., *Correct Meanings*, 292. Translations of this text in this chapter are my own.
29. Alternative translations of 理 are Pattern (capitalized), pattern (lowercase), pattern-principle, coherence, etc., which will be discussed more in chapter 8.
30. Wang et al., *Correct Meanings*, 289, with *Taiji* will be discussed more in chapter 7.
31. For a fine analysis on "Confucian theology," see Yong Huang, "Confucian Theology: Three Models," *Religion Compass* 1, no. 4 (2007): 455–78. Differing slightly from Huang's typological approach, I am dedicated here to demonstrating the robust continuity of theology (understood in the comparable Aristotelian sense) within the Ru tradition starting from its earliest commentaries of the *Yijing*.

32. Wang et al., *Correct Meanings*, 10.
33. All three texts are from Wang Ji 王畿, *Complete Works of Wang Longxi* 龍溪王先生全集 (南都萬曆乙卯刻本, 1615), Chinese Text Project, accessed July 2, 2024, https://ctext.org/library.pl?if=en&res=94250. They are "三教堂紀" in vol. 17, pp. 8–9; "三山麗澤錄" in vol. 1, pp. 20–21; "南遊會紀" in vol. 7, pp. 6–7. Although Peng does not use the concept of "seeded, open inclusivism," my understanding of the overall nature of Wang Longxi's thought is mostly indebted to Peng Guoxiang 彭国翔, *The Unfolding of the Learning of Conscientious Knowing: Wang Longxi and the Learning of Yangming in Middle and Late Ming* 良知学的展开: 王龙溪与中晚明的阳明学 (三联书店, 2005). I thank Paul Blair for his editing assistance in the translations of these three texts.
34. Ruism is also referred to as "the learning of sages" (聖學) in Wang Longxi's writing. "Lao" refers to Laozi, the legendary author of the *Dao De Jing* (道德經), a founding text of Daoism.
35. Wang Longxi understands Laozi's famous criticism of ritual as implying that when people are not intrinsically loyal and trustful, they will emphasize ritual to discipline themselves from without.
36. See *Analects* 11.1.
37. Xiangshan refers to Lu Jiuyuan (1139–1193 CE), a Ru contemporary of Zhu Xi.
38. Per Wang Longxi's understanding of Wang Yangming's "conscientious knowing," the innate moral consciousness is the manifestation of the constantly creative cosmic Dao in the human mind, and thus, its function pervades the entire universe and is not constrained by any concrete reality. Wang Longxi understands further this all-pervading nature of "conscientious knowing" as hinted by Kongzi's word "complete emptiness," and thus, his view is that Ruism from its beginning addressed metaphysical issues on which Daoism and Buddhism seem to particularly elaborate.
39. Buddhism holds that there are five basic components of sentience called the Five Aggregates. In Chinese, they are 色 (*se*, "form"), 受 (*shou*, "sensation"), 想 (*xiang*, "perception"), 行 (*xing*, "disposition"), and 識 (*shi*, "consciousness").
40. The Three Jewels of Buddhism: the Buddha, the Dharma (Buddhist teaching), and the Sangha (Buddhist monasticism).
41. Buddhism identifies six realms into which beings are reincarnated.
42. *Hao* and *li* are among the shortest units of length used in ancient China.
43. I have translated "祕" here as "esoteric" because there is a crucial component of Ruist self-cultivation which is deeply experiential and cannot be transmitted through words alone. This esoteric side of Ruism, however, does not tend to segregate itself from the mundane world. Rather, the salient feature of Ruist spirituality—in contrast to many other spiritual traditions—is that it always situates its mysticism in the depth of (rather than beyond) daily life in the here and now. In Wang Longxi's experience, the interactive process with his late teacher, Wang Yangming, on the bridge of Tianquan, may have been one of these esoteric moments, as referenced in the opening text in Wang Ji, *Complete Works*, vol. 1.
44. The Tang and Yu dynasties were those of Kings Yao and Shun, two of the earliest Ruist sage-kings. According to ancient Chinese texts such as the *Biographies of the Great Worthies* (高士傳), Chao and Xu were hermits who refused to serve the state even while it prospered and was ruled by the most enlightened of kings.

45. All these Ruist sayings are from the *Mengzi*.
46. For a fine analysis of these theologies of religions, see Marianne Moyaert, *Fragile Identities: Towards a Theology of Interreligious Hospitality* (Rodopi, 2011), 11–46.
47. Cornille, *Meaning and Method*, 53–60.
48. John J. Thatamanil, *Circling the Elephant: A Comparative Theology of Religious Diversity* (Fordham University Press, 2000), 63–69. The discussion is in reference to Paul J. Griffiths, *Problems of Religious Diversity* (Blackwell, 2015). Thatamanil later in the same book presents another Christian form of open inclusivism, as indicated by Martin Luther King Jr.'s theology, as he argues, "his [King's] is an inclusivism that actually includes new insights and practices from other religious traditions and so materially learns from them" (202). In comparison, the Ruist open inclusivism I advocate shares the same nature as King's to strive to include new insights, but it is different from King's in that I do not claim Ruism has achieved the fullness of divine disclosure.
49. Thatamanil discusses four criteria of a theology of religions, namely "difference without incommensurability," "truth," "critical theory of religion," and "intrinsic religious interest." *Circling the Elephant*, 42–45.

2. Comparative Theology as a Science

1. A general account by Aristotle on scientific knowledge is in *Posterior Analytics*, book 2.
2. Rudolf Carnap, "The Elimination of Metaphysics Through Logical Analysis of Language," *Erkenntnis* 2 (1932), trans. Arthur Pap, in *Logical Positivism*, ed. A. J. Ayer (Free Press, 1959), 60–81.
3. Immanuel Kant, *Prolegomena to Any Future Metaphysics That Can Present Itself as a Science*, ed. Jonathan Bennett (2017), particularly 74–77, retrieved September 1, 2021, at https://www.earlymoderntexts.com/assets/pdfs/kant1783.pdf.
4. Kant, *Prolegomena*, 53–54. An elaborated explanation can be found at the "First Antinomy," in the *Critique of Pure Reason*, book 2, chapter 2.
5. Thomas Aquinas, "On the Eternity of the World," in *Sancti Thomae de Aquino Opera omnia iussu Leonis XIII*, vol. 43 (Editori di San Tommaso, 1976), 85–89, trans. Robert T. Miller, in *Medieval Sourcebook*, retrieved September 1, 2021, at https://sourcebooks.fordham.edu/basis/aquinas-eternity.asp. Aquinas's thought on time and divine creation will be a major focus in chapter 6.
6. Kant, *Prolegomena*, 12–15 and 45–60.
7. Kant, *Prolegomena*, 60, and its elaboration in the "Appendix to the Transcendental Dialectics" of the *Critique of Pure Reason*, ed. Jonathan Bennett (2017), 292–301, retrieved September 1, 2021, at https://www.earlymoderntexts.com/assets/pdfs/kant1781part2_4.pdf.
8. René Descartes, *Principles of Philosophy*, ed. Jonathan Bennett (2017), 26, retrieved September 1, 2021, at https://www.earlymoderntexts.com/assets/pdfs/descartes1644.pdf.
9. See Imre Lakatos, *The Methodology of Scientific Research Programme: Philosophical Papers Volume 1*, ed. John Worrall and Gregory Currie (Cambridge University Press, 1978).
10. Chenyang Li and Franklin Perkins, eds., *Chinese Metaphysics and Its Problems* (Cambridge University Press, 2015) provides a "concentrated study of Chinese metaphysics that reflects the state of the art in the field" (1). Its editors define metaphysics as "theo-

ries regarding the nature, components, and operating principles of reality" (1) and emphasize that in the Chinese tradition, "the metaphysical and the moral are always intertwined" (7). My analysis here resonates with both this cross-cultural definition of metaphysics and its emphasis. I'll have further engagements with chapters in this book in chapter 7.

11. Wang Yangming 王陽明, *The Complete Works of Wang Yangming* 王陽明全集, ed. Wu Guang and Qian Ming (上海古籍出版社, 1992), 2.
12. See Chen Lai 陈来, *A Study on Master Zhu's Philosophy* 朱子哲学研究 (华东师范大学出版社, 2000), 221–25.
13. Learning of Principle (理學) and Learning of Heartmind (心學) are categories used by historians to sort out lineages of Ru thought in the Song and Ming periods. The mention of these two terms in this paragraph by no means implies that these are categories sufficient to divide thinkers of the concerned period into neatly bounded groups. Instead, keeping the complex nature of each studied Ru thinker in mind, I heuristically employ these categories to illustrate the nature of the metaphysical debate in the Ru tradition. For the origin and efficacy of these historiographical categories, please refer to Stephen C. Angle and Justin Tiwald, *Neo-Confucianism: A Philosophical Introduction* (Polity, 2017), 1–9.
14. Cheng Hao 程顥 and Cheng Yi 程頤, *Works of the Cheng Brothers* 二程集 (Zhong Hua Shu Ju, 1981), 188.
15. Wang Ji 王畿, *Complete Works of Wang Longxi* 龍溪王先生全集 (南都萬曆乙卯刻本, 1615), 17:19, *Chinese Text Project*, accessed July 2, 2024, https://ctext.org/library.pl?if=en&file=129711&page=213. Translations of Chinese texts in this chapter are my own.
16. "心也者, 人之神明, 而理之存主處也。豈可謂心即理, 而以窮理為窮此心哉!" Luo Qinshun 羅欽順, *Records of Knowing After Adversities* 困知記 (中華書局, 1990), 114. Original Chinese texts are selectively endnoted in this book.
17. Luo, *Records*, 18.
18. Luo, *Records*, 120.
19. Luo, *Records*, 123. My selection of references to Luo Qinshun is inspired by Yao Caigang 姚才剛 and Xiang Zhengxiang 向拯翔, "On Luo Qinshu's Critique to Wang Yangming's Learning of Heartmind 论罗钦顺对王阳明心学的辩难," 湖北大学学报 (哲学社会科学版) 39, no. 3 (2012): 46–49.
20. I further characterize the scientific nature of humanities studies—particularly the teaching of ethics within a grand metaphysical framework across various schools of ancient Greek philosophy—as a "science of self-transformation" in Bin Song, "As Ground of Being, God Favors Good over Bad Choices: A Confucian Response to Wesley J. Wildman," *American Journal of Theology & Philosophy* 45, no. 1 (January 2024): 50–68. I highlight the historical development of this science through the rise of modern natural science, the reinvention of empirical psychology and modern psychotherapy, and the decline of the humanities within academia. My call for a more thorough inclusion of subjective and conscious experiences of moral self-transformation in scientific inquiry suggests that it is the method—rather than any conclusive result—that defines the scientific character of a discourse. This call aligns with recent developments in the field of religion and science, which adopt a nonreductive approach to phenomena of consciousness, as seen in *Beyond Physicalism: Toward Reconciliation of Science*

and Spirituality, ed. Edward F. Kelly, Adam Crabtree, and Paul Marshall (Rowman & Littlefield, 2015).

21. Karl Popper, *Objective Knowledge: An Evolutionary Approach* (Oxford University Press, 1972).

22. As an exception, some of Zhu Xi's ethical ideas on principle border on Platonic dualism, as I will analyze in chapter 8.

3. The Transcendence Debate in the History of Christian-Ru Interaction

1. As indicated in the following, my use of the term "transcendence debate" emphasizes its long-standing historical expressions across different stages of the Christian-Ru interaction. However, other scholars use this term in different contexts as well. For instance, Jiang Wu asks what is the common denominator of "Confucian spirituality" given its varied expressions in modern times, and employs "transcendence debate" to specifically refer to the contemporary debate surrounding Tu Wei-ming's and Roger T. Ames's contested answers to whether "transcendence" should play any role in reviving Confucian spirituality. Wu concludes that to study and revive Confucian spirituality in modern times, the focus on *Jing Jie* (境界, spiritual realm) is more promising than the contested ontological commitment to transcendent reality. Jiang Wu, "What Is Jingjie? Defining Confucian Spirituality in the Modern Chinese Intellectual Context," *Monumenta Serica* 50 (2002): 441–62.

    A very recent effort by Roland Boer documents the critical reaction of mainly mainland Chinese scholars in recent decades to Mou Zongsan's thesis of "inner (or immanent) transcendence." Boer shows sympathy to these critical reactions and concludes that Mou's approach is a typical example of "using Western categories in an attempt to understand China" (98). Instead, Boer argues that the understanding of Ruist philosophy should focus more on concepts that highlight relationships rather than transcendence. Roland Boer, "Inner Transcendence and 'Beyond': The Debate in Chinese Philosophy," *Berlin Journal of Critical Theory* 7, no. 1 (January 2023): 83–102.

    Evidently, each of these studies focuses on one segment of the historical controversy that I have identified in this chapter. Regarding their theses, my response to Wu is that the aesthetic connotation of *Jing Jie* in traditional Ruist discourse cannot be illuminated absent a robust metaphysical analysis of ultimate reality, and therefore, a continual philosophical discussion of the transcendence debate is necessary for making Wu's case. My effort of connecting ontology (本體論) to the discourse on *Jing Jie* can be found at Bin Song and Stephen C. Angle, "A Ruist (Confucianist) Vision," in *What Is the Good Life? Perspectives from Religion, Philosophy, and Psychology*, ed. Drew Collins and Matthew Croasmun (Baylor University Press, 2023), 65–91.

    In response to Boer, I do not think transcendence is an entirely "Western category," since by using the comparative method of "vague category" in conjunction with "situational thinking," which I will detail in chapter 4, we can still use transcendence as a legitimate comparative category to fallibilistically and substantially explore traditional Ru metaphysics.

2. For a general approach to Matteo Ricci's missiology in China, please refer to Julia Ching, *Confucianism and Christianity: A Comparative Study* (Kodansha International,

1977), 20–25; John D. Young, *Confucianism and Christianity: The First Encounter* (Hong Kong University Press, 1983), 31–37; John Tong, "Catholic-Confucian Dialogue in Historical Perspective," in *Confucian-Christian Encounters in Historical and Contemporary Perspective*, ed. Peter K. Lee (Edwin Mellen, 1991), 2–3. Strictly speaking, Ricci was not the first to use Chinese to introduce Catholic theology. His precursor and mentor, Michele Ruggieri (羅明堅, 1543–1607), published *The True Record of the Lord of Heaven* (天主實錄) in 1584, earlier than Ricci's quoted work. However, I did not find a direct response to the Ruist *Li-Qi* cosmology in Ruggieri's work as I did in Ricci's, which may explain why Ruggieri's work did not generate the same scale of impact among Ruist scholars during their time. I thank Anonymous Reviewer 1 for reminding me of Ruggieri's work. For more on Ruggieri's introduction of Catholic ideas of creation, please refer to Sun Caixia 孙彩霞, "罗明坚《天主圣教实录》对创造本原论的阐讲及其启示," 基督教文化学刊, no. 32 (Autumn 2014): 65–82.

3. Wang Bi 王弼, Han Kangbo 韩康伯, and Kong Yingda 孔颖达, *The Correct Meanings of the Zhou Book of Change* 周易正义, in *Commentaries on the Thirteen Classics* 十三经注疏, ed. Li Xueqin 李学勤 (北京大学出版社, 1999), 292. The translation is my own. A philosophical analysis of *Xici*'s cosmology, ontology, and anthropology is a major theme of chapter 7.

4. Ricci's view on Ultimate Limit can be seen at Matteo Ricci, *The True Meaning of the Lord of Heaven (T'ien-chu Shih-yi)*, Chinese-English edition (Institute of Jesuit Sources, 1985), 61, 72, 82, 108–120. Scholarly analyses of Ricci's view can be found at Yang Hongsheng 杨宏声, "明清之际在华耶稣会士之《易》说," 周易研究 6 (2003): 41–51; Song Rongpei (韩) 宋荣培, "利玛窦的《天主实义》与儒学的融合和困境," 世界宗教研究 1 (1999): 50–59. Apart from construing Ultimate Limit as a general principle, Ricci also entertained the idea that Ultimate Limit is like Aristotle's prime matter (see Jacques Gernet, *Chine et christianisme: Action et réaction* [Gallimard, 1982], 41–42), although this idea isn't prominent in *T'ien-chu Shih-yi*. This entertained idea clearly impacted Ricci's followers' understanding of Ultimate Limit, as indicated in the following.

5. Julius Aleni 艾略儒, "Discussions at San Shan 三山论学," in *Collections of Thoughts and Writings of Jesuits in Late Ming and Early Qing* 明末清初耶稣会思想文献汇编, ed. Zheng Ande 郑安德, vol. 7 (北京大学出版社, 2003年), 333; and Alexandre de la Charme 孙璋, *Genuine Exposition on Nature and Principle* 性理真诠, vol. 2 (上海慈母堂, 1889).

6. Huang Zhen 黄贞, "Urgent Rectification to Venerate Ruism 尊儒亟镜叙," in Zheng Ande, *Collections of Thoughts and Writings*, vol. 57, 114. Translations from *Collections* are my own.

7. See Chen Houguang 陈候光, "An Initial Discussion on Distinguishing the Learning 辨学刍言," in Zheng Ande, *Collections of Thoughts and Writings*, vol. 57, 190.

8. Yu Chunxi 虞淳熙, "天主实义杀生辩 (To Comprehend That the 'True Meanings of the Lord of Heaven' Kills Lives)," in Zheng Ande, *Collections of Thoughts and Writings*, vol. 57, 202.

9. The virtual exclusivity of the Christian and Ruist worldviews regarding metaphysics is a key claim in Jacques Gernet, *Chine et christianisme: Action et réaction*, which focuses on the Ruist receptions of Christian missionaries in the late Ming and early Qing. Although I disagree with Gernet's thesis of intercultural incommensurability and instead intend to find comparable and communicable points between Christian and Ruist

metaphysics, Gernet's work provides historical context and ample examples of the *most visible* result of the first stage of Christian-Ru interaction regarding the transcendence debate.

I stress the phrase "most visible" in the last sentence because, given a tradition as historical and vast as Ruism, we should anticipate that there were alternative views among Ru scholars in the late Ming and early Qing who, though not converted to Christianity, less confrontationally anticipated or received Ricci's interpretation of Ru religiosity. For instance, Zhang Juzheng (張居正, 1525–1582) gets highlighted by Lauren F. Pfister, *Vital Post-Secular Perspectives on Chinese Philosophical Issues* (Lexington Books, 2020), because Zhang represents a Ru scholar who formulated his own theistic worldview several decades before the Jesuits arrived in China (105). The Jesuits drew upon Zhang's philosophy to articulate their own theism (114–15), which clashed with the Qing literati's preference for Zhu Xi's philosophy (121–22). Pfister even suggests a "pre-established harmony" (110) between Zhang and the Jesuits. Additionally, Dong fascinatingly identifies Wang Qiyuan (王啟元, ca. 1530–1600) as a Ru scholar who accused Ricci of usurping the ancient term "Lord-on-High" to translate the Christian God, and reinterpreted Ruism as a theistic religion resting upon the revelation of the genuine indigenous Chinese God, i.e., the Lord-on-High. Dong Fengxu, *Friendship and Hospitality: The Jesuit-Confucian Encounter in Late Ming China* (State University of New York Press, 2021), 168–75. In a hypothetical transcendence debate, these less-studied Ru scholars would agree with the first definition of transcendence that I'll identify later in chapter 3. They would assert that Ruism, in its core essence—not just in its pre-Confucian theistic forms—values this transcendent dimension. My subsequent analysis also implies that these Ru scholars' interpretation of their own tradition is in direct opposition to the perspective of Roger Ames and David Hall on transcendence. However, since these fascinating cases of theistic Ruists in the late Ming did not add new variations of the disputed concept of transcendence, and their influence upon the later stages of the transcendence debate is far less visible than the views of Ricci, his missionary followers, and Ru respondents identified in this section, my analysis in the main text of the book would have to bypass these cases. As I stressed at the beginning of this chapter, my selection of figures and texts is intended to identify patterns and repetitive themes across the stages of the transcendence debate, rather than to contribute unique and detailed scholarship on each stage.

As a side note, I should also mention that Ruist classics, as interpreted by Song and Ming Ruism, were translated and introduced into the European intellectual world in the seventeenth and eighteenth centuries via Jesuit sinologists' works such as François Noël's and Nicolò Longobardo's. These introductions created a considerable impact on the philosophical world of the European Enlightenment. Philosophers such as Nicolas Malebranche, Christian Wolff, and Gottfried W. Leibniz devised certain responses to Ruist conceptions of ultimate reality, and hence indirectly participated in the first stage of the transcendence debate. Although I have been fascinated by this topic and find a somewhat authentic understanding of Ruist theology, particularly in Leibniz's work, I have to omit an analysis of these materials in this book for the following reason: These mentioned works have neither been responded to by Ru scholars in ancient China nor seriously studied by contemporary Ru philosophers whose work

I will analyze in this chapter shortly. In fact, the Ruist impact on the birth of European modernity is a historical phenomenon that has been either largely overlooked or, in my view, generally underestimated by academia. Because of this limited impact of the European reception of translated Ruist thought on the dialogical process between Christianity and Ruism regarding transcendence, this book has to pass this very valuable topic to other future studies. For the most recently updated English research on Noël and Longobardo, please refer to Thierry Meynard's excellent works. For Enlightenment philosophers' reception of Ruist metaphysics and theology, I recommend Gottfried Wilhelm Leibniz, *Writings on China*, trans. Daniel J. Cook and Henry Rosemont Jr. (Open Court, 1994) as a starter. I thank Anonymous Reviewer 1 for prompting me to clarify the selection of figures and texts both at the beginning of this chapter and in the section on the first stage.

10. Norman J. Girardot, *The Victorian Translation of China: James Legge's Oriental Pilgrimage* (University of California Press, 2002), 266–68.
11. James Legge, *The Religions of China: Confucianism and Taoism Described and Compared with Christianity* (Scribner, 1881), 38.
12. James Legge, trans., *The I Ching* (Dover, 1963; the original version was published in 1899), 44.
13. Legge, *I Ching*, xvi.
14. Wang et al., *Correct Meanings*, 272.
15. Legge, *Religions of China*, 42.
16. Julia Ching, *Confucianism and Christianity: A Comparative Study* (Kodansha International, 1977), 118.
17. Ching, *Confucianism and Christianity*, 143.
18. Ching, *Confucianism and Christianity*, 30, 103.
19. Hyo-Dong Lee, *Spirit, Qi, and the Multitude: A Comparative Theology for the Democracy of Creation* (Fordham University Press, 2013), 34, 245.
20. Throughout this book, unless otherwise noted, Chinese philosophical terms such as Qi are capitalized in the main text but lowercased in parenthetical glosses.
21. Lee, *Spirit, Qi, and the Multitude*, 276.
22. Paulos Huang, *Confronting Confucian Understandings of the Christian Doctrine of Salvation: A Systematic Theological Analysis of the Basic Problems in the Confucian-Christian Dialogue* (Brill, 2009), 41.
23. Huang, *Confronting Confucian Understandings*, 41.
24. Huang, *Confronting Confucian Understandings*, 42.
25. In light of my discussion on Paulos Huang, I should use this note to mention another significant contemporary Christian comparative theologian, the Archbishop Stanislaus Luo Guang (罗光, 1911–2004). Because Luo's works haven't been translated into English and his academic impact has been largely confined to the Taiwanese area, I haven't taken Luo as a major Christian representative in the third stage of the transcendence debate. However, delving into his incredibly prolific writing on ancient Ru philosophy interpreted comparatively from a Scholastic perspective, readers will find a similarity between Luo's basic view regarding transcendence and Paulos Huang's.

Relying upon Zhang Zai's Qi-rooted cosmology that construes Ultimate Limit as primordial Qi (or Qi in general), Luo asserts that in Ruism, "the original state of the universe mysteriously and wondrously transforms as *Qi,* and this state is also called Ultimate Limit." Luo Guang, "Philosophy of Life生命哲学," in *Complete Works of Luo Guang* 羅光全書, vol. 2 (台灣學生書局, 1996), 88. Furthermore, relying upon the distinction between potentiality and actuality in Thomas Aquinas's Scholastic philosophy, Luo emphasizes that such an Ultimate Limit as primordial *Qi* is "blurred and uncertain," and "its nature remains unsettled." Luo Guang, *A Guideline of Chinese Philosophy* II中國哲學大綱 (下) (台灣學生書局, 1996), 20. Hence, the Ruist metaphysics prioritizing the creative potential of Ultimate Limit needs to be completed by the Christian faith toward God as a supreme substance of "pure act to be."

Here, we find a similarity between Luo Guang and early Jesuit missionaries such as Julius Aleni and Alexandre de la Charme regarding their interpretations of Ultimate Limit. We can also liken Luo's interpretation of Ultimate Limit to Huang's definition of Ultimate Limit as "producer" rather than "creator," and Luo's emphasis on the necessity of God as creator standing outside the world of cosmic changes to Huang's definition of transcendence as "objective-lying-beyond-the-limits." So, in Luo's view, if we define transcendence as something determinate and ontologically unconditioned by the existing world, there is no genuinely transcendent dimension of traditional Ru discourse except in the pre-Confucian belief in the *Shangdi.* Because of the identified similarities between Luo and other mentioned Christian theologians, my response to them in the final chapter can also be applied to Luo to a significant extent.

I thank Anonymous Reviewer 1 for prompting me to comment on Luo Guang's comparative work, and I also thank colleagues in the Department of Philosophy at Fu Jen Catholic University who hosted my visiting studies of Scholastic philosophy in the spring of 2010, when I was introduced to Luo's work for the first time. More detailed analyses of Luo's philosophy of creation can be found in Wu Qian 吴倩, "罗光儒学观研究," 学术交流, no. 9 (2017): 45–49; and Huang Zhipeng 黄志鹏, "论罗光生命哲学中的创造观," 原道, no. 2 (2018): 232–44.

26. Mou Zongsan 牟宗三, *Learning of the Life* 生命的學問 (三民書局, 1970), 74; Mou, *The Special Nature of Chinese Philosophy*中國哲學的特質 (上海古籍出版社, 1997), 21; and Mou, *Perfect Good*圓善论 (台灣學生書局, 1985), 340.
27. Liu Shu-hsien, "The Confucian Approach to the Problem of Transcendence," *Philosophy East and West* 22, no.1 (1971): 49.
28. Liu Shu-hsien, "The Openness of Confucianism," *Global Dialogue* 22, no.1 (2000): 93.
29. Mou, *Perfect Good*, 340, which instead champions "infinite awakening heartmind."
30. Tu Wei-ming, *Centrality and Commonality: An Essay on Confucian Religiousness* (State University of New York Press, 1989), 81.
31. Tu Wei-ming, "The Continuity of Being: Chinese Visions of Nature," in *Confucianism and Ecology: The Interrelation of Heaven, Earth, and Humans,* ed. Mary Evelyn Tucker and John Berthrong (Harvard University Press, 1998), 108.
32. Tu Wei-ming, "Neo-Confucian Ontology: A Preliminary Question," in *Confucian Thought: Selfhood as Creative Transformation* (State University of New York Press, 1985), 149–70.
33. Tu Wei-ming, *Centrality and Commonality*, 78, 106.
34. About the "correlative thinking" in ancient Chinese cosmologies, see Joseph Needham, *Science and Civilization in China,* vol. 2 (Cambridge University Press, 1956), 280, 302,

286, 582; A. C. Graham, *Yin-Yang and the Nature of Correlative Thinking* (Institute of East Asian Philosophies, 1986), 38.
35. Benjamin I. Schwartz, "Transcendence in Ancient China," *Daedalus* 104, no. 2 (1975): 57–68.
36. Paul R. Goldin, "The Myth That China Has No Creation Myth," *Monumenta Serica* 56 (2008): 1–22.
37. William Franke, *Apophatic Paths from Europe to China: Regions Without Borders* (State University of New York Press, 2018). Bin Song, review of *Apophatic Paths from Europe to China: Regions Without Borders*, by William Franke, in *Journal of the American Academy of Religion* 88, no. 1 (March 2020): 278–81.
38. Joshua R. Brown and Alexus McLeod, *Transcendence and Non-Naturalism in Early Chinese Thought* (Bloomsbury Academic, 2021). Bin Song, review of *Transcendence and Non-Naturalism in Early Chinese Thought*, by Joshua R. Brown and Alexus McLeod, *Notre Dame Philosophical Reviews*, March 1, 2021, https://ndpr.nd.edu/reviews/transcendence-and-non-naturalism-in-early-chinese-thought/.
39. David L. Hall and Roger T. Ames, *Thinking from the Han: Self, Truth, and Transcendence in Chinese and Western Culture* (State University of New York Press, 1997), 189.
40. Hall and Ames, *Thinking from the Han*, 190.
41. Roger T. Ames, *Confucian Role Ethics: A Vocabulary* (University of Hawaii Press, 2011), 226.
42. Hall and Ames, *Thinking from the Han*, 241.
43. Ames, *Confucian Role Ethics*, 245. Also refer to Roger T. Ames, "Confucian Harmony (he 和) as Creatio in Situ," in *Procedia: Social and Behavioral Sciences* 2 (2010): 7517–33.
44. Aristotle, *Metaphysics* 5.1019a2-14, trans. W. D. Ross, in *The Complete Works of Aristotle*, ed. Jonathan Barnes (Princeton University Press, 1991), 71.
45. Robert Cummings Neville, *Boston Confucianism: Portable Tradition in the Late-Modern World* (State University of New York Press, 2000), 150.
46. Neville, *Boston Confucianism*, 151.
47. Robert Cummings Neville, *The Good Is One, Its Manifestations Many: Confucian Essays on Metaphysics, Morals, Rituals, Institutions, and Genders* (State University of New York Press, 2016), 54.
48. Robert Cummings Neville, *Behind the Masks of God: An Essay Toward Comparative Theology* (State University of New York Press, 1991), 83.
49. I identify the major issue with Ames's methodology as its irrefutability. See Bin Song, "Robert C. Neville: A Systematic, Nonconformist, Comparative Philosopher of Religion," *American Journal of Theology and Philosophy* 40, no. 3 (September 2020): 11–30.
50. See a similar analysis in Robert W. Smid, *Methodologies of Comparative Philosophy: The Pragmatist and Process Traditions* (State University of New York Press, 2010), 123.

4. Methodologies of Comparative Theology, Religion, and Philosophy for the Progress of the Transcendence Debate

1. Francis Xavier Clooney, *Comparative Theology: Deep Learning Across Religious Borders* (Wiley-Blackwell, 2010), 7.

2. "Comparative studies of religion" is a broad category referring to any comparative study of religions or religion-like comprehensive traditions, and in this chapter, it includes three disciplines: comparative theology, comparative religion, and comparative philosophy of religion.
3. Catherine Cornille, "The Problem of Choice in Comparative Theology," in *How to Do Comparative Theology*, ed. Francis X. Clooney and Klaus von Stosch (Fordham University Press, 2018), 21–24.
4. Catherine Cornille, *Meaning and Method in Comparative Theology* (Wiley-Blackwell, 2020), 23.
5. Cornille, *Meaning and Method*, 26.
6. Max Müller, *Introduction to the Science of Religion: Four Lectures Delivered at the Royal Institution, in February and May, 1870* (Adamant Media, 2001), 16–24.
7. On postmodern critiques on comparison, please refer to Robert Segal, "In Defense of the Comparative Method," *Numen* 48, no. 3 (2001): 344–47, and Kimberley C. Patton and Benjamin C. Ray, eds., *A Magic Still Dwells: Comparative Religion in the Postmodern Age* (University of California Press, 2000), "Introduction" (1–22), and its related chapters.
8. Jonathan Z. Smith, *Relating Religion: Essays in the Study of Religion* (University of Chicago Press, 2004), 29.
9. Smith, *Relating Religion*, 22.
10. Smith, *Relating Religion*, 32.
11. Another excellent example would be Raimundo Panikkar, but I'll seek other publications to elaborate his fascinating case.
12. Robert Cummings Neville, *Behind the Masks of God: An Essay Toward Comparative Theology* (State University of New York Press, 1991), 168.
13. Neville, *Behind the Masks*, 165.
14. Robert Cummings Neville, *Ultimates: Philosophical Theology, Volume One* (State University of New York Press, 2013), location 180, Kindle.
15. Another relevant case is Lee H. Yearley's comparative study on Thomas Aquinas and Mengzi. See my analysis of this case in Bin Song, "Robert C. Neville: A Systematic, Nonconformist, Comparative Philosopher of Religion," *American Journal of Theology and Philosophy* 40, no. 3 (2019): 19–20.
16. Robert W. Smid, *Methodologies of Comparative Philosophy: The Pragmatist and Process Traditions* (State University of New York Press, 2010), 143.
17. Neville, *Behind the Masks*, 4.
18. Wesley J. Wildman and Robert Cummings Neville, "How Our Approach to Comparison Relates to Others," in *Ultimate Realities: A Volume in the Comparative Religious Ideas Project*, ed. Robert Cummings Neville (State University of New York Press, 2000), 213.
19. A similar concern is expressed by Smid, *Methodologies*, 203.
20. Aaron Stalnaker, *Overcoming Our Evil: Human Nature and Spiritual Exercises in Xunzi and Augustine* (Georgetown University Press, 2010), 17.
21. Stalnaker, *Overcoming Our Evil*, 17.
22. Stalnaker, *Overcoming Our Evil*, 286.

5. Creatio ex Nihilo *from Plato to Augustine*

1. *The Good News Translation* (GNT), the American Bible Society, 1976.
2. See N. Joseph Torchia, *Creatio ex Nihilo and the Theology of St. Augustine: The Anti-Manichaean Polemic and Beyond* (Peter Lang, 1999), 2.
3. Gerhard May, *Creatio ex Nihilo: The Doctrine of "Creation Out of Nothing" in Early Christian Thought*, trans. A. S. Worrall (T&T Clark, 2004), 7–8.
4. Torchia, *Creatio,* 2
5. Wisdom 11.17, as it is quoted by Torchia, *Creatio,* 3. In the GNT translation, it is "Your almighty power, Lord, created the world out of material that had no form at all. . . ."
6. May, *Creatio,* 21.
7. May, *Creatio,* 25.
8. *Phaedo* 99b–c, trans. G. M. A. Grube. Quoted translations of Plato's works are by different translators in Plato, *Plato: Complete Works*, ed. John M. Cooper and D. S. Hutchinson (Hackett, 1997). Page numbers of the quotes follow their Greek version marked on the margins. However, for the next section exclusively quoting Plato's *Timaeus*, I will simultaneously use the page numbers of the *Complete Works* as well.
9. The mode of ontological thinking in ancient Greek philosophy can be traced to philosophers earlier than Plato, such as in Parmenides's thought. However, compared with his predecessors, Plato's works in this regard are much more systematic. From the perspective of the intellectual history of *creatio ex nihilo*, Plato's ontology can be taken as its seed of thought.
10. *Phaedo* 99e–100d, trans. G. M. A. Grube.
11. *Republic* 509b, trans. G. M. A. Grube and rev. C. D. C. Reeve.
12. *Philebus* 27c.
13. *Philebus* 30b.
14. *Timaeus* 1234.28a, in Plato, *Complete Works*, trans. Donald J. Zeyl.
15. *Timaeus* 1235.29b.
16. *Timaeus* 1240.36e.
17. *Timaeus* 1254 and 1255.51a–51b and 52b–52c.
18. *Timaeus* 1237.31c–32c.
19. *Timaeus* 1246–47.42e–44c.
20. *Timaeus* 1236.29e. The use of the pronoun "He" follows the translation.
21. *Timaeus* 1236.30b.
22. *Timaeus* 1289.90d.
23. *Timaeus* 1250.48a and 1270.68e.
24. *Timaeus* 1241.38b.
25. *Timaeus* 1243.39e.
26. Living Thing is the thing with soul and intellect. In Plato's mind, the whole visible universe is a living thing with its own body and soul, which is furthermore an imitation of the model of Living Thing in the invisible and divine realm.
27. *Timaeus* 1241.37d–38b.
28. Plato's "Demiurge" was interpreted differently in middle Platonism and Neoplatonism. To maintain a consistency of term in my analysis of the intellectual history of *creatio ex nihilo*, I will use "God" to refer to any addressed supreme deity from this moment on.

29. See May, *Creatio*, 4–5.
30. Aristotle, "On the Heavens," book 1, 280a24–180a33, trans. J. L. Stocks, in *The Complete Works of Aristotle*, ed. Jonathan Barnes (Princeton University Press, 1991), 23.
31. Torchia, *Creatio*, 24. The original words of Taurus are in John Philoponus, *On the Eternity of the World Against Proclus*, ed. H. Rabe (B. G. Teubner, 1899), 145.
32. Torchia, *Creatio*, 24. The original thought of Albinus is in *Didaskalikos* 12.2 and 13.3, an English translation of which can be found at Albinus, *The Platonic Doctrines of Albinus*, trans. Jeremiah Reedy (PHANES, 1991).
33. See Torchia's discussion on Sallustinus's thought in Torchia, *Creatio*, 29. Sallustius's original work refers to Sallustius, *De diis et mundo* (Concerning the Gods and the Universe), in *Encyclopedia of Philosophy*, vol. 5, ed. Paul Edwards (Collier Macmillan, 1972).
34. See Torchia, *Creatio*, 25.
35. May, *Creatio*, 160. Theophilus's original thought on creation is expressed in *Ad Autolycum* 2.4.
36. I quoted Theophilus's words paraphrased in May, *Creatio*, 162. Theophilus's original words are from *Ad Autolycum* II, 10.
37. *Ennead* 3.2.3.5–10. All quotations of Plotinus come from Plotinus, *Plotinus*, trans. A. H. Armstrong (Harvard University Press, 1966).
38. See *Ennead* 6.8.6, and *Ennead* 6.8.13.15–20.
39. *Ennead* 6.8.8.
40. *Ennead* 6.8.7.40–50. The emphasis is my own.
41. *Ennead* 5.4.1.11.
42. *Ennead* 6.8.8.10–15.
43. *Ennead* 4.1.25–40. The emphasis is my own.
44. *Ennead* 6.8.12.14–17.
45. *Ennead* 6.8.7.54.
46. *Ennead* 5.2.1.5–10.
47. *Ennead* 3.2.1.22–27.
48. *Ennead* 6.7.17.41–44.
49. *Ennead* 6.8.8.1–6.
50. *Ennead* 5.4.2.27–29.
51. *Ennead* 5.3.15.26–35. The emphasis is my own.
52. Scholars interpret the One's activity differently in Plotinus's thought. For instance, Wesley J. Wildman envisions the emergence of distinct entities from the One as akin to "breaking off pieces from an endless and paradoxically edgeless chocolate bar" (Wesley J. Wildman, *Effing the Ineffable: Existential Mumblings at the Limits of Language* [State University of New York Press, 2018], 70), which is reminiscent of philosophers such as Aristotle, Spinoza, and Hegel, whose cosmogonical ideas of creation start similarly from an infinite yet formless abundance of being, rather than an unconditional "nothingness" stressed by the tradition of *creatio ex nihilo*. However, I think *Ennead* 5.2.1.5–10 and *Ennead* 5.3.15.26–35 provide strong evidence that the so-called "potency" of the One's emanation is beyond being, and cannot be understood as the self-differentiating plenitude of being as Wildman envisions. In

other words, I place Plotinus's thought more in the lineage of *creatio ex nihilo* than the one that Wildman identified. For my more robust engagement with Wildman's interpretations of Plotinus and other philosophical theologians, see Bin Song, "As Ground of Being, God Favors Good over Bad Choices—Confucian Response to Wesley J. Wildman," *American Journal of Theology and Philosophy* 45, no. 1 (January 2024): 50–68.

53. Aristotle, *Metaphysics* 5.1019a2–14, trans. W. D. Ross, in *Complete Works of Aristotle*, ed. Barnes, 71.
54. On this point, refer to Dominic J. O'Meara, "The Hierarchical Ordering of Reality in Plotinus," in *The Cambridge Companion to Plotinus*, ed. Lloyd P. Gerson (Cambridge University Press, 1996), 356–85.
55. *Ennead* 6.8.15.29–33.
56. *Ennead* 1.8.3.40 and *Ennead* 2.4.16.3. About the roles of "matter" and "evil" in Plotinus's thought, refer to Denis O'Brien, "Plotinus on Matter and Evil," in Gerson, *Cambridge Companion*, 171–94.
57. Plotinus's polemics against Gnosticism tinged his own thought with reminders of Gnostic dualism, as evidenced by the degraded role of matter in Plotinus's thought. The concern of dualism soon arose among Plotinus's followers in the Neoplatonic school, such as Iamblichus and Proclus, who refused the evil status ascribed by Plotinus to matter and intended to reform Plotinus's thought and practice surrounding the singularity of the One. For more on post-Plotinus Neoplatonic thought, refer to Gregory Shaw, "Platonic Siddhas—Supernatural Philosophers of Neoplatonism," in *Beyond Physicalism: Towards Reconciliation of Science and Spirituality*, ed. Edward F. Kelly, Adam Crabtree, and Paul Marshall (Rowman & Littlefield, 2015), 275–314. As my following analysis indicates, even Augustine's thought influenced by Plotinus is not fully exempt from dualism.
58. Karen L. King, *What Is Gnosticism?* (Harvard University Press, 2003), 4.
59. Bianchi, ed., *The Origins of Gnosticism / Le origini dello Gnosticismo: Colloquium of Messina, 13–18 April 1966, Texts and Discussions* (Brill, 1967), xxvi–xxvii. Quoted by King, *Gnosticism*, 170.
60. Adolf von Harnack, *History of Dogma*, vol. 1, trans. Neil Buchanan from the 3rd German ed. (Dover, 1961), 257–64. Quoted by King, *What Is Gnosticism?*, 62–63.
61. Harnack, quoted by King, *What Is Gnosticism?*, 62–63.
62. *De Genesi contra Manichaeos*, 1.17.28, trans. Edmund Hill. Unless otherwise noted, the English translation of Augustine's works refers to *The Works of Saint Augustine: A Translation for the 21st Century*, ed. John E. Rotelle (New City, 1991–2018). The original Latin works of Augustine that I occasionally quote are derived from the website www.augustinus.it, which primarily relies on the critical editions of *Corpus Christianorum Series Latina* (CCSL) and *Patrologia Latina* (PL) as its main sources for Augustine's Latin texts.
63. *Confessiones* 7.20.26, in *Works of Saint Augustine*, I/1, trans. Maria Boulding.
64. *Confessiones* 7.20.26.
65. The summarization of the three points is based on my reading of Torchia, *Creatio*, as well as Augustine, *Saint Augustine on Genesis: Two Books on Genesis Against the Manichees and on the Literal Interpretation of Genesis, an Unfinished Book*, trans. Roland J.

Teske (Catholic University of America Press, 1991), "Introduction," 1–38, along with other primary and secondary sources on Augustine's concept of creation. Augustine's idea of divine creation is a widely explored topic in scholarship. My analysis focuses on how this idea was shaped at the intersection of various accepted or rejected influences, such as Christianity, Platonism, and Gnosticism/Manichaeism. For a more general introduction, see Simo Knuuttila, "Time and Creation in Augustine," in *The Cambridge Companion to Augustine*, 2nd ed., ed. David Vincent Meconi and Eleonore Stump (Cambridge University Press, 2014), 81–98.

66. *Confessiones* 13.33.48; *De Genesi contra Manichaeos* 1.6.10 and 1.2.4. In the latter, Augustine also specifies that God's creation of matter out of nothing is different from His begetting His coeternal Son.
67. See the analysis by N. Joseph Torchia in Torchia, *Creatio*, 245 in reference to Augustine, *De continentia* 6.16.
68. *De Genesis contra Manichaeos* 1.2.4, in *Works of Saint Augustine*, I/13, trans. Edmund Hill.
69. *De vera religione* 17.34–18.35, in *Works of Saint Augustine*, I/8, trans. Edmund Hill. Emphasis is my own.
70. *Contra Secundinum Manichaeum* 8, in *Works of Saint Augustine*, I/19, trans. Roland J. Teske. I have slightly adapted the translation, changing "creation" to "the creature" as per the original Latin "de nihilo factam esse creaturam."
71. For a more in-depth analysis of the Trinity in relation to *creatio ex nihilo*, refer to Jared Ortiz, in *"You Made Us for Yourself": Creation in St. Augustine's Confessions* (Fortress, 2016). Ortiz contends that the Trinitarian conception of *creatio ex nihilo* is a central principle that makes the varying expressions of Augustine's autobiography in his *Confessions* a coherent whole. Ortiz summarizes that for Augustine's conception of God's *creatio ex nihilo*, the Father creates being from nothing, the Holy Spirit gives the creatures the power of "formation" toward their final end, and the Son "converts" the unformed matter of creation back to God (11–14).
72. See the analysis by N. Joseph Torchia in Torchia, *Creatio*, 171–72 in reference to *De natura boni contra Manichaeo* 8 and *Confessiones* 7.13.19.
73. *De diversis quaestionibus octoginta tribus* 46, in *Works of Saint Augustine*, I/8, trans. Boniface Ramsey. I slightly modified Ramsey's translation of "Deum irrationabiliter omnia condidisse" from "God created all things without good reason" to "God made everything irrationally."
74. *Confessiones* 13.33.46, trans. William E. Mann, "Augustine on Evil and Original Sin," in *Cambridge Companion to Augustine*, 2nd ed. (2014), 100. I prefer Mann's translation because the original Latin clause "simul tamen utrumque fecisti" explicitly conveys that "the form" is also made by God.
75. M. W. F. Stone, "Augustine and Medieval Philosophy," in *The Cambridge Companion to Augustine*, 1st ed., ed. Eleonore Stump and Norman Kretzmann (Cambridge University Press, 2001), 258.
76. Besides the quoted primary writings of Augustine, the following summary draws on Torchia, *Creatio*, 165–81; Mann, "Augustine on Evil and Original Sin"; and Knuuttila, "Time and Creation in Augustine."
77. *De civitate Dei* 11.22, in *Works of Saint Augustine*, I/7, trans. William Babcock.

78. *De libero arbitrio* 1.12.26, in Augustine, *On the Free Choice of the Will, On Grace and Free Choice, and Other Writings*, ed. and trans. Peter King (Cambridge University Press, 2010).
79. *De moribus ecclesiae catholicae et de moribus Manichaeorum* 2.1.1, in *Works of Saint Augustine*, I/19, trans. Roland J. Teske.
80. *Contra epistolam Manichæi quam vocant fundamentum* 38.44, in *Works of Saint Augustine*, I/19, trans. Roland J. Teske.
81. J. Kevin Coyle, "God's Place in Augustine's Anti-Manichaen Polemic," *Augustinian Studies* 38, no. 1 (2007): 88–89.
82. *De haeresibus* 46.2–3, in *Works of Saint Augustine*, I/18, trans. Roland J. Teske.
83. *De libero arbitrio* 2.17.46, in Augustine, *On the Free Choice of the Will*, ed. and trans. P. King, 65–66.
84. *De libero arbitrio*, 2.17.46.
85. Eleonore Stump, "Augustine on Free Will," in *Cambridge Companion to Augustine*, 2nd ed. (2014), 166–88; and Paul Rhodes Eddy, "Can a Leopard Change Its Spots? Augustine and the Crypto-Manichaeism Question," *Scottish Journal of Theology* 62, no. 3 (2009): 337.
86. *De libero arbitrio* 2.20.46, in Augustine, *On the Free Choice of the Will*, ed. and trans. P. King, 71.
87. A similar view about the necessary and not sufficient condition can be found in Christian Tornau, "Augustine of Hippo," *The Stanford Encyclopedia of Philosophy* (Summer 2024 Edition), ed. Edward N. Zalta and Uri Nodelman, accessed November 1, 2024, https://plato.stanford.edu/archives/sum2024/entries/augustine/.
88. The language of perpetual struggle derives from *De civitate Dei* 19.4. This perspective is expressed throughout Augustine's various writings. For further analysis, see James Wetzel, "Predestination, Pelagianism, Foreknowledge," in *Cambridge Companion to Augustine*, 1st ed. (2001), 55; Timothy Chappell, "Augustine's Ethics," in *Cambridge Companion to Augustine*, 1st ed. (2001), 223; Mann, "Augustine on Evil and Original Sin," 106.
89. *De gratia et libero arbitrio* 17.33, in *On the Free Choice of the Will*, ed. and trans. P. King, 169–70.
90. See the literature review by Brandon Fairbairn, "Manichaean Influences on Augustine's Catholic Theology," *Ipso Facto: The Carleton Journal of Interdisciplinary Humanities* 2 (2023): 11–22; Eddy, "Can a Leopard Change Its Spots?"; and J. Kevin Coyle, "Saint Augustine's Manichaean Legacy," *Augustinian Studies* 34, no. 1 (2003): 1–22.
91. *Ad florum* V, 31, PL 45, col. 1470, quoted by Mathijs Lamberigts, "Was Augustine a Manichaean? The Assessment of Julian of Aeclanum," in *Augustine and Manichaeism in the Latin West: Proceedings of the Fribourg-Utrecht Symposium of the International Symposium Association of Manichaean Studies (IAMS)*, ed. Johannes van Oort, Otto Wermelinger, and Gregor Wurst (Brill, 2012), 113–36. I translated the text from Latin into English in consultation with Peter Weigel.
92. Kurt Rudolph, "Augustinus Manichaicus—das Problem von Konstanz und Wandel," in *Augustine and Manichaeism in the Latin West*, 9.
93. Ludwig Koenen, "Augustine and Manichaeism in Light of the Cologne Mani Codex," *Illinois Classical Studies* 3 (1978): 159.

94. Lamberigts, "Was Augustine a Manichaean?," 135.
95. For instance, Colin E. Gunton, *The Triune Creator: A Historical and Systematic Study* (Edinburgh University Press, 1998); and Thomas Jay Oord, ed., *Theologies of Creation: Creatio Ex Nihilo and Its New Rivals* (Routledge, 2015).
96. Simon Oliver, "Augustine on Creation, Providence, and Motion," *International Journal of Systematic Theology* 18, no. 4 (2016): 379–98.
97. My writing on this section of Augustine has been significantly revised in light of the invaluable feedback from anonymous reviewers 1 and 2 on my original manuscript, to whom I extend my gratitude.

6. Creatio ex Nihilo *in Continuum: Aquinas, Descartes, Schleiermacher, and Tillich*

1. John F. Wippel, "Thomas Aquinas on the Ultimate Why Question: Why Is There Anything at All Rather Than Nothing Whatsoever?," in *The Ultimate Why Question: Why Is There Anything at All Rather Than Nothing Whatsoever?* (Catholic University of America Press, 2011), 89–90.
2. Wippel, "Ultimate Why Question," 90.
3. Wippel, "Ultimate Why Question," 90, as well as note 16 in reference to St. Thomas Aquinas, *Scriptum super Libros Sententiarum*, vol. 2, ed. Pierre Mandonnet (Lethielleux, 1929), 2, 18.
4. St. Thomas Aquinas, "On the Eternity of the World," trans. Robert T. Miller. Retrieved August 3, 2020, at https://sourcebooks.fordham.edu/basis/aquinas-eternity.asp. The original text is from St. Thomas Aquinas, *Sancti Thomae de Aquino Opera omnia*, ed. Leonine, vol. 43 (Editori di San Tommaso, 1976), 85–89.
5. Aquinas, "Eternity of the World," 85–89.
6. Thomas Aquinas, *Summa contra Gentiles*, bk. 1, chap. 15, trans. Anton C. Pegis (Image Books, 1955). The ontological dependence of all possible temporal modes of cosmic realities upon divine creation implies the nontemporality of divine creativity per se, and it also implies that once created, the continual existence of the world needs constant sustaining by God. As Peter Weigel reminds us, "In the United States, creation is often thought of as an event completed in the past, not something still happening." However, once the nature of divine causality in Aquinas's thought is clarified, we should realize that the doctrine of "continuous creation" is integral to Aquinas's teaching of *creatio ex nihilo*. Peter Weigel, *Reading Aquinas's Five Ways: The Arguments for God in Summa Theologiae* (Cambridge University Press, forthcoming), section IV of chapter 7. Here, I also thank Peter Weigel, a colleague in the Department of Philosophy and Religion at Washington College, for his continual support of my research leading to the formation of this book, and in particular, for his guidance on how to cite Aquinas's works professionally.
7. See Thomas Aquinas, *Summa theologica* I, reply to obj.7, q.46, a.2, trans. Fathers of the English Dominican Province (Cosimo Classics, 2013).
8. Wippel, "Ultimate Why Question," 88, in reference to *Summa contra Gentiles*, bk. 1, chap. 30.
9. Aquinas, *Summa theologica*, I, q.45, a.5, trans. Fathers of the English Dominican Province.

10. John F. Wippel, "Thomas Aquinas on Creatures as Causes of *Esse*," in *Metaphysical Themes in Thomas Aquinas II* (Catholic University of America Press, 2007), 180, in reference to Thomas Aquinas, *Leon.* 22.1.160:329–33.
11. Wippel, "Thomas Aquinas on Creatures," 180.
12. The fourth chapter of Gaven Keer, *Aquinas and the Metaphysics of Creation* (Oxford University Press, 2019) offers an excellent analysis of the distinction between a *per accidens* causal series and a *per se* causal series as well, as Keer succinctly summarizes on page 116 that God is "the primary cause of the *per se* series whose causality is *esse*."
13. Keer, *Aquinas and the Metaphysics of Creation*, 181, in reference to Aquinas, *Summa contra Gentiles*, bk. 2, chap. 21.
14. Augustine, *De libero arbitrio*, 3.1–5.
15. John F. Wippel, "Divine Knowledge, Divine Power, and Human Freedom in Thomas Aquinas and Henry of Ghent," in *Metaphysical Themes in Thomas Aquinas* (Catholic University of America Press, 1995), 258.
16. Wippel, "Ultimate Why Question," 91, in reference to *Summa theologica*, I, q.104, a.4.
17. Wippel, "Ultimate Why Question," 99, in reference to *De veritate*, q.23, a.4, Leon. 22.3.663:229–32.
18. Aquinas, *Summa contra Gentiles*, bk. 1, chap. 86, [3], trans. Anton C. Pegis.
19. Wippel, "Ultimate Why Question," 101, in reference to *Summa contra Gentiles*, bk. 1, chap. 86.
20. Aquinas, *Summa contra Gentiles*, bk. 1, chap. 84, trans. Anton C. Pegis. In particular, "whatever cannot be the object of the intellect is not an object of the will."
21. Keer, *Aquinas and the Metaphysics of Creation*, 70–71, delineates the "formal," "final," and "efficient" principles of divine creation in Aquinas's thought. While Keer's work does not address whether Aquinas adheres to the logic of ontological unconditionality in all three principles, his emphasis on these aspects of divine causality aligns with my own perspective.
22. Richard Cross, *Duns Scotus* (Oxford University Press, 1999), 50–51.
23. "À Mersenne, 15 avril 1630," in *Descartes: Oeuvres philosophiques*, vol. 1, ed. Ferdinand Alquié (Classique Garnier, 1992), 265. The edition is abbreviated below as "A." I once translated this and other quoted letters below, which speak to Descartes's theory of created eternal truth, from French into Chinese, and analyzed the theory in the context of the development of Descartes's metaphysical thought suitable for physics in Bin Song 宋斌, *Descartes' Metaphysical Philosophy—from the Perspectives of Metaphysics and Physics* 论笛卡尔的机械论哲学-从形而上学与物理学的角度看 (中国社会科学出版社, 2012), 41–49. However, back then, I didn't pay attention to the significance of Descartes's theory to the Christian tradition of *creatio ex nihilo*. My further learning experience with Robert C. Neville opened my eyes to this significance. Despite not being written in the strict style of intellectual history on *creatio ex nihilo*, the following words are among the most inspiring for my analysis of Descartes: "Some thinkers, Leibniz, for instance, are scandalized at the thought that intelligibility is created, which Descartes had claimed. For these thinkers, God the creator, as they identified ontological ultimate reality, is conceived to be perfectly intelligent, knowing all possibilities in choosing to create the world. Intelligibility thus is resident in the divine nature before creation. This view is in trouble, however, if the creator cannot be determinate because intelligibility

would have to be indeterminate, which is unintelligible." Robert C. Neville. *Ultimates: Philosophical Theology Volume One* (State University of New York Press, 2013), location 4795, Kindle. I thank Anonymous Reviewer 2 for prompting me to clarify the inspirational sources for my ideas on Descartes in this book.

24. Descartes, "À Mersenne, 15 avril 1630," A 1:259–61.
25. Descartes, "À Mersenne, 27 mai 1630," A 1:267–68.
26. Descartes, "À Mersenne, 27 mai 1630," A 1:265.
27. Descartes, "Règle utiles et claires pour la direction de l'esprit en la recherche de la vérité," in *Oeuvres de Descartes*, vol. 10, ed. Charles Adam and Paul Tannery (Librairie Philosophique J. Vrin, 1996), 368. The quoted title is Jean-Luc Marion's French translation of Descartes's original Latin work.
28. Descartes, "L'entretien avec Burman," *Oeuvres*, 5:148.
29. Please refer to the two letters written to Mersenne quoted above.
30. On the relationship between Descartes's metaphysics and physics, see Daniel Garber, *Descartes' Metaphysical Physics* (University of Chicago Press, 1992).
31. More detailed analyses on this point can be found at Bin Song 宋斌, "The Cartesian Circle and the Principle for the Certainty of Knowledge笛卡尔循环与知识的确定性原则," 中国现象学与哲学评论 15 (2014): 23–56.
32. Robert R. Williams, *Schleiermacher the Theologian: The Construction of the Doctrine of God* (Fortress, 1978), 35, in reference to Friedrich Schleiermacher, *The Christian Faith*, ed. H. R. Mackintosh and J. S. Stewart (T. & T. Clark, 1928), 4.3, abbreviated as GI in the following.
33. GI, 4.3, trans. Robert Williams in Williams, *Schleiermacher*, 36.
34. GI, 51.1, trans. Williams, 69.
35. GI, 54, trans. Williams, 90.
36. Willams, *Schleiermacher*, 69, in reference to GI, 167.1.
37. Willams, *Schleiermacher*, 88, in reference to GI, 52.
38. Willams, *Schleiermacher*, 94, in reference to GI, 54.4.
39. Willams, *Schleiermacher*, 39, in reference to Schleiermacher, *On Religion: Speeches to Its Cultured Despisers,* trans. John Oman (Harper & Row, 1958), 69. A fuller discussion on how Schleiermacher employs his pivotal concept of divine causality to interpret traditional divine attributes such as eternity, omnipresence, omnipotence, and omniscience can be found in Jon Paul Sydnor, *Ramanuja and Schleiermacher: Toward a Constructive Comparative Theology* (Pickwick, 2011), 95–102. In a comparative approach, Sydnor highlights the connection of Schleiermacher's concept of divine causality to the feeling of absolute dependence, as well as this connection's resulting resistance to the objectification and anthropomorphism of God. This is particularly helpful for my readers to gain a more well-rounded understanding of Schleiermacher's innovative approach to modern Protestant theology.
40. Williams, *Schleiermacher*, 94. The quotations of Schleiermacher are respectively from GI, 59, Postscript, and GI, 55.1, trans. Williams.
41. Leibniz's philosophy on creation is mainly embodied in his theory of the best possible world. Resonating with Schleiermacher's analysis quoted above, I decide not to include Leibniz among the figures for comparison because his thought does not represent modern Christian theology of *creatio ex nihilo* well. For a detailed presentation of Leibniz's

thought, please refer to Jesse R. Steinberg, "Leibniz, Creation and the Best of All Possible Worlds," *International Journal for Philosophy of Religion* 62, no. 3 (December 2007): 123–33.
42. Williams, *Schleiermacher*, 70.
43. Paul Tillich, *Systematic Theology*, vol. 1 (University of Chicago Press, 1973), 188–89.
44. Tillich, *Systematic Theology*, 1:188.
45. Tillich, *Systematic Theology*, 1:188.
46. Tillich, *Systematic Theology*, 1:188.
47. Because of this book's central theme of divine creation, my presentation of Tillich's thought on this theme follows a top-down, divine-to-human order. However, another order, which closely follows Tillich's original method of correlation, can be presented from the bottom up to emphasize that the existential state of humans' everyday life is always threatened by nonbeing, and it is God as the ground of being that provides the answer to overcome this menacing nonbeing. For this correlative approach to presenting Tillich's thought on creation, please refer to David H. Kelsey, "Paul Tillich," in *The Modern Theologians: An Introduction to Christian Theology since 1918*, 3rd ed., ed. David F. Ford and Rachel Muers (Blackwell, 2005), 62–75.

    I should also mention that the comparison of Tillich's thought on ultimate reality to Asian religions has generated a steady stream of scholarship in recent decades, as documented by Keith Chan Ka-fu and William Ng Yau-nang, eds., *Paul Tillich and Asian Religions* (De Gruyter, 2017). However, the comparative theme on nonbeing or nothingness has predominantly focused on the Buddhist and Daoist traditions, whereas a Ruist–Tillichian comparison typically centers on ethics. In this way, this book's core argument can be seen as contributing a Ruist chapter on the ontological comparison to this body of scholarship.
48. "Undialectical negation of being" refers to Tillich's view analyzed above that the *ouk on* full power of being in *creatio ex nihilo* "has no relation at all to being."
49. Tillich, *Systematic Theology*, 1:188.
50. I thank Anonymous Reviewer 2 for requesting that I state more explicitly the difference between Tillich and Augustine on this point.
51. Tillich, *Systematic Theology*, 1:190–91. The following views of Tillich on finitude and infinitude also derive from the same pages.
52. Paul Tillich, *Systematic Theology*, vol. 3 (University of Chicago Press, 1963), 307.
53. Tillich, *Systematic Theology*, 3:320.
54. Tillich, *Systematic Theology*, 3:373.
55. Tillich, *Systematic Theology*, 3:355, 358. Also see Bin Song, "The Utopian Seed of Modern Chinese Politics in Ruism (Confucianism)," in *Why Tillich? Why Now?*, ed. Thomas Bandy (Mercer University Press, 2021), 95–110.
56. Tillich, *Systematic Theology*, 3:400–401.
57. Tillich, *Systematic Theology*, 3:422.
58. Tillich, *Systematic Theology*, 3:421.
59. Tillich, *Systematic Theology*, 3:420.
60. Tillich's non-personalistic conception of God remains a strong reason for me to group Tillich's thought into the same de-anthropomorphizing lineage of modern theology starting from Descartes. However, in Tillich's earlier texts around 1913–16, he adhered

to the idea of God as the "absolute that has become personal." It was only under the influence of Martin Kähler's claim that "the absolute is an idol" that Tillich began to dissociate himself from the term "the absolute." Please refer to the fine analysis on this point by Martin Leiner, "Tillich on God," in *The Cambridge Companion to Paul Tillich*, ed. Russell Re Manning (Cambridge University Press, 2008), 48–49. An illuminating aspect of this transition is that the *ouk on* nature of *creatio ex nihilo* entails that any determinate characterization of God as a being, even a supreme, absolute being, violates the unconditional ontological status of *creatio ex nihilo*. Therefore, Tillich's decisive break from the traditional Christian idea of a personal God, in hindsight, greatly manifests the influence of the unconditional ontology of *creatio ex nihilo* on him.

7. Sheng Sheng *as* Generatio ex Nihilo *from Confucius to Wang Bi*

1. As explained in the introduction, I would not contest the composition of the texts analyzed in this chapter, since the transcendence debate has addressed mainly their received versions. I will still refer to the author of the *Dao De Jing* as the legendary Laozi.
2. Laozi, *Dao De Jing* (the received Wang Bi version), chapter 80. The translation of *Dao De Jing* is adapted by myself from multiple sources. For the original Chinese, refer to Chinese Text Project, accessed December 1, 2022, https://ctext.org/dao-de-jing/ens.
3. "The Unfolding of Rites (禮運)," in Zheng Xuan, Kong Yingda 郑玄 孔颖达, *The Correct Meanings of The Book of Rites*礼记正义, in *Commentaries on the Thirteen Classics*十三经注疏, ed. Li Xueqin 李学勤 (北京大学出版社, 1999), 658–59; the translation is my own. Although it is philologically arguable whether these words were said by Confucius, it is widely received within the Ru tradition that these words represent the social ideal of Confucius and the early Ru school. Also refer to *Li Yun* 1, Chinese Text Project, accessed December 1, 2022, https://ctext.org/liji/li-yun/ens.
4. The *Analects* 12.1, in Peimin Ni, *Understanding the Analects of Confucius: A New Translation of Lunyu with Annotations* (State University of New York Press, 2017), 279.
5. The term *Li* (禮, ritual) shares its pronunciation with another important philosophical concept, *Li* (理, pattern-principle), which is why these two entirely different Chinese characters appear in the same Romanized form. I will explain the relationship between these two concepts in more detail in chapter 8. As previously stated, unless otherwise noted, Chinese philosophical terms are capitalized in the main text, while lowercase is used in parenthetical glosses.
6. Benjamin I. Schwartz opines similarly on Daoism and Ruism in his "Transcendence in Ancient China," *Daedalus* 104, no. 2 (1975): 57–68.
7. The term "metaphysics," in my interpretation of both Western and Chinese thought, contains cosmology and ontology. My use of "cosmology" is close to "cosmogony," a theory or a narrative about how the cosmos originates and evolves. Whether there is an ontological dimension for a cosmology depends upon whether the cosmology addresses "nontemporal" characteristics of things in the cosmos. Please refer to chapter 2 for more details of my analysis of "metaphysics" in a comparative perspective.
8. Spinoza's and Hegel's thoughts on creation are not typical cases of *creatio ex nihilo*, and hence not included in this comparative study. See Richard Mason, *The God of Spi-*

noza: *A Philosophical Study* (Cambridge University Press, 1997) and C. Allen Speight, *The Philosophy of Hegel* (McGill-Queen's University Press / Acumen, 2008).

9. A more literal translation of 自然 is "what is as it is (然) of its own accord (自)," and the "law" mentioned in the translation therefore doesn't imply the existence of a "lawgiver." Please also refer to Paul R. Goldin, "The Myth That China Has No Creation Myth," *Monumenta Serica* 56, no. 1 (2008): 1–22 concerning 自然.

10. Or, it can be alternatively termed as an "undifferentiated whole of being-as-becoming" to highlight the processual nature of Laozi's thought.

11. This text was perhaps compiled in the time between Mencius (372–289 BCE) and Xunzi (313–238 BCE); even so, many scholars in the history of the Ru tradition ascribed its authorship to Confucius. Despite the uncertain authorship of the text, I maintain that, based on the affinity of the *Xici* with Confucius's thought in the *Analects*, as will be indicated later in this chapter, this text reflects the metaphysical development of Ru thought since the time of Confucius and is thus appropriate for comparative analysis.

12. *Xici*, chapter 1 of part 1, in Wang Bi 王弼, Han Kangbo 韩康伯, and Kong Yingda 孔颖达, *The Correct Meanings of the Zhou Book of Change* 周易正义, in *Commentaries on the Thirteen Classics* 十三经注疏, ed. Li Xueqin 李学勤 (北京大学出版社, 1999), 257–61. For the original Chinese, refer to *Xici* I.1, Chinese Text Project, accessed December 1, 2022, https://ctext.org/book-of-changes/xi-ci-shang. The chapter and part divisions of the *Xici* in my writing follow those in *The Correct Meanings*, although the Chinese Text Project adopts a different system of notation. Translation of *Xici* is adapted by me from multiple sources, including Richard John Lynn, trans., *The Classic of Changes: A New Translation of the I Ching as Interpreted by Wang Bi* (Columbia University Press, 2004) and Richard Rutt, trans., *The Book of Changes (Zhouyi)* (Routledge Curzon, 2002).

13. *Zhouyi* (*Zhou Book of Change*) was primarily a book of divination used in the Zhou dynasty (1046–256 BCE). *Yijing* (*Classic of Change*) adds a series of commentaries to the *Zhouyi* by early Ru thinkers, including the *Xici*, the focus of our analysis here. Subsequently, the *Yijing* emerged as one of the most significant classics in the Ruist canon, beginning from the Han dynasty. Please refer to chapter 1 of *Debating Transcendence* for more details of the formation of the classic.

Among all received Ru classics, the *Classic of Change* influenced my Ruist formation the most, and among countless scholarly works that have contributed to such formation, I honor two of the most important here: Cheng Yi 程颐, "A Cheng Commentary of the Zhou Book of Change 周易程氏傳," in *Collected Works of the Cheng Brothers* 二程集 (中華書局, 1981), 689–1026; and Zhu Bokun 朱伯崑, *History of Philosophy of the Yi Learning* 易学哲学史 (华夏出版社, 1994).

14. As I'll elaborate the rendering of 生 or 生生 at the end of this chapter, I may translate 生 as "create," "generate," or "give birth to" in varying contexts.

15. Wang et al., *Correct Meanings*, 292. An initial discussion of this quotation can be found in chapter 1 of *Debating Transcendence*.

16. Wang et al., *Correct Meanings*, 268–72; *Xici* I.5, Chinese Text Project, accessed December 1, 2022, https://ctext.org/book-of-changes/xi-ci-shang.

17. I will return to this point more elaborately in my analysis of Zheng Xuan's thought in a later section of this chapter.

18. It is noticeable that the *Xici* also includes a discourse on "nonaction," but its connotes a different meaning from its minimalist and austere version in the *Dao De Jing*. The *Xici* emphasizes the role of human endeavors in knowing and applying the pattern-principles of realities to expand human enterprise. Therefore, when the *Xici* describes how the *Zhou Book of Change*, as authored and operated by sages, can deliver results that resonate and penetrate (感而遂通) all causes under heaven in a way of "neither thought nor contrived action (無思無為)" (Wang et al., *Correct Meanings*, 282, which will be analyzed in more detail later in this chapter), such "nonaction" connotes an ideal consummation of knowing and applying pattern-principles, so that the sage could be at ease in aligning with all pattern-principles of realities that include the complexities of human endeavor in building and growing civilization. For a more detailed analysis of "nonaction" in varying pre-Qin philosophical texts, refer to Edward Slingerland, *Effortless Action: Wu-wei as Conceptual Metaphor and Spiritual Ideal in Early China* (Oxford University Press, 2003), though Slingerland hasn't focused on the text of *Xici*.

19. In *Analects* 15.29, Confucius also said, "It is humans who can broaden the Way, not the Way that can broaden humans" (Peimin Ni, *Understanding the Analects*, 366).

20. Wang et al., *Correct Meanings*, 288–90; *Xici* I.11, Chinese Text Project, accessed December 1, 2022, https://ctext.org/book-of-changes/xi-ci-shang. In light of quotations and discussions so far, the relationship between the concept of *Tian* (heaven or the cosmos) and the one of *Taiji* (Ultimate Limit) in Ruist metaphysics can be elaborated as follows. As the broadest ontological category, *Tian* refers to an all-encompassing constantly creative cosmic power or field that generates and contains everything in the universe. Within this all-encompassing cosmic field, the *Xici* exposits multiple layers of ontological pattern-principles to explain the order and existence of cosmic beings, such as two modes, four images, and eight hexagrams, etc. Among these pattern-principles, the one of *Taiji* is the highest, which is thought of by this quoted passage as the singular ontological pattern-principle generating everything else in the universe. Therefore, if *Tian* is understood as an all-inclusive container, *Taiji* will be what creates this container; if *Tian* is understood as the all-encompassing creative power, *Taiji* is the source from which this power ultimately derives. Because of the ultimate status of *Taiji*'s creative power in Ruist metaphysics, my discussions and comparisons in the later parts of the book will mostly focus on the concept of *Taiji*.

21. I create this diagram according to Zhu Xi, *Introduction to the Study of the Classic of Change (I-Huseh Ch'i-meng)*, trans. Joseph A. Adler (Global Scholarly Publications, 2002), figures 4, 5, and 6, pp. 17–18. The original figures used by Zhu Xi can be found at Hu Fangping 胡方平, *Explanations on the Introduction to the Study of the Classic of Change* 易學啟蒙通釋, vol. 1 (欽定四庫全書本, 1782), 25–31, Chinese Text Project, accessed June 30, 2024, https://ctext.org/library.pl?if=en&res=703. In light of this chart, it is also fitting here to discuss my translation of 太極 (*Taiji*) as Ultimate Limit. Current English translations of *Taiji* include "Great Ultimate" (Wing Tsit-Chan), "Supreme Polarity" (Joseph A. Adler), "Great Extreme" (W. H. Medhurst), and others. The term "Polarity" involves the concept of duality, whereas *Taiji*, as indicated by this chart, is the singular creative force of the universe that transcends the duality of *yin* and *yang*. For other translations, the difficulty lies in how to find a corresponding translation of 無極 (*Wuji*).

If *Taiji* is "Great Ultimate" or "Great Extreme," then *Wuji* would have to be "No Ultimate" or "No Extreme." However, the continuity of Ru metaphysical thought presented in chapters 7 and 8 of *Debating Transcendence* indicates that a crucial aspect of the Ru understanding of the relationship between *Wuji* and *Taiji* is that *Wuji* is not separate from *Taiji*; instead, it is just one way to characterize *Taiji*'s creative power as being unconditional. In other words, *Wuji* is by no means a negation of *Taiji*, but a reaffirmation of the supreme creative act of *Taiji*. Hence, the benefit of translating *Taiji* as "Ultimate Limit" is that *Wuji* can be rendered accordingly as "Non-Limit," "No Limit," or "Limitless," implying that the ultimately conditioning creative origin of *Taiji* is simultaneously unconditioned by anything else. No other listed translations offer such a benefit.

22. Wang et al., *Correct Meanings*, 291–92; *Xici* I.12, Chinese Text Project, accessed December 1, 2022, https://ctext.org/book-of-changes/xi-ci-shang.

23. Relying on relatively the same core material in the *Xici*, Robin R. Wang argues that a distinctive feature of Chinese metaphysics is its basic *yin/yang* cosmology, and that "Chinese metaphysics as *xing er shang* is rooted in a belief that there is no absolute and isolated substance, no transcendent entity independently existing beyond all things." Robin R. Wang, "Yinyang Narrative of Reality: Chinese Metaphysical Thinking," in *Chinese Metaphysics and Its Problems*, ed. Chenyang Li and Franklin Perkins (Cambridge University Press, 2015), 19. In a way that resonates with Wang's core argument, JeeLoo Liu in the same book also argues that the Chinese *Qi*-naturalism "consists of nothing but entities of the natural world and humans are part of the natural world." JeeLoo Liu, "In Defense of Chinese *Qi*-Naturalism," in *Chinese Metaphysics and Its Problems*, 38. Although Liu's article indicates a greater sensitivity toward the variety of Chinese metaphysics throughout its different historical periods, texts, and figures, neither Wang nor Liu has entertained the idea that there is a strong lineage of Chinese metaphysics that indicates an understanding of transcendence as per the second definition of transcendence identified in chapter 3 of *Debating Transcendence*. A major endeavor of my analysis in this and following chapters is to indicate how a lineage of Ru metaphysics tries to parse out the connotation of Ultimate Limit that is alleged by the *Xici* as beyond the basic *yin/yang* cosmology, which is a major demarcator of the difference between my understanding of Chinese metaphysics and that of both Wang and Liu.

24. Regarding the ineffability and fecundity of *Tian*'s creativity, Confucius also said in the *Analects* 17.19, "Does *Tian* say anything? Yet the four seasons rotate, and hundreds of things grow. Does *Tian* say anything?" Peimin Ni, *Understanding the Analects*, 401.

25. Wang et al., *Correct Meanings*, 268; *Xici* I.4, Chinese Text Project, accessed December 1, 2022, https://ctext.org/book-of-changes/xi-ci-shang.

26. Wang et al., *Correct Meanings*, 284; *Xici* I.10, Chinese Text Project, accessed December 1, 2022, https://ctext.org/book-of-changes/xi-ci-shang.

27. In the received version of *Zhuangzi*, the character here is "before" (先), meaning "temporally prior"; however, there are contemporary commentators who argue that the word here should mean "spatially beyond." In my view, these different interpretations do not matter much to *Zhuangzi*'s understanding of Ultimate Limit according to my analysis which follows.

28. The chapter of "Great Master (大宗師)" in the *Zhuangzi*; translation by James Legge, "The Writings of Chuang Tzu," 1891, which can be found at *Zhaungzi*, "The Great and Most Honoured Master," section 3, Chinese Text Project, accessed May 27, 2021, https://ctext.org/zhuangzi/great-and-most-honoured-master. Minor changes to the translation have been made.
29. Additional verses in the *Zhuangzi* that support this charted cosmological sequence can be found in chapters such as 天地, 至樂, and 庚桑楚. Here, the *Dao De Jing*'s stage of the undifferentiated whole could potentially be interpreted using the term "primordial vital-energy (元氣)," which is a frequently used term in later Chinese cosmologies. Moreover, the process by which the stage "One" in the Dao De Jing gives rise to subsequent stages is depicted in a more sophisticated manner. Nonetheless, it is clear that when presenting a cosmology, the intricate text of *Zhuangzi* takes the *Dao De Jing* as its fundamental framework.
30. John Knoblock and Jeffrey Riegel, trans., *The Annals of Lü Buwei* (Stanford University Press, 2001), 136–38. Minor changes to the translation have been made.
31. 淮南子 天文訓. The translation is adapted from multiple sources, including Evan Morgan, *Tao, the Great Luminant: Essays from Huai Nan Tzu* (Paragon Book Reprint, 1969) and John S. Major et al., trans. and eds., *The Essential Huainanzi* (Columbia University Press, 2012). 太昭 is alternatively written as 太始, which implies the same. The original text refers to He Ning 何寧, *Collected Exegeses of Huainanzi* 淮南子集釋 (中華書局, 1998年), 165–66; *Huainanzi* 1, Chinese Text Project, accessed December 1, 2022, https://ctext.org/huainanzi/tian-wen-xun.
32. 淮南子 精神訓. He, *Collected Exegeses*, 503–4; *Huainanzi* 1.
33. 淮南子 覽冥訓. He, *Collected Exegeses*, 454–56; *Huainanzi* 3, Chinese Text Project, accessed December 1, 2022, https://ctext.org/huainanzi/lan-ming-xun.
34. 淮南子 精神訓. He, *Collected Exegeses*, 551; *Huainanzi* 18, Chinese Text Project, accessed December 1, 2022, https://ctext.org/huainanzi/jing-shen-xun.
35. My reading of Zheng Xuan greatly benefits from Cheng Qiang 程強, "The Transformation and Change of the Concept of Taiji" "太极"概念内涵的流衍变化 (PhD diss., Shanghai Normal University, 2012). Though construing varying points of Zheng Xuan's thought differently, I keep in line with Cheng's basic insight that Zheng's thought pioneered Wang Bi's ontological works.
36. This term becomes well known after A. C. Graham's sinological works. Please see my explanation of "correlative thinking" in chapter 3.
37. "文淵閣本欽定四庫全書會要 經部 易緯 乾坤鑿度卷," *Qian Zao Du*, in Chinese Text Project, accessed September 1, 2021, https://ctext.org/library.pl?if=gb&res=82579, p.75. The translation is my own. This source will be written as *Qian Zao Du* in the following quotes.
38. *Qian Zao Du*, 80–82.
39. Zheng Xuan, 繫辭註*Commentary on the Xici*. This text is quoted from a fine compilation of Zheng's original writings in Lin Zhongjun 林忠軍, *An Exposition on Zheng's Learning of Zhou Yi* 周易鄭氏學闡微 (上海古籍出版社, 2005), 392. The translation is my own.
40. *Qian Zao Du*, 75. The source of Zheng Xuan's commentary on the *Qian Zao Du* refers to the same as the latter's, and the translation is my own.

41. *Qian Zao Du*, 80.
42. *Qian Zao Du*, 80.
43. *Qian Zao Du*, 81.
44. *Qian Zao Du*, 81.
45. Lin Zhongjun, *Exposition*, 400.
46. Among modern Chinese interpreters of Wang Bi, Tang Yongtong (湯用彤, 1893–1964) is the most prominent in stressing the role of traditional Ru classics in the formation of Wang Bi's thought, as well as the transitional role of Wang Bi in the ontological renovation of ancient Chinese metaphysics. As Tang Yijie and Sun Shangyang's introduction highlights, "As per Mr. Tang Yongtong, the ontology of the Learning of the Dark (玄学本体论), constructed by Wang Bi through interpreting how a hexagram in the *Yijing* is deduced, differs from Han scholars' cosmology (宇宙论或宇宙构成论) as heaven from earth." Tang Yongtong, *Essays on Wei-Jin Learning of the Dark* 魏晋玄学论稿 (上海古籍出版社, 2001), 5; translation is my own. One important article of Tang Yongtong in the *Essays* has been translated by Walter Liebenthal, "Wang Pi's New Interpretation of the I Ching and Lun-Y," *Harvard Journal of Asiatic Studies* 10, no. 2 (September 1947): 124–61, thereby rendering Tang's view on this point known to Western scholars.

    Nevertheless, disputants of the transcendence debate analyzed in chapter 3 haven't paid enough attention to Tang's studies, and in general, the Ruist nature of Wang Bi's metaphysics is an underexplored topic in English scholarship. Hence, my contribution in this section on Wang Bi and his follower Han Kangbo can be seen as presenting robust textual evidence of the transition identified by Tang Yongtong, hinting at its connection to later Song Ruists' thought, and, most important, analyzing this evidence from the perspective of the transcendence debate.
47. The translation of Wang Bi's commentary on the *Dao De Jing* is available in Richard John Lynn, *The Classic of the Way and Virtue: A New Translation of the Tao-te Ching of Laozi as Interpreted by Wang Bi* (Columbia University Press, 2004), and it is adapted by me here. The original Chinese text refers to Lou Yulie 樓宇烈, ed., *An Exposition on the Commentary of Laozi's Dao De Jing* 老子道德經註校釋 (中華書局, 2008), 117.
48. Lou, *Exposition*, 110.
49. Lou, *Exposition*, 17.
50. Lou, *Exposition*, 50.
51. "聖人體無, 無又不可以訓, 故不說也。老子是有者也, 故恆言無, 所不足。" He Shao 何劭, "Biography of Wang Bi" 王弼傳, originally quoted by "三國志 魏志 鐘會傳," in Peng Lin and Huang Pumin 彭林 黃朴民, eds., *A Collection of References in the Intellectual History of China: From Pre-Qin to the North and South Period* 中国思想史参考资料集 先秦至魏晋南北朝卷 (清华大学出版社, 2005年), 234. The translation is my own.
52. He, "Biography of Wang Bi," 234.
53. The current scholarship on Wang Bi in both English and Chinese languages increasingly recognizes the intermingling nature of Ruist, Daoist, and other ancient schools of thought in Wang Bi's philosophy. For instance, while exclusively focusing on the hermeneutical method of Wang's commentary on Laozi's *Dao De Jing*, Rudolf G. Wagner comments that Wang Bi's *Laozi* "is neither revealed by the highest deity, nor written by the Sage [Confucius]'s teacher, nor concocted by a mediocre thinker. And it is not Daoist as opposed to the Ruist teachings of Confucius." Rudolf G. Wagner, *The Craft*

of a Chinese Commentator: Wang Bi on the Laozi (State University of New York Press, 2000), 137.

On the side of Chinese scholarship, one of the most recent and significant contributions on clarifying the nature of Wang Bi's thought is by Li Lanfen 李兰芬, *The Charm and Confusion of Dark Thought—A Collection of Studies on Wang Bi and Tang Yongtong* 玄思的魅与惑— 王弼、汤用彤研究论集 (商务出版社, 2020). In the introduction of this book, Li writes:

> Traditionally, Wang Bi's *Learning of the Dark* (玄学, or Mysterious Learning) is considered an important milestone in the development of Daoist thought. The research of Tang Yongtong (1893-1964) on *Learning of the Dark* is still mostly regarded as a significant achievement in the study of Daoist thought (or Daoist philosophy). What kind of special way of thinking is involved in the Daoist thought or Daoist philosophy addressed in their ideas? What exactly is this special way of thinking aimed at, possessing both "charm" and "confusion"? In this collection of studies, I ask these questions from the perspective of the development of Ruist thought, aiming to present the charm and confusion of Dark Thought (玄思) as clearly as possible. (i–ii, my translation)

Clearly, the methodology of Li's study of Wang Bi highlights the continuity of Wang Bi's thought within the development of Ruism, which renews Tang Yongtong's legacy and resonates with my own approach to the study of Wang Bi. My effort in this and the next chapter is to highlight the Ruist metaphysical lineage of *generatio ex nihilo*, starting from the *Xici*, through Wang Bi, and downstream to Song Ruism—a laser focus on metaphysics and the transcendence debate that has not yet been equally shared by Li's book. However, Li's book provides sufficient historical study on issues such as how previous Ru scholarship in the Han dynasty stimulated Wang Bi's *Learning of the Dark*, the connection between Wang Bi's metaphysics and ethical/political thought, the differences between Wang Bi and other thinkers in the period of Wei-Jin Learning of the Dark (魏晋玄學), and the nature of the reception of Wang Bi's thought in later Ruism. All of these aspects complement my metaphysical analysis and can provide a well-rounded picture of Wang Bi's thought for my readers.

In comparison, despite noticing the intermingling nature of Wang Bi's thought, Rudolf G. Wagner's scholarship on Wang Bi, particularly exemplified by his more philosophical book, *Language, Ontology, and Political Philosophy in China: Wang Bi's Scholarly Exploration of the Dark (Xuanxue)* (State University of New York Press, 2003), predominantly focuses on Wang's commentary on *Laozi* and downplays the influence of the *Yijing* and other Ru classics on Wang's linguistic, ontological, and political thought. In this sense, the contributions of Tang Yongtong, Li Lanfen, and my own studies on Wang Bi can be seen as focusing on the Ruist side of Wang Bi's thought that hasn't been sufficiently stressed by Wagner's approach.

54. Wang et al., *Correct Meanings*, 279. My translation is adapted from Richard John Lynn, trans., *The Classic of Changes: A New Translation of the I Ching as Interpreted by Wang Bi* (Columbia University Press, 2004), 311.

55. These words of Wang Bi are quoted by Yang Shixun 杨士勋 in 《谷梁傳注疏》, which is furthermore discussed in Yang Jiansheng 杨鉴生, "王弼注《易》若干佚文考论— 兼论王弼注《系辞》問題," 中国文化论坛 4 (2010): 62–66. The translation is my own.

56. Wang et al., *Correct Meanings*, 289. My translation is adapted from Lynn, *Classic of Changes*.
57. Wang et al., *Correct Meanings*, 268.
58. "原夫兩儀之運，萬物之動，豈有使之然哉? 莫不獨化於大虛，欻爾而自造矣。造之非我，理自玄應; 化之無主，數自冥運，故不知所以然而況之神。是以明兩儀以太極為始，言變化而稱極乎神也。" Wang et al., *Correct Meanings*, 272.
59. In light of this clarification of the concept of "creation" in the Ruist context, it is also fitting here to discuss my translation of *sheng sheng* (生生) as "birth birth." Available translations of *sheng sheng* include "production and reproduction" (Wing Tsit-Chan), "creative creativity" (Liu Shu-hsien), and others, all of which try to provide a philosophical translation of the term. However, as indicated by my analysis in chapters 7 and 8, the philosophical connotations of *sheng sheng* are rich and multifaceted. Ontologically, *sheng sheng* portrays the way Ultimate Limit creates all ranks of derived realities in an order of ontological priority. Cosmologically, it primarily refers to Ultimate Limit's creativity unfolding as a constant cosmic advance into novelty. In the concluding chapter of *Debating Transcendence*, I will indicate that there are other philosophical connotations of *sheng sheng* as well. Therefore, I prefer rendering *sheng sheng*, when used as a stand-alone cosmological phrase, as "birth birth" mainly because this is a more literal translation, and hence, keeps closer to the syntax of the original Chinese phrase 生生. This translation does not intend to unpack the rich philosophical connotations of *sheng sheng* and therefore leaves more room for philosophers to pursue such interpretations. Regardless of the diversity of translations, I want to emphasize via my philosophical analysis of varying figures and texts in this chapter that the terms "creation," "generation," and "birth," in the context of Ruist metaphysics, all mean the same thing in the cosmic realm: something determinate spontaneously emerges from something else, and this process can be understood either cosmologically or ontologically. A final analysis of "creation" as a vague comparative category will be offered in the final chapter.

8. Generatio ex Nihilo *in Continuum: Zhou Dunyi, Zhu Xi, Cao Duan, and Luo Qinshun*

1. Wang Bi 王弼, Han Kangbo 韩康伯, and Kong Yingda 孔颖达, *The Correct Meanings of the Zhou Book of Change* 周易正义, in *Commentaries on the Thirteen Classics* 十三经注疏, ed. Li Xueqin 李学勤, ed. Li Xueqin 李学勤 (Bei Jing Da Xue Chu Ban She, 1999), 289. My translation is adapted from Richard John Lynn, *The Classic of Changes: A New Translation of the I Ching as Interpreted by Wang Bi* (Columbia University Press, 2004).
2. Wang et al., *Correct Meanings*, 268.
3. Zhou Dunyi 周敦頤, *The Collected Works of Zhou Dunyi* 周敦頤集 (中華書局, 1990), 3–5. My translation is adapted from Joseph Alan Adler, *Reconstructing the Confucian Dao: Zhu Xi's Appropriation of Zhou Dunyi* (State University of New York Press, 2014). Please refer to the original Chinese text at Chinese Text Project, accessed December 1, 2022, https://ctext.org/wiki.pl?if=gb&chapter=942058.

4. Zhou, *Collected Works,* 26–27. Also refer to the original Chinese text at Chinese Text Project, accessed December 1, 2022, https://ctext.org/library.pl?if=gb&file=153291&page=24.
5. An online version of the Diagram is in Joseph A. Adler, "Zhou Dunyi: The Metaphysics and Practice of Sagehood," available online at the Kenyon College website, accessed in June 2021, http://www2.kenyon.edu/Depts/Religion/Fac/Adler/Writings/Chou.htm.
6. Dong Zhongshu (董仲舒, 179–104 BCE), Zhang Zai (張載, 1022–1077 CE), and Luo Qinshun (羅欽順, 1465–1547 CE) are exemplars of this kind of understanding of "primordial *Qi*" in the Ru tradition. For them, "primodial *Qi*" means "*Qi* in general," and among the texts and thinkers I analyzed previously, we can find traces of this ontological construal of primordial *Qi* in Zheng Xuan's and Kong Yingda's commentaries on the *Xici*. According to this alternative conception of primordial *Qi*, *Qi* in general always runs and functions between Heaven and Earth, and its characteristics are shared by *yin/yang* vital-energies, which are the only concrete forms of vital-energy which we can find in a de facto way. Since my main purpose in chapter 7 is to highlight the thought process within those ancient Chinese cosmologies which lead to Wang Bi's and Hang Kangbo's shared ontology, I have analyzed the "primordial *Qi*" with a meaning of "*Qi* in general" very little. However, I believe readers have already found there to be an impressive difference between the Daoist understanding of "primordial *Qi*" and its Ruist counterpart: The primordial *Qi* in Laozi's version tends to be projected as temporally located at an earlier cosmological stage, while its Ruist conception of *Qi* in general tends to be ontologically located at a higher rank of cosmic realities. In this sense, whether to start the Ruist "chain of being" in an ontological cosmology with "*Qi* in general" or *generatio ex nihilo* can be seen as a watershed which distinguishes lineages within the Ru cosmological tradition. In other words, there are significant variations of cosmological thinking within the Ru tradition as well. As an example of this variation, Luo Qinshun's thought will be analyzed in more detail later.
7. Chen Lai exemplifies this interpretive approach to Zhou Dunyi in Chen Lai 陈来, *Song Through Ming Learning of Pattern-Principle* 宋明理学 (华东师范大学出版社, 2004), 10–20.
8. An example of this approach can be found in Shu Jincheng 舒金城, "A Study on the *Wuji* and *Taiji* in Zhou Dunyi's Thought 周敦頤的思想体系与'无极''太极'之辨," 孔子研究 3 (1999): 88–95
9. Zhu Xi 朱熹, "Unraveling the Explanation of the Diagram of Ultimate Limit 太極圖說解," in *The Complete Works of Master Zhu* 朱子全書, vol. 13 (上海古籍出版社, 2010), 73. My translation is adapted from Adler, *Reconstructing.*
10. Zhu Xi 朱熹, "Classified Dialogues of Master Zhu, vol. 75 朱子語類 卷七十五," in *Complete Works,* 16:2564–65. The dialogue, recorded when Zhu was seventy years old, is quoted in Chen Lai 陈来, *A Study on Master Zhu's Philosophy* 朱子哲学研究 (华东师范大学出版社, 2000), 98. I translate most of Zhu Xi's letters and dialogues myself after considering available English translations such as the ones in Justin Tiwald and Bryan W. Van Norden, eds., *Readings in Later Chinese Philosophy: Han Dynasty to the 20th Century* (Hackett, 2014).
11. Zhu Xi, "Classified Dialogues," in *Complete Works,* 16:2567.

12. Xu Shen, Duan Yucai, 許慎 段玉裁, *Commentary on To Explain and Analyze Characters* 說文解字注 (上海書店, 1992), 15.
13. Eric L. Hutton, trans., *Xunzi: The Complete Text* (Princeton University Press, 2014), 229.
14. Zheng Xuan, Kong Yingda 郑玄 孔颖达, *The Correct Meanings of The Book of Rites* 礼记正义, in *Commentaries on the Thirteen Classics* 十三经注疏, ed. Li Xueqin 李学勤 (北京大學出版社, 1999), 1387.
15. This is also the reason that I think Stephen Angle and Justin Tiwald's more recent way of translating *Li* as a capitalized "Pattern" in their book, *Neo-Confucianism: A Philosophical Introduction* (Polity, 2017), doesn't entirely fit. Whether capitalized or not, the word "pattern" cannot convey two meanings well, for *Li* are both normative ethical principles that human behaviors ought to comply with, and the ultimate ontological principle, Ultimate Limit, which creates and grounds all cosmic realities in the world.
16. Angle's rendering of *Li* as "coherence" is prevalent in Angle, *Sagehood*. This translation is adopted by other important researchers such as Brook Ziporyn, *Ironies of Oneness and Difference: Coherence in Early Chinese Thought—Prolegomena to the Study of Li* (State University of New York Press, 2012) and Brook Ziporyn, *Beyond Oneness and Difference: Li* 理 *in Chinese Buddhist Thought and Its Antecedents* (State University of New York Press, 2013). Ziporyn's books are among the most sophisticated in current English scholarship "to formulate and structure a global theory" about Chinese metaphysics as a whole, and in particular, about *Li* (*Ironies*, vii). Because Ziporyn's two books do not focus on the transcendence debate and the Ru lineage of interpretations on Ultimate Limit's ontological creativity, I cannot substantially engage with them here. However, one critique of mine concerning Ziporyn's overall position suffices to highlight the difference between his and my understanding of Chinese metaphysics.

    In contrast with Western thinking's obsessions with "sameness" and "essence," Ziporyn believes that Chinese thinkers tend to work without a concept of essence at all. Instead, every identity is "constitutively ambiguous," and "sameness and difference are negotiable" (*Ironies*, 7). This is because, as Stephen Angle's review of Ziporyn's books summarizes (*Dao: A Journal of Comparative Philosophy* 15 [2016]: 150), Ziporyn believes that in much of Chinese thinking, coherence is somehow prior to or more basic than the distinct, separate items which are said to cohere.

    My view is that Ziporyn's perspective may represent Tiantai Buddhism's or Zhuangzi's views on *Li* but is hard to square with the Ruist view, the lineage and continuity of which I try to illustrate in chapters 7 and 8. As indicated in these chapters, a major effort of Song and Ming Ruist thinkers is, in reliance upon interpretations of Ru classics, to deduce the normativity of moral virtues from the most generic traits of cosmic creativity, and furthermore, employ these moral virtues to anchor individual identity amid vicissitudes and changes of the mundane world. Quite often, the regulative power of these virtues is thought of by Ru thinkers as being unchangeable or even eternal, although these virtues indeed need to operate upon constantly changeable situations in everyday life. In other words, in my view, the Ruist view tends to be less negotiable than other schools of thought on the "sameness and difference" of things, and it clearly advocates for a morally robust individual identity rooted in the broadest context of realities afforded by the ultimate power of Ultimate Limit as *generatio ex nihilo*. As my analysis shows, this unique feature of Ru metaphysical ethics combines cosmological and ontological perspectives of an overall processual worldview.

In a word, I do not find that Ziporyn paid sufficient attention to the intertwined ontological-cosmological dimension of Chinese metaphysics. I would argue that Ziporyn's characterization of *Li* is more applicable to certain portions of Chinese metaphysics than others, and hence, is difficult to elevate onto an overall pattern of Chinese thought in comparison to its contrasting Western counterpart. A more detailed historical, philosophical, and sociological analysis of the Ru tradition's commitment to "constant virtue" can be found in Bin Song, "Contemporary Business Practices of the Ru (Confucian) Ethic of 'Three Guides and Five Constant Virtues (三綱五常)' in Asia and Beyond," *Religions* 12, no. 10 (2021): 895, https://doi.org/10.3390/rel12100895.

17. See Chen, *Study on Master Zhu's Philosophy*, 75–100. A major difference between Chen's and my interpretations of Zhu Xi on *Li* and *Qi* is that Chen mainly utilized an intratextual analysis of Zhu's writing to clarify whether *Li* is prior to *Qi* in different stages of Zhu's metaphysical thought. However, I focus on the continuity and innovation of Zhu's metaphysical thought in comparison with his Ru predecessors within the larger context of the comparative study of the transcendence debate. This major methodological difference leads to Chen's and my varying views regarding the core features of each stage of Zhu's metaphysical thought. For instance, Chen's discussions of Zhu didn't touch on the theme of *creatio ex nihilo*, and his interpretation of the second stage of Zhu's thought didn't address how ontologically unconditional Ultimate Limit's creative power could be.
18. Zhu Xi朱熹, "Unraveling the Diagram of Ultimate Limit 太極圖圖解," in *Complete Works*, 13:70.
19. Zhu Xi, "Unraveling," in *Complete Works*, 13:72–73.
20. Zhu Xi, "Appendix to Unraveling the Diagram of Ultimate Limit太極圖解 附論," in *Complete Works*, 23:77.
21. Zhu Xi, "A Third Letter to Chen Kejiu 答程可久第三," in *Complete Works*, 21:1642–43.
22. Zhu Xi, "Unraveling," in *Complete Works*, 13:72.
23. "不言無極則太極同於一物而不足為萬化之根，不言太極則無極淪於空寂而不能為萬化之根。" Zhu Xi, "A Reply to Lu Zimei 答陸子美," in *Complete Works*, 21:1560.
24. Zhu Xi, "A Reply to Lu Zijing 答陆子静," in *Complete Works*, 21:1568.
25. Zhu Xi, "Reply to Lu Zijing," 1567.
26. Zhou Dunyi周敦頤, *Collected Works of Zhou Lianxi* 元公周先生濂溪集 (岳麓书社, 2006), 22, quoted by Chen, *Study*, 91.
27. Zhu Xi, "Classified Dialogues朱子語類九十四，" in *Complete Works*, 17:3119.
28. Zhu Xi, "Classified Dialogues朱子語類四," in *Complete Works*, 14:200.
29. Zhu Xi, "A Reply to Liu Shuwen 答刘叔文," in *Complete Works*, 22:2146.
30. Zhu Xi, "A Reply to Yang Zizhi 答杨子直," in *Complete Works*, 22:2072.
31. Zhu Xi, "Classified Dialogues朱子語類一," in *Complete Works*, 14:116. The dialogue was recorded after Zhu turned sixty-nine, also quoted by Chen, *Study*, 95.
32. Zhu Xi, "Reply to Yang Zizhi," in *Complete Works*, 22:2072.
33. Zhu Xi, "A Reply to Chen Kejiu 答程可久," in *Complete Works*, 21:1643.
34. Zhu Xi, "Reply to Lu Zijing," in *Complete Works*, 21:1567.
35. Zhu Xi, "Reply to Lu Zijing," 1571.

36. Zhu Xi, "Reply to Lu Zijing," 1569.
37. In my view the challenge of the learning of heartmind to Zhu Xi mainly focuses upon the method of self-cultivation and ethics, despite such ethical critiques also having metaphysical connotations, as I analyzed in chapter 2.
38. Zhang Tingyu et al. 張廷玉等, *The History of Ming Dynasty*明史 (中華書局, 1974), 7238–39.
39. Cao Duan 曹端, "Preface to the Exposition of the Explanation of the Diagram of Ultimate Limit 太極圖說述解序," in *The Complete Works of Master Zhou* 周子全書 (商務印書館萬有文庫本, 1937), 5:79. The translations of Cao Duan are my own.
40. Cao Duan 曹端, *The Collected Works of Cao Duan*曹端集 (中華書局, 2003), 11–12.
41. Cao Duan, *Collected Works*, 5–7.
42. Cao Duan, *Collected Works*, 23–24.
43. Zhu Xi, "Reply to Yang Zizhi," in *Complete Works*, 22:2072.
44. Luo Qinshun 羅欽順, *Records of Knowing After Adversities*困知記 (中華書局, 2013), 68. The translations of Luo are my own.
45. Luo, *Records*, 38.
46. "僕從來認理氣為一物。" Luo, *Records*, 151.
47. Luo, *Records*, 4–5. Emphasis in the translation is my own.
48. Luo, *Records*, 29.
49. Luo's doubt about Zhu Xi's understanding of Non-Limit can be found in chapters 18 and 19 of Luo, *Records*, 19–20. About Luo's critique of the Daoist or Buddhist nihilism in relation to Ultimate Limit, please see Luo, *Records*, 13, 56.

Conclusion: Comparative Reflections on the Transcendence Debate

1. Thomas A. Metzger, *A Cloud Across the Pacific: Essays on the Clash Between Chinese and Western Political Theories Today* (Chinese University of Hong Kong Press, 2005), 21–31.
2. Friedrich Schleiermacher, *On Religion: Speeches to Its Cultured Despisers,* trans. John Oman (Harper & Row, 1958), 69.
3. Paul Tillich, *Systematic Theology II* (University of Chicago Press, 1957), 191.
4. I develop the nondualistic conception of the metaphysical goodness of divine creation from a Ruist perspective in Bin Song, "A Ru (Confucian) Theology of Nondualism in Light of Kongzi and Wang Yangming," in *Nondualism: An Interreligious Exploration*, ed. Jon Paul Sydnor and Anthony Watson (Lexington Books, 2023), 243–60.
5. Wang Yangming 王陽明, *The Complete Works of Wang Yangming* 王陽明全集, ed. Wu Guang and Qian Ming (Hang Hai Gu Ji Chu Ban She, 1992), 117.
6. See more details in Bin Song, "*Shengsheng* and the Confucian Sacred Canopy in the *Yijing*," in 周易研究*Zhouyi Studies* (English version) 9, no. 1 (June 2018): 33–55.
7. Zhou Dunyi 周敦頤, *Collected Works of Zhou Dunyi* 周敦頤集 (Zhong Hua Shu Ju, 1990), 22.

INDEX

Academy, of Plato, 19–20
agency, causality relation to, 92
Albinus, 96
Aleni, Julius, 55, 240, 241, 287n25
"all-encompassing wisdom," 91–92
Ames, Roger, 65–68, 71, 74, 257–58, 284n1
amorphous material, Demiurge and, 137–38
Angle, Stephen, 211, 213, 284n1, 309n16
Anglican Christianity, 80
"anonymous Christianity," 34
Anselm of Canterbury, 121
anthropocentrism, 127–28, 131, 132–33, 265
anti-cosmic dualism, 105–6, 107
antinomy, 42–43
Appended Texts. See *Xici*
Aquinas, Thomas, 27, 240; anthropocentrism and, 128; Augustine relation to, 126–27; on being, 124–25; *creatio ex nihilo* and, 9, 55, 71, 244–45, 246; Descartes compared to, 128; on divine causality, 296n6; on divine creation, 5, 122, 241, 242, 297n21; Huang compared to, 249; on knowledge, 252; on negation, 123; on nothingness, 121; Scotus compared to, 130–31; on time, 42
architectonic philosophy, 21
Aristotle, 27, 91, 102; Confucius compared to, 25; CT and, 22–23; metaphysics relation to, 21, 40; on priority, 66–67; on pure knowledge, 50; theology and, 22–23, 27, 278n3; on unmoved mover, 121
artificer, 136
atheism, 2

Augustine of Hippo: Aquinas relation to, 126–27; on *creatio ex nihilo*, 8–9, 66, 86, 106–8, 116, 120, 294n71; Descartes compared to, 128; on divine creation, 108–10, 111, 293n65; on evil, 262–63; on Gnosticism, 107–8; Huang compared to, 249; Manichaean dualism and, 114–15; Neville compared to, 84; on nonbeing, 139; on nothingness, 118; on philosophy, 20; on theodicy, 112–13, 119; Wang Bi *versus*, 11
authority, 3, 16, 20
awareness, 46–47; moral consciousness and, 49; of nonbeing, 190

becoming, 124, 187–88
being: becoming compared to, 124; chain of, 165, 204, 206, 219; *creatio ex nihilo* and, 141; creatures relation to, 126; *Dao* relation to, 151–52, 189; divine creation relation to, 125, 144; infinity relation to, 140–41; meaning and, 143; myriad things relation to, 186; nonbeing relation to, 148–49, 181–82, 185, 191, 220, 224; Wang Bi on, 189
being-as-becoming, 187–88
Benti (fundamental or original state), 275
bias, 82
the Bible, 86, 87–88
Big Bang theory, 151, 184
Bin Song, 284n1
birth birth. See *sheng sheng*
Boer, Roland, 284n1

Index

Book of Penetration (BP), 199, 203–4, 208, 213–14
Book of Rites, 212
Boston Confucianism, 5–6, 277n1
Boston Theological Interreligious Consortium, 5
Boston University, 12
Boston University Confucian Association, 5–6
BP. See *Book of Penetration*
bridge concepts, 83–84
Buddhism, 1–2; in China, 29; *Dao* relation to, 33–34; heartmind and, 33; metaphysics and, 30–31; ritual relation to, 29–30; Ruism relation to, 32; Tiantai, 309n16

Cao Duan, 227–29
Carnap, Rudolf, 41
Catholic missionaries, 53, 55, 59
Catholic Scholastic tradition, 15
causality: agency relation to, 92; *creatio ex nihilo* and, 91; divine, 134–36, 245, 296n6; natural philosophers and, 195–96; ontological dependence and, 89–90
centrality, 219, 275
centrality and commonality (*Zhongyong*), 56, 64, 219, 275
"chain of being," 165, 204, 206, 219
Chalcedon, 15
Change, 209; cosmic reality and, 163; Great, 179, 180–81, 182–83, 184, 196, 245; as *hunlun*, 178; Ultimate Limit and, 162, 166–67, 232
Chao, 31–32
Charme, Alexandre de la, 55, 240, 241, 287n25
Cheng Hao, 232–33
Cheng Qiang, 304n35
Cheng Yi, 46–47, 209, 229–30, 232–34
Chen Houguang, 56
China, 1, 53; Buddhism in, 29; Christian missionaries in, 56–57; Rites Controversy in, 56; science in, 44
Chinese cosmology, 12
Chinese Text Project, 301n12
Ching, Julia, 59, 71, 244
Christianity, 1; anonymous, 34; *creatio ex nihilo* and, 72, 86–87, 267, 277n3; creation relation to, 59; divine creation relation to, 108–10; Genesis and, 9; Gnosticism relation to, 104–6; inclusivism relation to, 35, 282n48; Neville relation to, 79–80; ontological dependence relation to, 121; philosophical theology and, 24–25, 27; philosophy relation to, 20; Plotinus relation to, 100; Ruism compared to, 4, 45, 53–54, 71, 165, 285n9; theology relation to, 17–18; *Tian* relation to, 58, 65–66; Ultimate Limit relation to, 56–58
Christian missionaries, 4; in China, 56–57; colonialism and, 58; Ruism relation to, 72, 74, 285n9. *See also* Catholic missionaries; Protestant missionaries
Christian mysticism, 9; divine creation and, 131–32; the One and, 101–2
Christian Scholasticism, 18
civilization: nonaction relation to, 160; ritual relation to, 145–47
civilized human (Ru), 213, 275
Classic of Change (*Yijing*), 10, 170, 250, 259–60, 301n13; knowledge and, 50; metaphysics and, 25, 44, 54; ontology of, 195; *Qian Zao Du* relation to, 177; Ruism relation to, 2, 275; Ultimate Limit and, 26–27. *See also Xici*
Clooney, Francis X.: CT of, 14–15, 24, 75–78, 278n1, 278n3; on faith, 16; Neville compared to, 17
"closed inclusivism," 35–36
"coherence," 213
Collected Commentary on the Great Learning (Zhu Xi), 254
colonialism, 58, 268
comparative philosophy, 84–85, 290n2
comparative religion, 76–80, 84, 290n2
comparative theology (CT), 5, 19, 278n1, 278n3, 290n2; Aristotle and, 22–23; comparative religion compared to, 76–80; creation and, 85; faith relation to, 14–15, 17; home tradition and, 15–16, 18, 75–76; impartiality and, 37; inclusivism relation to, 35–36; liberal arts and, 6, 24–25, 38, 73, 75, 239, 258; metaphysics and, 39; nonconfessional, 77, 81, 258; Ruism and, 14, 37–38, 52; of Ward, 24, 28
concupiscence, 118

confessional CT, 76–77
Confessions (Augustine), 294n71
Confucianism: Boston, 5–6, 277n1; creation relation to, 59, 244; Ruism relation to, 277n1
Confucian spirituality, 284n1
Confucius, 252; Aristotle compared to, 25; Laozi compared to, 145–47; Ruism relation to, 2–3; on Ultimate Limit, 180; *Xici* relation to, 58, 280n27, 301n11
conscientious knowing (*Liangzhi*), 28–30, 275, 281n38; cosmos relation to, 48–49; logic and, 47–48; self-cultivation relation to, 46; Three Teachings relation to, 33
Constant of *Tian*, 172
contemplation, 22–23
Contentions in the transcendence debate, 70
Cooper, John M., 279n14
Copernican astronomy, 43
Cornille, Catherine, 35, 76–77, 78, 80
Correct Meanings of the Zhou Book of Change (Kong Yingda), 193, 200–201
correlative cosmology, 177
"correlative thinking" school, 65
corruption, 114, 116–17
cosmic changes, 209, 236
cosmic evolution, 148
cosmic reality, 198, 231, 248; change and, 163; *Li* and, 156, 165, 168, 197, 212; Ultimate Limit and, 167, 233; *yin/yang* relation to, 158–59
cosmic soul, 91–92, 94
cosmogony: of Laozi, 187–88, 196, 206; in *Xici*, 243
cosmological succession, 89–90, 122–23, 134; in *Dao De Jing*, 164; *generatio ex nihilo* relation to, 245–46; Laozi relation to, 180; myriad things and, 149, 152–53; ontological dependence compared to, 10, 152, 166, 240, 261; order in, 135
cosmology: Chinese, 12; correlative, 177; in *Dao De Jing*, 147, 173; Daoism and, 12, 259; of *Huainanzi*, 174; of Laozi, 149–50, 154, 157, 159–60, 169–70, 183, 188–89; metaphysics relation to, 300n7; ontology relation to, 8, 255–57, 258, 260; open, 256–57; of Plato, 93; *Qi* and, 287n25; in *Qian Zao Du*, 178–79, 245; of Ruism, 156–57, 159–60, 163; social ideals and, 154; in *Timaeus*, 86, 87, 95; time relation to, 149; of *Xici*, 147, 154–56, 169–70; of *yin/yang*, 303n23; of Zhu Xi, 198
cosmontology, 255, 258
cosmos: "conscientious knowing" relation to, 48–49; *creatio ex nihilo* relation to, 256–57; *Dao* relation to, 161; humanity relation to, 160; Ruism and, 61; in *Xici*, 192; *yin/yang* relation to, 57. See also *Tian*
Council of Chalcedon, 278n8
Council of Nicaea, 8–9, 15, 106, 278n8
Courage to Be (Tillich), 140
created eternal truth, 9, 12, 132–33, 252, 261
creatio ex nihilo, 127–28, 297n21; Augustine on, 8–9, 66, 86, 106–8, 116, 120, 294n71; being and, 141; in the Bible, 87–88; Christianity and, 72, 86–87, 267, 277n3; cosmos relation to, 256–57; *creatio in situ* and, 66, 258; creation relation to, 249, 259–60; Creator-God relation to, 12; *Dao* compared to, 150–51; divine causality as, 135; divine creation and, 7, 71, 97, 101–2, 103, 131, 241, 242–43, 247, 249, 264; *emanatio ex nihilo* compared to, 100–101, 104; evil relation to, 262, 263; *generatio ex nihilo* compared to, 220, 250, 256–57, 269; Gnosticism relation to, 105–6; human cognition relation to, 130; human reason relation to, 132; interconnectedness and, 244; Manichaean dualism relation to, 114; nonbeing relation to, 116, 122, 137–40, 148; nothingness relation to, 119–20, 126, 292n52; ontological dependence and, 73, 89–90, 121, 125–26; ontological priority of, 246; ontological unconditionality of, 68, 126, 142, 168, 252, 268; ontology of, 299n60; Plato and, 90–91; Ricci and, 55; Ruism relation to, 166; science relation to, 245; self-consciousness relation to, 133–34; *sheng sheng* compared to, 196, 237–39, 250, 251; theodicy relation to, 112–13, 143; *Tian* compared to, 254–55; time and, 42, 137; Ultimate Limit compared to, 12–13, 167–68, 196–98, 200, 226; ultimate reality relation to, 143, 184, 195, 252, 254; Zhou Dunyi relation to, 209

creatio in situ, 66, 257, 258
creation, 8, 9, 55, 96, 127–28; Confucianism relation to, 59, 244; created eternal truth relation to, 12; *creatio ex nihilo* relation to, 249, 259–60; creatures relation to, 115, 123–24; CT and, 85; *Dao* relation to, 161, 187–88, 189, 261, 265; divine goodness and, 126, 143; emanation relation to, 98–100; evil relation to, 119; in Genesis, 88–89; *Li* relation to, 247; matter relation to, 197; of myriad things, 149; from nothingness, 121, 140; ontological dependence and, 8, 97; *Qi* and, 60, 243; Ruism relation to, 307n59; *Tian* and, 64, 253; ultimacy and, 67; Ultimate Limit relation to, 195, 242–43, 248–49, 253–54, 265; as vague category, 250; *yin/yang* and, 115–16. *See also* divine creation
Creator-God, 4, 8, 12, 53, 69
creatures: being relation to, 126; creation relation to, 115, 123–24; suffering of, 112–13
critical rationalism, 42
CT. *See* comparative theology
cultural devices, CT relation to, 15

Dao (the Way), 252–53, 275; being relation to, 151–52, 189; *creatio ex nihilo* compared to, 150–51; creation relation to, 161, 187–88, 189, 261, 265; great vacuum and, 225; heartmind and, 33–34; in *Huainanzi*, 174–75; humanity relation to, 162; *Li* relation to, 26, 159, 170; in *Lü Annals of Spring and Autumn*, 179; metaphysics and, 25–26; nonbeing relation to, 147–48, 152–54, 160, 183; ontological dependence on, 186; Ruism relation to, 36–37; self-cultivation relation to, 169; self-generation and, 245–46; Ultimate Limit relation to, 26–27, 56, 171, 187–88, 201; utensil-like things compared to, 214–15; *Xici* and, 157–59 182, 204; *yin/yang* compared to, 182, 192; *Zhouyi* relation to, 168
Dao De Jing (Laozi), 10, 12, 68, 157; being in, 181; cosmological succession in, 164; cosmology in, 147, 173; *generatio ex nihilo* relation to, 259; *Huainanzi* compared to, 174, 176; ritual-propriety in, 146; Ultimate Limit relation to, 171–72, 191–92; Wang Bi relation to, 185–89; *Xici* compared to, 159–60, 183; *Zhuangzhi* relation to, 304n29
Daoism, 1–2, 33–34; cosmological succession and, 10; cosmology and, 12, 259; heartmind and, 33; Legge relation to, 57; *Qi* and, 308n6; Ruism compared to, 156, 190–91; Ruism relation to, 32, 51–52; Zheng Xuan relation to, 180
"dao-logy," 27
Daoxue movement, 28
Daxu. *See* great vacuum
De Genesis contra Manichaeos (Augustine), 110
De libero arbitrio (Augustine), 115, 117
Demiurge, 92–95, 127, 223, 291n28; amorphous material and, 137–38; Trinitarian theology relation to, 109
demonic power, 140–41
De potentia (Aquinas), 124
Descartes, René, 106, 129–30; Copernican astronomy and, 43; created eternal truth and, 9, 12, 252, 261; on *creatio ex nihilo*, 127–28, 297n21; on divine creation, 132–33, 237, 249; on divine intelligence, 131; Newton *versus*, 44; Zhu Xi *versus*, 11
"determinate deity," 68
De vera religione (Augustine), 110
De veritate (Aquinas), 123–24
Diagram of Ultimate Limit (Zhou Dunyi), 154, 199, 207, 213–14, 219, 255. *See also Explanation of the Diagram of Ultimate Limit*
divination, 191
divine causality, 134–36, 245, 296n6
divine creation, 93, 237, 244–45, 293n65, 299n47; Aquinas on, 5, 122, 241, 242, 297n21; being relation to, 125, 144; Christianity relation to, 108–10; cosmic soul and, 94; created eternal truth relation to, 12, 132–33; *creatio ex nihilo* and, 7, 71, 97, 101–2, 103, 131, 241, 242–43, 247, 249, 264; Demiurge relation to, 92–95, 127; divine causality relation to, 136; divine will relation to, 111–12; eternal truths relation to, 129; Greek philosophy and, 87–88; nonbeing relation to, 142;

ontological dependence and, 66, 136–37, 296n6; ontological unconditionality of, 135; ontology and, 124–25; *Qi* and, 201; ratio of, 126–27; in *Timaeus*, 107, 137–38; time relation to, 94, 96
divine goodness, creation and, 126, 143
divine grace, 19, 117, 139; of divine creation, 144; free will relation to, 116
divine intelligence, 110, 257; divine will and, 128, 131; eternal truths and, 130
divine providence, 119, 141–42
divine punishment, 117–18
divine revelation: Aristotle relation to, 23; faith and, 14–15, 27; home tradition and, 24; mystery relation to, 16–17
divine will, 110; divine creation relation to, 111–12; divine intelligence and, 128, 131; human will compared to, 130
dualism: anti-cosmic, 105–6, 107; Gnosticism and, 293n57; Manichaean, 113–15, 118–19; ontological, 213–15; Platonic, 50–51, 94
Dupuis, Jacques, 34
dynamics, in physics, 77

Eckhart, Meister, 131
education, 25
EDUL. See *Explanation of the Diagram of Ultimate Limit*
emanatio ex nihilo, 100–101, 104, 108
emanation, 98–100
emotions, 190
emptiness, 29–30, 31
Ennead (Plotinus), 100
epistemological foundationalism, 133
"epistemological optimism," 251–52
escalated continuum, 161, 264
eschatological pantheism, 142–43
eschaton, 141, 263
"*eskhatos*," 141
esse. See being
essence, 172–73, 264
essentialization, 141–42, 264
eternal truths: created, 9, 12, 131–33, 252, 261; divine creation relation to, 129; divine intelligence and, 130; mathematical systems relation to, 128
ethical metaphysics, 208–9, 210

ethical realism, 207–8
ethics, 3, 22; bridge concepts and, 83; of pure knowledge, 51; Ruism relation to, 25, 203; science and, 283n20; self-cultivation relation to, 46, 311n37; vague category and, 84
eudaimonia (full flourishing), 22
Eurocentrism, 77, 246
evil, 9, 113, 144, 293n57; creation relation to, 119; free will relation to, 118–19; Gnosticism relation to, 106; Manichaean dualism relation to, 114; matter relation to, 104, 112; nonbeing relation to, 263; nothingness relation to, 118–19; Ruism relation to, 264–65; theodicy relation to, 94, 162, 262
exemplary person (*Junzi*), 25, 27, 51, 158, 275
existential now (*nunc existentiale*), 142–43
Explanation of the Diagram of Ultimate Limit (EDUL), 199, 203–4, 206–7, 213–14, 218, 234

faith, 14–17, 27
"faith seeking understanding," 79–80; membership community and, 23–24; theology as, 14, 17–19, 27
fallibilist methodology, 11–12
"family resemblance," 78
Five Aggregates, 29
formless and shapeless. See *Hunlun*
"formless thing," 165–66
forms, theory of, 89–90
free will, 113, 116–19, 263
full flourishing (*eudaimonia*), 22
fundamental, or original state (*Benti*), 275

generatio ex nihilo, 197, 230, 234–35, 248, 265; cosmological succession relation to, 245–46; *creatio ex nihilo* compared to, 220, 250, 256–57, 269; *Dao De Jing* relation to, 259; interconnectedness and, 244; *sheng sheng* relation to, 10, 255, 259, 261; *Tian* relation to, 266; Ultimate Limit as, 224, 243, 309n16; ultimate reality relation to, 252
Genesis, 9, 88–89, 94
Gernet, Jacques, 285n9

Gnosticism, 9, 293n57; Augustine on, 107–8; Christianity relation to, 104–6; creation in, 89; dualism and, 94; Greco-Roman philosophy and, 86–87
"Great Change," 179, 180–81, 182–83, 184, 196, 245
"Great Inception," 174
"Great Initial," 180–81, 182–83
Great Learning, 45–46, 51, 254
"Great Music" chapter, 172
"Great Vacuity," 63–64
great vacuum (Daxu), 148, 176, 181, 189, 194, 275; *Dao* and, 225; "Great Change" and, 196; nonbeing and, 153, 169; primordial *Qi* as, 190; *Qi* relation to, 202; quietude and, 160
great void, 194
Greco-Roman philosophy, 86–87
Greek philosophy, 20, 49, 108–9, 277n3, 291n9; creation in, 89; CT in, 18–19; Hellenistic Judaism relation to, 87–88
Griffiths, Paul J., 35–36, 282n48

Hadot, Pierre, 19, 279n14
Hall, David, 65–67, 71, 74, 257–58
Han dynasty, 51–52, 173–74, 177
Han Kangbo, 10, 167, 198, 241–42, 246, 259; Non-Limit relation to, 208; Ruism relation to, 180; on Ultimate Limit, 194; *Xici* and, 170, 193; Zheng Xuan relation to, 185
Harnack, Adolf von, 105
Harvard-Yenching Institute, 5
heartmind (Xin), 32, 275, 283n13; awareness relation to, 47; *Dao* and, 33–34; self-cultivation relation to, 45–46, 48; Zhu Xi and, 311n37
heaven, cosmos, or the universe (Tian). See *Tian*
Hedges, Paul, 17, 76
Hegel, 9, 148; idealism of, 222; Laozi compared to, 151
Hellenistic Judaism, 87–88
home tradition: CT and, 15–16, 18, 75–76; divine revelation and, 24; Neville relation to, 79; rooted tradition compared to, 36
Hong Kong, 58

Huainanzi, 170–71, 173–76, 179–80
Huang, Paulos, 60–61, 66–67, 71–72, 248–49, 287n25
Huang Zhen, 56
human cognition, *creatio ex nihilo* relation to, 130
human condition, 139
human consciousness, 129
humaneness, 160
human freedom, 125–26, 134, 141–42, 246
humanism, 142, 157, 162
humanitarian crisis, 51
humanities studies, science and, 283n20
humanity, or humaneness (*ren*), 146, 160, 162, 275
Human Limit, 206
human nature, 47–48, 116–17
human reason, *creatio ex nihilo* relation to, 132
human relationships, ethics in, 3
human will, divine will compared to, 130
Hunlun (formless and shapeless), 178, 181–82, 187, 245
hyle. See matter

Iamblichus, 293n57
the Ideal, 50
idealism, 222
immanence, 102
"immanent transcendence," 62
impartiality, 11–12, 37
imperialism, 268
inclusivism, 34–36, 52, 265, 270, 282n48
individuality, 211
infinity, 140–41
initiation, 137, 266
inner transcendence, 284n1
intellectual history, of China, 1
intellectualism, 111
interconnectedness, 244
intuition, 129–30
Irenaeus, 107
irrationality, 103

JeeLoo Liu, 303n23
Jesuits, 261–62, 285n9, 287n25
Ji. See ultimacy
Jiang Wu, 284n1

Jing Jie, 284n1
Julian, 118–19
Junzi (exemplary person), 25, 27, 61, 158, 275

Kähler, Martin, 299n60
Kant, Immanuel, 41–44
kinematics, in physics, 77
King, Martin Luther, Jr., 282n48
knowledge, 45, 102, 129, 252; created eternal truth and, 133; metaphysics relation to, 40, 42–43; by negation, 123; pure, 50, 51; research program and, 44; self-cultivation relation to, 46
Koenen, Ludwig, 119
Kong Yingda, 193, 200–2, 308n6
Kongzi, 29
Kun, 155, 156, 162, 166–67, 178

Lakatos, Imre, 44
Lamberigts, Mathijs, 119
Lao Dan, 29
Laozi, 151; Confucius compared to, 145–47; cosmogony of, 187–88, 196, 206; cosmological succession relation to, 180; cosmology of, 149–50, 154, 157, 159–60, 169–70, 183, 188–89; nonaction and, 166; on nonbeing, 153; on *Qi*, 184–85; Wang Longxi and, 281n35; Zhu Xi relation to, 224, 225–26. See also *Dao De Jing*
Learning of the Dark (Wang Bi), 305n53
Lee, Hyo-Dong, 59–60, 66, 71–72, 239–40, 248, 257; Oneness and, 244; ontological transcendence and, 74; on self-generation, 245
Legalism, 51–52
Legge, James, 57–58, 243
legitimacy, 82, 104
Li (pattern-principles), 148, 209, 275, 309n16, 309n17; cosmic reality and, 156, 165, 168, 197, 212; creation relation to, 247; *Dao* relation to, 26, 159, 170; metaphysics and, 309n16; *Qi* compared to, 210–11, 224–25, 229; *Qi* relation to, 198, 213–16, 220–23, 230–32, 235, 268; in reality, 158; Ruism relation to, 163; *Tian* in, 54–55; Ultimate Limit and, 194, 211–12, 213–14, 222, 227–29, 233, 236
Li (ritual, rite). See ritual, rite

Liangzhi (conscientious knowing), 28–30, 33, 46–49, 275, 281n38
liberal arts, 27; CT and, 6, 24–25, 38, 73, 75, 239, 258; full flourishing and, 22; membership community and, 23–24; Ruism relation to, 36
liberal democracy, 51
libertarian free will, 116–18
Li Lanfen, 305n53
Liu Shu-hsien, 5, 10, 62–63, 64, 71; Mou Zongsan compared to, 250–51; on *Tian*, 253
Liu Shuyi, 221
Liu Yuan, 232
Living Thing, 94, 291n26
logic: "conscientious knowing" and, 47–48; of ontological dependence, 202, 238, 250; of ontological unconditionality, 247, 297n21; of ontology, 269; science and, 40
logical possibilities, 136
Longobardo, Nicolò, 285n9
Lu, of Wutai, 32
Lü Annals of Spring and Autumn, 170–71, 176; *Qian Zao Du* compared to, 179; Ultimate Limit in, 172–73, 179–80
Lu Jiuyuan, 225, 235
Luo Guang, Stanislaus, 287n25
Luo Qinshun, 47–49, 55, 229–31, 240–41; Jesuits relation to, 261–62; on Ultimate Limit, 232–35
Lu Yuzhong, 30
Lu Zijing, 216–17, 218–19
Lu Zimei, 216–17

Manichaean dualism, 113–15; concupiscence relation to, 118; original sin relation to, 119
Manichaeism, 86–87, 107–8, 119
mathematical systems, 40; eternal truths relation to, 128; in nature, 129; Platonism and, 50; *Tian* relation to, 268; on *Zhouyi*, 163
matter, 9, 285n4; creation relation to, 197; divine creation relation to, 111; evil relation to, 104, 112; Manichaean dualism relation to, 114; the One relation to, 103–4; in Trinitarian theology, 109

320 Index

May, Gerhard, 87–88
meaning, being and, 143
medieval philosophy, 111–12
Meditations (Descartes), 132
membership community, 23–24
Mencius, 301n11
me on. See nonbeing
metaphysics, 196, 300n7; Buddhism and, 30–31; *Classic of Change* and, 25, 44, 54; created eternal truth and, 132–33; CT and, 39; ethical, 208–9, 210; knowledge relation to, 40, 42–43; *Li* and, 309n16; of Luo Qinshun, 234–35; Neville and, 41, 82; nonbeing relation to, 148; ontological dependence and, 67–68; Platonic dualism and, 50–51; of Plotinus, 104; Ruism relation to, 6–7, 26–27, 47–48, 49, 51, 54, 162; science and, 41, 43–45, 50, 52; theology and, 21, 40; of Ultimate Limit, 10; vague category and, 84; of Zhang Zai, 254–55; of Zhu Xi, 259, 261
Metaphysics (Aristotle), 21
Methodist Christianity, 80
middle Platonism, 9, 86–87, 95–97, 291n28
"Middle Zhe" school, 28
Ming dynasty, 1, 3
monotheism, 57, 95
moral consciousness, 47; awareness and, 49; self-cultivation relation to, 48
Mou Zongsan, 61–62, 64, 71, 250–51, 253, 284n1
Müller, Max, 77
myriad things: cosmological succession and, 149, 152–53; the One relation to, 185–86; *yin/yang* and, 241
Mysterious Female, 186–87
mystery, 16–17

Nag Hammadi codices, 104–5
natural phenomena, 156, 158, 213
natural philosophers, 89–90, 100, 195–96
natural theology, Aristotle and, 23
nature, 129, 211; corruption relation to, 114; *creatio ex nihilo* relation to, 122; human, 47–48, 116–17; of the One, 103; priority of, 102; science relation to, 40; Ultimate Limit relation to, 232
"Nebulous Vacuum," 175–76, 179

Needham, Joseph, 44
negation, 123, 143
Neoplatonism, 9, 98, 204, 291n28; Gnosticism relation to, 105; Greco-Roman philosophy and, 86–87; Plotinus and, 131
Neville, Robert Cummings, 15, 66–68, 239–40, 258–59, 269; Christianity relation to, 79–80; Clooney compared to, 17; *creatio ex nihilo* and, 71; metaphysics and, 41, 82; Smith compared to, 78; vague category and, 7, 74, 82–84, 85
Newton, Isaac, 43, 44
Noël, François, 285n9
"No Limit," 176
nonaction (Wuwei), 159, 160, 166, 275, 302n18
nonbeing, 115–16, 183, 200, 263–64; awareness of, 190; being relation to, 148–49, 181–82, 185, 191, 220, 224; *creatio ex nihilo* relation to, 116, 122, 137–40, 148; *Dao* relation to, 147–48, 152–54, 160, 183; divine creation relation to, 142; evil relation to, 263; nothingness compared to, 202; the One relation to, 185–86; ontological unconditionality relation to, 167, 191; *Qi* relation to, 201–2; in The Ruist Ontological Cosmology in the *Xici*, 195; Ultimate Limit relation to, 192, 204–5, 226, 246; vacuum relation to, 169, 189
nonconfessional CT, 77, 81, 258
Non-Limit (*Wuji*), 204–5, 302n21; Ruism relation to, 225; Ultimate Limit relation to, 207–8, 215–18, 235, 237–38
nonrationality, 103; of divine creation, 132
"no self-nature," 211
nothingness: *creatio ex nihilo* relation to, 119–20, 126, 292n52; creation from, 121, 140; free will relation to, 117–18; nonbeing compared to, 202
"Nous" (thought, or intellect), 21–23, 103, 110, 223
numinous and wonderful. *See shen*
nunc existentiale (existential now), 142–43

observable facts, 41
Old Testament, 107
Olivia, Simon, 119
omniscience, 125–26, 244

the One, 98–99, 102, 292n52, 293n57; *emanatio ex nihilo* relation to, 108; myriad things relation to, 185–86; ontological priority of, 248; ontological unconditionality and, 100–101, 103–4; order and, 110. See also *Dao* (the Way)
Oneness, 59–60, 223, 244–45
On the Heavens (Aristotle), 21
ontological contingency, 98–99, 134
ontological dependence, 102, 107, 269; cosmological succession compared to, 10, 152, 166, 240, 261; *creatio ex nihilo* and, 73, 89–90, 121, 125–26; creation and, 8, 97; on *Dao*, 186; divine creation and, 66, 136–37, 296n6; *generatio ex nihilo* relation to, 245; logic of, 202, 238, 250; metaphysics and, 67–68; myriad things relation to, 149; nonbeing relation to, 122; Plotinus and, 103–4; priority and, 66; *sheng sheng* and, 73, 165; *Tian* and, 71; on Ultimate Limit, 192; ultimate reality relation to, 183–84, 196; of *Xici*, 180
ontological dualism, 213–15
ontological hierarchy, 60
ontological priority, 196–97, 220, 246–48
ontological transcendence, 61–63, 65, 74
ontological unconditionality, 67, 259–60, 262; *creatio ex nihilo* and, 68, 126, 142, 168, 252, 268; of divine creation, 135; logic of, 247, 297n21; nonbeing relation to, 167, 191; the One and, 100–101, 103–4; of ultimate creativity, 197–99; of Ultimate Limit, 193, 239–40
ontology: of *Classic of Change*, 195; cosmology relation to, 8, 255–57, 258, 260; of *creatio ex nihilo*, 299n60; divine creation and, 124–25; logic of, 269; metaphysics relation to, 300n7; of Ruism, 180; of *sheng sheng*, 307n59; Ultimate Limit relation to, 171; ultimate reality and, 237; *Xici* and, 184, 243
open cosmology, 256–57
"open inclusivism," 35–36, 52, 270
order, 110, 127, 135
Origen, *creatio ex nihilo* and, 87
original sin, 118–19
orthodox theology, 106

Ortiz, Jared, 294n71
Otto, Rudolf, 131
ouk on. See nonbeing

Parmenides, 291n9
Parmenides (Plato), 90
patrimony, Ruism and, 32
pattern-principles. See *Li* (pattern-principles)
Peirce, 81
Phaedo (Plato), 89, 100–1
Philebus (Plato), 90, 91, 92
philosophical theology, 8–9, 23–25, 27, 79, 80
philosophy: architectonic, 21; comparative, 84–85, 290n2; Cornille and, 80; Greco-Roman, 86–87; Greek, 18–20, 49, 87–88, 89, 108–9, 277n3, 291n9; medieval, 111–12; metaphysics and, 49; religion *versus*, 19–20, 279n14; Ruism relation to, 52; of science, 42; theology relation to, 5, 17–19; of Wang Bi, 305n53; of Zhou Dunyi, 199
phronesis (practical wisdom), 21–22
physics, 43, 77
Physics (Aristotle), 21
Plato, 92–93, 100, 222, 259–60, 291n26; Academy of, 19–20; Aquinas compared to, 127; on causality, 195–96; on cosmological succession, 89–90; *creatio ex nihilo* and, 90–91; on creation, 88; on Demiurge, 223; Descartes compared to, 128; on divine creation, 94–95. See also *Timaeus*
Platonic dualism, 50–51, 94
Platonism, 107; Middle, 9, 86–87, 95–97, 291n28; Ruism relation to, 8, 268; science relation to, 50, 267
Plotinus, 98–100; on divine creation, 108; on evil, 106, 262; Gnosticism relation to, 105, 293n57; on intellect, 110; on matter, 112; Neoplatonism and, 131; on the One, 101, 292n52; on Oneness, 223; ontological dependence and, 103–4; on ultimate reality, 249
political reform, 3
political utopianism, 141
politics, 22, 25
Popper, Karl, 44, 50, 267

practical wisdom (*phronesis*), 21–22
pragmatic semiotics, 81
preexisting matter, 97
preservation, *creatio ex nihilo* and, 137
prime matter, 285n4
primordial *Qi* (Yuanqi), 187–88, 206–8, 215, 275, 287n25, 308n6; as great vacuum, 190; Laozi relation to, 184–85; Ultimate Limit as, 200, 204
princips tenebrarum, 119
priority, 66, 67, 102; ontological, 196–97, 246–47, 248; *Tian* and, 251
Proclus, 293n57
Protestant missionaries, in China, 53
Pseudo-Dionysius, 131
pseudo-science, science compared to, 44
public discourse, religion in, 51
pure knowledge, 50, 51
"pure transcendence," 62

Qi (vital-energy, or psychophysical energy), 164, 275, 309n17; being-as-becoming and, 187–88; creation relation to, 60, 243; in "Great Change," 180; Laozi on, 184–85; *Li* compared to, 210–11, 224–25, 229; *Li* relation to, 198, 213–16, 220–23, 230–32, 235, 268; nonbeing relation to, 201–2; in *Qian Zao Du*, 178; Ultimate Limit and, 26, 200–201, 202–3, 204–10, 240–41, 268–69, 287n25; *yin/yang* and, 156, 201, 214–15, 227, 233, 308n6
Qian, 155, 156; Kun compared to, 162; in *Qian Zao Du*, 178; Ultimate Limit and, 166–67
Qian Zao Du, 177, 181; cosmology in, 178–79, 245; Great Change in, 196; Ultimate Limit in, 180
Qi-naturalism, 303n23
Qufu, 1
quietude, great vacuum and, 160

Rahner, Karl, 34
ratio, of divine creation, 126–27
reality, 31, 207; creation relation to, 12; metaphysics relation to, 40, 41; nonbeing relation to, 139–40; philosophical theology relation to, 79; Ruism relation to, 63; science relation to, 44–45. *See also* cosmic reality; ultimate reality
religion, 1–2, 76, 290n2; bridge concepts and, 83; comparative philosophy of, 84–85; philosophy *versus*, 19–20, 279n14; in public discourse, 51; science of, 77; theology of, 36
ren (humanity, or humaneness), 146, 160, 162, 275
Republic (Plato), 90–91
Ricci, Matteo, 3, 7, 54, 285n9; *creatio ex nihilo* and, 55, 71; Ruism relation to, 56; Ultimate Limit and, 240, 241, 242–43, 285n4
rites. *See* ritual, rite
Rites Controversy, 56
ritual, rite (*Li*), 275, 281n35; Buddhism relation to, 29–30; civilization relation to, 145–47
ritual-propriety, 146, 154
rooted tradition, home tradition compared to, 36
Ru (civilized human), 213, 275
Rudolph, Kurt, 119
Ruism, 270; Christianity compared to, 4, 45, 53–54, 71, 165, 285n9; Christian missionaries relation to, 72, 74, 285n9; Confucianism relation to, 277n1; Confucius relation to, 2–3; cosmology of, 156–57, 159–60, 163; cosmos and, 61; creation relation to, 307n59; CT and, 14, 37–38, 52; Daoism compared to, 156, 190–91; emptiness relation to, 31; ethics relation to, 25, 203; evil relation to, 264–65; heartmind and, 33; inclusivism relation to, 34–36, 52; metaphysics relation to, 6–7, 26–27, 47–48, 49, 51, 54, 162; monotheism relation to, 57; Neville relation to, 79–80; nonaction relation to, 166; nonconfessional CT and, 81; Non-Limit relation to, 225; ontological dependence and, 10; ontological transcendence relation to, 65; ontology of, 180; patrimony and, 32; philosophy

relation to, 52; Platonism relation to, 8, 268; *Qi* and, 308n6; reality relation to, 63; Ricci relation to, 56; ritual-propriety relation to, 154; ritual relation to, 146–47; sage relation to, 190; science and, 39, 268–69; self-cultivation relation to, 50, 281n43; *sheng sheng* and, 72; theology relation to, 5, 25, 28, 49; *Tian* relation to, 4, 59; Ultimate Limit relation to, 4, 12–13; Wang Bi and, 10, 189; Zheng relation to, 180
Ruist heretic, 30
The Ruist Ontological Cosmology in the *Xici*, 170, 195, 255

sage (*Sheng*), 161, 190, 267, 275
Sagehood (Angle), 211
Sallustius, 96–97
Schleiermacher, Friedrich, 9, 246, 252, 261; *creatio ex nihilo* and, 133–35, 244–45; on divine creation, 136, 237, 249; metaphysics and, 41
Scholastic model, of theology, 80, 130
science, 184; comparative religion as, 84; *creatio ex nihilo* relation to, 245; CT as, 6, 239; humanities studies and, 283n20; logic and, 40; metaphysics and, 41, 43–45, 50, 52; philosophy of, 42; Platonism relation to, 50, 267; of religion, 77; Ruism and, 39, 268–69
Scotus, Duns, 128, 130–31
self-consciousness, 133–34
self-cultivation, 47, 188–89; *Dao* relation to, 169; ethics relation to, 46, 311n37; in *Great Learning*, 51; heartmind relation to, 45–46, 48; Ruism relation to, 50, 281n43; *Tian* relation to, 59
self-generation, 245–46
Shandong Peninsula, 1
Shangdi (supreme deity), 54, 58, 60–61, 150–51, 275
"sheer making," 101–2, 131, 249–50
shen (numinous and wonderful), 167, 256, 275
Sheng. See sage
sheng sheng (birth birth), 8, 71, 275, 307n59; *creatio ex nihilo* compared to, 196,

237–39, 250, 251; *generatio ex nihilo* relation to, 255, 259, 261; ontological dependence and, 73, 165; Ruism and, 72; sublime virtue and, 159; *Tian* as, 7; of Ultimate Limit, 10, 209, 242, 249, 255, 257, 261, 266–67
Shun, 31
situational thinking, 7, 82–83, 84, 85
Six Realms, 29
Smid, Robert, 81
Smith, Jonathan Z., 7, 77–78, 82–83, 84, 85
Smith, Wilfred C., 19
social Darwinism, 77
social ideals, 145–46, 154
solitude, 146
"Space-Time," 179
Spinoza, 9, 148
spiritual exercises, philosophy and, 19, 279n14
Stalnaker, Aaron, 78, 83–84
"strict transcendence," 65–66, 67
sublime virtue, *sheng sheng* and, 159
suffering, 112–13, 117, 154, 263
Summa theologiae I (Aquinas), 121
Sun Shangyang, 305n46
suppositional necessity, 127–28
supreme deity (*Shangdi*), 54, 58, 60–61, 150–51, 275
Su-un, 60
Systemic Theology I (Tillich), 137, 142

Taiji. See Ultimate Limit
Taiwan, 58
Tang dynasty, 31–32, 200
Tang Yijie, 305n46
Tang Yongtong, 305n46, 305n53
Taurus, Calvenus, 95–96
temporal beginning, 42
Ten Wings, 280n27
Tertullian, 107
Thatamanil, John J., 35–36, 282n48
theodicy, 8, 106, 119, 264; *creatio ex nihilo* relation to, 112–13, 143; evil relation to, 94, 162, 262
theological dialogue, 79

theology: Aristotle and, 22–23, 27, 278n3; in Catholic Scholastic tradition, 15; Christianity relation to, 24; divine revelation relation to, 16–17; metaphysics and, 21, 40; orthodox, 106; philosophical, 8–9, 23–25, 27, 79, 80; philosophy relation to, 5, 17–19; of religion, 36; Ruism relation to, 5, 25, 28, 49; Scholastic model of, 80, 130; science relation to, 41; Trinitarian, 60, 109. *See also* comparative theology

Theophilus of Antioch, 9, 86–87, 97–98, 100–101, 256

thought, or intellect ("Nous"), 21–23, 103, 110, 223

Three Teachings, 29–32, 33. *See also* Buddhism; Daoism; Ruism

Tian (heaven, cosmos, or the universe), 212–13, 250, 266, 275; Christianity relation to, 58, 65–66; Constant of, 172; *creatio ex nihilo* compared to, 254–55; creation and, 64, 253; Creator-God compared to, 53, 69; as "Great Vacuity," 63–64; mathematical systems relation to, 268; ontological dependence and, 71; ontological transcendence and, 61–63; priority and, 251; Ruism relation to, 4, 59; as *sheng sheng*, 7; Ultimate Limit relation to, 302n18; in *Xici*, 54–55; *yin/yang* relation to, 64–65

Tiantai Buddhism, 309n16

Tillich, Paul, 9–10, 27; Christian mysticism and, 131; on *creatio ex nihilo*, 137, 246, 299n60; on demonic power, 140–41, 252, 265; on divine creation, 237, 249, 299n47; on eschatological pantheism, 142–43; on essentialization, 141–42; metaphysics and, 41; on nonbeing, 138–40, 263–64

Timaeus (Plato), 86, 91–93; Christianity relation to, 106; cosmology in, 86, 87, 95; creation and, 197; *Diagram of Ultimate Limit* compared to, 199; divine creation in, 107, 137–38; matter and, 112, 121; ontological dependence and, 89; Theophilus relation to, 97; tripartite model in, 131; *Xici versus*, 11

time, 9; cosmology relation to, 149; *creatio ex nihilo* and, 42, 137; divine creation relation to, 94, 96; "*eskhatos*" and, 141; human consciousness relation to, 129; metaphysics relation to, 43; Space, 179

Tiwald, Justin, 309n15

To Explain and Analyze Characters, 212

Torchia, N. Joseph, 87

tranquility, 29, 31

transcendence, 69, 70. *See also specific topics*

transcendent reality, religion relation to, 19

transcultural universals, 83–84

transient religious experiences, 3

trigrams, 164, *164*

Trinitarian theology, 60, 109

tripartite model, 131

The True Meaning of the Lord of Heaven (Ricci), 54

Tu Wei-ming, 63–64, 71–72, 254, 284n1

Two Modes. See *yin/yang*

ultimacy (*Ji*), 67, 219

ultimate creativity, ontological unconditionality of, 197–99

Ultimate Limit (*Taiji*), 190, 225, 275, 302n21; change and, 162, 166–67, 232; Christianity relation to, 56–58; *creatio ex nihilo* compared to, 12–13, 167–68, 196–98, 200, 226; creation relation to, 195, 242–43, 248–49, 253–54, 265; Creator-God compared to, 8, 53, 69; *Dao De Jing* relation to, 171–72, 191–92; *Dao* relation to, 26–27, 56, 171, 187–88, 201; as *generatio ex nihilo*, 224, 243, 309n16; in *Huainanzi*, 174–76; *Li* and, 194, 211–12, 213–14, 222, 227–29, 233, 236; in *Lü Annals of Spring and Autumn*, 172–73, 179–80; nonbeing relation to, 192, 204–5, 226, 246; Non-Limit relation to, 207–8, 215–18, 235, 237–38; ontological dependence and, 71; ontological priority of, 246–47; ontological unconditionality of, 193, 239–40; prime matter compared to, 285n4; *Qi* and, 26, 200–1, 202–3, 204–10, 240–41, 268–69, 287n25; in *Qian Zao Du*, 178; Ruism relation to, 4, 12–13; *Shangdi* relation to, 60–61; *sheng sheng* of, 10, 209, 242, 249, 255, 257, 261, 266–67; *Tian* relation to, 302n18; trigrams from, 164; in *Xici*, 54–55, 64, 157, 165, 170–71, 180, 184–87, 212; *yin/yang* relation to, 26,

165–66, 184–85, 200, 204, 209, 216–20, 222–23, 228–29, 234, 256
"Ultimate One," 172
ultimate reality, 196–97, 251, 260–61; *creatio ex nihilo* relation to, 143, 184, 195, 252, 254; ontological dependence relation to, 183–84, 196; ontology and, 237; Ultimate Limit relation to, 249
unity, manifesting, 161
unmoved mover, 21–22, 121
utensil-like things (qi), 25, 157, 214–15, 275

vacuum, 43; *Dao* relation to, 153; "Great Change" as, 181; Nebulous, 175–76, 179; nonaction and, 159; nonbeing relation to, 169, 189. *See also* great vacuum
vague category, 7, 74, 82–84, 258, 259, 269; creation as, 250; situational thinking and, 85
vital-energy, or psychophysical energy. *See Qi*
void, 29, 33, 194
voluntarism, 111

Wagner, Rudolf G., 305n53
Wang, Robin R., 303n23
Wang Bi, 12–13, 68, 167, 198, 305n46; Augustine *versus*, 11; on *Dao*, 246, 253; *Dao De Jing* relation to, 185–89; on nonbeing, 200, 224; Non-Limit relation to, 208; philosophy of, 305n53; Ruism relation to, 10, 180; on sage, 190; on Ultimate Limit, 191–92, 237; *Xici* and, 170, 243; Zheng Xuan relation to, 176
Wang Longxi, 28, 31, 33–34, 47, 281n38; Laozi and, 281n35; "open inclusivism" relation to, 36; Wang Yangming and, 281n43
Wang Yangming, 28, 230, 265, 281n38, 281n43
Ward, Keith, 15–17, 24, 28, 76
Warring States period, 172
Washington College, 6
the Way. *See Dao*
"weft books," 177
Weigel, Peter, 296n6
Western culture, Ruism relation to, 4
Whitehead, Alfred, 41

Wildman, Wesley J., 292n52
Williams, Robert, 135–36
Wippel, John, 124
Wittgenstein, 78
World War II, 58
Wuji. *See* Non-Limit
Wuwei (nonaction), 159, 160, 275, 302n18

Xiangshan, 29
Xici (*Appended Texts*), 12–13, 167–68, 172, 191–93, 259, 275; change and, 163; Confucius relation to, 58, 280n27, 301n11; on cosmic reality, 198; cosmogony in, 243; cosmology of, 147, 154–56, 169–70; *Dao* and, 157–59, 182, 204; *Dao De Jing* compared to, 159–60, 183; Legge relation to, 57–58; metaphysics and, 25; on nonaction, 302n18; ontology of, 184, 243; *Qian Zao Du* relation to, 177–78, 179–80; The Ruist Ontological Cosmology in the, 195, *195*, 255; *Tian* in, 54–55; *Timaeus versus*, 11; trigrams in, 164; Ultimate Limit in, 54–55, 64, 157, 165, 170–71, 180, 184–87, 212
Xin. *See* heartmind
Xu, 31–32
Xunzi, 84, 212, 301n11

Yanzi, 29
yao, 31, 164, 275
Yijing. See *Classic of Change*
Yin-Senzhu, 60
yin/yang, 172, 275; cosmic reality relation to, 158–59; cosmological succession and, 152–53; cosmology of, 303n23; cosmos relation to, 57; creation and, 115–16; *Dao* compared to, 182, 192; in *Huainanzi*, 174; myriad things and, 241; *Qi* and, 156, 201, 214–15, 227, 233, 308n6; *Tian* relation to, 64–65; trigrams and, 164, *164*; Ultimate Limit relation to, 26, 165–66, 184–85, 200, 204, 209, 216–20, 222–23, 228–29, 234, 256; in *Xici*, 54–55
Yuanqi (primordial *Qi*), 55, 275. See also *Qi*
Yu Chunxi, 57
Yu dynasty, 31–32

Zhang Juzheng, 285n9
Zhang Zai, 63, 72, 240–41, 254–55, 287n25
Zheng Xuan, 176, 180, 185, 245–46, 304n35; on *Dao*, 252–53; on "Great Change," 182–83, 184; on *hunlun*, 181–82; on *Qi*, 308n6
Zhongyong (centrality and commonality), 56, 64, 219, 275
Zhou Book of Change. See *Zhouyi*
Zhou Dunyi, 55, 68, 72, 226, 234; *creatio ex nihilo* relation to, 209; *Diagram of Ultimate Limit*, 154; on Non-Limit, 208; philosophy of, 199; on sage, 267; on Ultimate Limit, 202–4, 205–6, 237–38; Zhu Xi relation to, 10, 13. See also *Diagram of Ultimate Limit*
Zhou dynasty, 145, 154

Zhouyi, 155–56, 163, 276, 280n27, 302n18; cosmic reality relation to, 165; *Dao* relation to, 168
Zhuangzhi, 170–71, 303n27; *Dao De Jing* relation to, 304n29; *Huainanzi* compared to, 175; Ultimate Limit in, 171
Zhu Xi, 60, 72, 202, 209, 227–30, 233–34; on centrality, 219; cosmology of, 198; on *Dao*, 158–59; Descartes *versus*, 11; *Diagram of Ultimate Limit* relation to, 255; heartmind and, 311n37; Laozi relation to, 224, 225–26; on *Li*, 211–12, 220–22, 247, 309n17; metaphysics of, 259, 261; ontological transcendence and, 74; on Ultimate Limit, 55–56, 210, 213–16, 217–18, 222–23, 237–38, 242, 246–47, 253–54; *Xici* and, 243; Zhou Dunyi relation to, 10, 13
Ziporyn, Brook, 309n16
Ziran, 276

BIN SONG is Associate Professor of Philosophy and Religion at Washington College, specializing in Confucianism, early modern philosophy, and comparative theology, with a focus on metaphysics, ethics, spirituality, and the intersections of Confucian and Christian thought. He is the author of *Descartes's Mechanical Philosophy* (in Chinese), a study on metaphysical foundations of modern science, and has published translations of early modern European philosophy into Chinese and ancient Confucian meditation texts into English.

Comparative Theology / Thinking Across Traditions

SERIES EDITORS
Loye Ashton and John Thatamanil

Hyo-Dong Lee, *Spirit, Qi, and the Multitude: A Comparative Theology for the Democracy of Creation*

Michelle Voss Roberts, *Tastes of the Divine: Hindu and Christian Theologies of Emotion*

Michelle Voss Roberts (ed.), *Comparing Faithfully: Insights for Systematic Theological Reflection*

Francis X. Clooney, S.J., and Klaus von Stosch (eds.), *How to Do Comparative Theology*

F. Dominic Longo, *Spiritual Grammar: Genre and the Saintly Subject in Islam and Christianity*

S. Mark Heim, *Crucified Wisdom: Theological Reflection on Christ and the Bodhisattva*

Martha L. Moore-Keish and Christian T. Collins Winn (eds.), *Karl Barth and Comparative Theology*

John J. Thatamanil, *Circling the Elephant: A Comparative Theology of Religious Diversity*

Catherine Cornille (ed.), *Atonement and Comparative Theology: The Cross in Dialogue with Other Religions*

Daniel Soars, *The World and God Are Not-Two: A Hindu–Christian Conversation*

Daniel Soars (ed.), *God at Play: Līlā in Hindu and Christian Traditions*

Bin Song, *Debating Transcendence: Creatio ex nihilo and Sheng Sheng*

www.ingramcontent.com/pod-product-compliance
Lightning Source LLC
Chambersburg PA
CBHW020352080526
44584CB00014B/996